Regional Development Banks in the World Economy

Regional Development Banks in the World Economy

Edited by

JUDITH CLIFTON,
DANIEL DÍAZ-FUENTES, AND
DAVID HOWARTH

OXFORD
UNIVERSITY PRESS

OXFORD
UNIVERSITY PRESS

Great Clarendon Street, Oxford, OX2 6DP,
United Kingdom

Oxford University Press is a department of the University of Oxford.
It furthers the University's objective of excellence in research, scholarship,
and education by publishing worldwide. Oxford is a registered trade mark of
Oxford University Press in the UK and in certain other countries

First Edition published in 2021

Published in the United States of America by Oxford University Press
198 Madison Avenue, New York, NY 10016, United States of America

British Library Cataloguing in Publication Data
Data available

Library of Congress Control Number: 2020947372

ISBN 978–0–19–886108–9

DOI: 10.1093/oso/9780198861089.001.0001

Preface

This volume on regional development banks has its origins in an open, competitive call for research projects launched by the Santander Financial Institute (SANFI) in 2015. Daniel Díaz-Fuentes, of the University of Cantabria, Spain, together with a group of scholars interested in bringing together knowledge on the origins and history of global banking and finance, led by Carlos Marichal, of El Colegio de México, and Andrés Hoyo Aparicio, also from University of Cantabria, were successful in their bid to obtain funding for a three-year period. Díaz-Fuentes was responsible for the contemporary period of international banking and finance within this multidisciplinary, long-term study. From this project grew the idea of this volume, based on the fact that, whilst multilateral development banks attract considerable attention from scholars of economics and political science, regional development banks remained rather neglected. Díaz-Fuentes, together with Judith Clifton, University of Cantabria, and David Howarth, University of Luxembourg, embarked on the work which culminated in this volume. The SANFI conference held at SANFI headquarters in Santander, in May 2017, was the first major milestone involving the presentation of research and constructive feedback. This was followed by a second workshop at the World Economic History Congress, hosted by the MIT in Boston, in July-August 2018. Ana Lara Gómez assisted throughout this period, helping to organize events, editing as well as contributing to the research project as a PhD candidate at the University of Cantabria. We are very grateful for her help throughout. The editors would also like to extend their thanks to a number of academic institutions. Judith Clifton completed the preparation of this book while a Visiting Academic at the European Studies Centre, University of Oxford. Daniel Diaz-Fuentes prepared the final version of this book at the University of Oxford's Department of International Development from September 2019 to March 2020, with funding from the competitive Salvador de Madariaga Fellowship scheme, which he took up between September 2019 and March 2020. David Howarth would like to thank his co-editors and Helen Kavvadia, European Investment Bank visiting fellow at the University of Luxembourg, whose knowledge of the EIB and other regional development banks is vast. He completed the preparation of the final manuscript of this volume as a Visiting Fellow at the Institute of Political Science, Leiden University.

Santander, Oxford, and Luxembourg

Contents

PART TWO: COMPARATIVE AND POLICY ANALYSIS

List of Figures

List of Tables

List of Abbreviations

ADB	Asian Development Bank
ADF	Asian Development Fund
AfCFTA	African Continental Free Trade Area
AfDB	African Development Bank
AfDF	African Development Fund
AG	Andean Group
AIIB	Asian Infrastructure Investment Bank
ALBA	Alternative for Latin America and the Caribbean
AoA	Articles of Agreement
ASEAN	Association of Southeast Asian Nations
AUC	African Union Commission
BCEAO	Central Bank of West Africa (Banque Centrale d'Afrique Occidentale)
BDEAC	Development Bank for Central African States
BNDES	Brazilian Development Bank (Banco Nacional de Desenvolvimento Econômico e Social)
BOAD	West African Development Bank
BoD	board of directors
BoG	board of governors
BRICS	Brazil, Russia, India, China, South Africa (large emerging economies)
CABEI	Central American Bank for Economic Integration
CACM	Central American Common Market
CAF	Andean Development Corporation (Corporación Andina de Fomento)
CAFIC	China-Africa Fund for Industrial Cooperation
CARICOM	Caribbean Community
CCCC	callable capital of countries with convertible currencies
CDB	Caribbean Development Bank
CEE	Central and Eastern Europe
CEEP	European Centre of Employers and Enterprises providing Public Services and Services of general interest
CEI	compliance, effectiveness, and integrity
CEMAC	Economic and Monetary Community of Central Africa (Communauté Économique et Monétaire de l'Afrique Centrale)
CEPAL	Comisión Económica para América Latina y el Caribe (see UN-ECLAC and ECLAC)
CGD	Centre for Global Development
CIDA	Canadian International Development Agency
COMECON	Council for Mutual Economic Assistance
DAC	Development Assistance Committee
D/E	debt-to-equity (ratio)

DFID	Department for International Development (UK)
DFI	development finance institutions
DG	directorate-general
DMCs	developing member countries
EAC	East African Community
EADB	East African Development Bank
EBRD	European Bank for Reconstruction and Development
ECA	Economic Commission for Africa (see UN-ECA)
ECAFE	Economic Commission for Asia and the Far East (see UN-ECAFE)
ECB	European Central Bank
ECLA/ECLAC	Economic Commission for Latin American and Caribbean (see UN-ECLAC)
ESCAP	Economic and Social Commission for Asia and the Pacific (see UN-ESCAP)
ETAD	ADB—Economic and Technical Assistance Department
EEC	European Economic Community
EFSI	European Fund for Strategic Investments
EIB	European Investment Bank
EPEC	European PPP (Public-Private Partnership) Expertise Centre
EPSU	European Federation of Public Service Unions
ERDF	European Regional Development Fund
ESG	environmental, social, and governance
ETAD	Economic and Technical Assistance Department
EU	European Union
FDI	foreign direct investment
FI	financial intermediary
FIRII	Fund for Integration Infrastructures (Fondo de Infraestructuras de Integracion)
FSO	Fund for Special Operations
G5	Group of Five
G7	Group of Seven
G20	Group of Twenty
G24	Group of Twenty-Four
GDP	gross domestic product
GMS	Greater Mekong Sub-region
GNI	gross national income
GAO	Government Accountability Office
HAEU	Historical Archives of the EU
IAB	Inter-American Bank
IADB	Inter-American Development Bank
IBEC	International Bank of Economic Cooperation
IBRD	International Bank for Reconstruction and Development
ICT	information and communication technology
IDA	International Development Association
IED	Independent Evaluation Department

IFC	International Finance Corporation
IFI	international financial institution
IIC	Integration Industries Convention
IMF	International Monetary Fund
IO	international organization
IPE	international political economy
IPG	international public good
IPPF	Infrastructure Project Preparation Facility
IR	international relations
IsDB	Islamic Development Bank
ISI	import-substitution industrialization
JASPERS	Joint Assistance to Support Projects in European Regions
JEREMIE	Joint European Resources for Micro to Medium Enterprises
JESSICA	Joint European Support for Sustainable Investment in City Areas
KFW	German National Development Bank (Kreditanstalt für Wiederaufbau)
LEGG	loans, equity investments, grants, and guarantees
MDB	multilateral development bank
MECOFIN	Mechanism of Confirmation and Financing of Credit Lines and Imports
MENA	Middle East and North Africa
MIC	middle-income country
MIGA	Multilateral Investment Guarantee Agency
MOU	Memorandum of Understanding
NDB	National Development Bank (Germany)
NGO	non-governmental organization
NHS	National Health Service (UK)
NIB	Nordic Investment Bank
NTF	Nigeria Trust Fund
OAS	Organisation of American States
OCR	Ordinary Capital Resources
ODA	overseas development aid
ODECA	Organisation of Central American States
ODI	Overseas Development Institute (UK)
OECD	Organisation for European Co-operation and Development
OEEC	Organisation for European Economic Cooperation
PDR	People's Democratic Republic
PFI	private finance initiative
PPIAF	Public-Private Infrastructure Advisory Facility
PPP	Public-Private Partnership
PPPLRC	Public-Private-Partnership Legal Resource Centre
PRC	People's Republic of China
RBC	risk-bearing-capital (ratio)
RDB	regional development banks
RDI	research, development, and innovation
REMU	Regional Economic Monitoring Unit
RMB	Renmimbi (Chinese International Currency)

RoE	return-on-equity (ratio)
RPG	regional public goods
SAFICO	Sistema de Financiamiento del Comercio Andino
SDG	Sustainable Development Goal
SIECA	Secretariat for Central American Economic Integration
SME	small and medium-sized enterprise
SPS	Safeguard Policy Statement
SUNFED	Special United Nations Fund for Economic Development
TAG	temporary alternate governors
TENS	Trans-European Networks
UK	United Kingdom
UN	United Nations
UNASUR	Union of South American Nations (Unión de Naciones Suramericanas)
UNCTAD	United Nations Conference on Trade and Development
UN-ECA	United Nations Economic Commission for Africa
UN-ECAFE	United Nations Economic Commission for Asia and the Far East
UN-ECLAC	United Nations Economic Commission for Latin America
UN-ESCAP	United Nations Economic and Social Commission for Asia and the Pacific
US	United States
USAID	United States Agency for International Development
USD	United States dollar(s)
USSR	Union of Soviet Socialist Republics
WAEMU	West African Economic and Monetary Union
WB	World Bank
WBI	World Bank Institute

List of Contributors

José Antonio Alonso is Full Professor of Applied Economics, Complutense University, Madrid.

Sarah Babb is Professor in the Department of Sociology, Boston College.

Dominique Barjot is Emeritus Professor in Economic History, Sorbonne University, Paris; Professor in Economic History, Renmin University, Beijing.

Carlos Andrés Brando is former Dean of Economics at Universidad Jorge Tadeo Lozano, and is currently Adjunct Lecturer in Economic History at Colegio de Estudios Superiores de Administración CESA in Bogota.

Judith Clifton is Full Professor of Applied Economics in the Department of Economics, University of Cantabria.

José Cuesta is a Lead Economist in the Social Sustainability and Inclusion Global Practice of the World Bank, Washington.

Alberto Cortés is Full Professor in the School of Political Science and Researcher at the Center for Research and Political Studies, University of Costa Rica.

Daniel Díaz-Fuentes is Full Professor of Applied Economics in the Department of Economics, University of Cantabria.

José Efraín Deras is Chief of the Independent Evaluation Office at the Central American Bank for Economic Integration (CABEI) and Visiting Professor at the Technological University of Centroamericana (UNITEC).

Guillermo Funes is a former Board Director of the Central American Bank for Economic Integration (CABEI) and an Independent Consultant.

Ana Lara Gómez is Assistant Professor of Applied Economics in the Department of Economics, University of Cantabria.

David Howarth is Full Professor of European Political Economy in the Institute of Political Science, University of Luxembourg.

Helen Kavvadia is Researcher in Residence in the Institute of Political Science, University of Luxembourg.

Erika Kraemer-Mbula is Professor of Economics, DST/NRF/Newton Fund Trilateral Chair in Transformative Innovation, the 4IR and Sustainable Development, at the University of Johannesburg.

Pierre Lanthier is Associate Professor of Modern History in the Department of Humanities at the University of Quebec, Trois-Rivières.

Moritz Liebe is a Postdoctoral Research Fellow in the Department of Political Science, Trier University, Germany.

Pablo J. López is Finance Minister for the Province of Buenos Aires and Professor of Macroeconomics in the Faculty of Economics, University of Buenos Aires.

Steven D. Roper is Professor of Political Science, in the Department of Political Science, Florida Atlantic University.

Marcelo Rougier is Professor of Economic History in the Faculty of Economics, University of Buenos Aires.

Stuart Shields is Senior Lecturer in International Political Economy in the School of Social Sciences, University of Manchester.

Jiajun Xu is Assistant Professor of International Development in the Institute of New Structural Economics, National School of Development, Peking University.

1

Regional Development Banks in the World Economy

Judith Clifton, Daniel Díaz-Fuentes, and David Howarth

1. Why study regional development banks, and why now?

This volume focuses on regional development banks (RDB) and provides a comprehensive, comparative, and empirically informed analysis of their origins, evolution, and contemporary role in the world economy. A volume on RDB is timely for four major reasons. First, since their establishment, the importance of RDB lending has increased significantly. To illustrate, the European Investment Bank (EIB) alone lent more overall than the World Bank, the world's largest global multilateral development bank (MDB), from 1991 onwards (Robinson 2009; Clifton et al. 2014, 2017b).[1] Even when specific RDB lend less in total than their MDB counterparts, the loans that these RDB make to their member states are often larger than the loans received from MDB.[2] In other words, RDB may be more important to their regions than the MDB.

A second reason for the timeliness of this volume is that RDB have experienced a renaissance over the past few years. In the age of what Angus Maddison and the OECD (2010) label 'Shifting Wealth', we are witnessing the relative decline of the West and the rise of new economic powers in the East and South. Global MDB and most RDB were established during a specific historical moment—at the end of the Second World War and over the following decade—and their governance and shareholder structures reflect this specific political-economic juncture. As the relative size of member state economies shifts, along with their political clout or even military might, a major question is the extent to which the banks' governance and shareholder arrangements will be changed to reflect this development (Ravallion 2016). Jakob Vestergaard and Robert Wade (2013, 2015) argue

[1] The EIB officially rejects its status as an RDB.

[2] This higher volume of RDB compared to MDB lending to member countries is seen notably in a number of Latin American and Asian RDB. For the Central American Bank for Economic Integration (CABEI), see Deras et al. Chapter 6, this volume; for the Andean Financial Corporation (CAF), see Brando, Chapter 7, this volume; and for the Asian Development Bank (ADB) see Barjot and Lanthier, Chapter 4, this volume.

Judith Clifton, Daniel Díaz-Fuentes, and David Howarth, *Regional Development Banks in the World Economy* In: *Regional Development Banks in the World Economy.* Edited by: Judith Clifton, Daniel Díaz-Fuentes, and David Howarth, Oxford University Press (2021). © Oxford University Press. DOI: 10.1093/oso/9780198861089.003.0001

that there has been determined resistance from the US, Japan and a number of European governments to power sharing with rising economic powers within the World Bank and International Monetary Fund (IMF). The debate over power sharing is only going to intensify as the economic and political weight of players in the East and South, and particularly, the People's Republic of China (PRC), increases (Mahbubani 2013). This re-assertion of East and South has included the establishment of new national development banks (NDB) and RDB. In particular, the creation of the Asian Infrastructure Investment Bank (AIIB) can be explained in large part by Chinese government frustration with the operation of existing RDB and global MDB and as an expression of Chinese ambitions for the future (Bhattacharya and Kharas 2016; Xu, Chapter 9, this volume).

A third reason for the timeliness of this volume is that RDB remain under-researched, when compared, for example, to global MDB. Of the existing body of academic work on RDB, the main focus has tended to be the principal advantages of RDB in comparison to global MDB (Griffiths-Jones et al. 2008). A major line of analysis associated with this literature is the extent to which RDB have advantages associated with greater geographical, economic, and cultural proximity, with regard to their shareholders and the countries to which they provide loans, than global MDB. RDB are thought to be better positioned to give voice to their members, especially to small or medium-sized countries, which may otherwise struggle to be heard in global MDB. This in turn leads to the expectation that RDB are better placed to respond to the needs and demands of their members. RDB are also considered to be more flexible, relying often on informal mechanisms of peer pressure, as opposed to harder conditionality. Furthermore, RDB are thought to present an arena in which agreements through negotiation are easier than in global MDB, largely based on the assumption that members are both lenders and borrowers (Griffith-Jones et al. 2008). Given the increased importance of RDB it is important to study them on their own terms.

Fourth, the time is ripe to examine RDB in the context of the aftermath of the international financial crisis and the Great Recession of the late 2000s, as criticism of the role of both global MDB and RDB has intensified. This recent wave of criticism is not unprecedented. Each major international economic and financial crisis that occurred since the Second World War triggered a re-assessment of the very foundations and sustainability of global MDB and RDB. The first wave of criticism emerged in parallel to the debt crisis after the collapse of the Bretton Woods system in the 1970s (Babb 2013). Criticism intensified again in the aftermath of the Cold War in the 1990s, with the collapse of most political regimes that had pursued a command economy, particularly the Union of Soviet Socialist Republics (USSR), followed by their economic transition to a form of capitalism and an era of rapid globalization. Since the 2008 crisis—which mainly affected the richest countries, notably the United States (US) and in Europe—critics have asserted that development banks did not do enough (Griffiths-Jones et al. 2008). Beyond crisis-related challenges, questions have been asked with regard to what extent global MDB and RDB perform in a manner that corresponds satisfactorily to their original mandates, particularly, that of development. To what extent has the role of banks become increasingly influenced by private forces. Has 'mission creep' occurred? Recommendations have also been made with regard to how global MDB and RDB can use public finance more efficiently to reconstruct, develop, and innovate economies around the world, and to identify mechanisms and institutions to overcome and, preferably, avoid future crises (see Alonso and Cuesta, Chapter 14, this volume).

In section 2, we present the categories and the analytical framework that we apply to examine RDB, and specifically a form of rational choice institutionalism—Principal-Agent analysis. In section 3, we apply the categories and framework to each RDB in its specific political economy context, with a view to setting out and analysing the similarities and differences among RDB. We demonstrate and explain an important evolution in the main objectives of RDB lending activities over three distinct periods: from regional integration and development, to market promotion and development, and then to geographical expansion—and multi-polarity promotion for some RDB—and a more strategic interventionism in the market, that includes market shaping activities including industrial policy. We explain this evolution in terms of the agency of the RDB in relation to their multiple principal—the shareholder national governments.

2. Regional development banks: a framework for analysis

Our analytical framework builds on—extends and updates—previous studies of RDB, in particular White (1970 and 1972) whose volumes on RDB cover only those in the Global South. White (1970) classified RDB in geographical-functional terms. Starting with geographical considerations, some definitions are required. The term 'region' is understood as constituting a unit of analysis with broadly similar geographical, historical, cultural, and political features. The largest unit to which the term region could be applied is the 'continent' (White 1970: 22), of which, according to different definitions, there are between five and seven. Below the unit of the region is the 'Sub-region', understood as a group of countries that agree to cooperate. The first period of Continental RDB creation included the establishment of the Inter-American Development Bank (IADB), the African Development Bank (AfDB) and the Asian Development Bank (ADB). Sub-regional RDB, on the other hand, consisted of national governments within a region which decided to cooperate to establish a development bank; this was the case for the Central American Bank for Economic Integration (CABEI) and

CAF.[3] With regard to functions, the Continental RDB—the IADB, ADB, and AfDB—all focused on promoting development across most of—but not all—the countries in their respective continents. Both donors and recipients were found within the continent. However, where asymmetry existed, the donor would be typically outside the continent, lending to the recipient within the continent. In contrast, the major function of the Sub-regional RDB would be to promote integration as well as development among the members of the club, a task that often included supporting the poorest members. Hence, when established, the IADB, the AfDB, and the ADB could be classified as Continental RDB, and the EIB, CABEI, and CAF as Sub-regional integration RDB.

Based on this initial classification, our study updates and expands on the original work by White (1970). We take into consideration the historical context of the constitutive moment when each RDB was established, and track and evaluate the subsequent evolution of the major RDB. We include in our analysis those major RDB in the Global North. To track the evolution of RDB, we consider the changing nature of cooperation and conflict in the international system in which the RDB have operated, which have shaped both the global and regional economies, contributing to both enhanced economic and political integration and, occasionally, disintegration of the world's regions. Post-colonialism also influenced the emerging RDB. From the end of the Second World War to the 1980s, most

[3] This volume does not cover all RDB. In particular, it does not analyse small Sub-regional RDB, such as those in the Caribbean and Africa, which were created with the aims of contributing to the decolonization process, or maintaining monetary stability and financial links with their former colonial powers. This volume omits, for example, the Caribbean Development Bank (CDB), established in 1970, originally constituted by sixteen economies (including dependent British Overseas Territories) that held 60 per cent of the voting shares as well as the United Kingdom and Canada, which held the remaining 40 per cent, in their capacity as non-regional donor members. Although the CDB is associated with the Caribbean Community (CARICOM), established in 1973, the CBD does not have mandates or functions in CARICOM as a Sub-regional integration RDB. Other RDB not covered in this volume include a group of Sub-regional RDB which emerged in Africa to support currency unions in former British and French colonies. Cases include the East African Development Bank (EADB), the West African Development Bank (BOAD) and the Development Bank for Central African States (BDEAC). The EADB was established in 1967, by Kenya, Tanzania and Uganda, to promote cooperation in the East African Community (EAC). As a result of regional conflicts, the EADB and the EAC disintegrated in 1977 and were re-established in 2000, adding Rwanda in 2008. BOAD was established in 1973 by the country members of the West African Monetary Union (1959) through the Central Bank of West Africa (BCEAO) as shareholders. From 1994, BOAD became a specialized financial institution to attain the objectives of the West African Economic and Monetary Union (WAEMU), including Benin, Burkina-Faso, Côte d'Ivoire, Guinea Bissau, Mali, Niger, Senegal, and Togo (IMF 2018). The BDEAC was established in 1977 by members of the Economic and Monetary Community of Central Africa (CEMAC), which included Cameroon, Central African Republic, Chad and Guinea Equatorial, Republic of the Congo, and Gabon (IMF 2018). A further set of small but notable RDB not covered in this book are the Council of Europe Development Bank (1956), which is oriented to social and emergency projects, and the Nordic Investment Bank (NIB), created in 1975 by Denmark, Finland, Iceland, Norway, and Sweden. Finally, this volume does not include other development banks the membership of which is based on religious and legal principles, such as the Arab Bank for Reconstruction and Development (1974), which includes eighteen members of the League of Arab States, and the Islamic Development Bank (1975) which includes fifty-seven countries across four continents.

international cooperation through RDB was driven by regionalism, and political and military rivalry between the West and the East. Later, in the post-Cold War period, international cooperation became characterized by globalization, a mistrust of government intervention at the national and international levels, and a relatively open multilateral regionalism among heterogeneous members—including countries with different levels of development and with, often, considerable geographical distance between them. Most recently, the shift of wealth to the East and South has resulted in an increasingly 'multi-polar' world economy, characterized by the relative decline of both the economic weight and political influence of Western countries and the emergence or re-emergence of new players.

These shifts in the world economy had a significant impact upon the establishment and subsequent evolution of RDB. We specify five RDB functions—development, regional integration, market promotion, multi-polarity reinforcement, and interventionist market shaping, or industrial policy—which have risen and declined in relative and real importance over time. There were three historical junctures when RDB were established. The first period of their creation, from the 1950s to the 1960s, was covered by Singh (1969) and White (1970, 1972). First, there were Continental RDB which promoted development across most countries in the continent in which they were based. This function responded to the objectives defined by political elites working in the specific Continental context, for example, within a Continentally focused organization in the Americas, Africa, or Asia. The second major function undertaken by some RDB was to promote Sub-regional integration as well as development. Integration included both negative integration—the elimination of, inter alia, tariff and non-tariff barriers—and positive integration—the creation of common rules, infrastructure, and public goods (Cook and Sachs 1999).

These development banks were established officially to correct for market failure. RDB provided long-term and high-risk financing to advance public policy objectives—and notably the construction of basic infrastructure that provided for positive externalities—where commercial banks and private capital markets were unwilling or unable. This kind of market failure was particularly acute in developing countries where investment risks could be significant and financial markets under-developed. Furthermore, national government fiscal resources, NDB, or other state-owned financial institutions—especially those in the developing world—often lacked sufficient capital to finance large infrastructural projects. Official development assistance from international bodies or other national governments was too piecemeal with the bulk directed to social sectors. Thus, RDB filled an important funding niche.

The second major period of RDB creation occurred in the 1990s. In this period, the function prioritized by newly established RDB was associated more closely with activities promoting market forces and a withdrawal of state intervention in national economies. In addition, already existing RDB also embarked—albeit unevenly—on more market-oriented functions. These functions involved RDB placing emphasis on the use of finance to support and promote private activities in the markets, towards increased competition and privatization. Hence, the original Continental and Sub-regional integration RDB of the first period transformed into banks that pursued 'market-led development'—whilst keeping their Continental and Sub-regional integration functions. This shift towards market-led development was particularly manifested in the so-called Washington Consensus approach (Caroll et al. 2019) that influenced most of the existing RDB, including the IADB (as demonstrated in Babb, Chapter 11, and López and Rougier, Chapter 2, both this volume), the AfDB (as seen in Kraemer-Mbula, Chapter 3, this volume), and the ADB (as shown in Barjot and Lanthier, Chapter 4, this volume). Market-led development also influenced Sub-regional integration RDB, including CAF (Brando, Chapter 7, this volume), CABEI (Deras et al., Chapter 6, this volume), and, to a lesser extent, the EIB (Clifton, Díaz-Fuentes, and Revuelta 2014; and Clifton, Díaz-Fuentes, and Gomez, Chapter 5, this volume). Market-led development inspired particularly the newly established European Bank for Reconstruction and Development (EBRD), the lending activities of which focused upon Central and Eastern Europe and Central Asia (see Shields, Chapter 8, and Roper, Chapter 10, both this volume). Hence, in this second period, Continental RDB were transformed into 'Continental market-led' RDB whilst Sub-regional integration RDB were transformed into 'Sub-regional market-led integration' RDB.

Finally, in the most recent period of RDB creation and evolution from the beginning of the twenty-first century, a more ambitious geo-political and market shaping approach can be detected. Geo-political ambition is most evident in the establishment of the AIIB under Chinese government leadership. Furthermore, a number of existing RDB which had previously focused mainly on their immediate region became increasingly active beyond that region. Hence, Continental RDB have expanded their borrowing and lending beyond their continent (to become '+continent'). Where there is asymmetry between donor and recipients, it is often in the opposite direction as before—that is, increasingly, the donor is based within the continent whilst the recipient is beyond the continent. Regarding Sub-regional RDB geographically, these, likewise, have tended to become much more active beyond their club members, with regard to both borrowing and lending (to become '+Sub-regional').

With regard to function, RDB have continued to develop the continent/region and pursued market-oriented activities—while extending these activities beyond the continent/region. At the same time, over the past decade, we detect a greater caution with regard with neoliberal market creating policies: a number of RDB have also re-asserted or rediscovered the merits of a more interventionist investment policy, including industrial policy. RDB have gone beyond the correction of market failure—and notably the absence of financial services willing to invest in large infrastructure projects, especially in developing countries—and engaged in market shaping (Mazzucato and Penna 2016). A number of RDB have become engaged in long-term strategic development of entire industrial sectors. In addition, in this period, RDB increasingly pursue the provision of international public goods (both global and regional public goods (RPGs)) with a particular focus on environmental sustainability, including decarbonization of the economy and energy transitions. Another important feature in this period is that many RDB have increased their involvement with the private sector in their operations, through the development of new instruments including the greater use of public-private partnerships (PPPs; see Howarth and Liebe, Chapter 13, this volume), known as 'blending'. RDB are also increasingly involving sub-sovereign actors, including local and regional governments as well as public corporations and entities. This amounts to a change in their business model. RDB must now operate in a more agile way in order to lend to both sovereign and sub-sovereign actors as well as to the private sector. These RDB have emerged as what we label '+Continental strategic market' RDB and '+Sub-regional strategic market integration' RDB. Both kinds of RDB have expanded geographically outside of the original area of financing and lending, whilst their functions have gravitated further towards more interventionist market shaping activities including industrial policy.

By way of illustration of these geographical and functional developments, we can take the case of the EIB. Originally established as a Sub-regional RDB to promote integration in Western Europe, the EIB from the 1990s, whilst remaining a Sub-regional integration RDB, expanded strongly into market-promoting functions, especially from the 1990s, whilst also lending outside the Sub-region. In recent years, the EIB has also engaged in a putative industrial policy through the European Commission's Investment Plan for Europe and European Fund for Strategic Investment. Furthermore, at the end of 2019, the EIB launched a new climate strategy and energy lending policy, stating that it will stop all lending to fossil fuel energy projects from the end of 2021. The EIB has developed a new business model from 1999 (see Kavvadia, Chapter 12, this volume) and its involvement of the private sector has developed through PPPs in this period (see Howarth and Liebe, Chapter 13, this volume). Another example is CAF, also originally a Sub-regional integration RDB, this time among the Andean Group national economies, which expanded its shareholders and lending activities significantly beyond its original club of members, whilst its function moved towards market promotion, albeit to a lesser extent than the EIB. Again, in the more recent period, CAF has seen a re-assertion of a more interventionist market shaping and industrial policy.

An analytical framework drawn from the political science and political economy literature assists our examination of the operation of RDB and their development: the Principal-Agent approach—a version of rational choice institutionalism.

To what extent can the Principal-Agent approach shine a light on these geographical and functional transitions? For many years, neoliberal institutionalism and intergovernmentalism dominated the scholarship on the role and development of international organizations (IOs) in international political economy (IPE). However, over the past two decades, a greater diversity of approaches has been applied. An influential rationalist analytical framework adopted to analyse the role and development of IOs and issues in the politics of international finance and economics more generally has been the Principal-Agent approach (Hawkins et al. 2006; Vaubel 2006). Through delegation to an agent, principal(s) hope to manage externalities, facilitate collective decision-making, resolve disputes, enhance credibility, and/or lock-in commitments (Weingast and Moran 1983; McCubbins and Schwartz 1984; Kiewiet and McCubbins 1991).

The Principal-Agent approach has been used to study the evolution of conditionality in approving loans to member states of the IMF (Martin 2006), American foreign aid policy (Lyne et al. 2006), and negotiations in the WTO (Elsig 2011), and the political economy of financial liberalization (Singer 2007). Most relevant to our analysis of RDB, the approach has also been applied to explain changes in the World Bank's lending portfolio (Nielson and Tierney 2003; see also Vaubel 2006). The added value of the Principal-Agent approach is in explaining puzzles where a group of member states are seemingly willing and potentially able to control the action of an IO but fail to do so. Since Principal-Agent analyses focus upon the strategies of rational actors, the approach is particularly relevant when analysing short- and medium-term action, when actors' preferences and interests are fixed (Ben-Artzi 2016).

One of several unique features of delegation at the international level is that this involves multiple principals and, specifically national governments (Nielson and Tierney 2003; Hawkins and Jacoby 2006). In the case of global MDB and RDB, these national governments are shareholders, the relative influence of which is determined in large part by the national share. While national shareholders have involvement in the governing boards of global MDB and RDB, this involvement will vary by institution. The board of directors of the global MDB and RDB will have some degree of autonomy—which again varies by institution—to manage the day-to-day affairs of the bank. The agreed preferences of the member state shareholders are set out in the terms of delegation—often referred to as articles of agreement. However, these terms will never provide precisely defined rules according to which the agent (the bank) will have to operate in all situations. Thus, the agent will have to use its discretion to adopt policies (inter alia, on funding sources and loans) in a manner that is deemed to correspond to the preferences of the multiple principal.

The principal(s) and the agent bargain over the extent of agent autonomy. The principal(s) prefer that the agent use its autonomy to further their interests, but 'agency loss'—when the preferences of the agent diverge from those of the principal—is inevitable due to information asymmetries and fundamentally different underlying interests (Hawkins and Jacoby 2006; Vaubel 2006). Bureaucratic agents possess greater information than principals and are not subject to electoral pressures—which many, if not all, national governments must face. Furthermore, bureaucratic agents (here, RDB boards of directors) are frequently driven by underlying interests that involve resource expansion: 'more staff, a larger budget and increasing competencies' (Vaubel 2006: 127). For these reasons—asymmetric information and different underlying interests—agents (here, RDB boards of directors) are prone to develop different preferences from the principal. 'Agency losses'—that is, shirking, slippage, or even sabotage—occur. 'Shirking' refers to the agent failing to act in a manner that best serves the interests/preferences of the principal, that is, putting no effort into fulfilling the delegated task or less effort than necessary, concentrating instead on promoting its own interests; 'slippage' involves the agent following its own preferences which diverge from those of its principal(s); while 'sabotage' involves the agent acting in outright conflict with the principal's preferences and underlying interests (Bendor et al. 2001). The principal can adopt a range of *ex ante* and *ex post* mechanisms through which to control the agent (McCubbins and Schwartz 1984). Moreover, the preferences of the principal might shift over time—away from the terms of delegation—due to a number of factors, including new members. In detecting the form of 'agency loss' it is crucial to take into consideration a possible shift in the principal's preferences and the danger of 'observational equivalence' (Weingast and Moran 1983).

The preferences of the RDB agent to what we refer to as the five functions of regional development banking—development, regional integration, market promotion, multi-polarity reinforcement, and interventionist market shaping, including industrial policy—may come to differ from that of its multiple principal. Given the RDB's day-to-day focus on core lending activities, we can draw the hypothesis that the RDB agent would tend to engage in 'slippage' and prioritize development and, notably, market promotion over the more political goal of regional integration which is specifically noted in all RDB articles of agreement. The RDB agent continued to pursue regional integration and, more recently, geopolitical ambitions involving multi-polarity, but only as secondary goals to development, market promotion, and, most recently, market shaping. We have evidence of most of the RDB studied in this volume having demonstrated agency in attempting to expand their resources, as predicted in Principal-Agent analysis. Furthermore, we argue that most RDB have made deliberate use of their advantages in information and expertise in relation to their national government principals, to shift the main *de facto* goals and activities of RDB. Thus, RDB officials have played a central role in the shift from Continental and Sub-regional integration RDB to Continental market-led and Sub-regional market-led integration RDB, and then to +Continental strategic market and +Sub-regional strategic market integration RDB. The multiple principal—the board of governors /

national government shareholders—could have made use of *ex ante* and *ex post* control mechanisms to rein in the RDB agent and prevent slippage. However, we see few examples of national governments blocking RDB activities to promote markets during the second period of RDB development or, in the third period, engage in more interventionist market shaping. The degree of RDB autonomy is also determined in large part by the composition of the board of governors, and notably whether they are technical or political, and whether they are residential or not. The autonomy of the management team is more restricted when the board of governors' members are technical and resident because they are better able to follow the details of RDB operations. By way of examples, in the case of the EIB, the bank's management has greater autonomy because of the political and non-residential nature of the board of governor appointments; while in the case of the EBRD, the board of governors' members have greater expertise and are resident in London, thus maintaining greater control over the management of the bank.

3. The regional development banks

In this section, we provide an overview of the establishment and evolution of the major RDB in the world economy from the post-war period to the present with insights from an application of the Principal-Agent approach. Here we develop upon the five main RDB functions and how these have shifted over time: development, regional integration, market construction, multi-polarity reinforcement, and strategic market shaping/industrial policy.

The World Bank: a precursor of RDB?

Our comparative analysis of RDB takes as its point of departure the establishment of the world's first global MDB, the International Bank for Reconstruction and Development (IBRD) or the World Bank, created in 1944. Most studies locate the institutional origins of the main Continental and Sub-regional integration RDB in the IBRD. In particular, a number of authors argue that the RDB created in the years after the IBRD were influenced by its statutes, mandates, policy objectives, operations, technical assistance, and policy advice at the regional level—see, for example, Singh (1969); White (1970 and 1972); Culpeper (1994, 1997); Marichal (2011); and Raghavan (2016).

The apparent 'global' scope of the IBRD as its name would suggest hides at least two important motivations in the logic behind its creation: reconstruction in Europe and development in Latin America. With regard to European reconstruction, Hans Singer (1995) demonstrated that the IBRD, in fact, had a European rather than universal scope, at least during its early years of operation.[4] With regard to the Americas, the first proposal to create a Continental RDB dates back to the 1890s and had been presented at the First Pan-American Conference. In fact, the IBRD had been inspired by a US proposal for a Continental RDB for the Americas, the Inter-American Bank (IAB). Following the outbreak of the Second World War in 1939, the Roosevelt administration returned to work on an earlier proposal on the IAB for presentation to Congress. Oliver (1971) describes how Dexter White—the American architect of the Bretton Woods institutions—had been inspired directly by the draft proposal of the IAB in his contribution to plans on the IBRD.[5] In sum, the institutional model for the IBRD did not emerge from plans to address the global objectives of reconstruction and development (Helleiner 2017). Rather, it was borne of longstanding discussions, ideas, and projects designed for RDB to deal with political and economic challenges, in particular, in Europe and the Americas.

However, in the immediate post-war period, the reconstruction and relief tasks of the IBRD for Europe became less important, due to the introduction of the European Recovery Plan (Marshall Plan 1947-51) and the establishment of the Organisation of European Economic Cooperation (OEEC), which had been selected to disburse US aid to Western European countries (Clifton and Díaz-Fuentes 2011a, 2011b). As tensions increased between the USSR and the Western powers, and the shadow of the Cold War deepened, the central aim of the Marshall Plan and the OEEC was to promote strong market economies as an alternative to the command or planned economies led by the USSR. In this context, the IBRD assumed global development as its main function—which at the Bretton Woods conference had been pursued by Latin American and Caribbean countries, and which would be supported by an increasing number of newly independent countries in Africa, Asia, and the Pacific Rim. Under the presidency of Eugene Black (1949-63), the IBRD operated as a semi-autonomous agent. With close ties to the Wall Street financial elite—Black had previously been vice-president of the Chase Manhattan Bank—the president and the bank's board of directors, oriented the World Bank Group mainly to productive investment projects (inter alia, dams, power stations, and railroads) to promote economic development and market construction in market economies (Alacevich 2008, 2009). Thus, the world's first development bank set the precedent for MDB and RDB agency.

[4] Singer (1995) describes how the IBRD was originally conceived by American and British policy-makers as an RDB for Western Europe before the outbreak of the Second World War, as an alternative mechanism to bring about European economic development to counter Walter Frank's ambitions through the Nazi's 'New Order' plan.

[5] Although the IAB never materialized, it did, nonetheless, provide a blueprint which shaped later discussions on the creation of the IBRD.

Though the IBRD assumed its global role as a world development bank, the challenges of each continent and region were significantly different. Member states, therefore, as well as newly emerging countries post-independence, argued that the creation of RDB would be the best way to address the specific needs of each continent and region (White 1972; Culpeper 1994; Griffith-Jones et al. 2008). When subsequent RDB were created, both Continental and Sub-regional variants adopted key elements of the World Bank's statutes, mandates, policy objectives, and governance institutions, but adapted them to regional-specific challenges and the needs of their members.

Creating Continental and Sub-regional integration RDB

The model of the IBRD—an international government-owned institution with statutes, mandates, and objectives to invest in development projects, particularly infrastructure, under favourable long-term conditions, including low interest rates—was transferred directly into the design of three RDB which prioritized the development of the continent or continents in which they were established: the IADB, established in 1959; the AfDB, in 1964; and the ADB, in 1966. These RDB resembled the IBRD in many respects, including its mandates and approach to financial cooperation. These banks were established to provide specific forms of multilateral funding, technical assistance and policy advice to less-developed member countries in their respective continents.

Despite sharing several common basic features, these three RDB were different in a number of important respects. First, they differed in terms of the heterogeneity of member countries with regard to economic, political, cultural, institutional, and social characteristics. On a continuum, the IADB was the most homogenous RDB in linguistic and socio-political terms. In contrast, the AfDB was the bank with the greatest heterogeneity among member states, bringing together as it did newly independent countries, which were constituted by distinct groups based on colonial inheritance and official language. In addition, representatives of soon-to-be independent colonies worked towards the project of creating the AfDB. Hence, the dynamics of the internal relationships among members in the governance of these three RDB differed sharply. Second, the ways in which shareholding power was distributed differed. From the outset, the US was the largest shareholder of the IADB, which meant it could influence the bank's policy across the Americas. Along with Japan, the US was also the largest non-borrowing shareholder in the ADB. In contrast, the US—like other countries outwith the African continent—was originally excluded from holding shares in the AfDB. It was only from 1982 onwards that the US emerged as the major shareholder of the AfDB Group.

The IADB can be understood in terms that reflect the manifestation of US financial hegemonic power across the Americas and the Caribbean. Among the forty-four states that attended the Bretton Woods conference—a main purpose of which was to establish the IBRD in 1944—there were twenty Latin American and Caribbean countries that demanded that the IBRD prioritize active financing for their development and not just relief and reconstruction for Europe (Helleiner 2017). Once the UN system was established, with its original fifty-one member states, its Latin American and Caribbean members proposed the creation of a Sub-regional body, the Economic Commission for Latin America and the Caribbean (UN-ECLAC), in order to promote industrialization and infrastructure projects for development in the region. From the outset, the US and Canada were opposed to establishing the UN-ECLAC, fearing they could be excluded, and because they wanted to be part of a Continental inter-American Organization (as they had been in the Inter-American Treaty of Reciprocal Assistance, signed in 1947, and the Organization of American States, founded in 1948). The original opposition to the UN-ECLAC was not only from the US but also from the USSR, the United Kingdom, and France. Despite this, one year later, in 1948, the UN-ECLAC was established with a broad UN agreement and with the membership of all Latin American and Caribbean countries, plus the US, Canada, France, the Netherlands, and the United Kingdom. Thus, a decade before the IADB was established, in 1959, the UN-ECLAC members had already set up an integrated institutional framework through which industrial and infrastructural projects for development could be conceived and funded. Additionally, the need for an RDB focused on Latin America had been called for from 1948 by the UN-ECLAC, on the grounds that the IBRD did not pay sufficient attention to the development of their continent. The IADB was finally established in 1958, with the support of the US and Canada. The US would be its main, non-borrowing, and dominant shareholder, even though the Latin American and the Caribbean members collectively enjoyed a majority of voting power. As argued by Pablo López and Marcelo Rougier (Chapter 2, this volume), as the IADB evolved, its relationship with NDB began to weaken and, during the 1990s, its loans became increasingly conditioned by market criteria, including the implementation of market-oriented policies in line with the Washington Consensus.

By the end of the 1950s, the economic and political situation in Africa was very different to that in Latin America. Most African countries were still colonies or occupied territories that were struggling for independence from European colonial powers. At the Conference of the Peoples for Africa held in 1960, a resolution was approved to create an international financial institution (IFI) on a Continental scale. The agreement for an RDB was prepared and signed by the governments of twenty-two new African states in 1963 at the Conference of African Ministers of Finance in Khartoum, Sudan (AAI 2015). Thus, when the AfDB began operating in 1964, its member countries had experienced less than a decade of independence, whilst colonies still en route to independence were represented by provisional authorities. Given ongoing divisions rooted in different colonial legacies and new divisions derived from different approaches to development, AfDB member state governments failed to agree upon a clear common strategy for Continental development. The strong cultural, linguistic, and regional differences were reflected within the management and shareholding structure of the AfDB. Shareholders' voting patterns tended to align with a myriad cultural, geographical, and linguistic blocks, including Francophone, Anglophone, northern, eastern, central, western and, later, southern African blocks. The failure to develop a clear common strategy can also be blamed on the UN-Economic Commission for Africa (UN-ECA), which had been established in 1958, following the establishment of the UN-Economic Commission for Asia and the Far East (UN-ECAFE) in 1947 and the Latin American version, UN-ECLAC, in 1948. The UN-ECA was largely focused upon the basic needs of building national economic and social institutions under conditions of conflict and extreme poverty. Moreover, newly independent African governments baulked at the imposition of financial conditionality from donor countries outside of their continent—and non-African control, particularly if they were former colonial powers, but also the US and the USSR. Thus, initial AfDB capital was subscribed exclusively by newly independent African countries, excluding the participation of non-African countries (Schiavone 1997). Indeed, as Erika Kraemer-Mbula (Chapter 3, this volume) observes, the AfDB's national shareholders intended to preserve African ownership and identity. However, given the immense economic and social deprivations of the continent, as well as the financial restrictions imposed by its initial capital governance reserved exclusively for Continental members, the AfDB board of executive directors demonstrated agency by pushing actively to extend membership to wealthier countries outwith Africa (see Kraemer-Mbula, Chapter 3, this volume). In 1972, AfDB member state governments agreed to create an African Development Fund (AfDF) which would be open to countries beyond the continent as donors. The objective of the AfDF was to finance, on concessional terms, the poorest African countries. Despite this, there remained a lack of resources from which to draw. Hence, in 1982—following years of active recommendation from the AfDB itself—the AfDB member state governments finally allowed countries beyond the continent, including the US, to join as non-borrowing shareholders, albeit with a much smaller subscribed capital and voting power than in the IADB and ADB. Officially—if not in practice—non-African shareholders were permitted as long as the bank preserved its 'African character'. In her chapter (Chapter 3) for this volume, Kraemer-Mbula offers an important contribution exploring the historical evolution of the AfDB with regard to its efforts to tackle key issues related to industrial diversification, the protection of the natural environment, inclusion, and innovation, and the extent to which the bank is effectively positioned to develop present and future 'African solutions to African challenges'.

In the case of Asia, during the 1950s, the problems in the region were similar to those in the African continent, though on a much larger scale, as the region represented more than half of the world's population. Following the Second World War and, in the context of decolonization and the spread of communism, Asia witnessed some of the worst conflicts of the Cold War period. However, with regard to the international economic and financial institutions for development, there were more similarities between Asia and Latin America than with Africa. In 1947, the UN approved the creation of the UN-ECAFE (which was renamed UN-ESCAP in 1974). Originally, the UN-ECAFE had been established for post-war relief and reconstruction, the reduction of extreme poverty, and post-colonial institution building. In the 1960s, the UN-ECAFE played an important role in the definition of the main lines of regional development and financial cooperation. The Vietnam War, like the Cuban Revolution in 1959 in Latin America, made it imperative for the US government to increase its involvement in Asia, in particular, with a view to preventing the spread of communism (through its policy of containment). Hence, the US administration supported the creation of the ADB in 1965 to support the spread of capitalism and financial cooperation across the continent. From its establishment, the ADB's shareholder structure and the distribution of votes to countries from beyond the continent were more open than the AfDB and, even, the IADB. Some nineteen of its original members were from Asia and the Pacific, whilst twelve were countries outside of Asia. However, while the IADB included the majority of Latin American and Caribbean countries, the ADB had a more limited geographical scale, with the absence of non-capitalist countries—such as the Peoples' Republic of China until 1986—and Iran and Russia—which are still non-members to the present day (see Lanthier and Barjot, Chapter 4, this volume).

Hence, the ways in which each of the RDB's shareholder governance was established in the initial period differed significantly. The involvement of the US was greater in the Latin American and Asian RDB than in the African case. The US enhanced its involvement in the IADB and the ADB as part of its response to the Cuban revolution and the Vietnam War, whilst, in the African case, foreign involvement was perceived with suspicion by the AfDB's member state governments and initially rejected.

Just as the IBRD model was adapted into the three RDB working across continents, so it was also translated into those RDB that prioritized Sub-regional integration. The most important of these RDB were in Europe—the EIB, founded in 1958—and in the Americas, CABEI, established in 1960, and CAF, set up in 1968. The Soviet Union established a bank for the Council for Mutual Economic Assistance (COMECON) countries—the International Bank of Economic Cooperation (IBEC)—which also presented itself as a bank promoting integration. However, this bank was a short-lived and, ultimately, flawed attempt to integrate the command economies of Central and Eastern Europe.

The first RDB for integration emerged as part of the European Economic Community (EEC): the EIB, founded in 1958, was known as the 'Community's

Bank'. After the Second World War, a project for uniting Western European countries gained support, with the aim of maintaining peace, containing Soviet influence, and strengthening national economies by opening them to increased competition and economies of scale in markets. The EIB became, then, the main precedent for the establishment of a regional bank in charge of promoting the economic development and integration of its members. The creation of the EIB reflected above all Italian and French demands for financial support to compensate for their comparatively weak competitiveness and under-developed regions and sectors (Bussière et al. 2008). Later, the possibility of EIB finance to reduce regional disparities served to attract other European countries to join the EEC / European Union (EU) (Clifton et al. 2018). EIB finance thus became an important symbolic and practical element of the integration process (see Clifton et al., Chapter 5, this volume).

In 1960, CABEI was set up for the Central American Common Market (CACM). Over the next six decades, the CACM proved to be surprisingly stable despite the considerable political and economic upheavals in Central American and one of the most stable regional integration areas in the Global South. In parallel to the establishment of the EEC and the EIB, policy-makers in Central America became increasingly strong advocates for closer regional economic integration, particularly from the late 1950s until the 1970s. Both the EEC and the EIB directly inspired Central American leaders who signed the General Treaty on Central America Economic Integration, which included the establishment of CABEI (García 2015). Moreover, during the 1960s, a number of Central American leaders also undertook efforts to establish a monetary union, but the project lacked broad political support and institutional capacity (Desruelle and Schipke 2008). José Efraín Deras, Alberto Cortés, and Guillermo Funes (Chapter 6, this volume) examine the contribution by CABEI to economic and social development and regional integration. CABEI changed its focus from an original 'closed regional' approach to a more 'open regional' approach during the 1990s. However, the overwhelming bulk of its activities remained focused on the region itself. At the same time, CABEI engaged in agency slippage to re-orient its lending activities towards the private sector and to attract private international investors, though this activity was rather modest (see Deras et al., Chapter 6, this volume).

In the late 1960s, a second integration RDB was established in Latin America, this time, composed of the members of the Andean Group (Bolivia, Chile, Colombia, Ecuador, Peru, and, later, Venezuela). CAF emerged as an instrument to foster the economic and political integration of the Andean Group. Carlos Brando (Chapter 7, this volume) demonstrates how CAF—unlike the IADB and the IBRD but like the AfDB—was founded as a RDB by developing countries, intending to lend to other developing countries. In other words, the corporation was developed 'by the poor, from the poor, and to the poor' (Brando, Chapter 7, this volume: 131). CAF has been successful without being dependent on external powers, in particular, the US. The corporation began operation in June 1970 to promote regional integration and development. Despite the fact that the Andean Group did not progress as had been originally envisaged, and some of its founding member states abandoned the Sub-regional integration process in subsequent decades (Chile in 1976 and Venezuela in 2006), CAF maintained all the original shareholders and went on to expand its Sub-regional membership. Brando argues that CAF has been successful in allocating voice to some of its smaller members, such as Bolivia and Ecuador, as well as performing in line with its original mandates and constitutive principles. However, Brando also shows how, from the 1990s onwards, CAF demonstrated agency by expanding its activities beyond the integration focus of its original five Andean country shareholders, focusing instead principally upon development and market-making activities, leading to it becoming Latin America's largest development bank.

While most RDB were established in market economies, the command economies also attempted to promote their own IFI and RDB. Though the USSR, Poland, and Czechoslovakia participated in the Bretton Woods conference in 1944, they refused to take part in the IBRD (World Bank) and IMF, which they labelled instruments of imperialism and colonialism (Schröder 1982). In 1949, the USSR established the COMECON with five East European countries (Bulgaria, Czechoslovakia, Hungary, Poland, and Romania). One of COMECON's founding objectives was to create alternative IFI to the IMF and IBRD with the aim of facilitating international trade and to better integrate the infrastructure among its members. However, it would take more than a decade, in the shadow of the Cold War in 1963, for the IBEC—the Soviet Bank—to be established (Bednarik 1966). The IBEC was mainly an instrument of Soviet domination of the COMECON command economies. However, shortly after its creation, the IBEC expanded geographically beyond Central and Eastern Europe to integrate other command economies in Far Eastern Asia and the Caribbean (Mongolia in 1963, Cuba in 1974, and Vietnam in 1977). With the collapse of the USSR in 1991, the IBEC phased out its financial and trade functions (based on transferable roubles) and accounting activities (Conway 1995).

Regional development banks and the turn to the market

As we have seen, the RDB established in the 1950s and 1960s focused upon Continental development and Sub-regional integration, and operated in capitalist economies—with the exception of the IBEC. In the aftermath of the Cold War and, with the collapse of most of the command economies, there was renewed attention to market promotion. This period saw the emergence of new RDB, which were characterized by different priorities to those established in the 1950s and 1960s. At the same time, those already-existing RDB from the first period underwent a shift towards market promotion—which we explain in large part in terms of RDB agency—albeit to differing degrees.

After the command economies collapsed, a new challenge emerged in Europe. Central and Eastern European countries were faced with huge financial needs, which most of the EEC member states were keen to meet with a view to helping these countries transition towards market economies. The idea, promoted by French President François Mitterrand, to create a new RDB, gained strength. While the EIB would focus on the EEC member states, a newly proposed institution would work in parallel to and complement the EIB, and focus on supporting the transition of Central and Eastern Europe towards market economies.

The EBRD was set up in 1991 with forty national shareholders. The EBRD was not just a new RDB for economic and political transition in the former communist countries. It was also representative of a change in the approach, objectives and functions of other RDB. The EBRD was established at a rapid speed on 29 May 1990 and was operational less than a year later, in contrast to other RDB which took years or decades to become operational. The new bank was an important source of transition knowledge and expertise for Central and Eastern Europe, and beyond, and was to guide these countries towards an open-market economy (see Shields, Chapter 8, this volume). EBRD economists Willem Buiter and Steven Fries (2002a, 2002b) disagreed with the traditional view that RDB and global MDB should be fiscal agencies for the allocation of grants either to ensure international redistribution or to finance international public goods. Rather, they asserted that the EBRD and other RDB should foster market reform by investing primarily in privatization. Stuart Shields (Chapter 8, this volume) argues that the EBRD is something of an anomaly among RDB, to the extent it is officially a development bank but actually resembles a merchant bank, due to its use of commercial criteria, its focus on private sector development, and the manner in which it produces knowledge, with the aim of promoting competitiveness, and the establishment of 'correct institutions'. Steven D. Roper (Chapter 10, this volume) compares the design of EBRD to that of IADB, both established in regions undergoing dramatic economic and political change—Central and Eastern Europe from the 1990s after the collapse of communism in that region and Latin America in the shadow of the Cold War in 1959. Finding their structures to be quite similar, but their mandates rather different, Roper argues that the reason the IADB has been able to focus on social development and poverty reduction loans, whilst the EBRD has concentrated on private sector development can be largely explained by the fact the IADB has ultimately been controlled by its borrowers, whereas the EBRD has been controlled by its lenders.

In the political and intellectual climate of the 1980s, many of the existing RDB shifted towards a more market-oriented focus. A re-orientation towards the market economy was also developing within the global MDB, notably within the

World Bank and the IMF. A key event in this period was the debt crisis that hit Latin America and Africa particularly hard. The shift to market promotion can be seen very clearly in the case of the IADB. Sarah Babb (Chapter 11, this volume) uses newly declassified documents from the US National Archive as well as information retrieved through the Freedom of Information Act to explore how the IADB was gradually subjected to greater control by the US at the expense of influence from Latin American countries during the 1980s (Tussie 1995). In 1982, though the IADB operated under a Latin American majority, with the US holding only 34.6 per cent of the votes, the bank became the target of the Reagan administration's policy to reduce the scope of public intervention by both domestic and international institutions. When Mexico and Brazil declared a foreign debt moratorium in 1982, the US Treasury made US participation in RDB and global MDB conditional upon policy reforms, stating that borrowing countries would be 'graduated' (non-eligible for loans) once they reached a certain level of GDP per capita and met thresholds of reliance on private finance (ODI 1991). Babb (Chapter 11, this volume) argues that, through the Baker Plan (1985), a decision was taken to attach conditionality strictly to loans to Latin America. Specifically, the Reagan administration imposed market-oriented policies upon Latin American governments seeking to benefit from IADB lending. The IADB was placed under supervision of the World Bank and became the third financial institution to push so-called Washington Consensus policies, after the World Bank and the IMF. The Reagan administration also insisted that lending programmes should promote privatization, trade, investment liberalization, and neoliberal economic policy reforms (Lustig 1997). Gradually, the IADB moved from a traditional project loan approach to a conditionality approach based on adjustment loans which were regularly associated with austerity measures similar to those imposed at the time by the World Bank and the IMF (Babb, Chapter 11, this volume). Thus, in the case of the IADB, it would be problematic to assign a decisive role to RDB agency in the move to market construction. Clearly, senior IADB officials may have supported the transformation of Bank lending policies. However, the role of US administration pressure was crucial.

Similar pressures in favour of market promotion and a more programme-based lending were experienced by the ADB and the AfDB (ODI 1992). By the 1990s, those RDB that had originally focused on development of the continent had experienced a shift away from a development approach towards the promotion of structural adjustment as advocated by US administrations and inscribed in the so-called Washington Consensus (ODI 1996; Rana 2014). However, while this development reflected pressure from the US government shareholder, our chapter authors also argue that the ADB and AfDB demonstrated considerable agency in pushing the new approach to lending (Barjot and Lanthier, Chapter 4, and Kraemer-Mbula, Chapter 3, both this volume).

In the EEC/EU, the EIB had long played a role in promoting both market integration and liberalization. Clifton et al. (2017) examine EIB lending from the 1960s to the 2000s demonstrating a move away from the EIB's initial focus upon reducing regional and national disparities in the EEC/EU to lending that was proportional to shareholding. In their chapter (Chapter 13) for this volume, Howarth and Liebe argue that the EIB promoted market/private sector solutions to public funding needs—specifically PPPs—from the late 1980s. In this, the EIB was only the first of most of the RDB to engage in the promotion of market forces. The EIB was able to direct a massive policy network on PPPs reaching across European Commission directorates-general, down to national, regional, and local authorities, and to private sector operators (both financial and infrastructural companies). The EIB initially promoted PPPs through major EU transport, energy, and communication infrastructure projects—the Trans-European Networks (TENS). From 1998, the EIB began to discuss the usefulness of PPPs in its monthly newsletters (EIB 1998). The EIB promoted PPPs at both EU and national levels as potentially being more efficient than alternative mechanisms of public financing, with lower maintenance costs, better risk management, better quality, and faster implementation. The EIB also raised the possibility of PPPs when it focused upon investment in less-developed areas and accession countries. The EIB's efforts were bolstered from 2008 by the creation of the European PPP Expertise Centre (EPEC) within the bank, with the official mandate of capacity-building among participating member states and as a forum for information exchange among members. By early 2020, EPEC had thirty-one national units as members and an addition eight sub-national (regional) units. EPEC was thus explicitly created with the aim of helping to strengthen the capacity of its national public sector members to enter into PPP transactions. Furthermore, the EU Commission and Council agreed upon the requirement that all countries seeking EIB funding were obliged to establish PPP units. The EIB was regularly present when PPPs were discussed at the European level, with the aim of preparing and facilitating a 'window of opportunity' which—while opened an inch or two for a couple of decades—was fully opened in the years following the outbreak of the international financial crisis (from 2008) and then euro area sovereign debt crisis (from 2010). Through this activism, the EIB agent engaged in agency slippage, going well-beyond its mandate set by its shareholder principals and promoting a financing mechanism that a number of member states had previously discouraged at the national level. Howarth and Liebe (Chapter 13, this volume) also point to the rapid growth in PPP promotion and usage by almost all RDB throughout the world. This promotion and usage has been encouraged through co-financing and expertise from the World Bank Group and the EIB, and by the British government through its development aid.

Regional development banks, Shifting Wealth, and the return of the 'policy that should not be named'

The third and most recent period of RDB creation occurred in parallel to the economic and geo-political rise or re-emergence of countries in the South and East. Though this shift is largely a consequence of the re-emergence of a global economic power—the PRC—it is also associated with the gradual relative decline of traditional Western economic powers and the faster growth in a number of newly emerging economies, including Brazil, India, Indonesia, Mexico, and Russia. Alice Amsden (2001) predicted early on that, by following specific policy approaches, notably forms of state intervention in industrial policy, the 'rest' could attempt to catch-up with the West, resulting in an increasingly 'multi-polar' world economy (Clifton and Díaz-Fuentes 2014). Mahbubani (2013) argues that the rise of these new players from the Global South will lead to strategies whereby existing institutions—here, the global MDB and RDB—are increasingly challenged by countries in the Global South, after experiencing them as insufficiently flexible and attentive to their needs and demands.

There are two main shifts in this third period of RDB creation, one affecting the geography of RDB, the other, their function. Starting with geography, both the new and already existing RDB—as well as the new and existing NDB—have adopted a broader and more ambitious vision of the geography in which they can operate (Mazzucato and Penna 2016; Griffith-Jones and Ocampo 2018; Mertens and Thiemann 2019). Newly established NDB, such as the China Development Bank in 1994, and the redeveloped NDB in Brazil (BNDES) in the first decade of the 2000s, provide examples of development banks that operate beyond their national space. These NDB have also designed the New Development Bank (the Bank of the BRICS (Brazil, Russia, India, China, and South Africa)) as a global MDB, as opposed to an RDB (Humphrey 2016; Wang 2017; Wang 2019). Both the AIIB and the New Development Bank offer an increasingly important source of alternative finance than that provided by the existing RDB.

With regard to the function of RDB, there has recently been an important—albeit uneven—shift in the form of renewed attention to a role for industrial policy. The traditional function of RDB was to leverage public funds, acting as catalysers for entrepreneurial and innovative investment when capital was scarce, whilst also playing a countercyclical role, providing access to capital during economic downturns, when private investors were reluctant to invest. Recently, however, RDB have entered into new funding areas, including new technologies and the global green economy (Griffith-Jones and Cozzi 2017). RDB (as well as NDB) are increasingly adopting—or being urged to adopt—a longer-term perspective, in order to cope with the risks associated with the funding of innovation.

This shift in function can be understood as a rebalancing of the trend towards the market, as discussed with regard to the second period of RDB creation, and is part of a global trend. IMF chief economists have expressed support for the re-emergence of industrial policy—the 'policy that shall not be named' (Cherif and Hasanov 2019a, 2019b). The attitude to industrial policy differs markedly by region. Whereas in Asia, industrial policy has largely remained a legitimate tool of government throughout the post-war period (Wang 2017), in Europe—where it went out of fashion in the 1980s—there is a revival (Mertens and Thieman 2018; Naqvi, Henow, and Chang 2019; Mertens, Thieman, and Volberding forthcoming).

The AIIB is the harbinger of new RDB created in the context of Shifting Wealth. This bank was set up in 2014 with the stated aim of covering the infrastructure financing gap in developing countries worldwide, and developing Asia in particular. Jiajun Xu (Chapter 9, this volume) argues that the creation of the AIIB reflects nothing less than the rising challenge by China to US hegemony. China has adopted a 'two-legged' approach (ODI 2015; Xu 2017 and Chapter 9, this volume): it has continued to vie for power within the already existing MDB but, at the same time, has focused on the creation of new development banks at the international, regional, and national levels. In the absence of sufficient international political will to change the voting power within existing multilateral and regional institutions—for example, as chronicled by Vestergaard and Wade (2013) at the World Bank—China decided to act. The AIIB was established with a capital of USD 100 billion and fifty-seven founding member countries, which increased to seventy-seven prior to the start of AIIB operations in 2016. Xu explores how the design of AIIB governance, membership, capital stock, financial instruments, mandates, and lending practice reflect these shifts, comparing this new bank to the World Bank and the ADB in particular. For example, with regard to RDB voting power, whilst in the ADB, Japan and the US together can potentially veto a decision, in the AIIB, the PRC alone holds this power. The AIIB's reach goes far beyond the continent in which it is based: rather, geography seems irrelevant, as the bank seeks out countries with an interest in and need for its 'shared vision'. Therefore, rather than pursuing traditional regional integration, the AIIB officially seeks to promote lending and borrowing well beyond the region. In the space of a few years, most of the world's largest economies have become shareholders, with the notable exceptions of the US and Japan, which continue to prioritize the role of the ADB in Asia and the Pacific.

In addition, previously established RDB have become more ambitious as to their reach. In Latin America, CAF is an important example, having extended its lending activities beyond the Andean Group. From the middle of the 2000s, CAF expanded to include additional and larger members, and notably Argentina and Brazil. This expansion allowed the bank to access increased capital and offer more loans with lower conditionality restrictions than applied by other RDB in Latin America, including the World Bank and the IADB (Babb,

Chapter 11, this volume). This has made CAF a particularly attractive source of funding for Latin American countries. In 2005, the founding statute of CAF was modified to allow non-founding members (Argentina, Brazil, Panama, Paraguay, Uruguay, and Trinidad and Tobago) to become full members. The bank was renamed the CAF Development Bank of Latin America. This was not just a simple rebranding exercise but indicative of an explicit ambition to become the largest Latin American RDB in the 2010s (Brando, Chapter 7, this volume; CAF-Banco de Desarrollo de América Latina 2016).

The AfDB has demonstrated both tendencies of the third period (see Kraemer-Mbula, Chapter 3, this volume). First, it has continued to expand its membership beyond the African continent, a process started in the early 1980s. Of the AfDB's eighty member states, twenty-six today come from outwith the continent. To counter US and European influence, the AfDB group accepted both Indian and Chinese government membership as early as 1982 and 1985, respectively. The importance of joint initiatives with the PRC have increased considerably over the past two decades and China has become the thirteenth largest contributor to the AfDF.[6] Second, the AfDB has recently embraced a return to a more interventionist market shaping policy, notably through the bank's 'High 5s' development priorities adopted in 2016 (AfDB Group 2019). The 'High 5s' include energy production and supply, and agricultural infrastructural projects but also a priority focused upon industrialization (see Kraemer-Mbula, Chapter 3, this volume). This interventionism has come hand in hand with a renewed focus on economic integration in the continent.

In Europe, too, RDB are adapting. The EIB is a good case in point. In the aftermath of the Great Recession of the late 2000s and early 2010s, the EIB came under criticism for overly conservative lending patterns and for failing to meet long-term development goals in the region and beyond (Clifton et al., Chapter 5, this volume). In 2015, the European Commission advocated a 'promotional role' for the EIB in supporting the Commission's Investment Plan for Europe and European Fund for Strategic Investment (European Commission 2015; Kavvadia, Chapter 12, this volume). Moreover, there is some evidence of the EIB performing the role of an activist agent by pushing in favour of interventionist market shaping. For example, the EIB president, Werner Hoyer, claims that he conceived the Investment Plan for Europe and promoted it to the Commission (Hoyer 2015). Simultaneously, several European countries have established new 'promotional' NDB (European Commission 2015; European Parliament 2016). Examples are the British Business Bank (2014) and the Green Investment Bank (2012) in the UK, the Strategic Banking Corporation (2014) in Ireland, and the Instituição Financeira de Desenvolvimento (2014) in Portugal. Moreover, existing NDB,

[6] https://www.afdb.org/en/countries/non-regional-member-countries/china

such as the German KfW (Kreditanstalt für Wiederaufbau) and the Spanish ICO (Instituto de Crédito Oficial: Official Credit Institute) have renewed their development functions to respond to the EU's investment plans (Mertens and Thiemann 2019; Clifton et al. 2019). Over the past decade, for example, the EIB has become a world leader in the promotion of green bonds. Moreover, in 2019, a High-Level Group of Wise Persons argued that the EIB and EBRD required urgent restructuring to avoid inefficiencies and duplications, with a view to bolster a strong development global action plan beyond Europe, particularly, in view of the challenges in Africa and as a result of climate change (Wieser et al. 2019; Kavvadia, Chapter 12, this volume).

4. Conclusion

In this chapter, we offer a revised categorization of RDB, through an analysis of their changing geographical operations and their changing prioritization of five functions—development, regional integration, market promotion, multi-polarity reinforcement, and strategic market shaping/industrial policy—over three periods. We argue that most RDB moved from a prioritization of regional development and integration towards a prioritization of regional development and market promotion and then to a prioritization of geographic expansion and, for a few RDB, multi-polarity and strategic market interventionism and industrial policy. We also argue that in the twenty-first century at least one RDB—the AIIB—one MDB, and a number of NDB have been created to promote multi-polarity in the world. Over the past two decades, a number of older RDB have extended their activities geographically beyond their original area of operation—be it a continent or a sub-region. Furthermore, we detect the re-assertion by a number of RDB of an industrial policy designed to promote regional development. The RDB that were created in the 1950s and 1960s were categorized by White (1970, 1972) as 'Continental and Sub-regional-integration' RDB. These transformed into what we label Continental market-led and Sub-regional market-led integration RDB in the second period and, in the third period, to +Continental strategic market and +Sub-regional strategic market integration RDB.

To explain these transformations, we argue that most RDB have operated as semi-autonomous agents engaged in 'slippage'. Most of the RDB that we examine in this volume developed preferences on their activities that diverged from their multiple principals—their member state government shareholders—because of different underlying interests and information asymmetries. During the second period, all of the existing RDB sought to prioritize market-led policies: hence, RDB such as the EIB that promoted integration focused on 'market promotion', whilst Continental RDB pushed a market-led development (Carroll et al. 2019).

During the third period, a number of RDB sought to increase the geographical spread of their membership and lending patterns, while engaging in more interventionist market shaping activities. There is clear evidence that the AfDB, CAF, and the EIB pushed their member state shareholders in this direction. Vaubel's (2006: 127) claims regarding World Bank interests—that it sought 'more staff, a larger budget and increasing competencies'—were paralleled in the efforts of most RDB similarly focused on resource expansion. During the third ongoing period, if we are to witness the development of an increasingly interventionist RDB industrial policy, this would also likely reflect semi-autonomous agency and these underlying interests.

Having made this argument in favour of the usefulness of the Principal-Agent analysis to explain the development of RDB activities over the past sixty years, it is nonetheless important to recognize the limits to the explanatory merits of this approach. RDB agency was constrained in a number of cases—notably where member state shareholders asserted political objectives. RDB agency was also constrained in cases—notably the IADB and the ADB—where a powerful element of the principal—respectively, the US government and the Japanese government—actively shaped the development of the RDB in favour of market promotion during the second period. However, in these two cases, US and Japanese government preferences on the prioritization of market promotion broadly aligned with the preferences of most RDB at the time.

In their concluding chapter to this volume (Chapter 14), José Antonio Alonso and José Cuesta ask if 'we still need regional development banks today (and tomorrow)?' Although they avoid a conclusive answer to this question, they nonetheless point to the important position of RDB in the global economy. In addition to tackling market failure—and specifically overcoming the unwillingness of private sector finance to invest in long-term and costly infrastructural projects in many parts of the world—RDB are particularly well-placed to overcome collective action problems related to the provision of RPGs, given the complexity and the supranational scope of these kinds of goods. Bridging huge gaps in infrastructure financing is crucial for development in many parts of the world. Furthermore, in the context of slower global economic growth, investment in infrastructure offers a strategy for immediate growth but also a way to invest in climate friendly technology that promotes environmentally sustainable growth. The recent creation of the AIIB indicates both the frustration of the Chinese government with existing RDB and its recognition of the ongoing relevance of RDB. At the same time, the AIIB creates a potential challenge as an innovative RDB. Its emergence combined with the rising profile of a number of RDB (such as the CAF Latin American Development Bank) provide traditional RDB with possible guidance to reform their organization, administrative procedures, infrastructure investment, and even policy remit.

References

AAI (The Africa-America Institute) (2015). *From the Archives: Establishment of the African Development Bank*, 15 April. Available online at: http://www.aaionline.org/from-the-archives-establishment-of-the-african-development-bank/ (Accessed 25 January 2018).

AfDB Group (African Development Bank Group) (2019). *Annual Development Effectiveness Review: Integrating Africa, Connecting People*. Abidjan: African Development Bank.

Alacevich, M. (2008). *The World Bank's Early Reflections on Development: A Development Institution or a Bank?* Washington, DC: The World Bank.

Alacevich, M. (2009). 'The World Bank's early reflections on development: a development institution or a bank?', *Review of Political Economy*, 21(2): 227–44.

Amsden, A.H. (2001). *The Rise of "The Rest: Challenges to the West from Late-industrializing Economies*. Oxford: Oxford University Press.

Babb, S. (2013). 'The Washington Consensus as transnational policy paradigm: its origins, trajectory and likely successor', *Review of International Political Economy*, 20(2): 268–97.

Bednarik, M.K. (1966). 'The Moscow Bank: The International Bank for Economic Cooperation', *The American Review of Soviet and Eastern European Foreign Trade*, 2(1): 3–8.

Ben-Artzi, Ruth (2016). *Regional Development Banks in Comparison: Banking Strategies versus Development Goals*. New York: Cambridge University Press.

Bendor, J., Glazer, A., and Hammond, T. (2001). 'Theories of delegation', *Annual Review of Political Science*, 4: 235–69.

Bhattacharya, A. and Kharas, H. (2016). *The Role of Regional Development Banks in the New Global Agenda*. Washington, DC: Brookings.

Boitan, I.A. (2017). *Examining the Role of National Promotional Banks in the European Economy: Emerging Research and Opportunities*. Hershey, PA: IGI Global.

Buiter, W. and Fries, S. (2002a) 'Quelle devrait être la mission des banques multilatérals de développement?' , *Revue d'économie du développement*, 10: 171–204.

Buiter, W.H. and Fries, S.M. (2002b). *What Should the Multilateral Development Banks Do?* London: European Bank for Reconstruction and Development.

Bussière, É., Dumoulin, M., and Willaert, É. (eds.) (2008). *The Bank of the European Union: The EIB, 1958–2008*. Luxembourg: European Investment Bank.

CAF-Banco de Desarrollo de América Latina (2016). *25 años de gestión*. Caracas: CAF.

Carroll, T., Clifton, J., and Jarvis, D.S.L. (2019). 'Power, leverage and marketization: the diffusion of neoliberalism from North to South and back again', *Globalizations*, 16(6): 771–7.

Cherif, R. and Hasanov, F. (2019a). *The Return of the Policy That Shall Not Be Named: Principles of Industrial Policy*. Wp 19/74. Washington, DC: International Monetary Fund.

Cherif, R. and Hasanov, F. (2019b). 'The leap of the tiger: escaping the middle-income trap to the technological frontier', *Global Policy*, 10(4): 497–511.

Clifton, J. and Díaz-Fuentes, D. (2011a). From 'club of the rich' to 'globalisation à la carte'? Evaluating reform at the OECD. *Global Policy*, *2*(3): 300–11.

Clifton, J. and Díaz-Fuentes, D. (2011b). The OECD and phases in the international political economy, 1961–2011. *Review of International Political Economy*, 18: 552–69.

Clifton, J. and Díaz-Fuentes, D. (2014). 'Is the Organisation for Economic Co-operation and Development ready for China?', *Emerging Markets Finance and Trade*, 50: 21–36.

Clifton, J., Díaz-Fuentes, D., and Gómez, A.L. (2018). 'The European Investment Bank: development, integration, investment?', *JCMS: Journal of Common Market Studies*, 56(4): 733–50.

Clifton, J., Díaz-Fuentes, D., and Revuelta, J. (2014). 'Financing utilities: how the role of the European Investment Bank shifted from regional development to making markets', *Utilities Policy*, 29: 63–71.

Conway, P. (1995). *Currency Proliferation: The Monetary Legacy of the Soviet Union*. Princeton: Princeton University Press.

Cook, L.D. and Sachs, J. (1999). 'Regional public goods in international assistance'. In I. Kaul, I. Grunberg, and M. Stern, et al. (eds.), *Global Public Goods: International Cooperation in the 21st Century*. Oxford: United Nations Development Program / Oxford University Press, pp. 436–49.

Culpeper, R. (1994). 'Regional development banks: exploiting their specificity', *Third World Quarterly*, 15(3): 459–82.

Culpeper, R. (1997). *The Multilateral Development Banks: Titans or Behemoths?* Boulder, CO: Lynne Rienner / Ottawa: The North-South Institute.

Desruelle, D. and Schipke, A. (eds.) (2008). *Central America: Economic Progress and Reforms*. Washington, DC: IMF.

EIB (European Investment Bank) (1998). 'The EIB and Public-Private Partnerships', *EIB Information*, 97(2): 4–6.

Elsig, M. (2011). 'Principal-Agent theory and the World Trade Organization: complex agency and "missing delegation"', *European Journal of International Relations*, 17(3): 495–517.

European Commission (2015). 'Working together for jobs and growth: the role of national promotional banks (NPBs) in supporting the Investment Plan for Europe'. Communication from the Commission to the European Parliament and the Council, COM(2015)361. Available at: https://eur-lex.europa.eu/legal-content/en/TXT/?uri=CELEX%3A52015DC0361 (Accessed 28 February 2020).

European Parliament (2016). 'New financial instruments and the role of national promotional banks'. Study by Directorate General for Internal Policies. Policy Department D: Budgetary Affairs. Available at: https://www.europarl.europa.eu/RegData/etudes/STUD/2016/572687/IPOL_STU(2016)572687_EN.pdf (Accessed 28 February 2020).

García, M. (2015). 'The European Union and Latin America: "transformative power Europe" versus the realities of economic interests', *Cambridge Review of International Affairs*, 28(4): 621–40.

Griffith-Jones, S. and Cozzi, G. (2017). 'The roles of development banks; how they can promote investment, in Europe and globally'. In A. Noman and J.E. Stiglitz (eds.), *Efficiency, Finance, and Varieties of Industrial Policy: Guiding Resources, Learning, and Technology for Sustained Growth*. New York: Columbia University Press, pp. 131–55.

Griffith-Jones, S. and Ocampo, J.A. (eds.) (2018). *The Future of National Development Banks*. Oxford: Oxford University Press.

Griffith-Jones, S., Griffith-Jones, D., and Hertova, D. (2008). 'Enhancing the role of regional development banks'. G-24 Discussion Paper Series No. 50, July. UNCTAD: New York. Available at: http://www20.iadb.org/intal/catalogo/PE/2009/02608.pdf (Accessed 28 February 2020).

Hawkins, D. and Jacoby, W. (2006). 'How agents matter'. In Darren Hawkins, David Lake, Daniel L. Nielson, and Michael J. Tierney (eds.), *Delegation and Agency in International Organizations*. Cambridge: Cambridge University Press, pp. 199–228.

Hawkins, D., Lake, D., Nielson, D., and Tierney, M.J. (eds.) (2006). *Delegation and Agency in International Organisations*. Cambridge: Cambridge University Press.

Helleiner, E. (2017). 'The Latin American origins of Bretton Woods'. In M. Margulis (ed.), *The Global Political Economy of Raúl Prebisch*. London: Routledge, pp. 96–112.

Hoyer, W. (2015). 'The investment plan for Europe'. Bridge Forum Dialogue, 27 October. Available at: https://forum-dialogue.lu/wp-content/uploads/discours-du-president-hoyer.pdf (Accessed: 28 February 2020).

Humphrey, C. (2016). 'The invisible hand: financial pressures and organisational convergence in multilateral development banks', *The Journal of Development Studies*, 52(1): 92–112.

IMF (International Monetary Fund) (2018). *Program Design in Currency Unions*, Policy Paper. Washington, DC: International Monetary Fund.

Kiewiet, D.R. and McCubbins, M.D. (1991). *The Logic of Delegation: Congressional Parties and the Appropriations Process*. Chicago: University of Chicago Press.

Lustig, N. (1997). 'The United States to the rescue: financial assistance to Mexico in 1982 and 1995', *Cepal Review*, 67: 41–61.

Lyne, M.M., Nielson, D.L., and Tierney, M.J. (2006). 'Who delegates? Alternative models of principals in development aid'. In D. Hawkins, D. Lake, D.L. Nielson, and M.J. Tierney (eds.), *Delegation and Agency in International Organizations*. Cambridge: Cambridge University Press, pp. 41–76.

Mahbubani, K. (2013). *The Great Convergence: Asia, the West, and the Logic of One World*. New York: Public Affairs.

Marichal, C. (2011). *Los antecedentes históricos de la creación del Banco Interamericano de Desarrollo: reflexiones a partir del archivo de Eduardo Villaseñor*. Mexico City: El Colegio de México.

Martin, L. (2006). 'Distribution, information, and delegation to international organizations: the case of IMF conditionality'. In D. Hawkins, D. Lake, D.L. Nielson, and M.J. Tierney (eds.), *Delegation and Agency in International Organizations*. Cambridge: Cambridge University Press, pp. 140–64.

Mazzucato, M. and Penna, C.C. (2016). 'Beyond market failures: the market creating and shaping roles of state investment banks', *Journal of Economic Policy Reform*, 19(4): 305–26.

McCubbins, M. and Schwartz, T. (1984). 'Congressional oversight overlooked: police patrols versus fire alarms', *American Journal of Political Science*, 28(1): 165–79.

Mertens, D. and Thiemann, M. (2018). 'Market-based but state-led: the role of public development banks in shaping market-based finance in the European Union', *Competition & Change*, 22(2): 184–204.

Mertens, D. and Thiemann, M. (2019). 'Building a hidden investment state? The European Investment Bank, national development banks and European economic governance', *Journal of European Public Policy*, 26(1): 23–42.

Mertens, D., Thieman, M., and Volberding, P. (forthcoming). *The Making of European Field of Development Banking*. Oxford: Oxford University Press.

Naqvi, N., Henow, A., and Chang, H.-J. (2019). 'Kicking away the financial ladder: German development banking under economic globalisation', *Review of International Political Economy*, 24(6): 759–70.

Nielson, D.L. and Tierney, M.J. (2003). 'Delegation to international organizations: agency theory and World Bank environmental reform', *International Organization*, 57(2): 241–76.

ODI (Overseas Development Institute) (1991). *The Inter-American Development Bank and Changing Policies for Latin America*. London: Overseas Development Institute.

ODI (Overseas Development Institute) (1992). *The African Development Bank: Facing New Challenges*. London: Overseas Development Institute.

ODI (Overseas Development Institute) (1996). *Rethinking the Role of Multilateral Development Banks*. London: Overseas Development Institute.

ODI (Overseas Development Institute) (2015). *Multilateral Development Banks in the 21st Century: Three Perspectives on China and the Asian Infrastructure Investment Bank*. London: Overseas Development Institute.

OECD (Organisation for Economic Co-operation and Development) (2010). *Perspective on Global Development: Shifting Wealth*. Paris: OECD.

Oliver, R.W. (1971). *Early Plans for a World Bank* (No. 29). Princeton: International Finance Section, Princeton University.

Raghavan, V. (2016) 'The World Bank and regional development banks'. *Proceedings of the Annual Meeting* (American Society of International Law), 110: 273–7.

Rana, P.B. (2014). 'From a centralized to a decentralized global economic architecture: an overview', *New Global Economic Architecture*, 11. In M. Kawai, P.J. Morgan, and P.B. Rana (eds.), *New Global Economic Architecture: The Asian Perspective*. Cheltenham: Edward Elgar Publishing.

Ravallion, M. (2016). 'The World Bank: why it is still needed and why it still disappoints', *Journal of Economic Perspectives*, 30(1): 77–94.

Robinson, N. (2009). 'The European Investment Bank: the EU's neglected institution', *Journal of Common Market Studies*, 47(3): 651–73.

Schiavone, G. (1997). *International Organizations: A Dictionary* (4th edn). London: Macmillan.

Schröder, K. (1982). 'The IMF and the countries of the Council for Mutual Economic Assistance', *Intereconomics*, 17(2): 87–90.

Singer, D. (2007). *Regulating Capital: Setting Standards for the International Financial System*. Ithaca: Cornell University Press.

Singer, H.W. (1995). 'An historical perspective'. In P. Streeten, M.U. Haq, R. Jolly, and M. Ul Haq (eds.), *The UN and the Bretton Woods Institutions*. Basingstoke: Palgrave Macmillan, pp. 17–25.

Singh, M. (1969). 'Regional development banks', *International Conciliation*, 38(1): 576. (January.)

Tussie, D. (1995). *Inter-American Development Bank*, Vol. 4: *Collection 'The Multilateral Banks'*. Boulder, CO: Lynne Rienner Publishers / Ottawa: The North-South Institute.

Vaubel, R. (2006). 'Principal-agent problems in international organizations', *Review of International Organizations*, 1: 125–38.

Vestergaard, J. and Wade, R.H. (2013). 'Protecting power: how Western states retain the dominant voice in the World Bank's governance', *World Development*, 46: 153–64.

Vestergaard, J. and Wade, R.H. (2015). 'Still in the woods: gridlock in the IMF and the World Bank puts multilateralism at risk', *Global Policy*, 6(1): 1–12.

Wang, H. (2017). 'New multilateral development banks: opportunities and challenges for global governance', *Global Policy*, 8(1): 113–18.

Wang, H. (2019). 'The New Development Bank and the Asian Infrastructure Investment Bank: China's ambiguous approach to global financial governance', *Development and Change*, 50(1): 221–44.

Weingast, B.R. and Moran, M.J. (1983). 'Bureaucratic discretion or Congressional control?', *Journal of Political Economy*, 91: 765–800.

White, J. (1970). *Regional Development Banks. A Study of Institutional Style*. London: Overseas Development Institute.

White, J. (1972). *Regional Development Banks: The Asian, African and Inter-American Development Banks*. New York: Praeger.

Wieser, T., Alonso, J.A., Barbut, M., Berglof, E., Dominik, J., Kleiterp, N., Kloppenburg, N., Passacantando, F., and Ulbaek, S. (2019). *Europe in the World: The Future of the European Financial Architecture for Development.* October. Brussels: General Secretariat of the Council of the EU. Economic and Financial Affairs.

Xu, J. (2017). *Beyond US Hegemony in International Development: The Contest for Influence at the World Bank*. Cambridge: Cambridge University Press.

PART ONE

THE RISE OF THE REGIONAL DEVELOPMENT BANKS

2

Transformations, Ruptures, and Continuities in the Inter-American Development Bank's Policy from 1980 to the Present

Pablo J. López and Marcelo Rougier

1. Introduction

Although there are a considerable number of studies about multilateral development banks (MDB), specific literature about the Inter-American Development Bank (IADB) is not as prolific, especially research with a long-term historic view. This void in the economic literature includes the lack of a consistent periodization of the IADB's development and its transformation since its founding. This chapter analyses the policy lines followed by the IADB from its creation to the present, focusing particularly on the last four decades. Our objective is to investigate how the IADB's lending policy from the 1980s to present has expressed the transformation in mainstream perspectives regarding the 'best' policies to boost economic development and how those changes defined the successive phases that characterized the Bank's policy guidelines. At the same time, we explore whether a larger participation of the borrowing countries in the IADB's governance influenced the kind of credit lines the Bank granted in response to the specific needs of regional development, unlike the lending policies of other multilateral banks that confer donor countries more voting power in the governance of those institutions. With the creation of the IADB in 1959, Latin American countries gained a regional bank to finance projects related to their economic development. These countries also gained a source of foreign currency in a context of recurring balance of payment crises.

This chapter shows that, although the IADB's mandate remained unchanged over the course of more than fifty years from its launch, the Bank's lending policies in the region changed over time, consistent with the prevailing policy framework in developed countries. Unlike in other MDB with a presence in the

Pablo J. López and Marcelo Rougier, *Transformations, Ruptures, and Continuities in the Inter-American Development Bank's Policy from 1980 to the Present* In: *Regional Development Banks in the World Economy.* Edited by: Judith Clifton, Daniel Díaz-Fuentes, and David Howarth, Oxford University Press (2021).
DOI: 10.1093/oso/9780198861089.003.0002

region—especially the World Bank—Latin American countries played a bigger role in the IADB's decision-making process from the very moment the regional bank was created. However, donor countries enforced IADB policy guidelines, with a varying degree of conflict over the different periods.

In terms of the IADB's transformation, we establish that the institution underwent a transition phase, which began in the 1980s, marking a move away from a developmental role associated with state-led industrialization processes. The IADB became a supporter of liberalization and deregulation policies in the 1990s, an orientation that remained almost unchanged until the 2008–9 global crisis, during which the institution played an important countercyclical role and noticeably increased its total loans. With more competition from national and other regional development banks (RDB), starting in 2010, while maintaining market-friendly fundamentals, the IADB lending policy focused heavily on the development of physical infrastructure in the region, seeking to boost competitiveness to promote free trade, and the transformation of economies towards more environmentally sustainable models.

In recent years, numerous studies have differentiated MDB from RDB, highlighting the particularities of the latter.[1] In addition, several studies compare the different characteristics of RDB, including the IADB.[2] Although a handful of specific studies about the IADB were published in the 1990s—including Griffith-Jones (1994), Tussie (1995), and Scheman (1997)—research updates or new studies are few and far between. Chapter 11 by Sarah Babb in this volume sheds light on the significant changes in the IADB's policy during the 1980s as a result of United States (US) pressure on MDB and Latin American countries, whereas this chapter is a contribution to a more comprehensive, long-term characterization of IADB policy guidelines and their transformation over time.

The chapter is comprised of five additional sections. In section 2, we describe the historical context that led to the creation of the IADB. In section 3, we consider the general objectives and mandates under which the IADB was created. Section 4 focuses on IADB funding. Next, in section 5, we examine the evolution of the IADB from the 1980s to the present, considering three subperiods for the analysis. Finally, in section 6, we present the main findings of our research.

[1] In their analysis of some aspects of bank governance, a number of authors agree that the main strategic advantage of RDB is the participation of both donors and borrowing countries in their decision-making structure (Griffith-Jones 2002; Birdsall 2003; Vivares 2013). There has also been considerable progress in the study of the financial dimension of RDB and their role in development processes (Rodrik 1995; Sagasti and Alcalde 1999; Meltzer 2000; Ratha 2001; Birdsall and Rojas-Suarez 2004).

[2] Sagasti (2002), Sagasti and Prada (2006), Prada (2012), and Humphrey and Michaelowa (2010), among others, compared the IADB to other supranational financial development institutions.

2. Setting up the IADB

After the Great Depression of the 1930s, the creation of mechanisms and institutions to provide long-term financing of industry and large-scale infrastructure was problematic for Latin American countries. Under-developed capital markets and the absence of large, experienced banks to carry out this task were major barriers. In the 1940s, the public sector began to play an active role in efforts to address these lacunae in financial markets, by promoting industrialization and generating the long-term financing mechanisms needed to boost this industrialization. In fact, different types of state-owned financial institutions were created to provide funding for economic development. In some cases, these public financial institutions had a mission that went beyond fixing financial market failures: they engaged in economic planning, creating markets, and developing entire sectors in the industrial structure (Mazzucato and Penna 2015).

However, import-substitution industrialization (ISI) required funding not only in domestic currencies but in foreign currency as well. Increasing demand for imports of technology, inputs, and capital goods clashed with the scarce foreign currency generated by primary exports. From the 1950s onwards, balance of payments crises were widespread throughout the region. Although foreign direct investment, especially from the US played an important role, it was insufficient to cover the external financing needs of the ongoing processes. In this context, the creation of multilateral financial development institutions was an opportunity to obtain external financing required by the ISI processes.

Indeed, the first MDB and RDB were created in the postwar period with the main objective of accelerating the development of developing countries in Africa, Asia, and Latin America. In a geo-political context favourable to regional integration, MDB and RDB were conceived as essential instruments in the promotion of development, especially in the 1950s and 1960s (Mistry 1995; Vivares 2013). The World Bank was the first institution in which Latin American countries placed their trust and expectations, but they were soon disappointed. The multilateral bank did not prioritize the region in its lending policy and focused its credits on infrastructure projects, leaving a gap in the financing needs of the local productive sectors. The US, which held a dominant position in the World Bank's decision-making process, believed that private foreign investment should play a leading role in providing the funding for developing countries' needs, and MDB should play a secondary role (Babb 2009). In fact, only a few developing countries were able to afford the interest rates charged by the World Bank.

In this respect, authors such as Sagasti (2002) and Humphrey (2012) point out that the creation of a specific RDB such as the IADB was related to the financial needs of productive sectors (industrial and agricultural) in the region. According to these authors, Latin American countries demanded foreign financing in greater quantities for productive sectors, while the World Bank, through the International

Bank for Reconstruction and Development (IBRD), lent small amounts basically for electrical and transport infrastructure.

However, it was the decision of the US administration, rooted in its concern regarding communist expansion throughout Latin America, that ultimately made possible the creation of the IADB towards the end of the 1950s (Nelson 2015). The interest of US administrations to consolidate US power in the region increased during the 1950s, as did Latin American resentment towards this power. The US was not especially committed to regional development. It was mainly interested in security-related issues and the expansion of its own trade and financial interests. However, the discontent of important sectors of the population in Latin American countries increased as their demands for economic support for national development plans remained unmet. Both the United Nations and the Organisation of American States (OAS) were important venues through which Latin American governments increased their pressure on the US during the 1950s (Babb 2009).

It was in this context that the Eisenhower administration agreed to create a regional bank with emphasis on the economic and social development of Latin American countries. The Eisenhower administration sought to avoid conflict and approached the largest countries in the region, even though it remained reluctant to give substantial financial support. As a regional financial institution for the development of its members, the IADB was created in 1959, with the participation of the US in a hegemonic position (although with no majority in the voting power of the institution), and eighteen other countries in the region.

3. Objectives and mandates of the IADB over time

The IADB was created with the comprehensive objective of enhancing the economic development of its member countries. Given that the institution was created, in part, as a consequence of US concern regarding the expansion of communism in Latin America, it was given an initial mandate associated with providing resources to social projects and to fighting poverty. In terms of its governance, the US held more than 40 per cent of the IADB's voting power during its first decade, thus having veto power in some major decisions that required a special 75 per cent majority—such as granting concessional loans, capital increases, or changes in the constitutive agreement. Borrowing member countries held a majority position in the IADB's decision process. This aspect differentiated the IADB from most other MDB and RDB in which donor members maintained significant majorities, even higher than 70 per cent.[3]

[3] For this reason, Humphrey (2012) distinguishes the IADB from the World Bank, which has a majority of non-borrowing countries, and the Andean Development Corporation (Corporación

After successive capital increases and the incorporation of new non-regional donor member countries, the voting power agreement, amended under the 'Eighth General Increase in the Resources' of the IADB, agreed upon in 1994, and ratified in 1995, established that the voting power of the borrowing countries should not fall below 50.005 per cent and that of the US should not be less than 30 per cent. Therefore, while borrowing countries had the simple majority for most decisions, the US maintained its veto power for some crucial decisions, and could reach simple majority allying with a small number of other countries. The IADB country shareholders agreed upon this balance of power for the Bank's governance.

According to its articles of agreement, the IADB had to fulfill the following functions: promote the investment of public and private capital for development purposes of the member countries; prioritize loans and guarantee operations which contribute more effectively to economic growth; encourage private investment and supplement it when private capital is not available at reasonable terms and conditions; cooperate with the member countries to orient their policies towards a better use of their resources in ways compatible with the promotion of orderly foreign trade growth; and provide technical assistance for the preparation, financing, and execution of development plans and projects (IADB 1959).

Like other MDB and RDB, the IADB created a soft-loan window, the Fund for Special Operations (FSO), to lend money to borrowers unable to meet market financial criteria. With this special fund, the IADB could provide concessional loans with more flexible requirements than those imposed on ordinary loans (or hard-loan window).[4] In addition, the institution could make direct loans to the private sector without need for government guarantees, being more flexible than other MDB and RDB in this respect (Humphrey 2012).

Although the IADB's articles of agreement did not specify the objective of stimulating member country industrial sectors, in its early years the Bank supported national development plans based on ISI (Tussie 1995; Vivares 2013). In fact, unlike the World Bank—which had allocated 75 per cent of its funds to finance infrastructure projects and only 3 per cent to productive sectors by the end of the 1950s—in the first five years, the IADB channelled almost 50 per cent of its loans to industry, mining, and agriculture while social sectors received more than 30 per cent of total loans. Infrastructure projects, on the contrary, received only 20 per cent of the IADB's loans (IADB *Annual Reports* 1960–5).

Andina de Fomento; CAF), in which all member countries are borrowers. The African Development Bank (AfDB) is one of the few other RDB where borrowing countries have always maintained a majority of votes (see Kraemer-Mbula, Chapter 3, this volume).

[4] However, over the IADB's long history, concessional lending represented only a very small part of the IADB's total lending (IADB *Annual Reports* 1960–2016).

In its first decade of operation, the IADB lent more money to the region's productive sectors than the World Bank ever had. Over the course of the decade and a half prior to the creation of the IADB (1947-60), the World Bank lent Latin American countries USD 1.16 billion in loans almost entirely to finance infrastructure. During the following decade, the World Bank allocated USD 3.3 billion to the region, with the lion's share once again going to finance infrastructure. In contrast, over a similar period—from 1961 through 1969—the IADB granted USD 3.5 billion in loans in Latin America, a substantial part of which was allocated to productive sectors. As a result, the IADB quickly became the region's main development bank, especially for financing its productive sectors.

In the 1970s, in spite of an exponential increase of MDB and RDB loans to the region, the share of these loans as a percentage of total external financing of Latin American countries declined. MDB and RDB loans represented 40 per cent of foreign financing granted to the Latin American national public sectors during the period 1966–70 and more than 15 per cent of the total foreign funding. However, by the end of the 1970s, MDB and RDB financing did not exceed 5 per cent of the total external financing received by the public and private sectors of the region. On the contrary, the participation of international private banks increased from 10 per cent of Latin American external financing at the beginning of the decade to 56 per cent in 1980.[5]

As for the sector-based distribution, in the first five years of the IADB's operation, economic infrastructure received less funding than productive and social sectors. However, this trend in the Bank's lending distribution soon reverted, as industrial and social sectors gradually lost significance. The infrastructure sector's share of IADB loans increased to such an extent that it averaged approximately 45 per cent of its total portfolio between 1961 and 1980.[6] Therefore, the initial differentiation between the World Bank and the IADB with its policy-based lending, then called 'sector lending', tended to disappear in the 1970s. The IADB, which had been created to finance sectors that were not prioritized by the World Bank, quickly emulated this MDB's credit policy.

In its early years, the IADB was characterized by its firm intention to contribute to the progress of national development plans, in a context of a widespread commitment among regional governments to promote industrialization using strong intervention tools. This developmental role explains the IADB's cooperation, and the synergies it displayed, with national public institutions in that first stage of its operation. In fact, state-owned financial development institutions became important mechanisms for the IADB to channel part of its resources

[5] See Griffith-Jones (1984) and Vivares (2013).

[6] These final percentages are consistent with the goals set by the IADB (*Annual Reports* 1975–8).

towards achieving the objective of contributing to the acceleration of the region's economic growth and social and economic development.

4. IADB funding

The IADB's capital structure was divided into two components: paid-in capital from member countries and callable or guarantee capital. As in the case of other MDB and RDB, this structure allowed the IADB to raise money in capital markets while sustaining a strong credit rating (and low interest rates), and eliminated the need for its member countries to pay in cash for their share in the institution's capital. However, the IADB's funding structure changed over time. The initial authorized capital was USD 850 million: USD 400 million in paid-in capital and USD 450 in callable capital. Paid-in capital was supposed to be paid in three annual and consecutive installments. The US was the main donor with 40 per cent of the ordinary capital of the Bank, followed by Argentina and Brazil, with 12.44 per cent each. In order to make loans, the IADB could use the paid-in capital, retained earnings and funds raised in international markets. It played an active role as a borrower in capital markets with a growing participation. At the beginning of the 1970s, while the IADB's ordinary capital was over USD 4 billion, its total net borrowing was USD 1.1 billion, with more than USD 100 million raised per year (IADB *Annual Report* 1972).

In the following decades, the share of the US was reduced to 32 per cent of ordinary capital (and also paid-in capital), but it remained the main donor, followed by Argentina and Brazil. Although ordinary capital increased considerably, and non-regional countries became members,[7] the paid-in capital to callable capital ratio declined. At the beginning of the 1980s, paid-in capital was barely 10 per cent of the total ordinary capital. However, the volume of callable capital was crucial to the IADB's access to capital markets and its triple-A debt rating granted by the three largest US rating agencies. In fact, in the 1980s, borrowing in capital markets became the main source of the IADB's funding. The debt-to-equity ratio, which exceeded 100 per cent at the beginning of the decade, was near 300 per cent at the start of the 1990s.

This funding structure was underscored in the following decades. By the end of the 1990s, the ratio of paid-in to callable capital was already under 5 per cent and has remained at that level up to the present. In contrast, the debt-to-equity ratio averaged 320 per cent from 1995 to 2015. The IADB's dependence on borrowed funds to carry out its lending strategy increased over time, making it critical that

[7] During the 1970s, fourteen European countries plus Japan and Israel became members of the IADB.

it meet all the necessary conditions in order to hold onto its AAA-rating from the rating agencies.

5. The IADB's trajectory from the 1980s to 2010

The 1980s: the transition leading up to the Washington Consensus

In the early 1980s, the sudden stop in private capital inflows to Latin American countries and the resulting debt crises marked the beginning of a transition period in favour of neoliberal economic policies. In this new context, government intervention in the economy, state ownership of companies and banks, and the policy of ISI came under fire. The IADB's credit policy would also suffer a profound transformation, shifting away from the prioritization of economic and social infrastructure projects and industrial activities, moving towards the promotion of programmes linked to the implementation of structural reforms. The programme of structural reforms was schematized by the so-called Washington Consensus at the end of the 1980s. It consisted of fiscal discipline and changing priorities in public spending; trade, financial, and foreign investment liberalization; reform in tax regimes; privatization of state-owned enterprises; and deregulation in goods and labour markets.[8]

During the 1970s, large amounts of foreign private financing for developing countries at extremely low interest rates and without conditionalities reduced the importance of international financial institutions (IFI) in those countries. In contrast, at the beginning of the 1980s, with developing countries in need of foreign financing and restricted access to private capital markets, the ability of the MDB, RDB, and the International Monetary Fund (IMF) to impose policies and reforms increased considerably. For the US, it was the perfect environment to impose market-friendly policies in developing countries using IFIs as a key instrument. After some initial hesitation, the US government definitively assigned the World Bank and the IADB a leading role in overseeing the changes in Latin America's development model.[9]

This new conception about IFIs was clearly connected to the crisis of Keynesian-type policies that dominated macroeconomic policy-making during the post-Second World War period, and the rebirth of neoclassical orthodox economic ideas that spread throughout the world from the oil crisis at the beginning of the 1970s. In this context, developed countries became more cautious about IFI. On the one side, revitalized fiscal austerity implied that donor countries should become more sensitive towards their monetary contributions to lending

[8] See Williamson (1990).

[9] See Bacha (1987), Babb (2009), and Stallings (2014).

institutions and more demanding with the result of their credit lines. On the other side, trust in market forces fuelled the idea that multilateral banks should withdraw from some activities to leave them to the private sector and help generate private sources of financing. In short, a new idea spread among developed countries championed by US administrations: in the context of budgetary constraints, the scarce resources of the MDB and RDB should be used to assist developing countries in applying structural reforms. From this perspective, lending should be allocated principally to countries with approved economic policies.

This transformation towards neoclassical orthodoxy did not happen at the same pace in all lending institutions. The IMF became immediately the key IFI to deal with the debt crisis in Latin American countries. The World Bank, as an institution where donor countries had the majority of votes and great influence on the lending decisions, began almost immediately to tie its credits to the implementation of specific market-friendly economic policies by borrowing countries, in coordination with the IMF.

The US government's concern was how to generate selectivity to favouring those countries with solid macroeconomic foundations, and conditionality to tie loans to the implementation of market-friendly economic policies and privatization of state-owned companies. For the IADB, which had allocated the majority of its loans to specific projects without conditionalities, this meant re-assessing and re-evaluating its credit policy and guidelines. But this transformation was not going to be easy. Although the US had veto power over some key IADB policies, borrower members held a majority in the decision-making process and these members faced great difficulties accessing private bank loans. In this context, during the first half of the 1980s, the IADB fluctuated between the objective of completing projects already underway and maintaining support for industrial sectors seriously compromised by the crisis. At the time, the IADB as an agent had no intention of allowing the Bank to become an instrument to impose structural reforms.

In 1985, with James Baker as treasury secretary, US pressure on IADB lending policy intensified. At the end of 1985, Baker proposed a plan to deal with the debt crisis in the form of the so-called Baker Plan.[10] The plan called on MDB and RDB to become promoters of market-friendly policies in developing countries and to establish stricter terms of conditionality in order to refuse to give loans when established conditions were not met.[11] MDB and RDB would need to develop 'country strategies' consistent with structural reforms in order to guide the lending policy for each country.

An essential element for a loan's conditionality to be successful was coordination among IFI, so that borrowers would not be able to bargain for different

[10] For more information on the Baker Plan, see Ocampo et al. (2014).
[11] See Babb (2009) and Stallings (2014).

kinds of requirements with different IFI. This coordination started working very well between the IMF and the World Bank. The World Bank quickly adopted a stance in which it would wait until a borrower had reached an agreement with the IMF before engaging in a programme with a country. The IMF, as well, expanded its conditionality menu, including structural reforms, and privatization, which were specific World Bank requirements up to that moment. The Baker Plan implied that RDB had to coordinate their actions in the same way with the World Bank. Also, according to the US government's view, some reforms needed to occur in the internal organization of the IADB before it was ready to assume the new role expected of the Bank.

In that context, negotiations on the IADB's 'Seventh General Capital Increase and Replenishment', which had begun in 1986, hit a roadblock, reflecting the increasing US pressure on the Bank. For the IADB, a period of financial strangulation began. For the first time since its creation, total loans decreased, as shown in Figure 2.1.

According to Babb (2009), the US offered an important financing package to the IADB in exchange for a number of reforms to the institution's policies and governing structure, in line with the Baker Plan's requirements. The IADB initially opposed the reforms. As a consequence, it ran short of resources and abruptly reduced its loans. Shortly thereafter, the Bank started to give into the pressure. Finally, by the end of 1988, after the resignation of IADB president, Ortiz Mena (succeeded by Enrique Iglesias), the Bank embarked on an internal restructuring, and donor countries approved a USD 26.5 billion increase in the

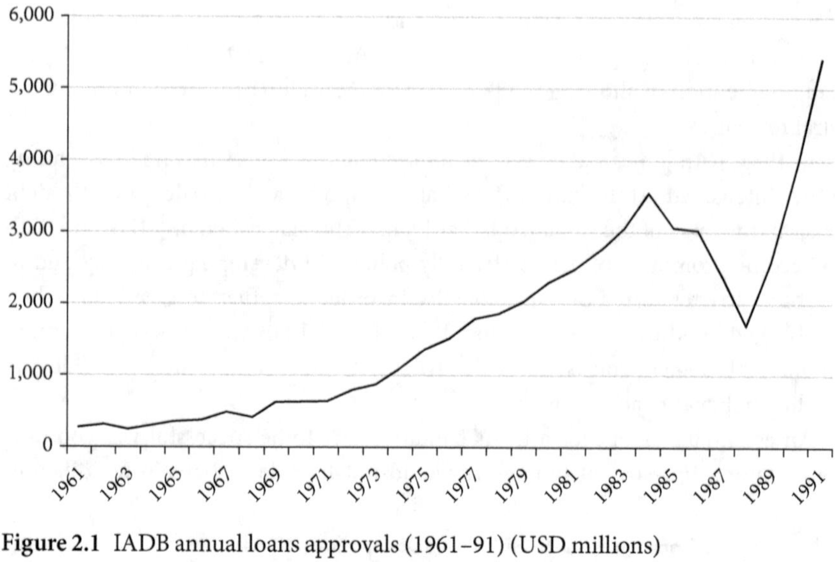

Figure 2.1 IADB annual loans approvals (1961–91) (USD millions)
Source: Authors based on IADB *Annual Reports* (1961–91).

IADB's resources. The IADB agreed to ensure that all loans would 'support policy reform and self-sustaining growth', and the Bank committed to conducting its lending under the supervision of the World Bank for two years (Babb 2009). 'From that point forward, the IADB would be much more responsive to US-led policy initiatives and relations between the Treasury and the IADB management [were] more cordial' (Babb 2009: 143). In line with Babb's analysis, after dropping for four years in a row, the IADB's total annual loans recovered in 1989 and reached a new historical high in 1990. As an illustrative element of the new role of the IADB in the region, the topic of 'macroeconomic policies' was created to carry on the political dialogue with the governments of borrowing countries.

Although the Baker Plan ultimately failed to resolve fully the problem of Latin American countries' debt crisis, the statement contained in Baker's programme about the new role of international organizations had a significant impact upon the IADB due to US pressure exerted on the institution. After the IADB's 1987–8 crisis, the institution focused on promoting structural reforms in Latin American countries, working in tandem with the IMF and the World Bank, in particular. Therefore, by the end of the 1980s, MDB and RDB (including the IADB) and the IMF were seen as key institutions for the new consensus handed down from Washington to the world.

While the IADB's original mandate, which consisted of boosting economic development, was not modified, the mainstream interpretation of the best policies to achieve that goal did change. According to the Washington Consensus, market-oriented policies and structural reforms would enhance growth in developing countries mainly through improved resource allocation. The Office of Chief Economist of the IADB described this shift in development policies as follows:

> The development model based on protection of domestic markets and state intervention was replaced by a set of policies overwhelmingly oriented toward the goal of improving efficiency, facilitating the working of markets and reducing the distorting effects of state intervention on economic activities. (Lora 2012: 2)

In the 1990s: promoting structural reform and dealing with its consequences

After a lost decade for the region in terms of growth and development, the 1990s was the decade of structural reforms in Latin American countries (Lora 2012). In this new context, the IADB became the main source of IFI financial assistance, promoting through its loans financial, economic, and political reforms. While the IADB's loans to the region totalled more than USD 70 billion during the decade, the World Bank reached almost USD 60 billion and the Andean Development Corporation (Corporación Andina de Fomento; CAF) contributed USD 23 billion.

However, private international markets were by far the main source of foreign financing for the region, especially from 1993, when new issues of sovereign bonds increased dramatically. Latin American countries issued sovereign debt of more than USD 140 billion during the 1990s (Titelman 2002).

Given the persistence of the problems generated by the debt crisis, from 1989 onward, Latin American countries started applying the Brady Plan—the successor of the Baker Plan. The plan called for the conversion of debt held by commercial banks into sovereign bonds, which could then be traded on secondary markets. The IADB became an agent for the implementation of the Brady solution in the region. For that purpose, Latin American countries needed to commit to making greater advances—or moving more quickly, depending on each case—to implement structural reform programmes, in order to receive funds from the World Bank and the IADB to acquire US Treasury bonds, which would serve as guarantee for the new Brady bonds. The IADB's commitment to this strategy was evident; in fact, the institution created a credit line for 'debt reduction and debt services reduction to help borrowing countries to decrease their external public debt and debt service with commercial banks' (IADB *Annual Report* 1990: 10).

In this context, the allocation of the IADB's loans for 'Public Sector Reform'—a category that did not exist until 1990—represented more than a quarter of the total funds provided by the institution over the following decade. 'Productive sectors' obtained a little more than 10 per cent of IADB funds, while 'physical infrastructure' received about 20 per cent of total loans, accentuating their declining position in IADB lending, as seen in Figure 2.2.

The other significant element observed in Figure 2.2 is the increasing importance of 'social sectors' in the IADB's loan portfolio. In 1994, during the 'Eighth Capital Increase', the IADB's Board of Governors established that funds assigned

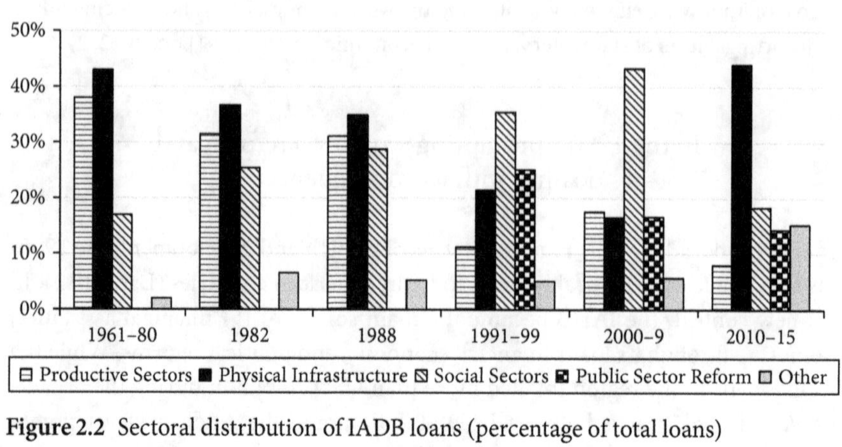

Figure 2.2 Sectoral distribution of IADB loans (percentage of total loans)
Source: Authors based on data from IADB's *Annual Reports* (several years).

to poverty reduction should be increased in order to represent no less than 40 per cent of the Bank's total lending in the following years. This concern for poverty levels and social sectors had to do with recognition of the negative consequences of the structural reforms proclaimed by the Washington Consensus and promoted by the IMF, MDB, and RDB—including, as noted above, the IADB. In its 1990 *Annual Report*, the IADB admitted: 'drastic fiscal adjustment, inflation, and stabilisation programs have unquestionably exacerbated the problems of poverty existing at the beginning of 1990' (IADB *Annual Report* 1990: 7).

Therefore, after inducing Latin American countries to apply structural reforms during the first half of the 1990s, the IADB increased its efforts to compensate for the effects of those policies on the most vulnerable social sectors, with credit lines that were merely palliatives. Consequently, there was an increase in the share of 'social sectors' in the IADB's total annual loans. However, the IADB's commitment to structural reforms remained intact. In fact, its 'Eighth Replenishment' mandate included essentially, 'the promotion of stability and economic growth by backing macroeconomic reform, anchoring improvements already undertaken, and supporting "second-generation" reform programs' (IADB *Annual Report* 1995: 9).

In line with these policies, the IADB also assumed an active role in providing resources to restore macroeconomic equilibrium in situations of financial crisis, such as the support given to Mexico and Argentina in 1995 in the middle of the Mexican currency crisis. That year, the IADB granted Mexico USD 1 billion in loans and USD 750 million to Argentina to strengthen their financial systems and financial institutions, in a nod to the two countries' pursuit of macroeconomic reform. The relative importance of the support for these countries is demonstrated by the fact that it accounted for more than 20 per cent of the total funds granted by the IADB in 1995.

Something similar occurred in 1997 and 1998, respectively, when the Asian and the Russian crises spread to the rest of the developing countries, which suffered severe macroeconomic destabilization in their financial systems and a decline in commodity prices, putting pressure on international reserves and reducing access to foreign financing. Once again, the IADB allocated important amounts of resources to assist large Latin American countries (especially Argentina and Brazil) to stabilize their economies, acting in coordination with the IMF and the World Bank (IADB 1997). For example, a USD 2.5 billion loan was granted to Argentina to support sector adjustments and banking system safeguards. In fact, in 1998, the IADB's total loans increased more than 65 per cent compared to the previous year and almost 40 per cent of total loans were allocated to Argentina. In the case of Brazil, the IADB, the IMF, and the World Bank put together a package for USD 41.5 billion 'to support several policy efforts in Brazil while strengthening its international reserve position' (IADB *Annual Report* 1998: 2).

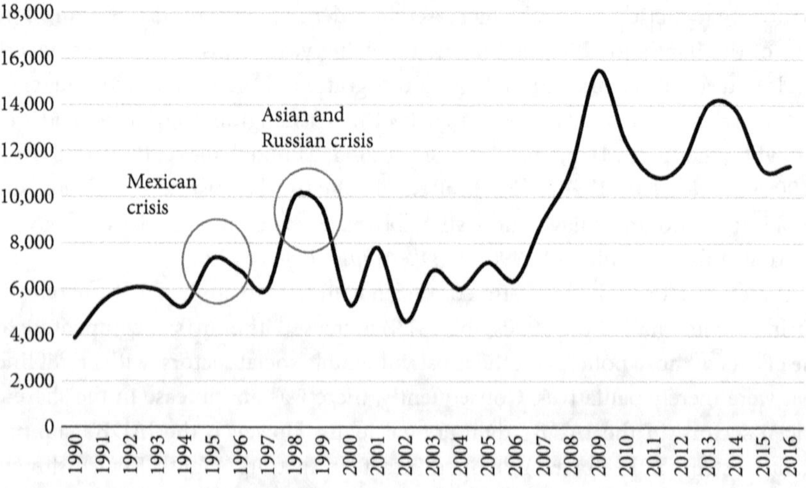

Figure 2.3 IADB annual loans approvals (1990–2015) (USD millions)
Source: Authors based on IADB *Annual Reports* (1990–2015).

Therefore, peaks in total IADB loans during the decade occurred during and after these episodes of crisis as shown in Figure 2.3. The intention was to grant loans to countries that were already applying the Washington Consensus recipes so that they could deepen the implementation of market-type structural reforms. It is no coincidence that the large economies of the region, which had advanced in the implementation of structural reforms starting in the late 1980s, suffered greatly from the financial crises of the decade, and required large aid packages from financial international organizations, like the IADB. The opening of economies to trade and capital flows left these economies highly vulnerable to the volatility of short-term capital movements. Consequently, the IMF, MDB, and RDB (including the IADB) needed to intensify the injection of resources during these episodes as the only possible way to give continuity to structural reforms in the region. In fact, the distribution of the IADB's loan portfolio, which had always shown a high degree of concentration in the largest countries, accentuated this tendency in the episodes of crisis in the 1990s, as shown in Figure 2.4.

In the 2000s: the IADB in the new century

As shown in Figure 2.3, during the 2000s, in terms of sector distribution, the IADB accentuated the trend observed in the 1990s: on the one hand, the share of social sectors increased, receiving almost 45 per cent of IADB loans; on the other hand, physical infrastructure barely received 15 per cent of IADB loans, and the share of productive sectors was practically nil. In 2006, the IADB emphasized

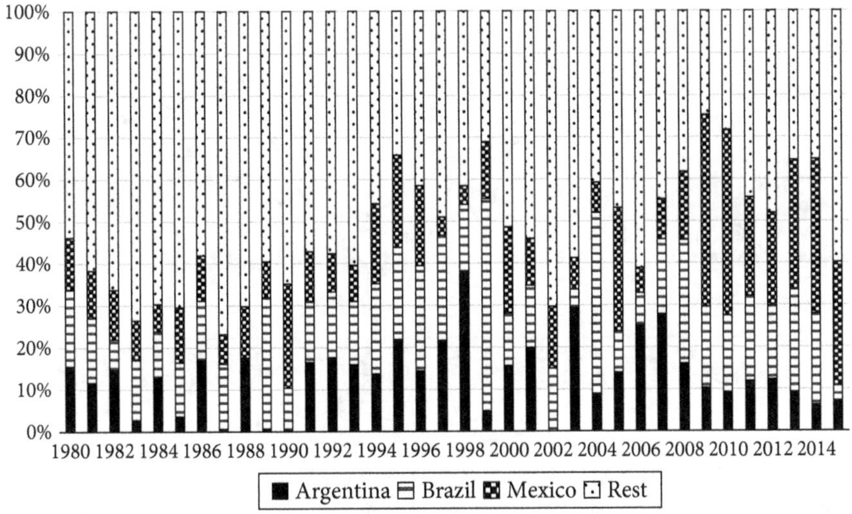

Figure 2.4 IADB loans distribution to selected countries (in percentage of total loans)
Source: Authors based on IADB *Annual Reports* (1980–2015).

that, considering the goal established in 1994 to allocate at least 50 per cent of operations and 40 per cent of funds to poverty reduction, 'the cumulative percentage for the period 1994-2006 [reached] 46 per cent of the number of projects and 49.3 per cent of the volume of loans' (IADB *Annual Report* 2006: 12).

In terms of the IADB's importance to the region, it lost its previous predominance held during the first part of the decade, until the outbreak of the international crisis in 2008. In fact, the quantitative relevance of its resources for the region between 2000 and 2006 was lower in absolute terms than at the end of the 1990s. Indeed, according to Prada (2012), between 2003 and 2006—for the first time—net flows from the IADB to Latin American countries were negative, due to the repayments to the Bank, especially by the biggest countries. At the same time, the CAF's role as a regional bank, especially as a source of financing for infrastructure projects and for productive sectors, increased, as seen in Figures 2.5 and 2.6.

In 2008-9, when Latin American growth decelerated considerably as a result of the international financial crisis, the IADB increased significantly its lending to the region, thus pursuing a classical countercyclical role with few precedents. The IADB declared: 'amid these difficult conditions, in which both sovereign and private-sector borrowers found capital markets hard to access, the IADB rose to the occasion and delivered countercyclical response of unprecedented proportions' (IADB *Annual Report* 2009: 7). In fact, both in absolute value and in terms of gross domestic product (GDP), IADB financing to the region saw a significant increase during the international financial crisis, as seen in Figure 2.7. The IADB was not the only institution to respond in this manner; other MDB and RDB and central banks around the world also reacted with aggressive expansionary

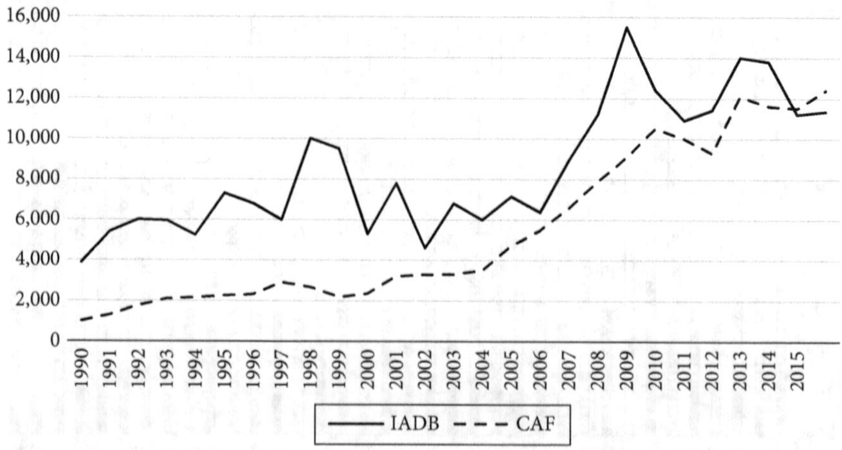

Figure 2.5 IADB and CAF: total loans (USD millions)
Source: Compiled by authors based on IADB (*Annual Reports* 1990–2016) and CAF (*Annual Reports* 1990–2016).

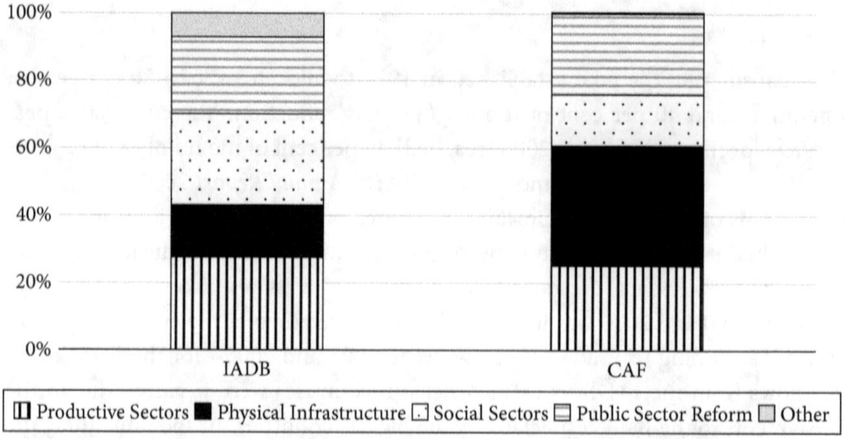

Figure 2.6 IADB and CAF: sectorial distribution of loans (2006) (USD millions)
Source: Compiled by authors based on IADB (*Annual Report* 2006) and CAF (*Annual Report* 2006).

responses. In this context, the IADB created a new Liquidity Programme for Growth Sustainability for USD 6 billion and increased the concessionary funds available, as well as those for its Trade Finance Facilitation Programme.

As Humphrey and Michaelowa (2010) demonstrate, during the two major crises of the last thirty years, in 1998 and in 2009, IADB and World Bank lending increased considerably, and in fact, the IADB took an even more aggressive stance than the World Bank. As seen in Figure 2.7, annual loans measured in constant dollars hit historic peaks in 1998 and 2009. When measured in terms of the size of regional economies, the IADB's total loans also showed a countercyclical a role

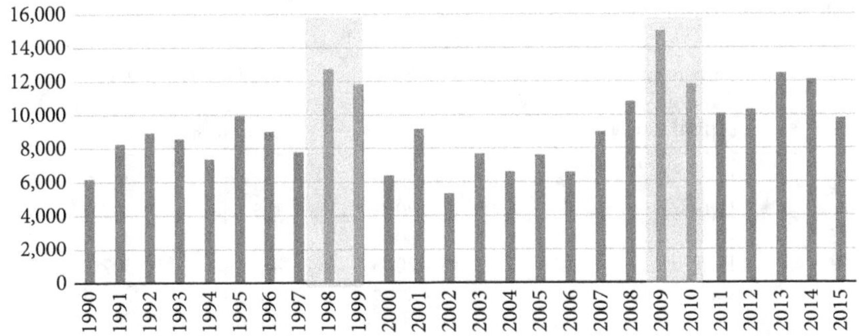

IADB Annual Loans (as a percentage of regional GDP)

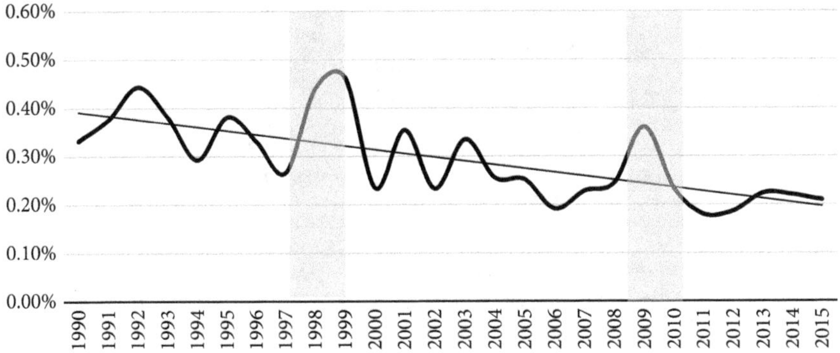

Figure 2.7 IADB annual loans (USD 2007 thousands)

Source: Authors based on data from IADB (*Annual Reports* 1990–2015) and the World Bank (2019) database.

in 1998 and 2009, but in the midst of a declining tendency from 1990 onward. In order to fulfil this countercyclical role, the Bank increased its borrowing markedly in both periods. As Table 2.1 shows, the Bank's debt-to-equity ratio increased from 320 per cent in 1997 to 446 per cent in 1999, and rose from 243 per cent in 2007 to 351 per cent in 2011.

The declining contribution of the IADB's loans to the regional GDP can be attributed, on the one hand, to the growth of private capital markets and, on the other, to developing countries' stronger balance of payments in the new century. In fact, as a result of the rise in commodities prices, international reserves of Latin American economies increased from less than USD 200 billion at the beginning of the new century, to more than USD 800 billion by 2012. In an unprecedented episode, between 2003 and 2007, the region obtained a cumulative current account surplus of more than USD 130 billion (World Bank 2019).

In terms of sector distribution, during 2009 and 2010, the IADB Board of Governors discussed the 'Ninth General Capital Increase'. The institutional priorities for the IADB's credit policy for the following years were established as

Table 2.1 IADB funding structure

Year	Paid-in to Callable capital %	Debt to equity (1) %	Year	Paid-in to callable capital %	Debt to equity (1) %
1983	11.3	94.7	2000	4.8	359.9
1984	16.6	89.3	2001	4.6	342.0
1985	10.8	140.3	2002	4.5	355.8
1986	10.1	247.5	2003	4.5	307.2
1987	10.1	288.4	2004	4.5	263.8
1988	9.5	260.5	2005	4.5	249.1
1989	8.3	254.6	2006	4.5	235.6
1990	8.3	275.4	2007	4.5	243.5
1991	8.3	291.8	2008	4.5	272.9
1992	8.3	294.5	2009	4.5	320.2
1993	7.4	307.1	2010	4.5	329.5
1994	7.4	327.4	2011	4.5	351.8
1995	6.2	316.6	2012	4.3	345.9
1996	6.2	309.6	2013	4.3	312.3
1997	5.8	320.3	2014	4.3	348.6
1998	5.5	394.5	2015	4.1	340.1
1999	5.0	446.6			

(1) Equity includes paid-in capital plus retained earnings and reserves
Source: Authors based on IADB *Financial Statements*, 1984–2016

follows: social policy for equity with emphasis on productive insertion of the poor, improving the quality of education and promoting equity health outcomes; infrastructure for competitiveness and social welfare; institutions for growth and social welfare, focused on improving lending for small business, fiscal efficiency through decentralization; competitive regional and global integration; and protection of the environment, responding to climate change and ensuring food security.[12]

These new priorities shaped the sectoral distribution of the IADB's lending policy for the period 2010–15, with greater emphasis on infrastructure to enhance the competitiveness of regional economies, and associated with the intention of financing production of sustainable energy and mitigating climate change. As shown in Figure 2.3, physical infrastructure represented more than 40 per cent of the IADB's resources as of 2010, while the social sectors fell to less than 20 per cent. It is also noticeable that the decrease in the participation of the productive sectors was accentuated, a tendency seen starting in the 1980s, receiving less than 10 per cent of the IADB's lending between 2010 and 2015.

These new priorities of the IADB's lending policy were aligned with a development model that can be seen as a continuity of the Washington Consensus principles, with some variants that emerged from the 2007–8 international financial

[12] See IADB (*Annual Reports* 2009 and 2010).

crisis. On the one hand, developed countries recognized the increasing weight of developing economies in the global economy, and the need of financing to deal with their deficits and funding gaps. On the other hand, the essential market-friendly economic ideas remained untouched. In its first declaration in November of 2008, G20 members argued that 'reforms will only be successful if grounded in a commitment to free market principles, including the rule of law, respect for private property, open trade and investment, competitive markets, and efficient, effectively regulated financial systems' (G20 2008: 4).

The IADB's lending policy during the period 2010–15 must be interpreted in this context. The greater emphasis on financing infrastructure to improve competitiveness was related to a development model based on the benefits of free trade. But also, MDB and RDB in general, and the IADB in particular, increased their support for infrastructure projects as an expression, at least to some extent, of the evident infrastructure gaps in developing countries and the increasing importance of these countries in the global economy.[13] Additionally, the IADB's policy in recent years expressed a broader vision of development models, associated with the need to reconvert economies to environmentally sustainable development schemes; a vision that has been gaining strength in developed economies since the 2008 international financial crisis.[14]

6. Conclusions

This chapter has demonstrated that the orientation of the IADB's lending policies for the region has evolved over time. Although the IADB's mandate remained unchanged over more than fifty years of the Bank's existence, a transition phase clearly started in the 1980s, moving away from a developmental role associated with state-led industrialization processes, to the liberalization and deregulation policies promoted in the 1990s and the pursuit of a countercyclical role in major crises episodes.

During the 1980s, a substantial transformation took place in the role of the MDB and RDB, which became key agents for the implementation of structural reforms in Latin American countries. In the case of the IMF and the World Bank, this transformation happened almost immediately when the debt crisis exploded in the region. The case of the IADB was different because of borrowing countries'

[13] 'We request the regional development banks (RDB) and the World Bank Group (collectively, multilateral development banks, or MDB) to work jointly to prepare action plans that increase public, semi-public and private finance and improve implementation of national and regional infrastructure projects' (G20 2010: 1).

[14] For example, since 2011, the G20 included fostering clean energy, green growth, and sustainable development, and pursuing the fight against climate change among its main objectives in its Leaders' Declaration (G20 2011).

larger voting power in the institution's lending decisions. However, the weakness of Latin American national economies during the debt crisis, and the relevance of the US as the main source of funds with veto power in some IADB decisions, led to the Bank's role as an agent for the application of market-friendly policies and structural reforms programmes by the end of the decade, thus replacing its active role in the financing of economic infrastructure and productive sectors during the first two decades after its creation.

Therefore, the IADB ended up aligning its actions with the Washington Consensus strategy, much like the IMF and the World Bank, in spite of the greater voting power of borrowing countries in its governance structure. The IADB's lending policy focused mainly on supporting structural reforms and, also, on fighting poverty because of the negative consequences of market-friendly policies and the openness of the economies (as described in the Bank's 'Eighth General Capital Increase'). This orientation of IADB strategy remained almost unchanged until the 2008-9 international financial crisis. During the crisis, the IADB played an important countercyclical role and increased noticeably its total lending. While maintaining the market-friendly fundamentals promoted by the Washington Consensus of the early 1990s, the IADB lending policy has become more strategic, focusing heavily on the development of physical infrastructure in the region since 2010, seeking to boost competitiveness to promote free trade and to accelerate the transformation of economies towards more environmentally sustainable models.

References

Babb, S. (2009). *Behind the Development Banks. Washington Politics, World Poverty, and the Wealth of Nations*. Chicago: The University of Chicago Press.

Bacha, E.L. (1987). 'IMF conditionality: conceptual problems and policy alternatives', *World Development*, 15(12): 1469–82.

Birdsall, N. (2003). 'Why it matters who runs the IMF and the World Bank'. Working Paper No. 22, Center for Global Development, Washington, DC.

Birdsall, N. and Rojas-Suarez, L. (2004). *Financing Development: The Power of Regionalism*. September. Available online at: http://dx.doi.org/10.2139/ssrn.2560932

CAF (Andean Development Corporation / Corporación Andina de Fomento) (1990–2016). *Annual Reports*. Caracas: CAF.

G20 (Group of Twenty) (2008). 'Declaration: summit on financial markets and the world economy', November. Washington, DC: G20. Available online at: http://www.g20.utoronto.ca/2008/2008declaration1115.html (accessed 20 February 2020).

G20 (Group of Twenty) (2010). 'The G20 Seoul Summit: Annex II. Multi-year action plan in development', November. Seoul: G20. Available online at: http://www.g20.utoronto.ca/2010/g20seoul-development.html (accessed 20 February 2020).

G20 (Group of Twenty) (2011). 'Final Summit Cannes Declaration', November. Cannes: G20. Available online at: http://www.g20.utoronto.ca/2011/2011-cannes-declaration-111104-en.html last access 20–2.2020 (accessed 20 February 2020).

Griffith-Jones, S. (1984). *International Finance and Latin America*. New York: St. Martin's Press.

Griffith-Jones, S. (1994). *Assessment of the IADB Lending Programme, 1979–92*. Sussex: Institute of Development Studies.

Griffith-Jones, S. (2002). 'Governance of the World Bank'. Working Paper, DFID.

Humphrey, C. (2012). 'The business of development: borrowers, shareholders, and the reshaping of multilateral development lending'. PhD thesis. London: The London School of Economics and Political Science.

Humphrey, C. and Michaelowa, K. (2010). 'The business of development: trends in lending by multilateral development banks to Latin America, 1980–2009'. CIS Working Paper No. 63, Center for Comparative and International Studies. Zurich: ETH Zurich and University of Zurich.

IADB (Inter-American Development Bank) (1959). *Agreement Establishing the IADB*. Washington, DC: IADB.

IADB (Inter-American Development Bank) (1997). *Latin America after a Decade of Reforms*, September. Washington, DC: IADB.

IADB (Inter-American Development Bank) (various, 1960–2016). *Annual Reports*. Washington, DC: IADB.

Lora, E. (2012). 'Structural reform in Latin America: what has been reformed and how it can be quantified (updated version)'. IADB Working Paper Series, No. IADBWP-346. Washington, DC: IADB.

Mazzucato, M. and Penna, C. (2015). 'Beyond market failures: the market creating and shaping roles of state investment banks', *Journal of Economic Policy Reform*, 19: 305–26.

Meltzer, A. (2000). *Report of the International Financial Institutions Advisory Commission*. Washington, DC: International Financial Institutions Advisory Commission.

Mistry, P. (1995). *Multilateral Development Banks: An Assessment of their Financial Structures, Policies and Practices*. The Hague: FONDAD.

Nelson, R.M. (2015). 'Multilateral development banks: overview and issues for Congress', December. Washington, DC: Congressional Research Service.

Ocampo, J.A., Stallings, B., Bustillo, I., Belloso, H., and Frenkel, R. (2014). *La crisis latinoamericana de la deuda desde la perspectiva histórica*. Santiago de Chile: Comisión Económica para América Latina.

Prada, F. (2012). 'World Bank, Inter-American Development Bank, and Subregional development banks in Latin America: dynamics of a system of multilateral development banks'. ADBI Working Paper Series, No. 380, September. Washington, DC: ADBI.

Ratha, D. (2001). 'Complementary between multilateral lending and private flows to developing countries. some empirical results'. Political Research Working Paper No. 2746. Washington, DC: World Bank.

Rodrik, D. (1995). 'Why is there multilateral lending?' Working Paper No. 5160, June. Cambridge: National Bureau of Economic Research.

Sagasti, F. (2002). *La banca multilateral de desarrollo en América Latina*. Series: Financiamiento del desarrollo 119. Santiago de Chile: CEPAL.

Sagasti, F. and Alcalde, G. (1999). *Development Cooperation in a Fractured Global Order: An Arduous Transition*. Ottawa: International Development Research Centre.

Sagasti, F. and Prada, F. (2006). 'Bancos regionales de desarrollo. Una perspectiva comparada'. In José Antonio Ocampo (ed.), *Cooperación Financiera Regional*. Santiago de Chile: CEPAL.

Scheman, D. (1997). 'Banking on growth: the role of the Inter-American Development Bank', *Journal of Inter-American Studies and World Affairs*, 39(1): 85–100.

Stallings, B. (2014). 'La economía política de las negociaciones de la deuda. América Latina en la década del ochenta'. In J.A. Ocampo, B. Stallings, I. Bustillo, H. Bellos, and R. Frenkel (eds.), *La crisis latinoamericana de la deuda desde la perspectiva histórica*. Santiago de Chile: CEPAL, pp. 53–82.

Titelman, D. (2002). *Multilateral Banking and Development Financing in a Context of Financial Volatility*. Series: Financiamiento del Desarrollo 121. Santiago de Chile: ECLAC.

Tussie, D. (1995). *The Inter-American Development Bank*. Collection: The Multilateral Development Banks, Volume 4. Ottawa: North-South Institute.

Vivares, E. (2013). *El Banco Interamericano de Desarrollo en la década neoliberal*. Quito: FLACSO.

Williamson, J. (1990). 'What Washington means by policy reform'. In John Williamson (ed.), *Latin American Adjustment: How Much Has Happened?* Washington, DC: Institute of International Economy.

World Bank. (2019). *DataBank: World Development Indicators*. Washington, DC: World Bank.

3

The African Development Bank

'African Solutions to African Problems'?

Erika Kraemer-Mbula

1. Introduction

Despite Africa's economic upswing over the last three decades, the fruits of growth have eluded the majority of Africans. Persistent challenges remain at the core of African development. The continent's current dependence on commodities and extractive industries is a reflection of the slow progress made in terms of economic diversification. Physical and digital infrastructure still lags behind other developing regions. Progress on the development of skills and competencies has been insufficient, along with innovation and technology development. All these challenges acquire a new magnitude under the threats posed by climate change and the quest for sustainability guided by the Sustainable Development Goals (SDGs).

However, the continent has been battling these issues for a long time. The appeal to find 'African solutions to African problems' gained prominence in policy discourse in the early post-colonial period. The year 1960 was pivotal for African development, with seventeen African countries gaining independence from their colonial rulers. It was at that stage when plans emerged for the creation of a development bank for the African continent, an institution intended to help build the economies of the new states.

Against this backdrop, the African Development Bank (AfDB) was established in 1964 with a strong commitment to addressing African interests and priorities. It was based on a collective vision to set a new path for the continent, based on self-reliance through cooperation among African states. At the time, it was understood that political independence went hand in hand with economic emancipation. In this regard, African leaders acknowledged the importance of regional integration as a tool for economic emancipation, to create regional markets, exploit economies of scale, and pool resources for critical investments, especially in infrastructure. These ideas were visible in the preamble to its 1964 agreement:

> The Governments on whose behalf this Agreement is signed;
>
> Determined to strengthen African solidarity by means of economic co-operation between African States,...

Erika Kraemer-Mbula, *The African Development Bank: 'African Solutions to African Problems'?* In: *Regional Development Banks in the World Economy.* Edited by: Judith Clifton, Daniel Díaz-Fuentes, and David Howarth, Oxford University Press (2021). © Oxford University Press. DOI: 10.1093/oso/9780198861089.003.0003

> Realizing the importance of co-ordinating national plans of economic and social development for the promotion of the harmonious growth of African economies as a whole and the expansion of African foreign trade, and in particular, inter-African trade;...
>
> Have agreed to establish hereby the African Development Bank. (AfDB, 1964)

The AfDB had the official goal of promoting African ownership. All twenty-three original member states were African countries, with the location of the secretariat also set in Africa, in Abidjan, Côte d'Ivoire. (In 2003, the secretariat moved to Tunis due to instability in Côte d'Ivoire but returned to Abidjan in 2015.) At the time of the AfDB's establishment, membership was limited to independent African states. The agreement establishing the AfDB (1964) indicates in its Article 29 that 'All the powers of the Bank shall be vested in the Board of Governors', and Article 30 stressed that the Board of Governors must be composed by 'nationals of the member States'. Regional ownership was seen as an important feature that was intended to help ensure the preservation of African interests and generate trust among recipient countries.

However, in its early years of operation and in the absence of wealthy non-regional members, the Bank struggled to access capital. African members were under financial stress, and operated in a heavily constrained financial environment, which limited the Bank's ability to fulfil its mission and serve the continent. In 1982, driven by its need to access external resources, the Bank rewrote its original Charter and started accepting non-regional members in its Board. This was a controversial move and had important implications for its approach to governance and decision-making. Today, the African Bank Group has eighty member countries, comprising fifty-four regional members and twenty-six non-regional members; although the rules ensure that it remains majority-owned by African governments.

When examining the AfDB activities, it is important to bear in mind the particular difficulties of its working environment as compared to other regional development banks (RDB). The AfDB was set up in the turbulent political and economic context of post-independence Africa. Even today, thirty-three out of the forty-seven least developed national economies in the world can be found in Africa. These countries comprise 52 per cent of the population of the AfDB's borrowers. The AfDB Group consists of three separate but connected institutions: the AfDB, the African Development Fund (AfDF), and the Nigeria Trust Fund (NTF). The AfDB gives loans to creditworthy African countries (mainly middle-income countries) on commercial terms. The two funds give loans on preferential terms or even outright grants to poorer African countries (low-income countries). Therefore, the AfDB Group separates its concessionary lending function from the non-concessionary (the Bank and the funds), which makes the Group distinct from other RDB. Although each one of these three organizations maintains distinct operations, voting systems, and lending modalities, they all fall under the AfDB Group umbrella and share the same objectives, policies, staff, management, and premises.

The colonial legacy of Africa left the continent fragmented and with extremely dependent political and economic structures. Therefore, the main *de facto* objectives of the AfDB Group was (and continues to be) the preservation of the continent's autonomy, representing Africa's interests, and representing a conduit for African integration, as reflected in various strategic documents such as 'The African Development Bank's Strategy for 2013–2022'. This chapter reviews the origins of the AfDB, its evolution and achievements in driving regional integration in the continent, and its ability to preserve its autonomy as it strives to find 'African solutions to African challenges'.

The rest of the chapter is organized as follows. The next section (section 2) reviews the existing literature on the AfDB Group, including the main academic contributions as well as the main publications produced by the Bank itself. Section 3 provides a brief overview of the context in which the AfDB Group was established, pointing to areas in which the AfDB Group was particularly important. Section 4 is devoted to exploring the evolution of the AfDB Group, how its functions have changed over time, and to evaluate its performance, especially in the area of regional integration. The final section (section 5) reflects on the evolution of the bank and considers the future contribution of the AfDB Group to regional integration and autonomy.

2. Review of literature on the AfDB Group

In comparison to other RDB and international financial institutions (IFI) more generally, the AfDB Group has been under-studied. Most of the analyses and reports on the AfDB Group have been produced by the AfDB Group itself or by its former staff. However, there are some studies that provide more critical analyses of specific dimensions of the AfDB's operations; these are discussed below. Early accounts of the AfDB Group tend to be descriptive, providing details about its establishment, main structures, functions, and operations. One of the earliest academic analyses of the AfDB by John White (1972) describes the efforts and severe challenges the Bank faced in attracting foreign funding prior to the creation of a 'special fund'. Yewou Amegavie in 1977 (cited by Mingst 1990) also describes the early operations and 'expansion' strategy of the Bank up until 1973. Kwame Donkor Fordwor served as president of the AfDB Group between 1976 and 1979, a stage marked by internal conflict, resulting in the termination of his position. His book (Fordwor 1981) provides his detailed interpretation of various events, especially the controversial debates that preceded the admission of non-regional members in 1982. Robert Gardiner, the executive secretary of United

Nations Economic Commission for Africa (UNECA) at the time and one of the major driving forces in the establishment of the AfDB Group, later co-authored the 'official' history of the Bank (in Gardiner and Pickett 1984).

The AfDB was the first Continental RDB that was founded and original 'owned' exclusively by its regional members. From the outset, the AfDB assumed a clear resolution to reject leadership and control from high-income external creditors. Preserving the autonomy of the AfDB has been central to its operations since its foundation, and this aspect has received substantial interest from various authors who have examined the Bank's power and governance structures. Voting systems are a central dimension of governance, shaping decision-making processes on loan approvals, as well as building consensus on contentious issues. In its voting system, the AfDB Group remains an exception among the other RDB, holding a 60/40 per cent vote split between regional and non-regional members (essentially between borrowers and non-borrowers)—in other RDB non-borrowers hold at least 50 per cent of the votes. Being borrower-dominant provides borrowers a clear sense of ownership among African members and the shaping of day-to-day operations. However, this feature also limits the ability of non-borrowing creditors to vote and exercise influence in the AfDB Group's decisions, which may affect their confidence and willingness to contribute resources.

A study by Krasner (1981) explores the influence of external powers in guiding the behaviour of the AfDB Group, comparing it with its counterparts in Latin America (the Inter-American Development Bank) and Asia (the Asian Development Bank). Krasner's analysis leads to the conclusion that by the early 1980s, the AfDB Group had achieved more autonomy from non-borrowing countries (external powers) than either of its counterparts. The heavy cost of such autonomy manifested in a severe constraint to access external funds. A similar conclusion is reached by Mingst (1990) and later Ben-Artzi (2016), both describing the AfDB Group as the RDB that has managed to retain the highest autonomy from hegemonic powers.

Strand (2001) analyses how the addition of non-regional members in 1982 affected the voting power relations in the AfDB Group. This study concludes that formal power relations were greatly altered by the addition of non-regional members, concentrating power in a subset of members, partly due to the rise of authoritarian regimes among the AfDB Group's voting members. More recently, Birdsall (2018) examines whether governance structures in general and voting systems in particular, affect the long-term financial prospects of RDB. In her analysis, Birdsall highlights the dilemma posed by the AfDB Group's governance structure. One the one hand, its governance arrangements and African 'ownership' make it the preferred development partner for African borrowers, as compared to the World Bank and other MDB, RDB, and bilateral donors. On the other hand, the voting system and regional presidency (held by a borrower) are not conducive to the Bank's creditworthiness and long-term ability to raise resources. Such financial constraints may curtail the Bank's ability to respond to regional developmental needs.

Fewer studies have examined the performance of the AfDB Group in achieving its development objective. One of the few exceptions is English and Mule (1996) who examine the impact of its operations on growth, poverty, the environment as well as social development. Even fewer scholars have paid attention to the role of the Bank in achieving African integration. Barnes (1984) explores the role the Bank has played in promoting regional integration in West Africa, with a follow-up study by Adarkwah (2016) who replicates and updates Barnes' study for the same sub-region. The latter identifies countries in West Africa, such as Ghana, where the AfDB has been criticized for being 'over-responsive to incumbent governments to the extent that it sometimes becomes inconsistent with the need for a firmer, more fundamental and coordinated stand in policy dialogue' (Adarkwah 2016: 6).

In addition to the academic literature, the AfDB Group produces a wealth of reports and studies, which include annual reports, statistical resources, and a plethora of specialized studies, assessments, and toolkits for its member states. In addition to its annual report, the AfDB Group produces multiple periodic publications, which have become key reference material for those interested in Africa's development. These flagship publications include *The African Economic Outlook*, which is produced annually. This publication has become a main reference, and presents the continent's state of affairs as well as a forecast for the coming few years. *The African Economic Outlook* examines the continent's performance in several key areas, including macroeconomics, external financial flows and tax revenues, trade policies and regional integration, human development, and governance. Each year it focuses on a specific theme of particular interest. The AfDB Group publishes *The Annual Development Effectiveness Review* (*ADER*) which provides an update of Africa's progress in relation to its development goals, and assesses the contribution made by the AfDB to that progress. The AfDB Group also produces 'The African Development Report' annually and provides in-depth reflections on specific themes that affect the overall development of the continent. 'The Africa Competitiveness Report', first published by the AfDB Group in 1998, has, since 2007, been a biennial project highlighting areas that require policy action and investment to ensure Africa's sustained growth. The report is a collaborative effort by the AfDB Group, the World Bank Group, and the World Economic Forum. Its statistical resources aim to provide users with quality statistical information and inform Africa's development initiatives. *The African Statistical Yearbook* is the result of the coordinated efforts among the three main Continental institutions (AfDB, the African Union Commission (AUC), and UNECA). The AfDB Group's *The Africa Infrastructure* aims to monitor progress on infrastructure development across the continent, thus contributing to the AfDB Group's resource allocation within the framework of AfDF replenishments.

Other statistical resources provide indicators for a range of thematic areas such as agricultural systems, tourism, visa openness (mobility of people), natural resources, gender, poverty, and environmental sustainability.

3. Background

The establishment of the AfDB was a major element of the governments of newly independent African countries' efforts to achieve emancipation from colonial economic structures, reframing Africa's aspirations and addressing its structural weaknesses. By the end of the 1950s and early 1960s, the continent was left with economies largely dependent on cash-crop production and mineral extraction for exports, with limited infrastructure and an almost inexistent manufacturing base. Independence brought a sense of urgency to rebuild the continent from within and to improve the living standards of African people. In the words of Dr Kwame Nkrumah, the first president of independent Ghana and an influential advocate of Pan-Africanism: 'We shall achieve in a decade what it took others a century…and we shall not rest content until we demolish these miserable colonial structures and erect in their place a veritable paradise' (Nkrumah 1957, quoted in Ayittey 1999: 7). Despite the low point of departure at independence, African gross domestic product (GDP) grew at a reasonably good rate across the continent during the 1960s and 1970s, at an annual average of over 4 per cent (Table 3.1).

Moreover, between 1965 and 1980, twelve African economies were increasing their GDP at a consistent rate of 6 per cent or above annually, which was well above the world average, and at times above the best performing East Asian economies. For example, over this period, the Kenyan economy was growing at a similar speed to that of Malaysia, Indonesia, and Thailand; and the economy of the Ivory Coast grew faster than that of the Philippines (Table 3.2).

The small size of many African national economies gave rise to the recognition that African integration should constitute an important tool to facilitate economic growth and development in the recently decolonized African economies. Such discourse was led by key figures including Nkrumah who advocated for full

Table 3.1 Average annual GDP growth in Africa (1965–99)

	1965–1969	1970–1979	1980–1989	1990–1994	1994–1999
Africa	4.5	4.2	2.5	0.9	3.5
North Africa	5.3	6.7	4.2	2.1	4.2
Sub-Saharan Africa	4.2	3.3	1.7	0.4	3.2
* Excluding South Africa	2.4	4.0	2.1	0.8	3.9
* Excluding Nigeria	3.5	3.9	2.5	0.3	4.2

Source: World Development Indicators (2017)

Table 3.2 Top twelve fastest growing African countries (1965–80)

Country	Average Annual GDP growth 1965-1980
Botswana	13.3
Gabon	8.0
Kenya	7.1
Seychelles	6.8
Tunisia	6.5
Algeria	6.4
Swaziland	6.4
Malawi	6.3
Rwanda	6.3
Cote d'Ivoire	6.3
Morocco	6.1
Lesotho	6.0

Source: World Development Indicators (2017)

Continental integration as a necessary means to reposition post-independence Africa on the world stage. African élites also understood that Africa's trading structures and relationships needed to be drastically reconstructed due to the distortions of the colonial past. Despite some achievements, such as the recently established African Continental Free Trade Area (AfCFTA)—further mentioned below—African regional economic integration remains limited, with intra-African trade accounting for 14.4 per cent of total trade in 2018—by comparison, interregional trade in Asia accounts for 59 per cent of total trade (AfDB 2019).

At the early stages of the AfDB, the mobility of goods and people in the continent was limited by the poor and deteriorating state of the continent's physical infrastructure. Africa's population is distributed over vast distances, and increasing intra-regional trade requires inter alia good roads and ports. In this respect, various studies, such as Mkandawire and Soludo (1999) have provided evidence on the poor state of Africa's physical infrastructure, providing a useful backdrop to the important mission that the AfDB Group had in supporting African integration through infrastructure development.

On the political front, post-independence transition was difficult for most African countries. The newly independent states lacked political unity, giving rise to a range of unresolved issues, including conflicting interests, competing power bases, and rival ethnic groups. The post-independence years were interrupted by political instability, often in the form of military coups or civilian takeovers. This situation created an environment of social tension and unrest, which had huge social and political consequences—in many countries, still present today. These were the trying circumstances in which the AfDB was established, launched its operations, and pursued the ambitious project of rebuilding Africa.

4. Evolution of the AfDB from its origin to the present

The early years: preservation of African identity

The origins of the idea of an African development bank have been traced back to various sources by different authors. In his account, Fordwor (1981) attributes the idea of establishing the bank to the Liberian delegation in one of the meetings of the UNECA. However, both White (1972) and Barnes (1984) link it to an initial proposal to set up a United Nations-based special fund for economic development—the Special United Nations Fund for Economic Development (SUNFED)—in which African countries would retain voting and decision-making power. Although this proposal was never realized, it generated an appetite to establish an 'African Bank' wholly owned by African nations, which would invest in African development. Fuelled by the independence movement and the strong sentiment of Pan-Africanism, the proposal was first presented at the All-African People's Conference in 1960 in Tunis. Taking up the proposal, UNECA further explored the possibility of establishing an AfDB by establishing a 'Committee of Nine', composed of experts from a small set of countries representing Africa that would consult with African governments and the international community.[1]

This committee debated contentious issues, such as whether the capital stock of the AfDB should be open or not to non-regional membership in order to preserve African ownership; whether greater voting power should be given to the larger contributing countries; or whether priority should be given to multinational or national projects. Negotiations on these matters led to a number of decisions. First, African ownership would be retained. The AfDB was assigned the function of securing additional capital from wealthy non-regional countries, although it proved to be extremely difficult to get non-African countries to commit funds to an institution in which they were denied voting rights. Also, there was a general reluctance from the international community to invest in an African organization with no experience or track record of performance. Second, to prevent the under-representation of smaller countries in decision-making, an agreement was reached to provide each member with a base of 625 votes and then, one additional vote for each share of the capital stock of the Bank held by that member. This arrangement provided a more equitable position between the large and small members while allowing large contributors greater voting power than under a system of 'one vote per country'. Third, to resolve the matter of national versus multinational, it was agreed to include in the Agreement establishing the AfDB (Article 2) a preference for projects that advanced regional development, but it did not preclude the possibility of national projects.

[1] The Committee of Nine included officials from Cameroon, Ethiopia, Guinea, Liberia, Mali, Nigeria, Sudan, Tanganyika (which formed Tanzania in 1964), and Tunisia.

The AfDB was founded by signatory agreement between twenty-three African member states on 14 August 1963 in Khartoum, Sudan, which became effective on 10 September 1964. The issue of non-regional membership would remain central for nearly two decades and had a range of important implications in the early years of the AfDB, affecting two key operational areas: access to skilled personnel and capital. Regarding the lack of skilled personnel, the exclusion of non-regional members implied that management had to look for its staff in Africa, finding at the time many difficulties in recruiting qualified personnel in a continent undersupplied with technical skills.

Regarding the issue of access to capital, since the membership of the AfDB was comprised of the poorest countries in the world, the financial weakness of its member states compromised the ability of the Bank to produce callable capital and access resources from the international marketplace. This was different from other RDB in the developing world, such as the Inter-American Development Bank and the Asian Development Bank, which fund their operations on the basis of borrowed capital. Instead, in its origins, the AfDB relied solely on the paid-in capital from the subscription of members, which became essentially a redistribution system.

Due to the lack of financial resources, the AfDB Group set up a loan ceiling policy in 1967, which limited its ability to fund multinational projects, resulting in a stronger focus on small national projects with lesser impact.[2] To reduce the risk of its lending, the AfDB was also reluctant to invest in projects in least-developed member countries. As a result, during its first decade, the AfDB channelled its limited funds to less risky projects in the strongest African economies at the time (such as Nigeria, Ivory Coast, Algeria, and Kenya), which eventually exacerbated regional disparities in the continent and did not serve the broader mission of regional integration.

The establishment of a soft-lending window and opening membership to non-regional members

There was a clear absence of AfDB lending to high-risk projects in the least-developed countries. However, raising funding for such projects was difficult on the sole basis of subscriptions irregularly paid by struggling African member states. The rationale to create a highly concessional funding mechanism became clear. Therefore, the Bank faced pressure to change its governance structure to attract funding from non-African members. Such a change had to be aligned with its strong desire to preserve its African character and autonomy. In 1972, the

[2] The AfDB's loan ceiling policy limited its loans to about USD 8 million for multinational projects and USD 3 million for national projects.

Table 3.3 Loan approvals by the AfD Group

	AfDB	AfDF	NTF	AfDB Group *Total*
1966–1975	312	139	–	451
1976–1978	457	408	64	929
1979–1981	894	811	21	1,726
1982–1984	1,467	1,071	37	2,575
1985–1987	3,087	1,795	53	4,935
1988–1990	5,428	2,825	47	8,300
1991–1993	5,735	3,151	72	8,958

Source: Extracted from English and Mule (1996)

AfDF was established, lifting restrictions against non-regional participation. The AfDF was inaugurated with total contributions of USD 87 billion from thirteen non-regional governments plus the AfDB itself. Non-regional participants would be members in the soft-lending window but not the hard-lending window. The AfDF remains an essential component of the AfDB Group in that, today, the majority of African borrower members depend entirely or in part on financing from its concessional window (Birdsall 2018).

By 1982 the resources of the AfDB Group had increased substantially (see Table 3.3), and in 1982 the African members voted in favour of extra-regional membership. For the first time, non-African donors were permitted direct influence in AfDB Group decision-making. Nevertheless, even after this adjustment of the institutional rules, the AfDB Group protected its unique African identity by ensuring that its headquarters remained in Africa, its president remained African, and the majority of its shares continued to be held by borrowing African member state governments.

From an initial authorized capital of USD 250 million, AfDB Group capital increased over nineteen years up to 1982 to USD 2.9 billion and jumped to USD 6.3 billion in 1983 as a result of the admission of non-regional countries in 1982. By 1987, AfDB Group capital further increased to USD 22.3 billion and this amount went up to USD 100 billion in 2010. The growing influx of capital allowed the Bank to channel resources under the concessionary loans to least-developed countries, reversing the previous trend and contributing to its mission of reducing regional disparities. This capital influx also allowed the AfDB Group to increase the size of its loans, thereby improving its ability to support multinational and large infrastructural projects. Moreover, the influx allowed the Bank to reduce its administrative costs and improve its record on the disbursement of funds. This success in the AfDB Group's resource mobilization was not without controversy, in that the ability of the Group to manage such a volume of loans was questioned by non-regional members. Such concerns and lack of confidence translated into a 25 per cent cutback in overall lending commitments by the early 1990s.

The troubled years

The 1990s were the years of 'Afro-pessimism'. The fast growth in the 1960s and 1970s was followed by the 'lost decade' which extended well into the mid-1990s. Structural adjustment programmes with the International Monetary Fund (IMF) were signed by thirty-six African countries in the 1980s. These programmes included the privatization of government entities, devaluation of local currencies, and trade liberalization. In many African countries, structural adjustment contributed to de-industrialization, rising unemployment, and a growing dependence on agricultural and raw mineral exports. In the 1990s, Africa's GDP growth dropped drastically and most African countries faced a growing debt problem which rose to unsustainably high levels.

With the AfDB Group close to bankruptcy, in 1995 it became the first ever Continental RDB have its credit rating downgraded to double-A rating by the main credit rating agencies. Furthermore, the AfDB Group was immersed in a number of corruption scandals. Some non-regional members questioned whether the Bank should continue to operate at all (Adams and Davies 1996). Finally, scrutiny of the AfDF nearly led to its closure, as non-regional members re-assessed whether their contributions to the Fund were, in fact, effective.

Cautiousness and repositioning

The 2000s were a decade of recovery and growth for many African economies, and in 2003 the AfDB Group managed to regain its triple-A creditworthiness rating. Since then, decision-making in lending has followed a cautious and risk-averse approach in order to maintain the triple-A rating. Such an approach to lending has limited the ability of the AfDB Group to fulfil its developmental goals. For instance, it poses limits to the AfDB Group's ability to expand lending to non-concessional countries due to existing country limits.

Another contemporary challenge that the AfDB Group has to confront is how to position itself concerning other financing sources. While it has managed to retain its character as an 'African Bank' serving 'African interests', African countries have more choices in terms of lending and frequently opt for sources other than the AfDB for various reasons—including more favourable economic terms or matters relating to political interests. Birdsall (2018) discusses the World Bank's International Development Association (IDA) and its window in Africa, as compared to the AfDF. Comparing the growth of the two funds over time,[3] her analysis suggests that 'donors prefer ensuring growth at IDA, even ultimately for lending to African members, over growth at the much smaller AfDF' (Birdsall 2018: 16).

Sub-regional banks in Eastern, Western, and Southern Africa have ambitious expansion plans and the New Development Bank (also known as the BRICS (Brazil, Russia, India, China, South Africa) Banks) became fully operational in 2016 with headquarters in China. Loans have already been approved for projects in areas such as renewable energy, transportation, water sanitation, and irrigation. Furthermore, African countries have a growing range of bilateral options (and, since the early 2000s, the Chinese government and public banks) to fund much needed large infrastructural projects, and other projects that may have more limited developmental impacts. Decisions on the source of loans are made in a context where African national governments are urgently seeking finance to close the massive infrastructural gap that continues to exist. In this respect, the AfDB Group has estimated that Africa needs an investment in infrastructure of USD 130–70 billion a year, with a financing gap of USD 68–108 billion (AfDB 2019). The AfDB Group's lending only reaches a small percentage of that amount (at USD 4–5 billion per year), meeting only a fraction of Africa's infrastructure and development needs. Many of these sought-after projects are beyond the capacity of the AfDB Group. Therefore, for the AfDB Group to be an effective force in regional integration through its investments in infrastructure, it is essential for it to partner and complement other sources of funding. Funding mega-projects, such as transport corridors, cannot be achieved by the AfDB Group alone, but requires cooperation.

In 2013, the AfDB Group adopted the 'AfDB Strategy for 2013–2022: At the Center of Africa's Transformation'. This strategy defines several key areas of focus that are well-suited to Africa's needs, which include: infrastructure development, regional integration, private sector development, and the special requirements of fragile states. In this respect, it has been noted that the impact of the AfDB Group would increase if the Bank reinforces its role as a catalyst and broker, more effectively partnering with other development funding providers, rather than aiming to spread across multiple focus areas less effectively (Humphrey 2016).

Within this ten-year strategy, in 2016 the AfDB Group crystallized its focus into five development priorities: the 'High 5s'. These include: 'Light Up and Power Africa' (energy production and supply projects), 'Feed Africa' (agricultural infrastructural projects), 'Industrialize Africa', 'Integrate Africa' (cross-national infrastructural projects), and 'Improve the Quality of Life for the People of Africa'.

[3] Birdsall (2018) indicates that IDA's replenishment in 2017 was about USD 75 billion compared to less than USD 7 billion replenishment of the AfDF for the same period, implying a larger impact by IDA in Africa than the AfDF.

These priorities have guided the AfDB Group's activities to the present day. Total approved lending has continued to increase, and in 2016 loans were 27 per cent higher than in 2015. Over half of the lending volume went to the 'Improve the Quality of Life' priority, followed by 'Light Up and Power Africa' (19 per cent), 'Feed Africa' (11 per cent), 'Industrialize Africa' (12 per cent), and 'Integrate Africa' (6 per cent).

The AfDB argues that all five priorities collectively contribute to the broad vision of African integration (AfDB Group 2019). In relation to this, a key milestone was achieved in 2019 towards a single economic space with the AfCFTA coming into force. AfCFTA is committed to removing tariffs on 90 per cent of goods, liberalizing tariffs on services, and addressing other non-tariff barriers across African countries. AfCFTA is expected to significantly increase the value of intra-African trade, with the official aim of reaching 23 per cent of total trade by 2025. Over the last decade, the AfDB has supported the vision of African integration—for example, by providing in April 2019 an institutional grant of USD 4.8 million to the African Union to help accelerate the implementation of the Agreement (AfDB Group 2019).

5. Conclusion

The AfDB has been deeply shaped by the continent's history. Fuelled by a sentiment of independence, the establishment of the AfDB was driven by a determination to create a regional bank run by Africans, funded by Africans, and serving African needs. African governments' desire for autonomy and the quest to break with distorted patterns created by Africa's colonial past have positioned the AfDB as the largest development institution dedicated solely to serve the needs of the continent. Over the years, and despite significant institutional reform, including the acceptance of non-regional members in its Board from 1982, the AfDB has managed to preserve its 'African identity'. In fact, regional members highlight the AfDB's 'Africanness' as one of the major reasons why it remains as a preferred development partner (Woods and Martin 2012). In 2021, a detailed assessment of the AfDB by its regional stakeholders suggests that one of the features of the Bank that is most appreciated is the way it ensures it is closer to Africa, understands the African way and African solutions, aligns with the priorities of regional stakeholders, and advocates for the continent in global forums as the 'African voice'. This unique feature positions the AfDB as a preferred and trusted partner among African borrowers—as compared to the World Bank and other MDB, RDB, and other bilateral donors (Woods and Martin 2012). This sense of ownership and trust among borrowers puts the AfDB in a leadership position in the region, with the potential to influence policy reforms among African member countries.

However, the same past has also brought severe limitations to its ability to attain resources. Being the smallest RDB, the African Bank Group faces ongoing difficulties to meet its objectives, supporting African integration through large multinational projects, providing concessional funding to its least-developed members, as well as supporting difficult economic reforms. The current governance structure provides few incentives to external donors to contribute with additional resources, especially in a context where other funding alternatives are increasingly available.

Approaching the complexity of the continent's challenges (at present and those ahead, especially related to the SDGs) requires further consideration of the existing governance structures within the African Bank Group, especially those related to voting rules. In addition, facing existing and new challenges also requires the willingness of external donors to recognize the unique position of leadership that RDB such as the African Bank Group have in their context and to increase the size of the AfDB and its concessional window. In sum, an approach based on cooperation rather than competition may result in better performance and more effective support for African development.

References

Adams, P. and Davis, A. (1996). 'On the rocks: the African Development Bank struggles to stay afloat', *Multinational Monitor*, 17(7/8): 30.

Adarkwah, G.K. (2016). 'Performance of the African Development Bank Group (AfDB) as a regional economic development partner in West Africa'. Master's thesis, Norwegian University of Life Sciences, Ås.

AfDB (African Development Bank) (1964). *Agreement Establishing the African Development Bank*. Khartoum, Sudan: AfDB.

AfDB (African Development Bank) (2019). *African Economic Outlook 2019*. Abidjan: AfDB, Organisation for Economic Co-operation and Development, United Nations Development Program.

AfDB Group (African Development Bank Group) (2019). *Annual Development Effectiveness Review: Integrating Africa, Connecting People*. Abidjan: AfDB.

Ayittey, G.B. (1999). *Africa in Chaos*. London: Macmillan.

Barnes, C. (1984). 'The African Development Bank's role in promoting regional integration in the economic community of West African states', *Boston College Third World Law Journal*, 4(2): 151–79.

Ben-Artzi, R. (2016). *Regional Development Banks in Comparison: Banking Strategies Versus Development Goals*. New York: Cambridge University Press.

Birdsall, N. (2018). 'The dilemma of the African Development Bank: does governance matter for the long-run financing of the MDBs? Working Paper 498. Center for Global Development, Washington, DC.

English, E.P. and Mule, H.M. (1995). *The African Development Bank*,Volume 1. London: Lynne Rienner Publishers.

Fordwor, K.D. (1981). *The African Development Bank: Problems of International Cooperation*. New York: Pergamon Press.

Gardiner, R.K.A. and Pickett, J. (eds.) (1984). *The African Development Bank 1964–1984: An Experiment in Economic Cooperation and Development*. Abidjan: AfDB.

Humphrey, C. (2016). 'The invisible hand: financial pressures and organisational convergence in multilateral development banks', *The Journal of Development Studies*, 52(1): 92–112.

Krasner, S.D. (1981). 'Power structures and regional development banks', *International organization*, 35(2): 303–28.

Mingst, K.A. (1990) *Politics and the African Development Bank*. Lexington, KY: University Press of Kentucky.

Mkandawire, T. and Soludo, C. (1999). *Our Continent, Our Future: African Perspectives on Structural Adjustment*. Trenton, NJ, and Dakar: Africa World Press and CODESRIA.

Strand, J.R. (2001). 'Institutional design and power relations in the African Development Bank', *Journal of Asian and African Studies*, 36(2): 203–23.

White, J.A. (1972). *Regional Development Banks: The Asian, African, and Inter-American Development Banks*. New York: Praeger Publishers.

Woods, N. and Martin, N. (2012). *The Preferred Partner? A Client Assessment of the African Development Bank*. Tunis: AfDB Group.

4

The Asian Development Bank

A Global Bank at the Service of Regional Growth

Dominique Barjot and Pierre Lanthier

1. Introduction

Since its creation in 1966, the Asian Development Bank (ADB) has grown to the point that many today hesitate to consider it a regional development bank (RDB), ranking it instead with multilateral development banks (MDB) such as the World Bank. This evolution may be attributed to three factors. First, the ADB always had two major economic powers among its members, Japan and the United States (US). Second, the ADB has long mobilized the world's richest countries in order to invest in Asian economies. Third, the Bank's Asian and Pacific developing members (which exclude Australia, New Zealand, and Japan) have flourished to such an extent that their share of the world's gross domestic product (GDP) has more than tripled in half a century, from 8 per cent in 1966 to 25 per cent in 2015. Many of these countries, notably South Korea, India, and People's Republic of China (PRC), have become leading players in the world economy. This growth has given more prestige and influence to the ADB worldwide.

These factors are noteworthy in light of the main theoretical issues discussed in this volume—principal-agent theory and market-failure theory—and the functions that a RDB typically pursues, such as development, market creation, and regional integration. Did the two-headed leadership enhance or diminish the principal's control over the ADB? How did the Bank's structural and financial evolution affect its role as an agent? A comparison of the ADB's financial operations with developing Asia's GDP (PRC excluded) shows that the Bank's operations oscillated from 0.5 to 0.8 per cent of GDP. After 2000, this percentage became even smaller, because of the exponential growth of Asia's economy. It is only after 2013 that the Bank's operations reached 0.5 per cent again (McCawley 2017). Can we conclude from these percentages that the ADB's contribution to market creation and development in Asia and the Pacific has been negligible? One can also wonder how efficient the Bank has been as a fixer of market failures.

Dominique Barjot and Pierre Lanthier, *The Asian Development Bank: A Global Bank at the Service of Regional Growth* In: *Regional Development Banks in the World Economy.* Edited by: Judith Clifton, Daniel Díaz-Fuentes, and David Howarth, Oxford University Press (2021). DOI: 10.1093/oso/9780198861089.003.0004

There are no simple answers to these questions. The relationship between the ADB and its market is complex. This chapter provides a survey of the Bank's evolution from its creation to its fiftieth anniversary.[1] After setting out details about the ADB's origins and its mandate, this chapter describes the Bank's membership, its organization, and its activities as a borrower and as a lender of capital. The theoretical issues will be addressed throughout the chapter and the findings will be summarized in the conclusion.[2]

2. Origins and mandate

The ADB owes its birth to the ambition of many countries and institutions which sought to stimulate the economic development of Asia. In 1966, Asia and the Pacific represented 51 per cent of the world's population with a GDP per capita at only USD 95. The region was torn apart by ideological and military conflicts, but it also provided immense opportunities for investment. During the second part of the 1950s, economists and politicians saw in the launching of a Continental development bank a way of promoting peace and economic growth. Solomon Bandaranaike, prime minister of Ceylon, put forward the idea of creating an RDB. The United Nations Economic Commission for Asia and the Far East (UN-ECAFE) also showed interest in a similar proposal. In 1963, the Tokyo study group, a Japanese team of economists and public officers close to the Ministry of Finance, conceived a plan to create a development bank for the entire Asian continent. The plan found a sympathetic ear within the UN-ECAFE, whose executive secretary, Sithu U Nyun, was particularly interested in development involving regional cooperation. The UN-ECAFE took the first steps that would lead to the ADB.

Nevertheless, the Japanese retained the leadership of the project. Ming Wan (1995) suggests that the Japanese sought to control a financial institution that would be as influential as the World Bank. However, without the support of the US, such a bank at a time when Asia was financially weak would not have been possible. Initially, the Americans were not keen on launching a competitor to the World Bank. However, they changed their minds, most likely because of the intensification of the Cold War following the Cuban revolution. In April 1965,

[1] It would have been interesting to analyse the Bank's evolution up to the present day. However, the ADB's 'Galaxy project', which became effective in 2017 (see below), altered the definition of many data. This has complicated, if not made impossible, a comparison of data after 2017 with data before that date.

[2] This chapter relies on the following references: ADB Charter (1965); ADB (1968–2016, 2016, 2019); White (1972); Watanabe (1973); Haas (1974); Huang (1975); Krasner (1981); Wilson (1987); Hirono (1991); Yasutomo (1993); Kappagoda (1995); Wan (1995); Dutt (1997, 2001); Bolt and Fugimura (2002); Naya (2002); Bull and Bøås (2003); Wesley (2003); Kilby (2006); Dent (2008); Lim and Vreeland (2012, 2013); Erquiaga (2016); Bulman et al. (2017); Delina (2017); and McCawley (2017).

President Johnson gave his full support to an RDB in Asia. Castro's victory made the Americans understand that the military option was not sufficient to fight communism. Policies that pursued economic and peaceful ends were needed. Among these was the creation of an RDB whose mission would be to ensure economic growth that would benefit the majority of the population. Already, in 1959, the Americans had contributed significantly to the establishment of the Inter-American Development Bank (IADB). Seven years later, with the escalation of the war in Vietnam, they played a similar role in Asia.

From 1963 to 1966, the ADB took shape. In 1963, UN-ECAFE set up a group of experts to prepare a proposal for the creation of an RDB, and in December of that year the First Ministerial Conference on Asian Economic Cooperation agreed to proceed with the project. A few months later, Rangaswami Krishnamurthy, head of the International Trade Division of UN-ECAFE, put together a group of bankers and financial experts to design the organization of the future bank. They were inspired by the organization of the World Bank. In March 1965, a Consultative Committee composed of representatives from nine Asian countries, including Japan, India, and Vietnam, was assigned the responsibility of looking for member countries both inside and outside of Asia. The Committee received a strong incentive from the American president when he declared that his country was ready to invest USD 1 billion in the social and economic development of South-East Asia, including a substantial contribution to the future ADB. More precisely, the US and Japan publicly committed to an investment of USD 200 million each. This support facilitated the Consultative Committee's efforts to recruit additional members. In October 1965, in Bangkok, the Charter of the ADB was adopted by a preparatory committee. The following month, Manila was chosen as the Bank's headquarters. In December 1965 and January 1966, thirty-one countries signed the Charter and the ADB officially commenced on 19 December 1966.

The Bank's Charter, which came into force on 22 August 1966, has not since been modified, with the exception of the articles relating to the amount of the capital and the number of directors. Article 1 of the Charter presents the general orientation of the Bank to:

> foster economic growth and cooperation in the region of Asia and the Far East (hereinafter referred to as the 'region') and to contribute to the acceleration of the progress of economic development of the developing member countries in the region, collectively and individually.

Article 36 specifies that in no way should the ADB take a political stand in its interventions. The eradication of poverty remains the Bank's prominent goal. Article 2 provides more detail on how this could be achieved: first, by stimulating public and private investment, either through equity investment or through loans;

second, by inciting its member countries to harmonize further their economic policies or to participate in common projects; third, by giving technical assistance in the realization of projects; and, fourth, by cooperating with the United Nations (UN; and in particular with the UN-ECAFE) as well as with any other international and national institution.

The creation of the ADB was closely associated with the Cold War. Moreover, the Bank was a means for Japan to gain more influence in relation to other Asian countries, without interfering in local politics. The Bank's objectives were above all developmental, mobilizing both private and public investments from over the world. Finally, under the influence of UN-ECAFE, the Bank sought to promote regional economic cooperation. Although these objectives remained constant over the years, the strategies put forward by the ADB to reinforce economic cooperation changed significantly, and the evolution of the membership played a non-negligible part in this transformation.

3. Membership and voting

From the outset, the Bank made it clear that it would mobilize funds from outside Asia. Consequently, its membership would include non-Asian as well as Asian countries. However, it was always understood that Asian countries would maintain a dominant voice within the Bank. The rules for becoming a member and for being given a specific voting right reflect the preoccupation of openness to non-Asian countries while protecting the prerogative of the Asian countries. According to the Charter (Article 3), all the members and associate members of UN-ECAFE, as well as all other countries of the region and all developed countries outside the region, provided they are members of the UN or of one of its agencies, can become members of the ADB. In 1966, there were thirty-one founding members, including nineteen from Asia and the Pacific and twelve from Europe and North America. The countries that became members after September 1966 needed the approval of two-thirds of the Governors' votes, provided they represented three-quarters of the voting power of existing members.

The number of shares to be allocated to each member is determined by the Board of Governors (BoG). The distribution of shares must be done in such a way that the percentage held by regional members should never be lower than 60 per cent. All members can ask to modify the percentage of their shares; however, priority must be given to members with less than 6 per cent (ADB Charter 1965, Article 5). Finally, each member's voting power is based on two considerations: 80 per cent depends upon the number of shares possessed by the member, and the remaining 20 per cent of the voting power is equally distributed among all the members. This means that the small members benefit from an improved voting power. This is noteworthy, because the members of an RDB consists of lenders and borrowers of capital. Normally, the first will prevail over the second. However, the ADB Charter tries to limit the domination of the lenders (and especially that of the non-regional members). To use the language of principal-agent analysis, one can say that the principals should not be submitted to the hegemony of one of their own, especially the hegemony of a non-regional member, and consequently the principals might not speak with one voice.

Table 4.1 summarizes the evolution of the ADB's membership since its creation. From its original thirty-one members in 1966, the number of members more than doubled to sixty-seven by 2007. Only one new member has been admitted since: Niue, in 2019. This evolution has many consequences. First, the non-regional members, whose share represented 38.7 per cent of the total membership in 1966, fell to 28.4 per cent in 2007. The newcomers among the regional members were mostly small countries, with the exception of Bangladesh and Myanmar in 1973 and the PRC in 1986. Newcomers were either ex-Soviet republics such as Kazakhstan, small but powerful economies such as Hong Kong and Singapore, or countries from the Pacific, many of them newly formed. Among the non-regional countries, one can mention Switzerland in 1967 and France three years later. Two countries remained noticeably absent: Iran and Russia. Both were invited to become founding members, but they declined.

The change in the membership is, however, more complex than the simple addition of new countries. From the outset, one could say that the members of the ADB were divided into two categories: developed countries (all the non-regional members along with Japan, Australia, and New Zealand) and under-developed countries (all of which were regional members). Gradually, either through the introduction of new members (Singapore and the PRC, for instance) or by the significant growth of some of the founding members (South Korea in particular), many of the regional members reached the level of emerging or, for some, fully developed countries. This has brought a new (and more complex) dynamic among the members.

The modification in the voting power reflects this evolution. According to the Charter, the voting power of the regional members must not be lower than 60 per cent. This minimum has been respected: in 1967, the regional members had 62.6 per cent of the votes; in 2015, 65.2 per cent. However, if we divide the voting power between the developed and the developing countries, a different image emerges. In 1967, according to the classification used by Nitish Dutt,[3] 64.7 per cent of the voting power was in the hands of developed countries, and most of these countries would share the views held by Japan and the US. This may explain why the Soviet Union and its satellites, as well as France, refused to become members of the ADB. France joined the Bank in 1970, after de Gaulle's departure.

[3] All the non-regional members, plus Japan, Australia, and New Zealand, are considered to be developed countries (Dutt 1997).

Table 4.1 The evolution of ADB membership (1966–2007)

December 31st	1966	1970	1980	1990	2000	2010	Total
Regional members	Afghanistan	Hong Kong (1969)	Papua New Guinea (1971)	Vanuatu (1981)	Mongolia (1991)	Timor-Leste (2002)	
	Australia	Fiji (1970)	Tonga (1972)	Bhutan (1982)	Nauru (1991)	Palau (2003)	
	Cambodia		Bangladesh (1973)	China (People's Republic of) (1986)	Tulavu (1993)	Armenia (2005)	
	India		Myanmar (1973)	Marshall Islands (1990)	Kazakhstan (1994)	Brunei Darussalam (2006)	
	Indonesia		Solomon Islands (1973)	Micronesia (Federated States of) (1990)	Kyrgyz Republic (1994)	Georgia (2007)	
	Japan		Kiribati (1974)		Uzbekistan (1995)		
	Korea (Rep. of)		Cook Islands (1976)		Tajikistan (1998)		
	Lao (People's Democratic Republic)		Maldives (1978)		Azerbaijan (1999)		
	Malaysia				Turkmenistan (2000)		
	Nepal						
	New Zealand						
	Pakistan						
	Philippines						
	Samoa						
	Singapore						
	Sri Lanka						

Continued

Table 4.1 *Continued*

December 31st	1966	1970	1980	1990	2000	2010	Total
	Taipei						
	Thailand						
	Viet Nam						
Sub-total	19	2	8	5	9	5	48
Non-Regional Members	Austria	Switzerland (1967)		Spain (1986)	Turkey (1991)	Portugal (2002)	
	Belgium	France (1970)				Luxemburg (2003)	
	Canada					Ireland (2006)	
	Denmark						
	Finland						
	Germany						
	Italy						
	The Netherlands						
	Norway						
	Sweden						
	United Kingdom						
	United States						
Sub-total	12	2	0	1	1	3	19
Total	31	4	8	6	10	8	67
Cumulative total	31	35	43	49	59	67	

Source: ADB 2016b.

Throughout all the capital increases, the developed countries managed to keep a majority of votes. However, their percentage diminished. In 1972, the developed countries' voting share was reduced to 58.3 per cent and, in 2015, to 54.5 per cent. On the other hand, if we add the newly developed regional countries (the PRC, South Korea, Hong Kong, and Singapore), their voting power increases to 65.1 per cent; and with emerging countries such as India, Indonesia, and Taipei, it reaches 76.3 per cent. Consequently, the ADB remains strongly in the hands of the developed countries. Nevertheless, the rising number of developed and emerging countries among the regional members tends to relativize the impact of the division between developed and developing countries, since the newcomers do not necessarily share the views of the traditional developed countries, and especially, those of Japan and the US.

Table 4.2 provides the voting percentage of the ten most important member countries from 1967 to 2015. The list remains quite stable. In 1980, Pakistan and the UK vanished, while Malaysia made its appearance; and, in 1996, the Philippines gave way to the PRC. However, the voting power of the top ten fell over 10 per cent from 1967 (71.9 per cent) to 2015 (61.4 per cent). Countries such as India and Australia declined, while Canada, South Korea, and Indonesia increased their voting share. The two dominant shareholders, Japan and the US, saw their share fall from 34.2 to 25.5 per cent. Initially, they had invested USD 200 million each, giving them an equal 17.1 per cent of the voting power. Later, their voting power was reduced, but at a different pace. In 1972, while the Americans' voting power was cut by half (8.4 per cent), the Japanese increased theirs to 20.2 per cent by investing USD 173.7 million in the ADB's capital.

Table 4.2 Voting power of the ten most important ADB members (1967–2015)

	1967	1980	1996	2015
Japan	17.12	14.05	13.2	12.8
United States	17.12	11.19	13.2	12.71
India	8.3	6.78	5.57	5.37
Australia	7.64	6.24	5.12	4.93
Philippines	3.51	2.84		
FGR /Germany	3.34	4.78	3.92	3.76
Pakistan	3.26			
South Korea	3.1	5.49	4.5	4.33
United Kingdom	3.1			
Indonesia	2.69	5.89	4.84	4.66
Canada	2.69	5.68	4.66	4.89
Malaysia		3.18	2.6	2.48
China (PRC)			5.66	5.46
Total	71.87	66.12	63.27	61.39

Source: ADB 1968-2016.

However, Japan's voting power went down to 14 per cent in 1980 and diminished further to 12.8 per cent in 2015. On their part, the US gradually increased its share to 13.2 per cent in 1996 and reduced it to 12.7 per cent twenty years later. To sum up, both countries have lost five percentage points, but their voting power still remains equal and predominant within the Bank's membership.

The leadership of Japan and the US in the ADB deserves attention. Many scholars argue that both Japan and the US use the Bank to promote and defend their respective interests in Asia (Yasutomo 1983; Wihtol 1988; Wan 1995; Dutt 1997, 2001; Dent 2008; Strand 2011; Ben-Artzi 2016). Some scholars focus on the relationship between Japan and the ADB. They emphasize the close personal and professional relations between the Bank's top executives and the Japanese Ministry of Finance. A few experts even depict the ADB as a political instrument for Japan to gain influence within international institutions such as the US Security Council. To be sure, Japan has made significant financial efforts to impose its presence over the ADB. However, the presence of the US must not be ignored. The Americans may have had a political purpose for investing in the Bank. However, they also saw in it a means to develop Asia to the extent that it would become advantageous to invest more in this continent. Both countries have shared political influence over the ADB. Christopher Kilby (2011) argues that while Japan has always had a strong financial and human presence in the ADB, the US managed to exercise influence through its economic and political presence throughout Asia, especially during the Vietnam War. At times, Japan and the US competed with each other to gain predominance over the ADB. This seemed to be the case during the 1990s, when the US, with the implicit support of other members, tried to curb the influence of Japan. After 2000, a new potential competitor made its appearance, the PRC, which was given a comfortable position in the ADB with some 5.5 per cent of voting power. Nevertheless, the PRC's influence remains limited within the Bank.

The double leadership of Japan and the US is interesting from the point of view of principal-agent theory. Both countries have expectations towards the ADB that can sometimes be limited by competition and by the growing presence of other member countries. With the advent of new members, a trend seems to emerge: the Japanese and the American influence over the other members, while indisputable, has tended to diminish. The two leading countries have not always been in total agreement, and the support of other members is likely to be essential. Voting power is not sufficient to determine the real influence of the members. The limitation of the two leaders' control favours the autonomy of the ADB as the agent. This is all the more true as the Bank is part of international institutions such as the World Bank, UN-ECAFE, and the IADB. These institutions share with the ADB an ideological commitment towards regional development and influence each other in their respective management.

4. The Bank's organization

The organization of the Bank can be analysed from two perspectives: the top management and the overall structure. Both increased in size and complexity over time.

The Bank's top management

The highest deciding authority in the ADB is the BoG, consisting of one representative per member country. A country nominates a governor and an alternative in case the former is incapacitated. The BoG meets once a year, but can call for special meetings if needed. The majority of the governors constitutes the quorum provided it represents at least two-thirds of the total voting power. The BoG holds all the Bank's power. However, it hands over part of its power to the Board of Directors (BoD). The BoG keeps exclusive authority on items such as the Bank's membership, the increase or decrease of capital, the election of the BoD and of the president, and cooperation with other international institutions. More importantly, the BoG's decision should always prevail over that of the BoD. In other words, the BoD is the instrument of the principals over the agent, the Bank.

During the first years, the governors were mostly the ministers of finance of their respective countries, while the alternates were top executives of their country's central bank. With time, the nature of the governors changed. In the 2012 annual meeting, there were important differences between the governors from regional countries and those from non-regional members. In their great majority (thirty-five out of forty-eight), the regional governors were ministers of finance (or the equivalent), the remaining being heads of central banks or senior government officials close to the Ministry of Finance. The governors from non-regional countries, for their part, were senior officers from Ministries of Finance (fourteen out of nineteen) or heads of a public institution with an international mission, such as the Canadian International Development Agency. The governors were accompanied by teams of temporary alternate governors (TAG) and advisers. The number of TAGs and advisers varied considerably from one country to another. In the 2012 meeting, Japan had four TAGs and thirty-four advisers; the US had two and twenty-eight, respectively; while Australia had two TAGs and five advisers; India had five TAGs and four advisers; and the PRC had two and eighteen, respectively. Moreover, some fifty to sixty observers attended the meeting. They represented institutions such as the World Bank or non-member countries such as the Russian Federation. The number of the TAGs, advisers, and observers changes from one meeting to the next, depending on the interests each member and non-member have in the issues to be debated. The meetings of the BoG are eminently political and draw a large number of participants.

The BoD must be permanently based in the ADB's headquarters in Manila. It is responsible for the general operations of the Bank, such as lending, borrowing, and authorizing guarantees, investment, and technical assistance. The BoD plans meetings as often as necessary. The required quorum is the majority, provided the directors attending the meeting represent at least two-thirds of the voting power.

The directors are elected by the BoG. Originally, there were ten directors, seven of whom represented the regional members and the other three the non-regional members. In 1969, their number was increased to twelve: eight regional and four non-regional directors. The election of a director follows a complex pattern. The candidates are proposed by the members of the BoG and they must not be governors themselves. Those nominated by regional members are elected by regional governors only; the candidates nominated by non-regional members are elected by non-regional governors. To be elected, a regional candidate must gather 10 per cent of the regional voting power and a non-regional candidate must obtain 17 per cent of the non-regional voting power. This means that Japan and the US will always elect the candidates they have chosen. The other members have no choice but to associate themselves to propose an eligible candidate. Some countries, under these circumstances, have enough voting power to invite smaller members to vote for their candidates. This is the case, for instance, for Australia and South Korea. Jonathan Strand (1999) describes them as 'dictators' because of their capacity to impose their choice for a director. If, after one election, there remain vacant seats, other elections will be held until all the seats are fulfilled. However, the votes during the second and the following elections are reserved for the members whose voices were not strong enough to choose a candidate in the previous election. The Bank makes sure that all its members have a director to represent them. This system tends to favour smaller members. Article 30 of the Charter also specifies that a candidate for the BoD must have solid economic and financial knowledge or competence. Each director is elected for two years and can be re-elected.

The BoD is chaired by a president who also heads a managerial team composed of vice-presidents and a managing director general. The president is elected by the BoG with a majority of voting power. He or she must originate from a regional country and be neither a governor nor a director. The president is elected for five years, and his or her mandate can be renewed. Although the president cannot vote at the BoG meetings or at the BoD meetings (except when the votes are equal), his or her influence is most important.

Table 4.3 shows that all the ADB presidents have been Japanese and have shared one previous affiliation: they all had an active career at the Ministry of Finance or, in the case of Shiro Inoue, at the Bank of Japan. Within the Ministry of Finance, many have spent years in the International Finance Bureau. Moreover, the majority of them have worked for the World Bank or the IMF. Two have previous experience at the ADB, Masao Fujioka and Tadao Chino. Consequently, the

Table 4.3 ADB presidents and previous institutional affiliations (1966–2019)

	Years	MoF	BoJ	OJPI	ADB	WB	IMF	TSE	ECAFE
Watanabe (Takeshi)	1966 to 1972	x				x	x		
Inoue (Shiro)	1972 to 1976		x			x			
Yoshida (Taroichi)	1976 to1981	x					x		
Fujioka (Masao)	1981 to 1989	x		x	x	x			
Tarumizu (Kimimasa)	1989 to 1993	x		x					
Sato (Mitsuo)	1993 to 1999	x					x	x	
Chino (Tadao)	1999 to 2005	x			x				x
Kuroda (Haruhiko)	2005 to 2013	x					x		
Nakao (Takehiko)	2013 to present	x					x		

Notes: MoF (Japan's Ministry of Finance); BoJ (Bank of Japan); OJPI (Other Japanese public institutions); ADB (Asian Development Bank); WB (World Bank); IMF (International Monetary Fund); TSE (Tokyo Stock Exchange); ECAFE (UN Economic Commission for Asia and the Far East).

Source: ADB. 2016b; McCawley 2017.

links between the ADB and Japan are reinforced at the top. These links are all the stronger since there is no statutory obligation for the Bank to elect a Japanese national as president. Scholars and journalists have criticized this practice and expressed hope that the next president will come from another country (*The Economist* 2016). However, some presidents made a point of defending the Bank's autonomy in relation to Japan's Ministry of Finance. This has been the case of Taroichi Yoshida. It seems that Japan endorsed Yoshida's stand, because the ADB, politically speaking, is better placed to invest across Asia and the Pacific than is Japan (Wan 1995). To a certain extent, the relative autonomy of the ADB as an agent benefits Japan's influence over Asia and Pacific.

The management staff are under the authority of the president, who is surrounded by vice-presidents recommended by the president but nominated by the BoD. The vice-presidents are chosen primarily on the basis of their academic background or professional experience. Originally, there was only one vice-president, C. S. Krishna Moorthi, an official with proven experience at the World Bank and as India's representative in a consultative committee of UN-ECAFE. He stayed for eleven years as vice-president and was replaced, in 1978, by two vice-presidents: another Indian, Ashok T. Bambawale, and an American, S. Stanley Katz. In 1983, a third vice-president was added: Günther Schulz, from West Germany. Other vice-presidents joined the team afterwards. In 2016, there were six, plus one managing director general, making up a total of seven individuals heading the management staff. Four originate from regional countries (the PRC, Australia, Indonesia, and India) and three from non-regional countries (the US, the Netherlands, and Spain). If three of them did have previous experience working for the ADB, all developed more experience outside the Bank—including working at the Ministry of Finance, World Bank, OECD, Central Bank, EBRD, and

USAID. It has long been a tradition in the Bank for the management to have acquired experience in other international institutions and, particularly, from other RDB. A good example is Günther Schulz, vice-president from 1983 to 1995, who had worked previously for the IADB. His successor in 1995, Pierre Ubel, came from the African Development Bank.

To sum up, the head of the ADB has become a complex entity over time. If the political decision-making is firmly in the hands of the BoG and the BoD, the management as such and the design of proposals to be voted by the political instances are under the responsibility of the president and his or her managing staff. One could say that the president is at the centre of the Bank's strategy and, being consistently Japanese, he or she makes sure Japan holds a key influence over the Bank. Nevertheless, his or her managing staff is not Japanese. Moreover, their experience, in nearly all the cases, includes working for other international institutions such as the IMF and the World Bank. The same is true of the vice-presidents. Seen from this perspective, then, the ADB looks less like a subsidiary of the Japanese Ministry of Finance and more as providing an opportunity for Japan to participate more efficiently in the development of Asia and the Pacific without exerting any direct form of hegemony. This situation is interesting from the point of view of principal-agent theory. On the one hand, the ADB, as the agent, benefits from a minimal autonomy in relation to the BoG and the BoD, the principals; on the other hand, this autonomy seems to be helpful to one of the principals in particular—Japan.

The evolution of the Bank's structure

The multiplication of vice-presidents is a sign of the evolution of the Bank's organizational structure. In 1966, the ADB had an organization closer to that of the World Bank than to that of other RDB. Under the president, there was one vice-president responsible for the functioning of five offices and three departments distributed in two sections: operations, consisting of the Operations Department and the Economic and Technical Assistance Department (ETAD), both dealing with projects and loans; and services, with an Administration Department and the five officers (treasurer, internal auditor, general counsel, secretary, and information/publicity officer).

The Bank constantly modified its structure. In 2016, the president has under his authority one department (the Strategy and Policy Department), five officers (ombudsperson, auditor general, anticorruption and integrity officer, public-private partnership officer, and special project facilitator), a managing director general, six vice-presidents, and one dean. The vice-presidents are at the head of nineteen departments or offices, under which there are eighty-four divisions or units and twenty-six resident missions. The vice-presidencies are divided into three sections: operations (three vice-presidencies: knowledge management and sustainable development; Operations 1, in charge of Central and West Asia and South Asia; Operations 2, responsible for East Asia, South-East Asia, and the Pacific), Finance (two vice-presidencies: private sector and co-financing operations; finance and risk management), and Administration (one vice-presidency: Administration and corporation management). For his or her part, the dean heads the Asian Development Bank Institute. Finally, above the president, the BoD has an office of the compliance review panel and an independent evaluation department.

Comparing change between 1966 and 2016, the differences are striking. From a simple structure, the ADB gradually built up a complex organization. Offices or departments have been renamed or split; under each department and office, divisions, units, and, later on, missions have multiplied. With these changes, it has become necessary to distribute the responsibilities between the president and the vice-president and add more vice-presidents. These transformations have come along with a continual growth of the Bank's staff. In 1967, there were 190 individuals working for the ADB. In 1986, their number reached 1,604 and in 2016, 3,092.[4] *The Economist* (2016) has deplored the complexity of the Bank's organizational structure on the grounds that it impairs its efficiency. Three reasons can be put forward to explain the evolution.

First, even if the ADB is an RDB, Asia and the Pacific are too wide and too culturally diverse to be considered as a region *per se*. Over the years, the Bank has divided the continent in regions, each of them requiring equal attention. This has contributed to the setting up of new regional departments, offices, and divisions, especially in 1973–4.[5] More importantly, it also led to the creation of missions in the field. In 1982, the Bank organized a first resident mission in Bangladesh in order to have a more efficient management of the ongoing activities in this country. Two years later, it created a second one, in Vanuatu. In the following years, the ADB multiplied missions around Asia and the Pacific: there were six in 1996, twenty in 2006, and twenty-six ten years later. In 2007, 19.7 per cent of the ADB's staff worked in these missions; in 2016, this percentage increased to 23.2. From one reform to the next, these missions have received more responsibilities for efficiency reasons. They certainly contributed to increasing the autonomy of the ADB as an agent in relation to the principals. They also facilitated the emergence of the specific way in which the ADB fulfilled its RDB mission, that is, development, market creation, and integration, within each region mentioned above of smaller transnational regional units. During the 1990s, Mitsuo Sato and his team designed

[4] In October 2019, the Bank had 3,381 employees. The ADB added almost 300 members of staff within three years.

[5] On regional development in Asia and the role played by the ADB, see Kuroda and Kawai (2002); Hamilton-Hart (2003); Kawai (2005); Rathus (2008); Jayasuriya (2009); Carroll (2012); and Uhlin (2016).

an explicit regional policy consisting of building up cross-border cooperation involving not only the public authorities but above all the private sector. The Bank would provide research and technical assistance and mobilize local as well as non-local investors. Moreover, it would open the chosen area to the global market, prompting it to boost its productivity and improve its infrastructure. This is what the ADB meant by 'open regionalism', a way of bringing not only growth and technical efficiency, but also Sub-regional integration. A first experiment was attempted in 1992 in South-East Asia, the Greater Mekong Sub-region (GMS), involving six countries. Under this programme, many projects became a reality, such as the Yunnan Expressway in the PRC and the Theun Hinboun Hydroproject in Lao People's Democratic Republic (PDR). The GMS served as a model for other projects set up by the ABD, such as the Jobor-Riau-Singapore programme and the Bay of Bengal Initiative for Multi-Sectoral Technical Economic Co-operation. These programmes were accompanied by organizational changes within the ADB. A Private Sector Group, an Economics and Development Resource Center, and an Office for Co-financing Operations made their appearance. In 1994, the two vice-presidencies 'Projects' and 'Operations' became 'Region West' and 'Region East', with Sub-regional divisions. In 2006, these divisions were replaced by five regional departments (East Asia, Central and West Asia, South Asia, South-East Asia, and the Pacific) under two vice-presidencies, Operations 1 (ex-West) and Operations 2 (ex-East).

The ADB's open regionalism has been criticized by many scholars as a way to implant liberalization and globalization in developing countries, with or without the participation of local public institutions (Oehlers 2006; Rosser 2009; Glassman 2010; Cammack 2016). Christopher Dent (2008) prefers to see in the ADB's regional policy as a manifestation of 'Japanese developmentalism', which consists of mobilizing institutions, local as well as international, to open local economies to the world market. He considers this approach more proactive than those of simple liberalization or deregulation.

Financial crises provide a second reason for the complexity of the ADB's structure. In 1997, in the middle of the Asian crisis, the ASEAN+3 (Association of Southern Asian Nations plus PRC, South Korea, and Japan) asked the ADB to set up a Regional Economic Monitoring Unit (REMU) with a mandate to follow the Asian financial market closely so as to prevent further crises. This unit became in 2005 the Office of Regional Economic Integration and added to its mission the promotion of economic cooperation. In 2002, a new vice-president position was created, knowledge management and sustainable development, with three departments including one responsible for economic research and regional cooperation.

The administrative re-organization of the top management represents a third reason for the increasing complexity of the organizational structure. It became important for the president not to be overwhelmed by demands and issues from above or below. In this context, the presidency has been reinforced by the addition of five offices, one department, and one institute which are under his or her direct control, and the setting up in 2003 of a managing director general as a coordinator. As a reaction, the BoD proceeded to create one office and one department to help its members evaluate the Bank's projects.

Hence, the ADB's organization has become complex, with a trend towards decentralization, especially with the increase of the number of missions. This trend, nevertheless, has been offset by the reinforcement of the top management and of the presidency in particular. The power given to the president favours Japan as a principal and Japan's vision of development and integration, not only in joining the forces of regions, but also in forging links with global partners (multinational firms, international financial agencies, etc.). This organization seems to provide an ideal field for internal competition opposing the BoD to the president, the president to the vice-presidents, and the resident missions to Manila. However, by practising the policy of open regionalism, these actors share the same vision of development, which contributes to a unifying of the Bank's strategy.

5. Assets and operations

Capital and borrowing

To be able to function normally, a development bank must rely primarily on borrowing and managing funds donated by members and outside institutions. The size of its operations depends on its capacity to attract investment. This is done by increasing the ordinary capital resources (OCR), consisting of the authorized capital, the funds obtained by borrowing, the funds earned from loans and guarantees, and funds from other sources (Charter, Article 7). Attracting capital is also done by managing special funds.

Capital increases

In November 1966, the authorized capital of the ADB was USD 1.1 billion, half of which was paid-in. There have been five general capital increases, plus many specific (and smaller) increases to accommodate new members, such as Spain and the PRC in 1986, or countries wishing to augment their share, such as South Korea and Canada in the 1970s. Any capital increase must receive the authorization of two-thirds of the BoG voices representing three-quarters of the total members' voting power (Charter, Article 4).

In 2016, the authorized capital was worth USD 154.09 billion. The subscribed capital is equal to $153.06 billion, the paid-in capital to USD 7.68 billion and the callable to USD 145.38 billion. Even if the callable capital is intangible, it plays a major role in backing up the ADB's bond issues. Until the 1990s, the general increases were relatively modest: USD 1.65 billion in 1971, USD 4.79 billion in 1976, and USD 8.16 billion in 1983. The 1994 increase was more significant, with USD 25.04 billion. This increase happened after negotiations that lasted from 1986 to 1993. The Japanese were in favour of such an increase, but not the US. The Americans feared this would give too much power to Japan. However, the increase was finally approved during the 1993 annual meeting. It was justified by a predicted growth from 7.7 to 10.5 per cent annually of the Bank's operations over the next six years. As a result of this decision, the Americans encouraged the new industrial nations of Asia to increase their participation in the ADB's capital in order to better contain the Japanese hegemony (Strand 2011).

In the aftermath of the Asian crisis, the Bank refrained from making any increase until 2009. The increase of that year, however, was the most important of the ADB's history, reaching USD 106.3 billion (of which USD 4.3 billion was paid-in). Such a large amount was justified by the need for more liquidity caused by the 2007–8 crisis and by the growth prediction of the Asian economy according to the Bank's 'Strategy 2020' programme.

Borrowings

The Charter allows the Bank to borrow from its members. However, it is important that the borrowers be as diversified as possible (Charter, Article 21). Until the 1980s, the ADB's borrowings were modest, making a point not to overpass the callable capital of the developed member countries with convertible currencies (CCCC). During the initial years, the Bank even restricted its borrowings to 75 per cent of its CCCC. From 1969 to 1974, the Bank borrowed close to USD 300 million only through public issues and private placements in Europe, North America, the Middle East, and Asia. However, in 1975–6, the ADB had to cope with inflation. During these two years, the Bank borrowed around USD 1.1 billion. Afterwards, the ADB constantly increased its borrowings (Table 4.4).

Table 4.4 ADB's decennial borrowings (1978–2016)

Years	*Amount*
1977–1986	6.4
1987–1996	12.4
1997–2006	53.0
2007–2016	144.0

Source: ADB 2016b.

The ADB was present across all the financial markets around the world. The Bank took a prudent approach by borrowing in low-interest currencies. Its credit rate soon reached triple-A level. However, in 1982, the Bank felt that the CCCC limit was too restrictive and, three years later, it abandoned this system. Using flexible market opportunities, the ADB was able to emit 'Dragon Bonds' in 1991, worth USD 300 million, in Hong Kong, Singapore, and Taipei. From 1997 to 2006, the ADB made 329 medium- and long-term borrowing transactions representing USD 39 billion, and 130 short-term transactions, reaching a total of USD 14 billion. Almost 30 per cent of these transactions were undertaken during the Asian Crisis. The Bank diversified its borrowings and included more regional members among the lenders. For instance, in 2006, it emitted USD 10 billion in Hong Kong and in the PRC; in 2014, it issued 3 billion rupees in the Indian market. From 2007 to 2016, the Bank raised an average of USD 14.4 billion annually in an increasingly diversified financial market.

Special funds

The ADB has been managing special funds independent from the OCR for long-term development lending. With a low interest rate, these funds are intended for its poorest members. To raise these funds, the Bank can mobilize up to 10 per cent of its paid-in capital or ask for extraordinary contributions from its members. These contributions have become the most important source for gathering (or replenishing) special funds. The donators, however, can impose conditions on the beneficiaries. The ADB can also have a free hand on the management of these funds, provided they have the explicit agreement of the contributors.

Before 1973, the ADB launched three major special funds: an agricultural special fund (USD 20 million from the Japanese government in 1968 intended for the South Asian countries); a multipurpose special fund (USD 25 million by the Canadian government in 1968); and a technical assistance fund (USD 250,000 from the US government). These funds received supplementary contributions from other countries subsequently. In 1973, the first two funds ended their replenishment period and the unused money was transferred into a new special fund called the Asian Development Fund (ADF). From 1973 to 2016, the ADF was replenished eleven times to a total of almost USD 63 billion. The first contribution was rather modest: USD 710 million for ADF I. The following replenishments were to be more substantial. ADF XI, for instance, raised USD 4.45 billion.

In 1977, the Bank drew up a priority list of its members to receive ADF loans. Some countries, such as Bangladesh, were fully eligible, while others, such as Indonesia, were only marginally eligible. Subsequently, the list was revised and new classification rules applied. Some countries, such as South Korea and Singapore, were excluded from the ADF programme because they were considered to be developed economies. However, in case of emergencies (an economic crisis or a natural disaster, for instance), these countries could become eligible again, but on an exceptional basis. In addition to the ADF, other special funds have been managed by the ADB. In 1988, a Japan Special Fund was created to contribute to the industrialization of its developing members through technical assistance and through interventions from the private sector. Regularly, Japan replenished the fund: USD 20 million in 1988; more than USD 100 million in 1995. In the years that followed, Japan participated in two more funds: Japan Fund for Poverty Reduction and Japan Fund for Information and Communication Technology. In the end, Japan remains the most important supplier of special funds. Already in 1967–72, Japan gave USD 122.6 million, while the US contributed only USD 1.25 million. Throughout the subsequent decades, the gap between the two countries' contribution has remained constant. In ADF VIII (2004), Japan gave USD 1.1 billion while the US gave USD 412 million. Other countries, such as Canada and Sweden, increased their donation. However, the most significant growth in contributions came from regional donors: already by the end of the 1970s, Hong Kong, Taipei, Indonesia, and South Korea had participated in an ADF. In the following years, South Korea increased its donations. At the turn of the century, for the first time, the special funds donations came equally from regional and non-regional countries. South Korea continued to increase its share; and the PRC, for the first time, participated in a fund.

However, there remains a problem with the ADF. This fund does not have a separate legal identity and, consequently, bonds cannot be issued to back up its loans. In 2014, the Bank proposed a new project, 'Galaxy', whereby the ADF was maintained, but its loan assets were absorbed by the OCR. The ADF was to concentrate on funding grants but was also to stop lending money. The 'Galaxy project' was accepted in 2015 and became effective in January 2017. The OCR equity, then, jumped from USD 18.3 billion to USD 50 billion, strengthening the Bank's capacity to borrow and lend. It is clear that Japan has been the biggest supplier of funds. From 1973 to 1986, Japan financed 29.4 per cent of the ADB's total borrowings, while the US provided 12.9 per cent, and the member countries from Europe together gave 45.1 per cent. From 1987 to 1993, Japan maintained its participation at 30.4 per cent, the US at 11.7 per cent, while the combined contribution of European countries fell to 39.8 per cent. The rest of the world, and mainly Asia, increased its share from 12.6 to 18.1 per cent. The predominance of Japan as a money lender may explain, at least in part, the difficulties in US-Japan relations during the 1990s. In more recent years, however, especially with the emergence of regional donors, the competition between the US and Japan seems to belong to the past. This is corroborated by the Bank's operations.

The Bank's operations

According to its Charter, the Bank lends money, gives technical assistance, grants, and guarantees, and makes equity investments. It also participates in

Table 4.5 ADB Loans, equity investments, grants, guarantees, and technical assistance (1967–2016)

	1967–1976	1977–1986	1987–1996	1997–2006	2007–2016
LEGG[a] (OCR)	2,466	10,758	30,082	50,013	110,663
Loans (ADF)	895	5,283	12,981	14,062	29,648
Technical Assistance[b]	25	125	882	1,383	1,540
Total	3,386	16,166	43,945	65,458	141,851

[a] LEGG = loans, equity investments, grants and guarantees.
[b] Grants funded by the Technical Assistance Special Fund.

Source: ADB 2016b.

co-financing, proposes projects, and facilitates cross-border cooperation. In equity investments, the Bank cannot take control of any enterprise, unless this is necessary. The total amount of the loans, equity investments, grants, and guarantees (LEGG) should not be superior to the subscribed capital, reserves, and surpluses included in the OCR. Moreover, equity investments should not exceed 10 per cent of the paid-in capital, plus reserves and surpluses. The Bank can make LEGG based on the value of its OCR. It can also make loans with money taken from the ADF. OCR loans are considered to be 'hard loans' and those of the ADF, 'soft loans'. The soft loans have a lower interest rate and their amortization lasts longer.

Table 4.5 gives the decennial evolution of the LEGG (OCR), of the lending attached to the ADF and of the grants funded by the technical assistance special fund from 1967 to 2016. Equity investments, grants, and guarantees do not add up much in comparison with loans. In 2016, for instance, the three of them put together represented only 6.3 per cent of the Bank's total operations, while the technical assistance funds were equal to 0.95 per cent.

The Bank granted its first loan in 1968. We can see that the loans attached to the OCR have always been more voluminous than those from the ADF and technical assistance put together. More importantly, from one decade to the next, the loans became bigger, especially over the last decade. The growth of the loans was slow and gradual until the Asian crisis, increasing from USD 42 million in 1968 to USD 5.3 billion in 1996. However, in 1997, this rose to USD 9.5 billion. During the first years of the 2000s, annual loans oscillated between USD 5 billion and USD 6 billion. In 2006, these went up to USD 8.1 billion and to USD 11.1 billion the following year. After 2010, these first stabilized at over USD 13 billion, only to reach USD 16.3 billion in 2015 and USD 17.5 billion in 2016. Market failures, such as the Asian crisis and the 2008 downturn, contributed to the sudden growth, but so did the Galaxy project in 2014.

If we examine the operations by sectors of activity (Table 4.6), we can see that the initial priority went to energy, transport, and agriculture. The 1973 oil

Table 4.6 ADB Loans, equity investments, grants, and guarantees by sectors (1967–2016)

	1967–1976	1977–1986	1987–1996	1997–2006	2007–2016
LEGG (millions of USD)[a]	3,361	16,041	43,064	64,075	140,311
Energy	23%	25%	26%	15%	25%
Transport and ICT[b]	20	12	24	27	29
Agriculture	19	31	16	9	6
Finance	18	10	11	23	12
Industry	10	3	5	2	2
Water	9	10	8	8	9
Education	1	5	5	4	4
Multisector	0.1	1	2	—	—
Health	—	2	2	3	1
Public Sector	—	—	—	9	13

[a] LEGG= loans (OCR and ADF), equity investments, grants and guarantees.
[b] ICT= information and communication technology.

Source: ADB 2016b.

crisis pushed forward the energy sector, especially in Thailand, the Philippines, and Pakistan. Investment in roads was also crucial, notably in South Korea. From 1977 to 1986, agriculture came first by a long margin, with projects such as irrigation and forestry, in particular in Indonesia, Pakistan, and Bangladesh. During the next decades, agriculture lost its predominance to become a secondary sector, even if, in 1980, the ADB set up a 'sector lending' programme in part to help agriculture. Energy remained among the most important lending sectors, except in 1997-2006, when the Asian crisis pushed energy behind finance and transport. The Bank adopted explicit energy policies, notably in 1995 and in 2009.

The Asian financial crisis convinced the Bank to implement a risk-based capital policy and various preventive measures after 2000. The crisis hit South Korea, Thailand, and Indonesia strongly. The ADB lent them respectively USD 15 billion, USD 1.2 billion, and USD 1.8 billion. After the crisis, the Bank created a Poverty Reduction Unit to fight poverty, and promote social development and good governance. The Bank supported the public sector, also hit by the crisis. The 2008 crisis had a similar impact, pushing the ADB to mobilize supplementary resources and set up various programmes. In 2009, for instance, the Bank lent USD 8.8 billion to forty-three projects as a support through the difficult times. The same year, it launched a Counter-cyclical Facility programme, consisting of short-term lending. Other sectors such as education or health never enjoyed a big share of the ADB's operations. Overall, crises, such as market failures, encouraged the ADB to gather new capital and invest more in fighting poverty.

Table 4.7 lists the five countries benefiting the most from the ADB's LEGG and technical assistance. Countries such as Pakistan and Indonesia remained permanently within the top five; so did the Philippines during the first three decades of the Bank's operations. According to Dutt (2001), the countries that received the most funds from the ADB in 1968–1972 supported US policies in Asia. This interpretation would be difficult to maintain for the subsequent decades. The tensions between Japan and the US during the 1980s and the 1990s would make it difficult for either of these two countries to impose their respective hegemony over the Bank. Moreover, the arrival of both India and the PRC as ADB borrowers in 1986 was decisive: these two countries would soon impose themselves as the first two beneficiaries, with a combined share of around 30 per cent. From 1986 to 1996 alone, the ADB lent USD 6.3 billion to the PRC and USD 6.6 billion to India to develop their transport and energy infrastructure. The presence of these two giant borrowers contributed to a sharp increase in the operations of the Bank. One can wonder whether their importance as borrowers inflated their influence within the ADB far beyond their respective voting power and at the expense of the leading principals. At the same time, Table 4.7 shows that the total percentage of the first five borrowers, after a height of 72.3 per cent in 1987–96, declined steadily to 56.6 per cent two decades later. This means that the cumulative share of the small borrowers has grown.

Technical assistance, in spite of the small amount its grants represent in the ADB's operations, should not be neglected, given the importance of its role on the ground. This activity consists of elaborating and supervising projects as well as giving advice. During the first years of the Bank's operations, technical assistance was undertaken through hiring technical experts or cooperating with institutions such as UN-ECAFE. However, with the advent of resident missions in the 1980s, the Bank managed the technical assistance more directly. Indonesia, Bangladesh, Pakistan, and, later on, India and the PRC were the main beneficiaries of this programme.

Co-financing also represents a major activity of the ADB. The first co-financing was settled in 1970 for a fertilizer plant in Indonesia. The ADB supplied USD 10 million for a USD 68 million venture. Its partners were the International Development Assistance, the US, and Japan. In 1982, the Bank created a Co-financing Unit, which rapidly bore fruit. From USD 29 million in 1967–76, co-financing reached USD 612 million the following decade, USD 4.6 billion in 1987–96, USD 5.7 billion in 1997–2006, and USD 68.3 billion in 2007–16. There have been many types of partners in co-financing: member countries of the ADB, other developing banks, public institutions such as the UN and the World Health Organisation, private foundations and companies (Rockefeller Foundation and Crédit Suisse AG, for instance).

Table 4.7 The five biggest beneficiaries of LEGG[a] and technical assistance[b] (1967–2016)

1967–1976		1977–1986		1987–1996		1997–2006		2007–2016	
South Korea	16.33%	Indonesia	21.11%	Indonesia	21.40%	PRC	18.51%	India	17.72%
Philippines	13.76	Pakistan	17.37	PRC	14.67	India	16.09	PRC	12.86
Pakistan	12.75	Philippines	12.22	India	14.50	Indonesia	13.08	Pakistan	9.25
Indonesia	11.23	Bangladesh	10.79	Pakistan	13.23	Pakistan	11.82	Vietnam	8.52
Thailand	9.27	South Korea	9.41	Philippines	8.53	South Korea	6.13	Indonesia	8.21
Total	63.28	Total	70.90	Total	72.33	Total	65.63	Total	56.56

[a] LEGG= loans (OCR and ADF), equity investments, grants and guarantees.
[b] grants funded by the Technical Assistance Special Fund.

Source: ADB 2016b.

6. Concluding remarks

Rivalry between the US and Japan and the economic growth of Asia have left their mark on the 'personality' of the ADB. In doing so, they provide interesting insights into the application of principal-agent theory on the RDB's mission and on the market-failure approach. Usually, the principal-agent theory opposes the owner (principal) to the manager (agent). The competition observed in the ADB opposes less the principals to the agent than the principals to each other. The ADB Charter makes sure that regional members have the majority of the voice and that the smaller members have a minimum of representation. Moreover, competition between the US and Japan in the 1990s encouraged other member countries to counterbalance the leaders' influence by increasing their share in voting power. The PRC's entry into the Bank in 1986 also contributed to diversifying the points of view among the member countries. The competition among the principals has, to a large extent, politicized the annual meetings of the BoG.

Japan understood that, to assert its dominance over the Bank, it was necessary to do more than just keep its share of the voting power. The country invested in the various funds available, such as the special funds and the ADF. Other countries, such as the US and South Korea, also invested in these funds. Nevertheless, Japan's financial participation has been far superior to those of other members taken individually. Japan also made sure that the Bank's president has always been a Japanese official with previous experience in the Ministry of Finance.

There is no doubt that the presence of two country leaders instead of one has had an impact on the capacity of the principals to control the agent efficiently. The emulation among the principals has certainly helped to increase the size of the agent. It must also have contributed to enhancing the Bank's autonomy. Already, the Bank is part of a wider set of international institutions associated with the UN and other development banks, regional or non-regional. An examination of the managing personnel shows how these institutions share their managerial personnel. Their common influence, although not studied here, is real, and many policies the Bank has adopted are in conformity with what has prevailed in other RDB. As an agent, the ADB consequently has a wide autonomy. As a principal, Japan did not oppose the ADB's tendency to become more autonomous. In fact, the Bank has been an indirect way for Japan to invest throughout Asia. One could describe this relationship between the principal and the agent as mutually fruitful.

The relationship between Japan and the ADB helped the Bank to define a specific development and integration policy. The Bank's 'open regionalism', consisting of going over the borders to create a Sub-regional project, of attracting capital from outside to ensure the development and integration of local projects into the global market through cooperation with private companies, has been implemented in large countries such as India and the PRC and in smaller ones such as Malaysia and Vietnam. Open regionalism is meant to go beyond policies, such as liberalization and deregulation, put forward by MDB during the 1990s and the 2000s. The ADB has set up an important network of missions throughout Asia to facilitate the implantation of its projects.

The ADB owes a large part of its growth to the remarkable development of the Asian economy. It would be difficult to pretend that the Bank played a decisive role in this growth, considering the minimal part of its contribution to Asia's GDP. In fact, the economic boom forced the ADB to increase its financial capacity. In order to keep pace with Asian growth, the Bank had to develop well beyond its previous financial capacities. This growth helped the Bank intensify another function: fixing market failures. The 1973 oil crisis was the first event that resulted in an increase in capital and in borrowings. The Asian crisis of 1997-8 and the 2008 international crisis led to additional—and massive—increases. These crises were not obstacles but opportunities to widen. In their aftermath, the Bank acted increasingly like a reserve bank, through the rapid mobilization of capital to tackle economic emergencies. Consequently, the ADB has acquired a dual personality: regional developer and market-failure fixer. These two functions reflect the Asian reality, a mixture of persevering poverty and of extreme wealth.

References

ADB (various, 1968–2019). *Annual Reports.* Manila: ADB.

ADB (2016). *ADB through the Decades Series.* Volumes 1 to 5. Manila: ADB. Available online at: https://www.adb.org/publications/series/adb-through-the-decades (accessed 20 February 2020).

ADB (2019). *Investing in a Prosperous, Inclusive, Resilient, and Sustainable Asia and the Pacific.* Manila: ADB. Available online at: https://www.adb.org/sites/default/files/institutional-document/191221/investor-presentation-201910.pdf (accessed 20 February 2020).

ADB Charter (1965). *Agreement Establishing the Asian Development Bank.* Manila: ADB. Available online at: https://www.adb.org/documents/agreement-establishing-asian-development-bank-adb-charter (accessed 20 February 2020).

Ben-Artzi, R (2016). *Regional Development Banks in Comparison: Banking Strategies versus Development Goals.* New York: Cambridge University Press.

Bolt, R., and Fujimura, M. (2002). *Policy-based Lending and Poverty Reduction: An Overview of Processes, Assessment, and Options.* Manila: ADB.

Bull, B. and Bøås, M. (2003). 'Multilateral development banks as regionalising actors: the Asian Development Bank and the Inter-American Development Bank', *New Political Economy*, 8(2): 245–61.

Bulman, D., Kolkma, W., and Kraay, A. (2017). 'Good countries or good projects? Comparing macro and micro correlates of World Bank and Asian Development Bank project performance', *Review of International* Organizations, 12(3): 335–63.

Cammack, P. (2016). 'World market regionalism at the Asian Development Bank', *Journal of Contemporary Asia*, 46(2): 173–97.

Carroll, T. (2012). 'Working on, through and around the state: the deep marketisation of development in the Asia-Pacific', *Journal of Contemporary Asia*, 42(3): 378–404.

Delina, L. (2017). 'Multilateral development banking in a fragmented climate system: shifting priorities in energy Finance at the Asian Development Bank'. *International Environmental Agreements. Politics, Law and Economics*, 17(1): 73–88.

Dent, C.M. (2008). 'The Asian Development Bank and developmental regionalism in East Asia', *Third World Quarterly*, 29(4): 767–86.

Dutt, N.K. (1997). 'The United States and the Asian Development Bank', *Journal of Contemporary Asia*, 27(1): 71–84.

Dutt, N.K. (2001). 'The U.S. and the Asian Development Bank: origins, structure and lending operations', *Journal of Contemporary Asia*, 31(2): 241–61.

Erquiaga, P. (2016). *A History of Financial Management at the Asian Development Bank: Engineering Financial Innovation and Impact on an Emerging Asia*. Manila: ADB.

Glassman, J. (2010). *Bounding the Mekong: The Asian Development Bank, China, and Thailand*. Honolulu: University of Hawai'i Press.

Haas, M. (1974). 'Asian Development Bank', *International Organization*, 28: 281–96.

Hamilton-Hart, N. (2003). 'Asia's new regionalism: government capacity and co-operation in the Western Pacific', *Review of International Political Economy*, 10(2): 222–45.

Hirono, R. (1991). 'Japan's leadership role in the multilateral development institutions'. In Shafiqul Islam (ed.), *Yen for Development: Japanese Foreign Aid and the Politics of Burden-Sharing*. New York: Council on Foreign Relations Press.

Huang, P. (1975). *The Asian Development Bank: Diplomacy and Development in Asia*. New York: Vintage Press.

Jayasuriya, K. (2009). 'Regulatory regionalism in the Asia-Pacific: drivers, instruments and actors', *Australian Journal of International Affairs*, 63(3): 335–47.

Kappagoda, N. (1995). *The Multilateral Development Banks*. Volume 2: *The Asian Development Bank*. Boulder, CO: Lynne Rienner Publishers.

Kawai, M. (2005). 'East Asia economic regionalism: progress and challenges', *Journal of Asian Economics*, 16(1): 29–55.

Kilby, C. (2006). 'Donor influence in multilateral development banks: the case of the Asian Development Bank', *Review of International Organizations*, 1(2): 173–95.

Kilby, C. (2011). 'Informal influence in the Asian Development Bank', *Review of International Organizations*, 6(3–4): 223–57.

Krasner, S.D. (1981). 'Power structures and regional development banks', *International Organization*, 35: 303–28.

Kuroda, H. and Kawai, M. (2002). 'Strengthening regional financial cooperation in East Asia', *Pacific Economic Papers*, 332: 1–35.

Lim, D.Y.M. and Vreeland., J.R. (2012). 'Supplemental appendix to regional organizations and international politics: Japanese influence over the Asian Development

Bank and the UN Security Council'. Available online at: http://scholar.harvard.edu/danielyewmaolim/publications (accessed 20 February 2020).

Lim, D.Y.M. and Vreeland, J.R. (2013). 'Regional organizations and International politics: Japanese influence over the Asian Development Bank and the UN Security Council', *World Politics*, 65(1): 34–72.

McCawley, P. (2017). *Banking on the Future of Asia and the Pacific: 50 Years of the Asian Development Bank*. Manila: ADB.

Naya, S. (2002). *The Asian Development Experience: Overcoming Crises and Adjusting to Change*. Hong Kong: Asian Development Bank.

Oehlers, A. (2006). 'A critique of ADB policies towards the Greater Mekong Sub-region', *Journal of Contemporary Asia*, 36(4): 464–78.

Rathus, J. (2008). 'China, Japan and regional organisations: the case of the Asian Development Bank', *Japanese Studies*, 28(1): 87–99.

Rosser, A. (2009). 'Risk management, neo-liberalism and coercion: the Asian Development Bank's approach to "fragile states"', *Australian Journal of International Affairs*, 63(3): 376–89.

Strand, J. (1999). 'State power in a multilateral context: voting strength in the Asian Development Bank', *International Interactions*, 25(3): 265–86.

Strand, J. (2011). *Regional Development Banks*. New York: Routledge.

The Economist (2016). 'The incumbent', 17 December: 66.

Uhlin, A. (2016). *Civil Society and Regional Governance: The Asian Development Bank and the Association of Southeast Asian Nations*. Lanham: Lexington Books.

Wan, M. (1995). 'Japan and the Asian Development Bank', *Pacific Affairs*, 68(4): 509–28.

Watanabe, T. (1973). *Towards a New Asia: Memoirs of the First President of the Asian Development Bank*. Manila: ADB.

Wesley, M. (2003). 'The Asian Development Bank'. In Michael Wesley (ed.), *The Regional Organizations of the Asia-Pacific: Exploring Institutional Change*. Houndmills and New York: Palgrave Macmillan.

White, J. (1972). *Regional Development Banks: The Asian, African, and Inter-American Development Banks*. New York: Praeger.

Wihtol, R. (1988). *The Asian Development Bank and Rural Development: Policy and Practice*. Basingstoke: Macmillan.

Wilson, D. (1987). *A Bank for Half the World: The Story of the Asian Development Bank, 1966–1986*. Manila: Asian Development Bank.

Yasutomo, D.T. (1983). *Japan and the Asian Development Bank*. New York: Praeger.

Yasutomo, D.T. (1993). 'Japan and the Asian Development Bank: multilateral aid policy in transition'. In B.M. Koppel and R.M. Orr Jr (eds.), *Japan's Foreign Aid: Power and Policy in a New Era*. Boulder, CO: Westview Press, pp. 305–40.

5

The European Investment Bank

From Development, Integration, and Investment to 'You Get What You Give'

Judith Clifton, Daniel Díaz-Fuentes, and Ana Lara Gómez

1. Introduction

Notwithstanding its importance, the European Investment Bank (EIB) has been neglected in European Union (EU) studies for decades. Despite its key role in tackling some of the main concerns of the European project, and the fact it emerged as the world's largest supranational lender—overtaking the World Bank as regards loan volumes from the mid-1990s (EIB 1994a)—the institution has surprisingly attracted little research. EU scholars urge that more attention should be paid to understanding this important but understudied regional development bank (RDB) (Robinson 2009; Liebe and Howarth 2020).

It has only been recently, in the context of the Great Recession, that the EIB has received more attention—in the form of intensified criticism. In particular, the EIB has been criticized for not prioritizing finance to the least-developed regions (Griffith-Jones and Tyson 2012). This criticism suggests the Bank is neglecting one of its original *raisons d'être*: to promote the development of less-favoured areas in the EU[1] in order to reduce economic disparities among regions. This heightened interest in the EIB motivates our study. The time is ripe to remedy the lack of research on this key EU institution, which is the world's largest lender.

Most, if not all, international financial institutions (IFI), multilateral development banks (MDB) and RDB were created with multiple lending objectives (Humphrey 2015; Mazzucato and Penna 2016). An analysis of EIB statutes and historical documentation[2] shows that, until the 1990s, its lending objectives can be essentially condensed to three: development, integration, and investment.

[1] At the time the European Economic Community (EEC). We use the term EU for all periods to harmonize the different names: EEC (1957–93), European Community (EC) (1993–2009), EU (2009–16).

[2] Historical archives of the EU, which include primary documentation and draft versions of the constitutional documents, including the official meetings and negotiations towards establishing the EIB.

Judith Clifton, Daniel Díaz-Fuentes, and Ana Lara Gómez, *The European Investment Bank: From Development, Integration, and Investment to 'You Get What You Give'* In: *Regional Development Banks in the World Economy*. Edited by: Judith Clifton, Daniel Díaz-Fuentes, and David Howarth, Oxford University Press (2021). © Oxford University Press. DOI: 10.1093/oso/9780198861089.003.0005

Importantly, the EIB was the first RDB created with a remit including regional integration (Clifton et al. 2018). This was initially understood as 'the balanced and smooth development of the Common Market' (EIB 1957b, Article 130) (we call this 'market integration'), and later, as loans to new member states (we label this 'enlargement'). In addition, its lending objectives included the alleviation of capital constraints (essentially, promoting investment) and facilitating economic development. Both investment and development had been included amongst the objectives of previously established MDB, such as the World Bank, but the combination of this three-pronged set of EIB lending objectives was unique at the time. This new mix of lending objectives can be explained by the historical context in which the EIB emerged, in the immediate postwar period, when it was feared that the creation of the EU would exacerbate the need for cross-border investment and cause 'rich regions to become richer at the expense of backward areas' (Licari 1969: 192). The EIB was conceived, then, to promote economic development and regional integration while contributing to meeting the pressing investment needs of a war-torn Europe. From the 1990s, however, concerns relating to the environment and the reduction of unemployment gained weight and the EIB attempted to include these new objectives (EIB 1991b, 1995b). Therefore, EIB lending objectives from the 1990s were five: economic development, integration, and investment (which we recognize as its original mission), the environment, and unemployment concerns, the latter two conforming with its extended mission. We analyse to what extent EIB lending reflects these major objectives.

This chapter analyses sixty years of EIB lending to its member states, from the start of operations in 1958 up to 2018. The chapter analyses total loans but focuses on infrastructure, by far the largest portion of all lending during the period considered. The extent to which lending reflects MDB and RDB lending objectives has preoccupied a body of scholars working on organizational effectiveness (Gutner 2005, 2010; Nielson et al. 2006). Another related strand of research on MDB and RDB has sought to uncover the determinants of lending, that is, the determinants of the country requesting a loan and the bank granting that loan (Knight and Santaella 1997; Vreeland 2004; Harrigan et al. 2006; Humphrey and Michaelowa 2013. Our approach follows the first line of analysis, assessing the extent to which EIB loans satisfied its core lending objectives. Both bodies of scholarship influence our analysis. Lending was reconstructed using data from the annual reports of the EIB as obtained from the Historical Archives of the EU (HAEU) and from the EIB (2019) official database. As will become clear, until the 1990s the EIB was the first RDB to promote regional economic integration and development over the alleviation of capital constraints. From the nineties onwards the EIB changed dramatically and capital subscribed started to determine EIB loans. The Bank has not completely been fulfilling its mandate in terms of the official goals stated, but it seems to be becoming the nucleus of a European investment state that promotes investment in specific sectors (Mertens and Thiemann 2019).

The chapter is divided into five sections. The next section (section 2) discusses the setting up of the EIB and identifies its original mission, embodied in three core initial lending objectives (development, integration, and investment) as derived from the EIB statutes and historical documentation. Section 3 analyses EIB lending from 1958 to 1995, considering development, integration, and investment; while section 4 analyses EIB lending from 1995 to 2018, considering its extended mission and taking into account the environment and unemployment goals that were introduced in the 1990s. We conclude in section 5, summarizing our results, their limitations, and possible directions for further research.

2. Setting up the EIB: a threefold mission

When the EIB was created in 1957, it was strongly influenced by the economic and political context, which permanently shaped its constitution and evolution. The Second World War had left European countries devastated (Temin 1994) and, it was perceived, highly vulnerable to the spread of communism (LaFeber 1999). The International Bank for Reconstruction and Development (IBRD) (today the World Bank) was created in 1944 to support Europe, but it was soon seen that more resources were needed, hence the United States (US) implemented the Marshall Plan as a short-term measure (1948–51). However, this was inadequate to cover the region's huge investment needs, to which the creation of the EU added two concerns: the extra need for cross-border investment (HAEU 1956a) and the fear integration would create divergence among the least-developed regions (HAEU 1956b). It was in this context that the EIB was created.

Analysis of the EIB statutes and constitutive primary documentation reflects that, essentially, lending would prioritize three core objectives: development, to prevent economic imbalances among members and encourage the economic growth of the least-developed regions (HAEU 1956b); integration, to encourage the 'development of the Common Market' (EIB 1957b, Article 130; HAEU 1956e); and investment, to rebalance capital markets through investments and the setting of interest rates (HAEU 1956a).

On the one hand, it was perceived the integration process exacerbated the need for additional investment in cross-border projects of common interest (besides the huge investment needs of each country) (EIB 1958a). However, obtaining long-term lending at low interest rates was particularly difficult due to financial constraints and the high-risk premium caused by long-term uncertainty (HAEU 1962; Frenkel 2008). Hence, a major problem facing the EU was underinvestment, particularly in infrastructure, one of the key elements in economic development (Hirschman 1958). A mechanism to facilitate access to capital was needed (EIB 1978b). To address this need, Germany and the Benelux countries favoured a bank independently operating from its members, focused on financing sound, profitable projects (HAEU 1956c). It should finance itself independently from member state interests, so it was not a burden, for which they requested it was denominated a 'bank' not a 'fund' to reflect its independence in the international financial markets. Following the example of the IBRD, the new institution should provide credit and reduce borrowing costs, the idea being that 'the sum of membership's credibility' would reduce 'borrowing costs for all members below what they would pay on their own' (Birdsall 2000: 121).

On the other hand, contemporary economic theories suggested the integration process could generate two opposing forces: convergence and divergence, either one with different impacts on members' welfare. Neoclassical growth theories predicted a positive impact through long-run gross domestic product (GDP) convergence and factor price equalization, while endogenous growth theories predicted a potential negative outcome with long-run GDP divergence. Particularly important for negotiations leading to the Treaty of Rome was the influence of Myrdal's (1957) theory, based on the Mezzogiorno experience (Licari 1969). This reinforced the conviction that, without measures to reduce divergence and inequality, integration—despite having an overall positive impact—could have a negative effect on countries like Italy (El-Agraa 2007).

Concerned that integration would cause richer nations to become richer at the expense of the poorer ones (HAEU 1956b; EIB 1978b), Italy and—to a lesser extent—France, called for a development institution (a 'fund') that would promote the development of the least-developed regions with financial support in the form of grants (HAEU 1956c). Both wanted member states to be able to influence this institution, which should also deal with social questions. Italy, where 1870 unification had resulted in sharp disparities between the north and south, was particularly concerned with the creation of such an institution (Licari 1969). France was also worried that the introduction of free competition would spoil its market for agriculture, and that financial aid would be needed (HAEU 1989; Ludlow 2005).

All these concerns and economic ideas were influential when, during 1956, the founding members reached a compromise: the EIB would promote development, integration, and investment. This nodded to all positions: the EIB would promote integration, be able to lend money to the least-developed regions, and as an independent bank, be able to raise money on the international financial markets (EIB 1957b, Articles 11, 13). This innovative institution resulted from different concessions in multiple directions. It would be called a 'bank' and would lend to sound, profitable projects, but it would not be as independent as Germany and the Benelux countries had desired, since countries would exert subtle control through the board of governors (as Italy and France wanted). Italy also succeeded in attaching a protocol to the statutes to help its economy (EIB 1957b). Germany and the Benelux countries accepted these requests so long as this did not damage the financial markets' perception of the Bank (HAEU 1956g), which should borrow from capital markets. Thanks to its superior rating[3] it would lend at attractive interest rates enabling it 'to meet its obligations, cover its expenses and to constitute a reserve fund' (EIB 1957b, Article 19), acting as an intermediary in the financial markets. Quantities would be expressed in units of account to signal independence from third countries (HAEU 1956h, Annex B) and lending would be made on a non-profit basis (EIB 1957b, Article 130). Moreover, the Bank could grant loans to both member states as well as countries 'outside the European territories' (EIB 1957b, Article 18). This, in practice, allowed the EIB to lend to most countries and, importantly, as we will see, to future members of the EU ('enlargement').

The 1990s brought two new objectives into scene: to protect the environment and to reduce unemployment. Concerns were raised that the environment was a crucial issue to be addressed and most MDB and RDB tried to conform to the new standards, including the EIB. The early 1990s recession, on the other hand, led to high unemployment rates and a deep sense that measures had to be taken to counteract the situation. Therefore, the EIB had what we call an original mission—economic development, investment, and integration—and an extended mission, which adds in the 1990s the environmental and unemployment concerns.

The regional institution, owned entirely by its borrowing countries, was a clever way to address countries' financial needs while tackling potential disparities that might be exacerbated during the integration process. EIB statutes specified three kinds of projects it would award: while the development objective has been explicitly reflected in project profiles, the integration, investment, environmental and unemployment goals have been intrinsic to all projects. First, the Bank finances 'projects for developing less-developed regions' to reduce economic disparities, as Italy had wished. Second, it finances 'projects for modernising or converting enterprises or for creating new activities... called for by the progressive establishment of the Common Market' to help industries' modernization and competition (a concession to France) in the face of the structural change the integration process was to induce. Third, it loans to projects considered 'of common interest to several Member States', where additional investment is needed for integration to succeed (HAEU 1956d, 1956f). So, the EIB was the principal financial instrument used to build the EU in close connection with other bodies, such as the Commission (EIB 1958a); moreover, its lending objectives reflected major concerns and economic ideas raised during negotiations (both the negotiations leading to the Treaty of Rome (EIB 1978b) and the subsequent negotiations).

[3] Bonds have been rated triple-A, the highest possible level (EIB 1975a) since the EIB made the first issue in the US in 1975.

Nevertheless, the relative importance of each objective has remained unclear, awarding the EIB flexibility, but also an undefined path to follow.

3. EIB lending (1958–95): development, integration, and investment?

Striking a balance between lending objectives is a major task for all MDB and RDB (Howarth and Quaglia 2016). In order to determine the extent to which EIB lending was oriented towards development, investment, and integration until the 1990s, we construct three hypotheses. First, we assume the loans are oriented to development when lending goes to the least-developed countries. Second, loans are oriented to investment when they contribute to the effectiveness of financial markets by reducing borrowing costs (Birdsall 2000), which is further complemented by the financial market's perception of a country's ability to repay. Third, loans promote integration when they encourage cross-border infrastructure projects, intra-European trade and enlargement. (Table 5.1.)

The early years: 1958–73

The first lending period can be divided into two sub-periods. From 1958 to 1966, the EIB focuses its resources largely on Italy (77.03 per cent), the least-developed member. Next, from 1967 to 1973, there is an effort to increase both lending volume and target countries. The EIB extends its reach to France (25.59 per cent), Germany (15.58 per cent), and the Benelux countries (4.46 per cent) though Italy remains the main beneficiary of lending (52.7 per cent).

In the immediate period from 1958, much of the lending was channelled to the Mezzogiorno, in southern Italy, at the time the least-developed region of the EU (with the lowest per capita GDP) and, hence, perceived as one of the main challenges confronting the integration project (EIB 1962a). Three other things contributed to turn Italy into the centre of EIB's lending until 1966. First, the annexed protocol to the statute recommended the implementation of a ten-year programme aimed at correcting disequilibria in the Italian economy (EIB 1957b). Second, two Italians, Pietro Campilli in 1958 and Paride Formentini in 1959, were consecutively appointed as EIB presidents (HAEU 1958, 1959) to watch over Italian interests. Lastly, the world economy was going through a period of expansion, which meant other countries did not have such drastic economic needs. In fact, Italy borrowed from the EIB at higher interest rates than national ones, indicating the magnitude of that country's need for financial support. During the early years, the Bank failed to be a good intermediary in the financial markets, neglecting its investment role in favour of development.

Table 5.1 EIB lending to European countries (2005 USD millions), by at successive enlargements

		1959-1968	1969-1978	1979-1988	1989-1998	1999-2008	2009-2018
1957	Belgium	181	608	1627	7951	7987	17627
	France	940	7385	14476	36642	49114	69793
	Germany	631	3152	4076	36724	76655	73710
	Italy	3666	15040	47415	61077	69830	98878
	Luxembourg	49	5	59	561	1220	1685
	Netherlands	–	478	811	5724	7692	18431
1973	Denmark	–	764	4979	11469	7884	5293
	Ireland	–	1571	6281	4258	5139	7504
	UK	–	7881	18323	39075	41171	52614
1981	Greece	424	289	5096	7840	14644	16883
1986	Portugal	–	699	3355	18984	20860	20139
	Spain	–	–	5007	43912	75212	104828
1995	Austria	–	270	455	2703	11629	17274
	Finland	–	–	–	2155	8232	13243
	Sweden	–	–	–	4008	9101	16318
2004	Czech Rep.	–	–	–	2752	10489	11122
	Cyprus	–	–	102	368	1630	2910
	Estonia	–	–	–	135	478	2474
	Hungary	–	–	–	2019	10267	12817
	Latvia	–	–	–	136	1867	1090
	Lithuania	–	–	–	225	450	3013
	Malta	–	–	89	73	293	308
	Poland	–	–	–	3759	19348	53508
	Slovakia	–	–	–	1015	2021	6812
	Slovenia	–	28	278	565	2920	4240
2007	Bulgaria	–	–	–	875	2820	2508
	Romania	–	–	–	1555	6221	8290
2013	Croatia	–	48	236	105	1791	4822
	TOTAL	5892	38218	112665	296665	466966	648138

Source: EIB *Annual Reports* 1958–2018; EIB *Financed Projects* 2019.

But there was another crucial determinant of EIB loans: market integration. Most infrastructure lending was channelled towards the transportation sector during this period. In line with EU efforts to establish an integrated network, the strategy of the EIB, not only for Italy, but for most countries, was to pursue an integrated transportation policy towards the implementation of the Common Market. Yet, despite efforts at the European level in 1961,[4] 1962[5] and again in 1964[6] (Turró 1999), transportation needs were still huge at the time of the first enlargement, which in turn exacerbated them. In 1967, the world economy

[4] Schaus Memorandum. [5] Action Programme for the Implementation of a CTP.
[6] Draft decision for Community control of infrastructure investment.

slackened off due to political tensions and conflicts which affected the Middle East and Africa (EIB 1967a). This second sub-period (1967–73) was a time of political agitation with countries experiencing a tendency towards cyclical recession. Thus, the EIB started to distribute loans to other countries besides Italy, particularly, to France. Simultaneously, an interest in telecommunications as a means to developing the market grew (Michalis 2007) and lending increased to this sector.

The situation deteriorated by 1970. Real economic growth slowed, interest rates rose, and some countries entered in recession (EIB 1970a). This was further aggravated when the convertibility of the US dollar to gold was cancelled in 1971. European countries decided to peg currencies to each other to maintain monetary stability (EIB 1972a), which marked the first step towards the introduction of the euro and reinforced the European compromise to encourage integration. In this context, the EIB increased its lending and presence in the financial markets to counteract the situation. Nevertheless, despite these efforts, its effectiveness was low. Those years saw higher inflation, rising unemployment, and production stagnation. It was in 1972, when, presaging the oil crisis, the European Commission (EC) became interested in the role of the EIB to diversify energy supplies (EIB 1972a). From that time onwards, as part of the integration objective, investments in energy became a core part of the Bank's priorities.

In a relatively short period, the EIB became a leading source of finance with two clear priorities: helping Italy and lending at the best possible conditions (HAEU 2003). However, in practice, the EIB failed to offer better rates, and lending served more the purposes of development and integration. Both Italy and France were satisfied with an institution that helped to develop the least-developed regions while also contributing to build the Common Market. Both were by far the largest beneficiaries during the period in terms of funding, particularly Italy (59.59 per cent), which more than doubled the capital subscribed (24 per cent).

First enlargement: 1973–81

Between 1973 and 1981, EIB lending continued to focus on integration and development, as seen in particular through a 'rewarding strategy' for new adherents and a 'least-developed strategy', providing credit to new members, as well as least-developed countries. The first EU enlargement, in 1973, coincided with the oil crisis caused by an oil embargo from Middle East oil-producing nations and the collapse of the Bretton Woods system. Under this scenario, with inflation, current account deficits, and high interest rates, the EIB targeted new members (Denmark, Ireland, and the United Kingdom (UK)) with lower interest rates than the national ones. This was insufficient, though, to solve their huge economic problems and the idea that a regional fund 'to reinforce economic and social cohesion' (*Official Journal of the EU* 2006, Article 2) was needed (as Italy had argued during the creation of the EIB) gained strength with the support of the UK and Ireland. The European Regional Development Fund (ERDF) was established in 1974 on the principle it should cooperate with the EIB (EIB 1974a). Did this mark a turning point as regards EIB loans?

Given the difficult economic background, policies to stimulate expansion were implemented. In an attempt to reduce the inflow of foreign capital, Germany, among other countries, encouraged a reduction in interest rates (EIB 1977a) which, in turn, reduced the demand for EIB loans. However, economic difficulties continued and, following the recommendations adopted by the European Council on 1977, the EIB decided to increase its lending (EIB 1979a) with an escalation of more, smaller loans. Italy, France, and the UK, which were going through difficult times and were among the countries with the lowest per capita GDP, received the largest amounts (in absolute terms), but also Ireland and Denmark were particularly advantaged in per capita terms. This suggests EIB lending was focused on integration and development through two combined strategies: a 'rewarding strategy' for new adherents as well as a 'least-developed strategy'.

On the other hand, infrastructure became increasingly important (73 per cent of all lending). By 1973, the oil crisis had been followed by a decision to reduce Europe's energy dependency (EIB 1973a), so loans started to be addressed to the energy sector. Simultaneously, water supply became considered as an 'investment with limited return' (Commission of the European Communities 1991), and served, together with the concession of the ERDF, as a bargaining chip to obtain the adhesion of the UK, which obtained EIB lending to establish ten regional water authorities (Water Act 1973).

Over the period 1973-80, the UK greatly benefited from EIB funding (27.62 per cent), together with Italy (38.38 per cent) and Ireland (8.43 per cent), more than offsetting the capital subscribed (21.74 per cent, 17.39 per cent, and 0.73 per cent, respectively). The EIB continued a clear effort to address lending to the countries with lower per capita GDP. However, integration, particularly 'enlargement', played an important role. Despite the creation of the ERDF, the EIB continued along the path of the previous period, the Bank finally attaining better lending conditions on financial markets.

Second enlargement: 1981–6

The third period, marked by the Greek accession, continued to reflect a lending pattern focused on development and integration and, to a lesser degree, investment. However, the integration objective increased, as compared to the previous period, at the expense of the development imperative. The second enlargement

(1981) was an outcome long awaited on both sides: from the outset, Greece sought to join the EU (HAEU 2004) and it also constituted a strategic site in the Mediterranean for the Community (Kaiser and Elvert 2004). The EIB granted Greece access to its resources thanks to the Ordinary and Special operations the moment the country signed the first association agreement of the EU (1961) (HAEU 1961), but the *coup d'état* of 1967 interrupted negotiations and funding. The access to lending was taken up by Greece after 1975, with the restoration of democracy, culminating in EU adhesion.

For two years after accession, Greece, one of the two least-developed members together with Ireland, received significant loans (7.19 per cent). However, Italy (48.3 per cent), France (14.97 per cent), and the UK (12.8 per cent) received more in absolute terms, while Ireland, Denmark, and, from 1984, Italy also received more in per capita terms. Even though over the period Greece more than offset the capital paid in at the EIB, on this occasion the Bank's mission on development was diluted by other considerations. There was an effort to help countries with more pressing economic needs, but, in contrast to previous years, this was not the whole story, to judge from per capita GDP. Instead, the EIB continued to pursue its 'enlargement' strategy.

Integration explains EIB lending in terms of 'enlargement' and 'market integration'. In countries like France or Ireland, the focus of loans was on transportation and telecommunications respectively, even if, as a whole, energy was still the main concern (with half of overall lending designated to it). In contrast, as had occurred during the first period analysed (1958–73), the EIB investment objective explains lending only weakly. Germany, the Netherlands, and Luxembourg barely received any loans because of their better interest rate conditions as compared to those of the EIB. Overall, though EIB lending continued to reflect a development imperative, this loses ground to integration.

Third enlargement: 1986–95

The pattern of the previous period is continued along the fourth period analysed, with integration driving the logic of an increasing share of loans, as development continues to lose ground while the investment role is weaker.

Adhesion to the EU of Portugal and Spain in 1986 implied a new challenge to the EIB in terms of resources, which had to increase, and countries' heterogeneity. As in the case of Greece, lending to both countries started well in advance of accession.[7] The Portuguese and Spanish accession coincided with EIB loans becoming more evenly distributed among members as well as a further

[7] Portugal from 1976; Spain from 1981.

distancing from the development objective. Whereas Portugal, Ireland, Greece, and Spain were the least-developed members of the period, they were not the main beneficiaries of funding. Italy, having by then a similar per capita GDP to France, was still the highest beneficiary in absolute terms (27.09 per cent), followed by Spain (15.88 per cent), and the UK (14.22 per cent). Similarly, the highest beneficiary in per capita terms, Denmark, was the second most-developed country (the first one being Luxembourg) as measured by per capita GDP. That said, lending was still explained by development to some extent, with Portugal, Spain, and Ireland among the least developed, getting a good share of loans.

In addition, Portugal and Spain were not only among the least developed but were also newcomers to please. As part of the 'enlargement' strategy, the EIB addressed a large proportion of its loans to these countries that from 1992 onwards received, in per capita terms, more lending than Italy. Most of these funds went to transportation, the main focus of the EIB from 1988, possibly influenced by the first action plans on trans-European networks that were to be adopted by the EC in 1990. Indeed, Portugal, Spain, France, Ireland, and the UK received loans primarily aimed at the transportation sector during this period, which served to encourage market integration (Clifton et al. 2014).

So, between 1986 and 1995, the development imperative declined with respect to previous periods. Increasingly, integration, both in market integration and enlargement, accounted for greater shares of EIB lending. In contrast, the extent to which investment explains lending is less clear cut, since some countries benefitted from the interest rates differential while others did not. The end of the Cold War broke sharply with the economic and political environment forged after the Second World War. In Europe, the period culminated with the Maastricht Treaty (1992), the Copenhagen criteria (1993), and the fourth enlargement (1995). This led to a new set of challenges for the EIB and a new lending pattern.

4. EIB lending (1995–2018): development, integration, investment, environment, and unemployment

The end of the Cold War, characterized by the German re-unification in 1990, set an end to the economic and political environment forged after the Second World War and brought a change of logic. EIB lending followed such exponential trend since the Bank's creation that it overcame World Bank loans volume in 1991 (EIB 1991a), becoming, since then, the largest lender worldwide. That year opened, for the Bank, a new post-Cold War period marked by the unification of Germany and the dissolution of the Soviet Union, but also by the creation of the EBRD and the establishment of the Single Market in 1993. As we will see, the 1990s seem to bring a change of logic. The integration project appeared, at that time, to be working and the EC arranged a fourth EU enlargement, to which the EIB would contribute. In fact, by 1991 the capital subscribed, which amounted to ECU 57.6 billion, was already benefiting all the twenty-eight members except for Croatia. As in previous years, loans were oriented towards development, investment, and integration, and, from the 1990s, towards the environment and unemployment as well (the two new concerns that arose in this period). We assume bank loans are oriented to the environment when projects contribute to its enhancement, while the loans are oriented to fight unemployment when they focus on those regions particularly hit by this problem.

Fourth enlargement: 1995–2004

Between 1995 and 2004, when the largest enlargement up to date took place, EIB lending reflected a pattern focused on integration and, to a lesser extent, on development. In practice, investment, the environment or unemployment were hardly relevant, despite the Bank's discourse. The adhesion of Austria, Finland, and Sweden in 1995 implied the signature of a new statute with new demands. On the one hand, a new protocol to promote regions with low population was approved under request of the new members. On the other, specific aid to 'certain areas' of the Federal Republic of Germany was conceded as compatible with the common market 'in order to compensate for the economic disadvantages caused by that division' (EIB 1995b). These requests implied new efforts to increase lending and, despite a slight decline during the early 2000s recession, on balance the Bank increased lending.

Challenges were multiple: Germany struggled to rebuild the former communist German Democratic Republic (East Germany), in need of investments; while the Gulf crisis (1990–1) increased oil prices (up to USD 40 a barrel) (Ibrahim 1990), leading to an increase in interest rates and a reduction in investments. Moreover, the war took a terrible toll in Yugoslavia (Papaioannou 2004). In this context, unemployment increased and brought the problem to the top of the EU agenda,[8] which affected EIB discourse (even if by the end of the decade the EU economy had started to recover). In this context, the fourth enlargement (1995) reinforced the start of a major change in the distribution of EIB loans. In absolute terms, for the period 1995–2003, Germany, together with Italy and Spain, benefited the most (despite Greece or Portugal still having a lower per capita GDP). The new statute (EIB 1995b, Article 92) approving specific aid to 'certain areas' of Germany bore fruit. Instead, France and the UK were net contributors, as in

[8] The 'White Paper on Growth, Competitiveness and Employment' (1993) launched a debate on the EU's economic and employment strategy by bringing the issue of employment to the top of the EU agenda for the first time (European Parliament 2019).

previous years. Data shows the EIB still lent like a development institution even though it also had other lending criteria.

Most EIB funding continued to be addressed to infrastructure, but its share decreased. Transportation took the largest share in this period, especially in Portugal and Spain, while in Italy the energy sector continued to be the priority. Credit lines for small and medium-sized enterprises (SME) started to gain importance in this period, highlighting a global change from projects to programmes (SME, environment). The importance given by the Maastricht Treaty to the Trans-European Networks (TEN) became reflected in the EIB strategy. Transportation and the energy sector were consolidated as the key pillars to strengthen the European project, accompanied by credit lines and industry loans.

The 11 September 2001 attacks in the US affected the world economy, seeing, among other things, a dramatic fall in the stock markets. In Europe, Germany, Switzerland, France, and the UK were hit the hardest. The world economy began to recover in 2002–3, until the global financial crisis of 2007 led to the Great Recession (2008–12), which in turn contributed to the European sovereign debt crisis.

Fifth enlargement: 2004–7

The pattern of previous periods broke partially with the 2004 enlargement. Particularly after the Nice Treaty (2003) reformed the European Community (EC) to face the enlargement of eight countries (in 2004) from Eastern and Western Europe (Slovakia, Slovenia, Estonia, Hungary, Latvia, Lithuania, Poland, Czech Republic) plus two Mediterranean countries (Cyprus and Malta), loans started to be redistributed quite evenly according to countries' capital share. While integration was still the underlying factor behind a considerable number of loans, increasingly, loans were correlated to the share of capital subscribed. In short, a system was born where 'you get what you give' (in percentage terms), so the least developed were not necessarily the largest recipients of funding.

Enlargement also affected the redistribution of power and meant an increase of resources, amounting to 163.65 billion euro, less than 5 per cent belonging to capital subscribed by the new members. The rise benefited Germany, Italy, and Spain, the largest recipients in absolute terms. Despite the willingness of the EIB to be considered an 'investment bank' we find that its role as an intermediary in the financial markets was limited during all these years. Undoubtedly, low interest rates were a key challenge during the first years of the EIB, but it does not seem to have been the major outcome. One possible explanation is that once financial markets had approved of the Bank's way of working and bonds were rated triple-A (the highest possible rating), the role of the EIB for investment would not have been a high priority when lending. In terms of sectors, transportation and energy continued to receive most of the attention. As a result, Italgas, Edison Gas SpA, AGIP, SNAM, and ENEL benefitted in Italy from EIB loans, as well as RENFE, Iberia, AENA, Air Europa, and Spanair in Spain. As mentioned, infrastructure loans were largely oriented towards integration. Credit lines to SME continued to gain importance in this period, combining the loans to big companies with those to SME.

Sixth enlargement: 2007–13

The financial crisis of 2007–8 began with a crisis in the subprime mortgage market in the US. The collapse of the investment bank Lehman Brothers in 2008 led to an international banking crisis magnified by the excess of risk-taking. To prevent the collapse of the financial system, massive public bailouts together with restrictive monetary and fiscal policies had to be taken (Hall 2018). This did not avoid, though, the Great Recession, one of the worst worldwide economic slowdowns. In Europe, the BNP Paribas was the first banking institution (in August 2007) to suffer the consequences of the US subprime mortgage market. The European debt crisis followed at the end of 2009. As a result of the public bailouts, private debts from the property bubble were transformed into sovereign debt. As the concerns regarding the solvency of the banking system and the sovereign debt increased, several member countries required assistance (Gambarotto and Solari 2015). The situation affected broad sectors of the population, which suffered the consequences for years.

It was precisely this new depressed economic environment of 2008 that forced the EIB to exert a countercyclical role by increasing its loan volume. Germany, Italy, and Spain persisted as the highest beneficiaries of EIB lending in absolute terms, while France and the UK carried on making the highest contributions. The increase in lending was accompanied by a rise in loans towards credit lines, energy, industry, and transportation. However, this was not sustained and from 2009 loans decreased (particularly energy and industry loans), hitting bottom in 2012, thereafter increasing again to coincide with the last enlargement of Croatia in 2013.

Seventh enlargement: 2013–18

Finally, the accession of Croatia (2013) diluted even more the alleged cooperation of the EIB, with smaller differences between the percentage of capital contributed and received, reinforcing the tendency towards a mechanized process of lending approval where 'you get what you give' (as a share of the total). Even though loans increased, a new decrease in 2015 put an end to this upward trend and loans have declined to date. Spain and Italy continued to be beneficiaries in absolute terms during the period, unlike Germany, which saw its loans diminish, with Poland being the only country to receive a percentage as much as four times the percentage of capital subscribed. On the other hand, France and the UK received a higher share of lending than before, reducing the differential (in percentage terms) between contributions and loans.

Lending was concentrated in credit lines, which increased, and transportation, despite a slight decrease in relation to the previous years. The Bank changed from financing different infrastructure projects to focusing on transportation and credit lines, sometimes accompanied by an emphasis on energy and industry. Overall, large, important companies such as Telecom Italia, Unión Fenosa Distribución, Telefónica, Abengoa, E.ON, and important banking institutions (Deutsche Bank AG, Banca Popolare di Milano, Intesa San Paolo, Bankinter, BBVA, Banco Santander) benefited from EIB loans, thanks to which the EIB continued to encourage their internationalization. It continued to disregard the agriculture, solid waste, and water and sewerage sectors, and despite the declared concern for the environment, those projects continued to be a minority concern.

5. Conclusions

The EIB was the first RDB created with the purpose of promoting regional economic integration rather than just alleviating capital constraints and promoting development, as previously established IFI, such as the World Bank. However, from a scholarly perspective, it remains a neglected EU institution. This chapter identified the extent to which development, integration, investment (until the 1990s), together with the environment and unemployment (from the 1990s) explained the pattern of EIB lending. It provided a first approach to the Bank's performance based on the destiny of its lending, used to understand its performance over time. After assembling and processing all data on EIB lending, we selected all finance destined for projects in Europe over the period 1958-2018. Until the mid-1990s, loans were particularly channelled towards the least-developed countries. So, despite the Bank's founders opting to call it an 'investment bank', it was more active in promoting development. Instead, the effectiveness of the EIB as an intermediary in the financial markets was quite limited. But, importantly, integration was a key factor for EIB lending. Two main approaches can be seen: market integration related to infrastructure lending and political integration supporting enlargement.

Our qualitative analysis identifies four periods demarcated by the enlargements within this first phase: 1958-73 with two priorities, helping Italy (the least developed) and promoting the Common Market; 1973-81, particularly focused on development and rewarding newcomers; 1981-6 and 1986-95, with a lesser emphasis on development but a clear interest in encouraging integration through the Common Market and enlargement.

The mid-1990s marked a change: capital subscribed gradually started to determine EIB lending and eventually dominating the general trend over the whole period 1995–2018. Even though just after the end of the Cold War the EIB was still taking a stand to encourage development and integration through lending to some of the less-developed countries and the promotion of the Common Market, this logic in terms of the Bank's scope became blurred after the 2004 enlargement. As evidenced by our analysis, capital subscribed became the major deciding factor in loans approved. While it is true that development is behind lending to Portugal and the high unemployment rate would explain the large amounts of lending to Spain, the quantitative analysis suggests that these examples are the exceptions rather than the rule.

This all amounts to quite rigorous evidence that EIB lending was destined towards development and integration and, to a lesser extent, investment until the mid-1990s. However, even if the EIB's discourse was maintained since its creation, its actions changed. The EIB was established by the Treaty of Rome (1957) with clear objectives, which were maintained and enlarged to new goals through the years. Nevertheless, the development of events shaped the institution's policy action without really fulfilling the stated goals. Instead, in time, the Bank evolved towards a more mechanized lending process, diverging from its core mission. Our chapter helps to shed light on the debate on the EIB and RDB as a whole. It is time to rethink the role and performance of RDB (as done by Alonso and Cuesta, Chapter 14, this volume). RDB such as the EIB are in a unique position to affect policy-making: the fact that EIB loans are increasingly misaligned with its core mission have consequences for its members that require further analysis.

Acknowledgements

This chapter draws heavily from, updates, and extends Clifton et al. 2018. We thank Wiley for permission to republish.

References

Birdsall, N. (2000). 'The World Bank of the future: victim, villain or global credit union?'. *The Brown Journal of World Affairs*, 7(2): 119–27.

Clifton, J., Díaz-Fuentes, D., and Revuelta, J. (2014). 'Financing utilities: how the role of the EIB shifted from regional development to making markets', *Utilities Policy*, 29: 63–71.

Clifton, J., Díaz-Fuentes, D. and Gómez, A.L. (2018). 'The EIB: development, integration, investment?' , *JCMS*, 56(4): 733–50.

Commission of the European Communities (1991). *Annual Report on the Implementation of the Reform of the Structural Funds 1989*. Luxembourg: EEC.

EIB (European Investment Bank) (various, 1958a–2018a). *Annual Reports*. Luxembourg: EIB.

EIB (European Investment Bank) (1957b). *Statute of the EIB*. Luxembourg: EIB.

EIB (European Investment Bank) (1978b). *EIB 20 Years: 1958–1978*. Luxembourg: EIB.

EIB (European Investment Bank) (1991b). *Statute of the EIB*. Luxembourg: EIB.

EIB (European Investment Bank) (1995b). *Statute of the EIB*. Luxembourg: EIB.

EIB (European Investment Bank) (2019). *Financed Projects*. Luxembourg: EIB. Available online at: https://www.eib.org/en/projects/loans/index.htm (accessed 5 May 2018).

El-Agraa, A.M. (2007). *The EU: Economics and Policies*. 8th ed. Cambridge: Cambridge University Press.

European Parliament (2019). *Employment Policy, Fact Sheets on the European Union*, May. Available online at: http://www.europarl.europa.eu/factsheets/en/sheet/54/employment-policy (accessed 22 January 2020).

Frenkel, R. (2008). *From the Boom in Capital Inflows to Financial Traps*. Oxford: Oxford University Press.

Gambarotto, F. and Solari, S. (2015). 'The peripheralization of southern European capitalism within the EMU', *Review of International Political Economy*, 22: 788–812.

Griffith-Jones, S. and Tyson, J. (2012). 'The EIB and its role in regional development and integration'. In Macedo Cintra and da Rocha Gomes (eds.), *The Transformations of the International Financial System*. Brasília: IPEA, pp. 411–40.

Gutner, T.L. (2005). 'Explaining the gaps between mandate and performance: agency theory and World Bank environmental reform', *Global Environmental Politics*, 5(2): 10–37.

Gutner, T.L. (2010). 'The politics of IO performance: a framework', *Review of International Organizations*, 5(3): 227–48.

HAEU (Historical Archives of the EU) (1956a). 'Conférence intergouvernamentale pour le Marché Commun et l'Euratom'. BEI-1001. MAE 322 f/56, 24 September. Brussels: EIB.

HAEU (Historical Archives of the EU) (1956b). 'Conférence intergouvernamentale pour le Marché Commun et l'Euratom'. Fonctionnement du Marché Commun. BEI-1002. MAE 329 f/56, 26 September. Brussels: EIB.

HAEU (Historical Archives of the EU) (1956c). 'Conférence intergouvernementale pour le Marché Commun et l'Euratom'. *Projet du process verbal des reunions du groupe*. BEI-1004. MAE 361/f56/js, 2 October. Brussels: EIB.

HAEU (Historical Archives of the EU) (1956d). 'Groupe ad hoc pour le Fonds d'investissement: résumé des travaux du 8 octobre 1956'. BEI-1007, 8 October. Brussels: EIB.

HAEU (Historical Archives of the EU) (1956e). 'Groupe ad hoc pour le Fonds d'investissement: résumé des travaux du 9 octobre 1956'. BEI-1008, 9 October. Brussels: EIB.

HAEU (Historical Archives of the EU) (1956f). 'Groupe ad hoc pour le Fonds d'investissement: résumé des travaux du 10 octobre 1956'. BEI-1009, 11 October. Brussels: EIB.

HAEU (Historical Archives of the EU) (1956g). 'Groupe ad hoc pour le Fonds d'investissement: résumé des travaux du 11 octobre 1956'. BEI-1010, 12 October. Brussels: EIB.

HAEU (Historical Archives of the EU) (1956h). 'BEI Creation 27/11/1956. Rapport sur les travaux du Groupe ad hoc pour le Fonds d´investissement'. BEI-1021, 27 November. MAE-621/f/56/gh. Brussels: EIB.

HAEU (Historical Archives of the EU) (1958). 'Procès-verbal du Conseil d'administration du 6 février 1958 à Bruxelles'. BEI-1023. CA-001–58, 6 February. Brussels: EIB.

HAEU (Historical Archives of the EU) (1959). 'Procès-verbal du Conseil d'administration du 25 mai 1959 à Bruxelles' BEI-1032. CA-009–59, 25 May. Brussels: EIB.

HAEU (Historical Archives of the EU) (1961). 'Association de la Grèce: signature de l'accord d'association de la Grèce à la CEE, le 9 juillet 1961 à Athènes'. BAC-003/1978_0265. Brussels: EIB.

HAEU (Historical Archives of the EU) (1962). 'L'historique de la Banque mondiale: création et évolution'. BEI-5560, 2 March. Brussels: EIB.

HAEU (Historical Archives of the EU) (1989). 'Interview with Sicco Mansholt: interview by Seminaire R. Griffiths. Firenze (EUI)', 17 April. Oral History Collections. INT012. Brussels: EIB.

HAEU (Historical Archives of the EU) (2003). 'Entretien avec Michel Albert par Bussière, E., Lavezzi, G. and Willaert, E. à Paris le 18/12/2003'. INT700. Brussels: EIB.

HAEU (Historical Archives of the EU) (2004). 'Entretien avec Francesco Fresi par Bossuat, G. et Legendre, A. à Paris le 5/02/2004'. INT727. Brussels: EIB.

Hall, P.A. (2018). 'Varieties of capitalism in light of the euro crisis', *Journal of European Public Policy*, 25: 7–30.

Harrigan, J., Wang, C., and El-Said, H. (2006). 'The economic and political determinants of IMF and World Bank lending in the Middle East and North Africa', *World Development*, 34(2): 247–70.

Hirschman, A.O. (1958). *The Strategy of Economic Development*. New Haven, CT: Yale University Press.

Howarth, D. and Quaglia, L. (2016). *The Political Economy of European Banking Union*. Oxford: Oxford University Press.

Humphrey, C. (2015). 'The invisible hand: financial pressure and organisational convergence in multilateral development banks', *The Journal of Development Studies*, 52(1): 92–112.

Humphrey, C. and Michaelowa, K. (2013). 'Shopping for development: multilateral lending, shareholder composition and borrower preferences', *World Development*, 44: 142–55.

Ibrahim, Youssef M. (1990). 'The Gulf Crisis forces a diminished OPEC to face reality', *The New York Times*, 16 December, section 3: 12. Available online at: https://www.nytimes.com/1990/12/16/business/the-gulf-crisis-forces-a-diminished-opec-to-face-reality.html.

Kaiser, W. and Elvert, J. (2004). *EU Enlargement: A Comparative History.* New York: Routledge.

Knight, M. and Santaella, J.A. (1997). 'Economic determinants of IMF financial arrangements', *Journal of Development Economics*, 54: 405–36.

LaFeber, W. (1999). 'The tension between democracy and capitalism during the American century', *Diplomatic History*, 23(2): 263–84.

Licari, J. (1969). 'The EIB'. *Journal of Common Market Studies*, 8(3): 192–215.

Liebe, M. and Howarth, D. (2020). 'The EIB as policy entrepreneur and the promotion of public-private partnerships'. *New Political Economy*, 25(2): 195–212.

Ludlow, N.P. (2005). 'The making of the CAP: towards a historical analysis of the EU's first major policy', *Contemporary European History*, 14(3): 347–71.

Mazzucato, M. and Penna, C.C.R. (2016). 'Beyond market failures: the market creating and shaping roles of state investment banks', *Journal of Economic Policy Reform*, 19(4): 305–26.

Mertens, D. and Thiemann, M. (2019). 'Building a hidden investment state? The EIB, national development banks and European economic governance', *Journal of European Public Policy*, 26(1): 23–43.

Michalis, M. (2007). *Governing European Communications: From Unification to Coordination*. Plymouth: Lexington Books.

Myrdal, G. (1957). *Economic Theory and Underdeveloped Regions*. London: Duckworth.

Nielson, D.L., Tierney, M.J., and Weaver, C. (2006). 'Bridging the rationalist–constructivist divide: re-engineering the culture of the World Bank', *Journal of International Relations and Development*, 9: 107–39.

Official Journal of the EU (2006). 'Regulation (EC) No 1080/2006 of the European Parliament and of the Council of 5 July 2006 on the ERDF and repealing Regulation (EC) No 1783/1999' published on the Official Journal L 210 of 31/07/2006. Available online at: https://eur-lex.europa.eu/legal-content/EN/ALL/?uri=CELEX%3A32006R1080

Papaioannou, G. (2004). 'The European Union in the 90's: fiscal conditions and concerns', *European Research Studies*, VII(3–4): 65–82.

Robinson, N. (2009). 'The EIB: the EU's neglected institution', *Journal of Common Market Studies*, 47(3): 651–73.

Temin, P. (1994). 'The Great Depression'. NBER Working Paper Series on Historical Factors in Long Run Growth. Historical Paper No. 62.

Turró, M. (1999). *Going Trans-European: Planning and Financing Transport Networks for Europe*. Amsterdam: Pergamon.

Vreeland, J.R. (2004). *Institutional Determinants of IMF Agreements*. London: UCLA International Institute.

6

The Role of the Central American Bank for Economic Integration in Regional Integration and Development

José Efraín Deras, Alberto Cortés, and Guillermo Funes

1. Introduction

From its establishment in 1960, the Central American Bank for Economic Integration (CABEI) has sought to support the Central American region by facilitating financial resources and providing technical assistance with a view to promoting integration and a balanced social and economic development—following its Constitutive Agreement (CABEI 2010). The CABEI was established as the first 'Sub-regional integration bank' (see the Chapter 1, this volume) in the Global South, on 13 December 1960 in Managua, Nicaragua. Four governments—those of Guatemala, El Salvador, Honduras, and Nicaragua signed the Bank's Constitutive Agreement—Costa Rica joined soon afterwards, in 1963. In May 1961, with an authorized capital of USD 16 million, the CABEI's official headquarters were established in Tegucigalpa, Honduras. Regarding the chronology of the establishment of regional development banks (RDB) in Latin America, the CABEI was only preceded by the Inter-American Development Bank (IADB), which had been created in 1959 with a capital of USD 1 billion, as a Continental RDB. After the creation of the CABEI, however, there was also a notable effort to create a second Sub-regional integration bank, in the form of the Andean Development Corporation (CAF), with an authorized capital of USD 25 million in 1968.

Prior to the official establishment of the CABEI, in June 1960, the Central American countries that would make up the CABEI signed an agreement with the United States (US) Agency for International Development (USAID) to establish a financial fund for Central America. These resources represented support by the US towards the Central American integration process, while they were also a means of trying to influence the free trade agenda in the region. Once established, the CABEI signed a Coordination Agreement with the IADB, in August 1962, with a view to promoting the economic and social progress of the countries of

José Efraín Deras, Alberto Cortés, and Guillermo Funes, *The Role of the Central American Bank for Economic Integration in Regional Integration and Development* In: *Regional Development Banks in the World Economy.* Edited by: Judith Clifton, Daniel Díaz-Fuentes, and David Howarth, Oxford University Press (2021).
DOI: 10.1093/oso/9780198861089.003.0006

Central America, in order to accelerate economic integration in the region (CABEI 2010). At that time, the governments of Central America hoped to achieve social development through an economic development agenda based on integration—mainly based on the belief that the import substitution model was going to deliver industrialization to the region (Deras 2012).

During the 1960s, the CABEI was the main source of resources to finance the development agenda in Central America. By the end of the decade, it had assumed a leading role by focusing on the correction of asymmetries among country members—asymmetries derived from the continued evolution of free trade. During this first decade of its existence, the Bank approved USD 96.4 million for infrastructure, USD 48.3 million for the manufacturing sector, USD 15.2 million for telecommunications, and USD 23 million for housing (CABEI 2010). By 1969, the CABEI staff calculated these projects had generated USD 112 million of added value, USD 82 million of foreign currency, around 18,000 direct jobs, and 1,745 housing units (CABEI 2010). During the 1970s and the 1980s, the CABEI continued to represent a relevant force across the region, this despite the fact that the integration process was facing obstacles which were not overcome until the 1990s, when a new integration phase began. From the mid-1990s, the CABEI received new support from both regional and extra-regional member states, converting the Bank into the most important source of multilateral funds for Central America. From 2010 onwards, the CABEI channelled more resources to Central America than the IADB or the World Bank (CABEI-ODE 2018).

2. 'Closed regionalism' and the origins of the CABEI

The establishment of the CABEI needs to be understood in the historical context associated with the desire to integrate the Central American region. According to Rull Sabater (1971), the dream of integrating the Central American region was a long-term one and, notwithstanding the failure of the early federation following independence in the 1820s, had continued to persist. In the 1950s, a series of factors conducive to economic integration arose in the region. In 1951, the Organisation of Central American States (ODECA) was established by the ministers of foreign affairs of five Central American countries—Guatemala, El Salvador, Honduras, Nicaragua, and Costa Rica. Once established, this organization was strengthened further by new bilateral trade treaties signed between countries in the region during the 1950s (Rull Sabater 1971). Intra-regional trade increased, with intra-regional imports increasing from USD 8.6 million in 1950 to USD 13.7 million in 1956 (Bulmer-Thomas 1994). It was also at this time that the Economic Commission for Latin America and the Caribbean (ECLAC), through the ODECA, proposed that Central American countries should open to intra-regional trade and simultaneously introduce external trade barriers to protect the region from the rest of the world. The aim of this regional integration was to promote industrialization and the diversification of production, which is known conceptually as the import-substituting industrialization (ISI) model under a 'closed regionalism' (Mariscal 1989).

The promotion of industrialization in Central American countries had presented difficulties previously, since the small size of the domestic industrial market undermined their potential for industrialization and the diversification of production. However, ECLAC proposed that the integration of the regional market could enable such industrialization to occur, given that companies could then develop economies of scale at the regional level. In this way, Central America could become more competitive in the international market. To facilitate this, the Committee of Economic Cooperation was created in 1952, which was formed by the ministers of economic affairs of the region, who were to develop the required regional framework (Schmitter 1970).

Movement towards the Central American Common Market (CACM) took time, however. After almost a decade working towards its implementation, the Multilateral Treaty on Free Trade and Central American Economic Integration was signed in 1958. This Multilateral Treaty allowed for regional free trade across 239 product groups, with provisions to establish total intra-regional free trade within the following ten years. The Treaty also incorporated the Integration Industries Convention (IIC), which advocated the formation of 'regional monopolies', that is, developing a regionally integrated industry which produced specific products in all the member countries—so-called 'industrial reciprocity' (Schmitter 1970; Bulmer-Thomas 1994). The IIC model had been promoted from the 1950s by ECLAC, although the US was against the creation of such 'regional monopolies', as it saw them. The main reason for the opposition of the US was that they saw this development as threatened their position as Central America's main trading partner. Following discussions both inside the bloc and with the US, the IIC was expected to help allocate capital investment among member states (Library of Congress 2010). This process generated more internal discussion due to the need of the Central American countries to tackle social pressure and improve economic growth. However, the opposition of US was focused on foreign trade issues, specifically, on how the creation of regional monopolies (such as the integration bloc that proposed common external tariffs against the rest of the world) was going to affect US trade (Deras 2012).

According to Bulmer-Thomas (1987), while the IIC had been established with a view to promoting the balanced development of industries among CABEI member states, by the end of the 1960s, it had only actually helped the emergence of a handful of industries. The year after the Multilateral Treaty was signed, in 1959, the Tariff Equalisation Convention (TEC), which introduced a common external tariff on products imported to the region, was approved (Schmitter 1970).

Bulmer-Thomas (1994) argues that, because the approval of the constitution of ECLAC had taken place, despite the opposition of the US in the United Nations in 1948, therefore, opposition from the US to the Central American integration process was to be expected, particularly as the initiative was proposed and supported by ECLAC. However, somewhat unexpectedly, the US agreed to support the initiative—with two 'caveats'. First, the US requested that the trade exceptions granted to the region's principal exports were rescinded, as it expected regional free trade to be the norm. Second, as noted above, the US disapproved of the IIC, which it feared would create regional monopolies to the detriment of US foreign trade policy. The US therefore requested the IIC be removed from the Treaty. The CACM members concurred, due to the high level of trade with, and foreign direct investment (FDI) from, the US. This imbalance is a continual scenario that has historically influenced the regional agenda in Central America. Their acceptance of the first of these conditions imposed by the US—and the emasculation and subsequent failure of the second IIC—led to a decision whereby the US released funds with the aim of helping promote the creation of regional institutions. A Tripartite Treaty with the US was signed by Guatemala, Honduras, and El Salvador in 1960 (Rull Sabater 1971; SIECA 2008), since Costa Rica and Nicaragua were opposed to regional free trade at this time. This was succeeded by the General Treaty of Central American Economic Integration (1960), signed in Managua by all the Central American republics, with the exception of Costa Rica.

The Multilateral Treaty saw the governments of Guatemala, El Salvador, Honduras, and Nicaragua re-affirm their commitment to jointly promote the development of Central America with a view to improving the living conditions of their citizens, as stated in the General Treaty of 1960 at the Secretariat for Central American Economic Integration (SIECA) (SIECA 2008). It was this treaty that provided the legal basis for the formation of the CACM and set a specific timetable for the gradual elimination of tariffs (Nugent 1974). The General Treaty entered effect for Guatemala, El Salvador, and Nicaragua in 1961, for Honduras in 1962, and for Costa Rica in 1963, and anticipated largely intra-regional free trade within five years (Nugent 1974). Once the CACM was functioning, from 1961, many regional institutions were formed to support the process of integration in Central America. The main institutions that emerged were the SIECA, the CABEI, the Central American Institution for Research and Industrial Technology, and other councils dealing with standardized trade classification, navigation, and sanitation (Nugent 1974; Mariscal 1989). During 1970s, the application of the CACM was interrupted due to civil wars in some Central American countries and conflicts among specific CACM members. In the 1990s, following peace agreements, the Protocol of Tegucigalpa and Protocol of Guatemala were signed, and the region was able to enjoy the gradual and ongoing construction of an 'open regionalism' with the signing of multiple bilateral free trade agreements and, most recently, the initiation of discussions to create a customs union.

3. The CABEI's institutional history: establishment and evolution during 1960s and 1970s

The CABEI was established as the financial arm for the integration of Central America and the promotion of the development agenda when regional governments decided to promote the CACM (Rull Sabater 1971). With intra-regional trade starting to increase and, as governments of Central American countries demanded an acceleration of the process of industrialization and diversification of production, the CABEI was expected to channel additional and complementary foreign resources towards financing the processes of economic and social development. On the one hand, the CABEI would finance manufacturing projects that could be viable under the new tariff regime that supported the ISI strategy in the region (Deras 2005). On the other hand, the CABEI would also have to finance infrastructure projects in transportation, communication, storage, energy, agricultural and social development. However, the financing of these projects attracted limited resources. This was largely due to the perspective which tended to prevail at the time within the CABEI which focused principally on urban-industrialization and intra-regional trade (CABEI 2010). It was clear from the CABEI's constitution that a 'balance in the credit policy for development' was required, which is expressed in Article 2 of its Constitutive Agreement. This article establishes that the Bank's objective is to promote economic integration as well as the balanced economic and social development of the Central American region.

The constitutive agreement of the CABEI stated that it was essential to accelerate the integration and development of member countries to contribute towards the promotion of social progress. In their original statutes, education, health, housing, and rural development priority fields were established as a strategy to complement the efforts of member countries in those fields—during the 1950s, regional per capita income was low, around USD 200, and around 70 per cent of the population was working in agriculture (Nugent 1974). However, industrialization and complementary competitive infrastructure were the main goals of the CABEI as an arm of the CACM integration system. On the one hand, the CACM was working towards the establishment of common external tariffs, the harmonization of trade, and the coordination of policies, all with a view to promoting economies of scale and intra-regional trade as part of the ISI strategy. As result of these policies, intra-regional trade increased from USD 32.7 million in 1960 to USD 258.3 million in 1968 (Bulmer-Thomas 1979). On the other hand, the CABEI, as the financial arm of CACM, increased significantly its funding from an original capital of USD 16 million in 1960 to nearly USD 200 million by the end the 1960s. Most of the CABEI financing in the 1960s funded projects that promoted economic development, with industry, infrastructure, telecommunications totalling around 75 per cent, and only about 25 per cent destined for social agenda targets such as health, education, and social housing (CABEI 2010).

During the 1970s, the CABEI faced different challenges, including the Honduran-Salvadoran war—known as the 'football war' of 1969 (Deras 2012), the Managua earthquake, the social and political conflict in Guatemala, El Salvador, and Nicaragua, and Hurricane Fifi in Honduras, amongst other events. However, in the 1970s, despite this, the CABEI could boast some achievements, such as the financing of water supply projects in all five capitals of the founding countries, the large hydroelectric generation projects of Chicory and Aguacapa-Escuintla in Guatemala and 'El Cajón' in Honduras, and the beginning of the project to interconnect large-scale electricity systems among the Central American countries (CABEI 2010). In the agricultural sector, the CABEI also played an important role in the reconstruction of the irrigation system of the Comayagua Valley in Honduras and, in general, in the expansion of sugar mills, the development of the dairy industry, and a set of projects within the rural agribusiness programme. In other sectors, the CABEI financed 'silo'[1] systems in Guatemala, El Salvador, and Honduras. In addition, airports were built and expanded in El Salvador and Honduras using CABEI loans. Moreover, support for the construction of roads, industrial parks, and tourist developments, such as Copán and Tikal, were intensified during the 1970s. By the end of the decade, the Bank had approved loans for USD 956.8 million.

4. The CABEI's debt reduction strategies in the 1980s and 1990s

During 1980s, as a result of the crisis of external debt that affected directly the domestic economic and political stability of the area (Esquivel et al. 1998), the regional integration process largely lost momentum and relevance in the political agenda of the Central American countries. Due to the concentration of its portfolio in the region, the CABEI experienced the consequences of the weakening of productive activity, combined with the resurgence of political-military confrontation in three of its member countries, and complications associated with the financial crisis of the external debt. This crisis generated unprecedented shortcomings, such as the neglect of the service of the external debt with the CABEI by the member states, a product of the illiquidity of these countries (Bulmer-Thomas 1994).

Despite the instability of the international economy, political-military confrontation, and the slowdown in regional economic activity during the 1980s (Almeida 2015), the CABEI was able to overcome these challenges and continue its activities. However, the Bank's ability to adapt also meant it would have to face three challenges: first, it had to ensure its own financial viability, second, it was charged

[1] A technique of storing grain to feed animal production during long dry seasons.

with maintaining its participation in the economic recovery of Central America; and, third, it had to honour timely payment to external sources. In order to reach the end of a decade during which the CABEI had become weakened, in June 1990, the Bank obtained the political backing of its founding member states. This support helped the CABEI to fulfil its obligations, approving new capital increases, and dollarizing its equity. Furthermore, in the spirit of the Antigua Declaration, in which economic issues were once again considered to be of the highest political level in the region, the Economic Action Plan for Central America was adopted.

Towards the end of the decade of the 1990s, the CABEI's founding members experienced the aftermath of the international financial crisis and the ravages of Hurricane Mitch and Tropical Storm Newton. In view of these challenges, at the end of 1998, the Bank's strategic position was defined in order to consolidate the reconstruction and development efforts of the founding member countries. The Bank actively participated in both the preparation of the Central American Reconstruction and Transformation Plan and, regarding the external debt of the countries, the CABEI coordinated with other international financial institutions (IFI) in the context of the Heavily Indebted Poor Countries Initiative (HIPC), with the incorporation of Nicaragua in 1997 and Honduras in 2000 to the initiative. In parallel, the Bank made coordinated efforts towards the implementation of the Emergency Trust Fund to Support the Countries of Central America in the Service of its Multilateral Debt. The CABEI's participation was the most vigorous of all MDB and RDB working within the region: the total debt relief assigned to the CABEI was USD 508.3 million.

During the 1990s, in the context of increasing cross-border financial flows around the world, which included international investors, private banks, and MDB, there was a re-orientation towards private sector initiatives. This led to the strengthening of both banking and non-banking financial institutions as regards their ability to expand their distribution channels to small and medium-sized enterprise (SME). The CABEI followed a similar pathway and undertook venture financial projects in energy, tourism, transportation, and telecommunications. It also made incursions into non-regulated financial intermediaries in order to support SME. At the same time, the CABEI continued its support of the export and social sector. By the end of the decade, the CABEI had contributed to around 30 per cent of the multilateral resources that had been disbursed to the region. The bank was able to attract over USD 2 billion to the region in total (CABEI 2010).

5. The CABEI's consolidation in the early twenty-first century

During the first decades of the twenty-first century, after half a century in operation, the CABEI is one of the few regional institutions that could be said to be durable and robust in the Central American context. From 2000, the Bank underwent a new growth in its operations (CABEI 2010). The underlying strength of the CABEI lies both in its balance sheet in terms of liquidity, capitalization, the quality of its assets, its capacity to generate income, as well as in the support of its shareholders, which are also its clients. During the period between 2000 and 2018, the CABEI's approved loans totalling USD 28.67 billion. Of these, 31 per cent (USD 8.88 billion) was approved in the area of productive infrastructure; 21 per cent (USD 5.89 billion) in financial system intermediation; 19 per cent (USD 5.47 billion) in energy; 16 per cent (USD 4.65 billion) in social infrastructure and human development; 8 per cent (USD 2.42 billion) in services for competitiveness; and 6 per cent (USD 1.36 billion) in rural development and environment. Of the approved amount, around one-quarter, or 24.5 per cent (USD 7.04 billion) was destined for Costa Rica; 17.6 per cent (USD 5.03 billion) for Guatemala; 17.3 per cent (USD 4.96 billion) for El Salvador; 14.5 per cent (USD 4.16 billion) for Nicaragua; 14.1 per cent (USD 4.05 billion) for Honduras; 5.9 per cent (USD 1.68 billion) for Panama; 2.7 per cent (USD 0.78 billion) for Dominican Republic; 2 per cent (USD 0.58 billion) for Colombia; 0.7 per cent (USD 0.20 billion) for Argentina; 0.5 per cent (USD 0.15 billion) for Mexico; and 0.2 per cent (USD 0.04 billion) for Belize.

As regards the relationships that the CABEI maintains with international cooperation organizations and the public and private sector, the Bank tends to be associated most with an actor seeking to support regional growth. By 2019, the CABEI had fifteen member states as shareholders, five of which are the original founders (Guatemala, El Salvador, Honduras, Nicaragua, and Costa Rica); three are regional non-founders (Belize, Panama, and Dominican Republic); and seven are extra-regional members (Argentina, Colombia, Spain, Mexico, the Peoples' Republic of China-Taiwan, Cuba, and South Korea). The CABEI has modified its Founding Agreement, which now includes all country members as beneficiaries, which opens up its portfolio for diversification to guarantee its long-term sustainability. Accumulated knowledge and its strong relationships with the main stakeholders have allowed the CABEI to develop in a strong and durable manner, and to create a solvent and efficient entity trademark in providing medium- and long-term resources to promote integration and development in the region. The financial backup of its partners and the status reached in capital markets has turned the Bank into one of the main sources of multilateral financing for the region—it contributes more to the region than the World Bank and the IADB. During the period 2010-18, the CABEI's resources to Central American countries have represented the equivalent of 40.5 per cent of public investment and some 23 per cent of total FDI (CABEI-ODE 2019).

6. Assessing the CABEI's impact on integration and development

During the period 2010–16, the three main development banks (CABEI, IADB, and the World Bank) that operated in the region approved more than USD

22.8 billion for Central American countries—the equivalent to the gross domestic product (GDP) of Honduras, nearly twice the GDP of Nicaragua and about 10 per cent of regional GDP. The CABEI represents around 44 per cent of the total approvals for the region during the period (USD 10.1 billion), the rest being distributed between the IADB and the World Bank. It is important to mention that almost 50 per cent of the amount approved by these banks was focused upon infrastructure and energy. From the amount approved by the CABEI, more than USD 5 billion was destined for infrastructure (mainly roads) and around USD 4.8 billion went to energy. The rest of the amount approved was destined for focus areas, such as agriculture, human development, competitiveness, financial intermediation, social investment, with contributions to regional integration as an important funding target (CABEI-ODE 2018).

Although most development banks claim they seek to work in a complementary way, avoiding competition, in the Central American region, there is little evidence of bank specialization or differentiation by sector. In this case, the three banks participate in nearly all the areas mentioned above. In fact, there are similarities in the regional specialization of the two main RDB: the CABEI and the IADB's main portfolio are both mainly focused on infrastructure and energy. Based on the changes as regards the banks' portfolios, it appears that the IADB has followed the strategy led by the CABEI in the region. Nevertheless, the World Bank seems to take a different approach, which can be differentiated from that of the CABEI and the IADB: the World Bank finances sectoral policy loans in health, education, and government institutional strengthening, with a degree of specialization. In general, the role of all of these development banks in the region is relevant and their activity has positively impacted the well-being of the Central American population. However, financing seems to be becoming a 'commodity' and the CABEI and IADB both need to re-orient their policies and move on from a traditional financing approach to one considering the additionality of financial services that create value to societies, particularly, knowledge, innovation, institutions, technical assistance, market creation, and sound policy (Abraham et al. 2019).

In this scenario, the CABEI has played an important role as regards regional integration and development as part of its institutional mandate. However, the CABEI's role needs to be subject to assessment, using scientific tools, in order to improve the accountability of its performance and results, and to learn from lessons to improve future decision-making. Hence, the CABEI is subject to an evaluation according to the so-called 'Balanced Scorecard' (Kaplan and Norton 2015) to measure institutional effectiveness in terms of its contribution to the development of its member states. To guarantee the fulfilment of the CABEI's strategic objectives according to its vision and mission, the Bank has traced its actions and the initiatives that act as guiding agents. These are measured through specific indicators alongside the execution of strategy, so that resources are effectively oriented towards its partner's priorities and its focus areas for development. The

Balanced Scorecard applied to the Bank's strategy focuses its strategic objectives using four perspectives: clients and beneficiaries (for the region)—where the countries expect that the CABEI should play a significant and positive impact on economic and social development in the region; finances—where the CABEI's financial sustainability is an essential requirement to provide resources that will allow it to impact on regional development in the long-term; structure and processes—with the aim of ensuring that the Bank continues to operate with state-of-the-art technologies and processes at an adequate cost, with efficiency and controls, all towards the service of the strategy; and organizational capacity (for the institution)—where the CABEI must work to strengthen its human capital. The execution of these four perspectives established indicators that are used to measure the impact of the Bank's activities on development. The indicator for development is important: this allows for the quantification of the impact on development of each operation through the incorporation of a series of economic and social indicators, both qualitative and quantitative. The indicator measuring resources dedicated to focus areas, or the financial net flows indicator for member countries, shows the difference between disbursed capital and capital recoveries. Some internal indicators stand out, notably: capital payments from the member countries to increase the capacities of the Bank to allocate resources to projects; (efficient) administrative expenses; and other internal indicators related to human resource development. These indicators together make up the Annual Institutional Performance Index, which establishes specific measures that are monitored annually to an institutional rating.

The CABEI defines country strategies as the instruments that allow the linking of institutional strategy with the socio-economic development priorities of each country. To measure the degree of accomplishment of country strategies, the CABEI implements the Evaluation Guidelines for Country Strategies, which are based on international standards (that include evaluation criteria and sub-criteria) recommended by the Evaluation Cooperation Group. The criteria adopted to evaluate country strategies are related to: relevance, that is, the degree to which the design and strategy are consistent with a country's needs and aligned with the government's development plans and priorities; efficiency; effectiveness; impact; and sustainability, that is, the certainty that present and expected results can persist over time despite risks, even after the strategy has been concluded.

In order to assess the role of the CABEI, it is possible to observe the relevance of the Bank in terms of development and integration using data for the period between 2010 and 2014. During this period, the CABEI approved USD 7.6 billion, divided into 176 operations, and disbursed USD 7 billion—disbursements being used as a proxy for implementation of approvals. Some 54.2 per cent of the total amount approved was dedicated to economic competitiveness, 33.3 per cent to social development, and 12.5 per cent to regional integration. Meanwhile, the disbursements replicated such behaviour, with economic competitiveness receiving 43.4 per cent, whereas social development and integration received 40.6 per cent and 16 per cent, respectively. According to the office of evaluation of the Bank (CABEI-ODE 2015), the contribution to economic development can be evidenced by the number of jobs created, due to the approvals made during the period 2010–14, with 127,875 permanent and 70,577 temporary jobs created; 40,550 houses built, mainly social housing to reduce regional deficits of around 40 per cent (including construction and improvements; and 2,660 hospital beds, just to mention the main contributions to development. In terms of integration, the main two contributions are, first related to trade, tourism, and transportation of passengers, with 1,592 kilometres of highways along the region, and, second, a boost to the Central American market of energy with new power generation to the Central American system of 1,745 Megawatts of electricity, focused 100 per cent upon renewable resources. Meanwhile, regarding the comparison of Bank disbursements against FDI in the region, it may be said that this is equivalent to nearly 25 per cent of the regional FDI for the period. The main conclusion at this point is that the CABEI plays an important role as regards the renewed agendas of integration, as well as efforts to overcome the development challenges of the region.

In terms of relevance for the countries,[2] considering official country development plans, the CABEI is present in nearly 60 per cent of the priority areas established by the countries of the region (CABEI-ODE 2018). On the other hand, when rating the Bank's participation inside MDB portfolio belonging to each Central American country, 45 per cent of the total was financed by the CABEI in 2018. Table 6.1 shows the individual participation for each MDB.

During the implementation of the 2015–19 strategic period, the CABEI approved USD 2.5 billion and disbursed USD 2.1 billion through forty-seven operations. Of these approved projects, the priority was economic competitiveness (46.7 per cent; USD 1.2 billion); followed by social development (32.8 per cent; USD 819 million), and regional integration (20.5 per cent; USD 511 million). Meanwhile, in terms of the disbursed funds, 63.3 per cent (USD 1.3 billion) was destined for economic competitiveness; USD 487 million (22.9 per cent) for social development; and 13.7 per cent (USD 292 million) for integration. A comparative analysis between the 2010–14 and the 2015–19 strategic periods reveals significant improvements as regards the extent to which social development and integration were positively impacted. For example, the rate of growth of the approved projects 2015-19 period turned out to be higher than 30 per cent in comparison to the 2010-14 period. This recent trend found in the CABEI's work validate its relevance by contributing to regional priorities that generate jobs,

[2] The Evaluation Cooperation Group (ECG), a specialized group established for the Evaluation Offices of the Multilateral Development Banks created its 'Big Book' of principles and best practices in evaluation, naming relevance, efficiency, effectiveness, impacts, and sustainability of the results as the main principles to apply for evaluators at country level, among other applications (ECG 2012).

Table 6.1 Relevance of the CABEI among MDB and RDB in Central America (2010–17)

	Amount of loans approved by MDB, millions of USD, 2010–2017					
	Costa Rica	El Salvador	Honduras	Guatemala	Nicaragua	Total
CABEI	2,813.4	2,164.8	2,220.2	2,007.6	2,301.6	11,507.6
IADB	2,069.2	1,927.7	1,888.2	1,877.4	1,874.2	9,636.7
IBRD	620.0	540.0	497.6	1,586.5	631.7	3,875.8
Total	5,502.6	4,632.5	4,606.0	5,471.5	4,807.5	25,020.1
	Percentage of the amount of loans approved by MDB, 2010–2017					
	Costa Rica	**El Salvador**	**Honduras**	**Guatemala**	**Nicaragua**	**Total**
CABEI	51.1	46.7	48.2	36.7	47.9	46.0
IADB	37.6	41.6	41.0	34.3	39.0	38.5
IBRD	11.3	11.7	10.8	29.0	13.1	15.5

Source: CABEI-ODE 2018 and 2019

physical infrastructure, access to credit, and human development. In relation to the contribution to development in regional economies, in the first years of the implementation of the CABEI's 2015–19 Institutional Strategy, the forty-seven approved projects created 132,740 jobs, contributed to 974 kilometres of improved and newly built highways for continuing to improve the connectivity of the region, 616.8 Megawatts of energy, mainly renewable; 11,237 houses, focused upon social housing; and infrastructure in the health and education sectors. Meanwhile, with respect to the comparison between public investment versus the Bank's disbursement, the ratio is of USD 2.3/USD 1.0, while the ratio against FDI in the region is of USD 4.4/USD 1.0.

7. Conclusions

The CABEI is one of the few modern regional institutions that has proved to be durable in the Central American context. Accumulated knowledge and the relationships with its main stakeholders have allowed it to develop strengths and to create an efficient and solvent entity in providing medium- and long-term finance to promote regional integration, and the economic and social development of the isthmus. The partners' commitment and the Bank's status achieved in international capital markets have turned the CABEI into the main RDB source of financing in the region and a strategic development institution for the future of the region. The underlying strength of the CABEI lies in its annual sheets in terms of liquidity, capitalization, the quality of its assets, and the capacity to generate income—thus it has gained the support of its shareholders who are also beneficiaries as clients.

The Bank has accompanied regional economic policy goals starting with the ISI model of the 1960s, debt sustainability in the 1980s, the open regionalism of the 1990s, and the current goals regarding to the Sustainable Development Goals (SDG), regional integration, social development and competitiveness, which the Bank is reconsidering in order to respond to the challenges and demands of the region. Like other RDB elsewhere, the CABEI is considering the possibility of diversifying its services beyond lending. As loans are becoming a 'commodity' in which the financial additionality for development and integration is not enough, the Bank is currently developing an agenda to offer 'non-financial additionality', such as the ability to formulate and re-address public policy, institutional strengthening, sectoral expertise, technical assistance, access to capital markets to reduce financial costs in the public sector, mechanisms to avoid public debt shortcomings, private-public partnerships, correction of market failures, creating development poles and new markets, among others.

In order to ensure the continuous improvement of the CABEI, a decision was taken to evaluate its performance in-house. This evaluation has become a strategic tool to assess efficiency and effectiveness as regards development and integration along time. Through this evaluation, the CABEI has been able to answer the following question: 'What have been the effects that interventions for development and integration have had upon its beneficiaries?' It is important that the conclusions of this assessment exercise show that the Bank's mandated goals of 'promoting economic integration and balanced social and economic development of Central American countries' are reached in a cost-effective manner, which is key to stakeholders. The CABEI's evaluation practice is today an important tool for the role played by the Bank in development and integration. These have been designed to focus upon each component of the Bank's strategic planning, with feedback at different stages, in a way that the findings and recommendations may contribute to the Bank's continuous improvement.

Acknowledgements

Thanks from José Efraín Deras to Pablo Flores, Luisa Noyola, Shirley Orellana, and Natasha Kronzonas, of the CABEI's Evaluation Office (CABEI-ODE), for the very important contributions regarding data and discussion of this chapter.

References

Abraham, F., Schmukler, S.L., and Tessada, J. (2019). 'Financial innovation and additionality: the power of economic analysis and data analytics', *Research and Policy Briefs 23*, June. Washington, DC: The World Bank.

Almeida, P. (2015). 'Neoliberal forms of capital and the rise of social movement partyism in Central America', *Journal of World-Systems Research*, 21(1): 8–24.

Bulmer-Thomas, V. (1979). 'Import substitution v. export promotion in the Central American Common Market (CACM)', *Journal of Economic Studies*, 6(2): 182–203.

Bulmer-Thomas, V. (1987). *The Political Economy of Central America since 1920*. Cambridge: Cambridge University Press.

Bulmer-Thomas, V. (1994). *The Economic History of Latin America since Independence*. Cambridge: Cambridge University Press.

CABEI (Central American Bank for Economic Integration) (2010). *CABEI's Contribution to the Development of Central America: 50 Years of History*. Tegucigalpa: Lithopress Industrial S.A.

CABEI-ODE (Central American Bank for Economic Integration-Evaluation Office) (2015). *Reports of Results of Ex Post Evaluation of CABEI Operations*. Tegucigalpa: CABEI.

CABEI-ODE (Central American Bank for Economic Integration-Evaluation Office) (2018). *Reports of Results of Ex Post Evaluation of CABEI Operations*. Tegucigalpa: CABEI.

CABEI-ODE (Central American Bank for Economic Integration-Evaluation Office) (2019). *Reports of Results of Ex Post Evaluation of CABEI Operations*. Tegucigalpa: CABEI.

Deras, J. (2005). *The Central American Common Market (CACM): An Application of the Gravity Model Approach to Analyze Trade of the CACM*. England, United Kingdom: The Eighth Postgraduates in Latin American Studies (PILAS) Conference, University of Cambridge.

Deras, J. (2012). *The Central American Common Market (CACM)*. Tegucigalpa: Spacio Gráfico.

ECG (Evaluation Cooperation Group) (2012). *Big Book on Evaluation: Good Practices*. Washington, DC: ECG.

Esquivel, G., Larraín, F., and Sachs, J.D. (1998). 'The external debt problem in Central America: Honduras, Nicaragua, and the HIPC Initiative', Development Discussion Paper No. 645. Cambridge, MA: Harvard Institute for International Development.

Kaplan, R.S. and Norton, D.P. (2015). *Balanced Scorecard Success: The Kaplan-Norton Collection*. Brighton, MA: Harvard Business Review Press.

Library of Congress (2010). 'The Central American Common Market'. Available online at: http://memory.loc.gov/frd/cs/nicaragua/ni_appnb.html

Mariscal, N. (1989). *Integración económica y poder-político en Centroamérica*. El Salvador: Universidad Centroamericana José Simeón Cañas.

Nugent, J.B. (1974). *Economic Integration in Central America: Empirical Investigations*. New York: Johns Hopkings University Press.

Rull Sabater, A. (1971). *La planificación económica y social en Centroamérica*. El Salvador: IEPAL.

Schmitter, P.C. (1970). 'Central American integration: spill-over, spill-around or encapsulation?'. *Journal of Common Market Studies*, 9(1): 1–48.

SIECA (Secretariat for Central American Economic Integration) (2008). *Estado de situación de la integración económica Centroamericana*. Guatemala: SIECA.

7

From Sub-Regional Industrial Financier to Latin America's Main Development Bank

The Andean Development Corporation

Carlos Andrés Brando

1. Introduction

In 2018, the Andean Development Corporation (CAF) acquired new lending commitments with Latin America and the Caribbean worth USD 13.6 billion. This amount is larger than that offered by the historically dominant multilateral development banks (MDB) and regional development banks (RDB) operating in the region; that is, the International Bank for Reconstruction and Development (IBRD) or the World Bank (WB) and the Inter-American Development Bank (IADB). In 2018, the former approved loans to Latin America totalling USD 4.3 billion, and the latter recorded lending commitments for USD 13.2 billion (CAF 2019; IADB 2019; WB 2019). This was not an anomaly, since, in recent years, the CAF has outperformed both the WB and the IADB as the single largest supplier of development finance to the region. This is an extraordinary situation, more so due to the very nature of financial entity that the CAF is. Unlike other MDB and RDB operating in Latin America and the Global South—bar the recently created Asian Infrastructure Investment Bank (AIIB)—with developed countries acting as (major) donor shareholders and developing countries as borrowers, the CAF was founded as an RDB by developing countries, intending to lend to the same member countries. For a number of years, the CAF also obtained the bulk of its financing resources from these countries. An RDB by the poor, from the poor, and to the poor has proved to be not only viable, but competitive at the highest of levels. The CAF's current standing as a solid financial institution in the global order, and as major provider of loans, grants, equity investments, and guarantees has not always been so, however. The history of the CAF has also been one of difficulty, transition, and—only more recently—success.

Carlos Andrés Brando, *From Sub-Regional Industrial Financier to Latin America's Main Development Bank: The Andean Development Corporation* In: *Regional Development Banks in the World Economy*. Edited by: Judith Clifton, Daniel Díaz-Fuentes, and David Howarth, Oxford University Press (2021). © Oxford University Press.
DOI: 10.1093/oso/9780198861089.003.0007

This chapter offers a long-run view of the CAF from its conception in the late 1960s to the present. The limited existing literature has tended to concentrate on the last two decades of the CAF's accomplishments, offering assessments of its contributions to regional integration, economic growth, and development (Sagasti 2002; Zúñiga 2003). Extant analyses have highlighted the increasing ascendancy of the CAF in regional lending, and its organizational uniqueness as an RDB (Humphrey 2012; Rubio-Vega 2015). Others have focused on the determinants of the CAF lending and financial policy (Humphrey 2014, 2015), and on the nature of the demand for these type of institutions (Seatzu 2014). None, however, has provided a complete picture of how the CAF transformed throughout its lifetime. This chapter traces the historical evolution of the CAF, according to its changing mandates, from its initial role as financial catalyst of economic integration to the expanding range of tasks it has assumed over time. This chapter also analyses the most salient trends and changes in the CAF's nearly fifty years of operations; specifically, by looking at patterns of loan allocations and the evolving origins of funding sources through the distinctive operational phases that have come to characterize concrete periods of its existence.

The analysis emphasizes the benefits enjoyed by two small-sized countries—namely, Bolivia and Ecuador—in exercising greater voice within the fold of the CAF, benefits that they would have probably been unable to obtain in any large/global international financial institution (IFI) (Griffith-Jones et al. 2008: 1–2). Further, this analysis shows, that by fulfilling the original mandate of treating less-developed countries within the group of founding members in preferential terms, the CAF conformed to one of the major political goals set by the Andean-region agreements which created the Corporation. Despite profound political change in all of the CAF's founding countries, this RDB has managed to continue to operate according to its constitutive principles.

Using quantitative and qualitative material from primary sources including the CAF annual reports, general balance sheets, official 'Memories', and income statements—available both online and in publicly accessible archives—and the CAF staff memoires, as well as material from the existing secondary literature, this chapter includes statistical series for a range of variables that reveal the most important changes and continuities in the evolution of the CAF from 1970 to 2016. Further data and information has been kindly provided by the CAF's staff headquartered in Caracas. The series for volumes of loans and their distribution by terms, geographical location, and economic sectors, combined with data on the composition of the CAF's liabilities, debt-to-equity (D/E) ratios and risk-bearing capacity, not only supply the necessary data for the intended comprehensive, long-run perspective offered, but also facilitate the elaboration of a novel periodization that sheds light on the trajectory of the Corporation. Tentative explanations regarding the behaviour of the key variables analysed, and intermittent critical commentaries on particular junctures and contexts serve to sustain the judgements offered for a distinctive characterization of the CAF's trajectory.

The chapter is divided into five further sections. Section 2 ('Origins') deals with the origins and foundation of the Corporation, putting the emphasis on both political agency and agenda, the national interests, and the wider international geo-political context that allowed for the emergence of this Andean RDB in the late 1960s, and its early operations over the following decade. Sections 3-5 chronologically examine the evolution of the CAF, and set out a new periodization for it, from 1970 to 2016. This periodization coincides with the distinctive mandates and financial performance that the entity exhibited over the years, and that thus justifies the division of the narrative into different phases or sub-periods. Section 3, 'The early years (1970-81)' considers the CAF's original mandate, explains its *modus operandi*, and tracks its initial lending and performance, deepening into the years of early hardship. Section 4, 'The transition years: crisis and recovery (1982-91)', registers the changes proposed in the CAF leadership to guarantee the Corporation's survival in the aftermath of the Latin American Debt Crisis, preparing the Corporation for better times. This section discusses how the CAF struggled, yet partially managed, to follow through its new directives. This section also details the difficulties faced by the Corporation to tap significant external resources free of conditionalities. In section 5, 'Consolidation and expansion: from Regional to Continental (1992-2016)', the analysis concentrates on the fundamental trends that transformed the CAF into Latin America's largest development bank, even restructuring its original membership and mandate as a regional integration bank for the Andean zone. Particular attention is given to the financial intermediation of the Corporation in international capital markets. Section 6 concludes the chapter by highlighting the CAF's unique features and distinctive evolution in relation to other RDB.

2. Origins

The CAF was born as the financial mechanism under-girding the economic integration aspirations of the Andean Group (AG). The Group initially included Bolivia, Chile, Colombia, Ecuador, and Peru, and was formalized in the Cartagena Agreement in 1969. The CAF's origins and eventual emergence as an RDB, thus, are part of the history of integration of these countries. The CAF was inspired to some extent by the example of Europe following the Second World War (and notably the European Economic Community from 1957). In part, the CAF was conceived as a means to advancing the ongoing processes of import-substituting industrialization. The CAF was also seen as a mechanism to sustain growth through the promotion of greater economic independence. Efforts at regional integration at the time took hold not only in the Andes, but in Central America

(Central American Common Market (CACM), 1960), and Latin America more generally (Latin American Free Trade Agreement (LAFTA), 1960), amongst other regions (Cai 2010: 73). In fact, the AG was designed to work with LAFTA, rather than to supersede it (Ffrench-Davis et al. 1998).

The Cartagena Agreement was to a significant degree the achievement of two political leaders. The presidents of Chile and Colombia: Eduardo Frei and Carlos Lleras. Though the two had met at the United Nations summit of experts in 1954 to consider Latin America's developmental problems, it was only after Lleras' electoral victory in 1966 that their integrationist ambitions were offered a real opportunity. Counting on the full support of Congress and the Christian-democratic political movement, Frei made the promotion of regional integration a cause of his own, and a key component of his government's foreign policy (Walker 1970; Ffrench-Davis et al. 1998). The Chilean president declared that he was not just an enthusiast but a firm believer that integration would bring the jobs, economic development and living standards Latin Americans so badly needed (Godoy 1965).

In 1966, the Colombian president-elect toured in earnest the countries of the future AG ahead of the meeting that would establish its foundations. Just nine days after inauguration, Lleras, along with the presidents of Chile and Venezuela, and the personal delegates of their Ecuadorian and Bolivian counterparts, signed the Bogota Declaration (16 August 1966), a document on which Lleras worked directly and which reflects his plans and ideas on integration (Ruiz Lara 1999). As conceived by the 'architects' of the agreement, the declaration emphasized the differentiated treatment that less-developed countries deserved in trade deals; namely, Bolivia and Ecuador, announced the concertation of a regional agreement, approved a programme for immediate action to promote and liberalize trade, coordinate industrial policy, and considered a special regime for foreign direct investment. Critically, the declaration envisioned the creation of an RDB tasked with the direct promotion of business as well as the provision of technical assistance to the private sector in the execution of projects of common interest for the member countries. The seeds of the CAF had been sown.

The presidents' convictions on integration coincided with national interests which were, in turn, shaped by shifting geo-political arrangements at the global level. Critical arguments from both Left and Right pointing to the limitations of the industrializing strategy and the inward-looking model, commonly referred to in Latin America as ISI exhaustion, orientated the (integrationist) direction of governments' responses. According to Rivera, both Chile and Colombia promoted the formation of the AG with the protection of domestic business from international competition, in particular avoiding the larger member states such as Brazil or Argentina (Rivera 2014: 181). In the Colombian case, many argued that it stood to benefit from trade expansion with the AG partners because it enjoyed a lead in manufacturing; specifically, in textiles and petrochemicals, and in the supply of raw materials for human-made fibres (Salgado 1970; Abel and Palacios 1991). Salgado also noted that Colombian exports remained practically stagnant during the decade prior to 1966, in a case of 'typical external throttle', which neatly motivated the AG's constitution (Salgado 1970: 190). Moreover, Lleras himself had demonstrated that the possibilities for industrialization depended on market size, and that by 1961, the Colombian market was not sufficiently large (Villamizar 2013). The case of Venezuela echoed such concerns. State-sponsored industrialization in non-traditional exports such as iron, aluminium, and finished goods complemented nicely with entry to the AG in 1973, as an international initiative aimed at 'collective self-reliance' (Werz 1990: 193). Finally, what amounted to a privileged status in trade and financial prospects for the less-developed members of the Group (Bolivia and Ecuador), under conditions they had never been granted before in regional trade deals, constituted an incentive attractive enough for these countries to join.

Nationalism and anti-Americanism also played their roles in the formation of the Group. The latter was perhaps most pronounced in Venezuela, where governments pursuing an independent foreign policy escalated efforts at multilateral cooperation, including the Organization of the Petroleum Exporting Countries, the Latin American Economic System, and the AG (Rivas 2006). In preparation for joining the Group in 1973, Venezuela is said to have denounced the trade treaty with the US two years earlier (Ewell 1992). A similar trajectory was followed by successive governments in Peru, which from 1963 onwards sought to distance themselves from the US. Belaunde's emphasis on modern infrastructure and the provision of large incentives to industrialization brought him closer to the regional developmentalist trend of the AG (Wise 2003). The Revolutionary Government of the Armed Forces that followed in 1968, under the leadership of Juan Velasco, characterized by third-worldism and non-alignment pretending to reduce further its external dependence on the US, also supported a pact which regulated foreign investment more rigidly.

At first glance, Colombia resembled such patterns. Lleras' rhetoric certainly pointed in the nationalist direction:

> it is natural that we long for foreign direct investment, but we cannot be pleased with the foreign takeovers of enterprises created and strengthened by Colombians... A semi-colonial economy, led from abroad, represents the exact opposite of what the majorities had wished for. (Villamizar 2013: 315)

Lleras had reservations about the slowness of the Alliance for Progress launched in 1961, and more importantly, about the lending policies of dominant IFIs (Randall 1992). Yet, it was his firm stand against the International Monetary Fund (IMF) in 1966 that propelled his confidence regarding the autonomy of the AG countries, substantiated in the Cartagena Agreement as the dorsal spine of the integration project, and flanked in the financial arena with the creation of the CAF, as well as the Andean Reserve Fund of Central Banks (Sanz 2009).

Historical contexts, in particular those pertaining to major international geopolitics and economics in the late 1960s and the 1970s, shaped both the conditions leading to the formation of the AG and the CAF, as well as the opportunities and challenges that they would have to face in their early years. Prominent at the time was the Cold War confrontation between two ideological blocks, each led by a superpower, which in one way or another touched all parts of the globe (Freedman 1998). The dynamics of international conflict and cooperation engendered by the Cold War contributed to setting the stage for the AG and the CAF. As the Cuban Revolution unfolded and the threat of communism spreading across Latin America loomed, US governments juggled to support anti-communist movements and regimes amidst growing anti-Americanism (McPherson 2006). In 1961, President Kennedy launched an ambitious USD 20 billion economic assistance programme to fund agrarian, health, and educational reforms to better the lives of Latin Americans and so counter the appeals of revolutionaries. The Alliance for Progress was effective at raising expectations of material improvement, democracy, and stability (Levinson and de Onis 1970; Fajardo 2003). But this Alliance started faltering rather soon as President Johnson changed the nature of the aid given to the region, and President Nixon redirected US foreign policy priorities away from Latin America (Fajardo 2003; Taffet 2006; Lawrence 2010).

Conflict in Asia soon overshadowed cooperation in Latin America. Whilst US loans and grants to Latin America, from 1961 to 1969, reached USD 6.1 billion, those flowing to Asia totalled USD 14.6 billion. Illustrating this point further, the amount of resources channelled to the six Andean countries combined, which would form the AG, equalled those destined to Pakistan alone, remained well below those advanced to Vietnam, and was only half those directed to India (Taffet 2006). US governments, however, essayed carrots and sticks with Latin America. As they extended economic aid, US governments' containment strategy was paralleled with military interventions in Cuba and the Dominican Republic, as well as covert campaigns against Marxist and liberal reformers in Brazil, Bolivia, Chile, and Guatemala, amongst others (McPherson 2006). It was in one of these operations that, with the assistance of the CIA, the democratically elected government of Allende was ousted from power, and the military coup led by General Pinochet installed a regime that rapidly withdrew Chile from the AG and the CAF. Given that Latin Americans feared, and were frustrated by, US policies, calls for solutions from within the region, with an eye on integration, gained force and legitimacy.

A second set of events and processes influencing the CAF relate to the post-Second World War growth of international finance and the economic expansion of the West. The 'Golden Age' of European accelerated economic growth, according to Eichengreen (2010: 31), resulted from high investment rates, rapid export growth, and wage moderation. Industrial exports matter in particular to this story, for European (especially German, Spanish, and Italian) manufacturers of capital goods, along with Japanese and American ones, also sought to place their products in Latin American markets. This concern amongst industrialized countries helps to explain why so many of their export/import banks exhibited interest in conducting businesses with the CAF, and facilitated a significant part of the loans and lines of credit that the Corporation received to fund its operations in the 1970s and 1980s. Perhaps this trade dynamic also explains why the IMF and the WB appeared tolerant of state-supported strategies of industrialization in the medium- and large-size economies of Latin America (Webb 2000). Thus, it would not be coherent to argue that an entity such as the CAF was born as a reaction to the anti-industrializing stand of IFIs.[1] Nor would this argument apply to the recently created IADB, which according to Webb (2000), had been financing industry with loans amounting to approximately a fifth of its total lending during the 1960s.

Shifting patterns of financial flows during the 1970s also affected the CAF's prospects at fundraising. To start with, the oil shocks that hit the globe in the form of price hikes effected a massive transfer of US dollars to the so-called Petro-states of the Middle East, which ended placing their surpluses in European and American commercial banks that turned into 'major controllers of world liquidity' (Adelman 2010: 118). Petro-dollars were compounded by the accelerating growth of the euro currency market—itself, ultimately a function of persistent US trade deficits—to nurture a global supply of abundant money to be lent (Shadlen 2007). Technical innovations in the banking sector were key in facilitating the recycling of dollars that took place across different regions of the world. The first was the syndicated loan, by which a pool of banks organized around a 'lead' institution to extend significantly large amounts of money, whilst diversifying risk at the same time. The second was an adjustable interest rate clause integrated into financial contracts, which transferred the bulk of the risk burden onto the borrower. It was in these changing conditions that the CAF managed to tap international financing sources during the 1970s to fund its operations. The largest loan advanced to the Corporation prior to the mid-1980s—a USD 50 million deal granted by the Bank of America in 1977—was obtained in, and due to, these circumstances.

[1] In fact, a pro-industrializing bias was created in the Bank's project selection and procurement procedures; see Webb (2000: 105).

3. Early years (1970–81)

The CAF was founded to serve as the financial mechanism of the AG's integration. Its main objective was to promote sustainable development and regional integration. According to the CAF's own coordinator of the Cartagena Board (subsequently the CAF and AG rector), the Corporation had to drive integration through the creation, expansion, modernization, and conversion of production firms, as well as the carrying out of studies and the preparation of projects (Camacho 1973). As an RDB, the Corporation sought to facilitate financial intermediation, and to mobilize investment resources, entrepreneurial capabilities, and technical assistance for integration endeavours. Originally, the CAF was tasked with supporting multinational projects or national ones with integrational content. It could also promote domestic ventures in the less-developed member states—Bolivia and Ecuador. As seen in Table 7.1, by the time of its foundation, and as expressed in gross domestic product (GDP) per capita, both of these countries were relatively more backward than the rest. Although Bolivia clearly remained so throughout the period, some of the differences in income were small, so much so that in certain years the other relatively less-developed country was not Ecuador, but Colombia, as in 1975, or more evidently, Peru, which for two decades, from 1985 to 2005, recorded lower GDP per capita levels.

The CAF started operating in June 1970, soon after a technical mission had visited member countries eyeing business prospects. A total of 220 initiatives in fields as diverse as infrastructure, manufacturing, and services were identified. To bring these to fruition, the Corporation could operate in a wide range of forms: providing technical assistance, facilitating financial resources from capital markets, contributing with equity capital and technology, or, most frequently, offering

Table 7.1 Andean Group: economic performance (1970–2015)

GDP per/capita (Constant 2010 USD)						
	Bolivia	**Chile**	**Colombia**	**Ecuador**	**Peru**	**Venezuela**
1970	1.392	4.656	2.800	2.486	3.381	14.329
1975	1.659	3.913	3.287	3.392	3.887	14.369
1980	1.646	5.242	3.808	3.687	3.727	14.119
1985	1.343	4.726	3.806	3.672	3.303	11.809
1990	1.358	5.947	4.310	3.720	2.679	11.830
1995	1.504	8.051	4.912	3.847	3.140	12.545
2000	1.616	9.469	4.764	3.678	3.310	11.597
2005	1.720	11.249	5.312	4.286	3.831	12.237
2010	1.981	12.860	6.230	4.657	5.022	13.961
2015	2.392	14.893	7.461	5.352	5.937	13.709

Sources: World Bank (2019b).

credit, as well as grants, guarantees, and underwriting services to both public and private sectors.

In some basic respects, the CAF resembled other MDB and RDB, such as the WB, the IADB (established in 1959) and, in particular, the Central American Bank of Economic Integration (CABEI, established in 1960) and the European Investment Bank (EIB, established in 1958). First, the Corporation was a legal entity of international private law. Secondly, as Humphrey (2012: 63) notes, 'CAF followed the model of a corporation, owned by six shareholder governments who contributed the initial capital and were the final arbiters of its policies'. Thus, it was an international state owned bank controlled by its members—without dominant donor countries and the conditionalities derived from such dominance. Finally, the Corporation could use its equity capital and financial resources to lend at attractive terms for development and integration.

Similarities with the EIB's core objectives are thus striking (Clifton et al. 2018). As with its European counterpart, the CAF promoted the economic development of the AG with an eye to preventing imbalances among members, and to encouraging catch-up growth from the less-developed ones. Further, it intended to finance infrastructure development and productive national projects aimed at strengthening the economic integration of the region—harnessing market expansion and easing trade. Finally, the CAF had to facilitate financial intermediation and mobilize investment resources for integration purposes.

Yet the CAF was different and even unique in several aspects. To start with, its shareholding composition was comprised of only developing countries—five countries from 1969 to 1973 (Bolivia, Colombia, Chile, Ecuador, and Peru), temporarily six from 1973 to 1976 (with Venezuela joining in 1973) and five again in 1976 (after Chile dropped out).[2] These were developing countries and the very same ones expecting to borrow from the Corporation. Moreover, these shareholding countries exerted broadly equal control over the CAF (Humphrey 2012). In addition, the Corporation was endowed with the ability to build partnerships through the subscription of risk capital in multinational enterprises—an unusual competence for international entities of this type (Camacho 1973). Lastly, the CAF ought to observe the 'rational specialisation and the equitable distribution' of investments within the area (El-Agraa and Hojman 1988), whilst taking into account effective actions in favour of less-developed Bolivia and Ecuador.[3]

[2] At the time, the other RDB exhibiting this shareholder-borrower structure was the African Development Bank (AfDB), founded in 1964. This entity, however, when confronting difficult financial conditions during the late 1970s and early 1980s, took the controversial decision to accept non-regional members as shareholders, and in doing so compromised (in practice) its 'African character'; see Kraemer-Mbula (Chapter 3, this volume). As a result of this modification, both the US and Japan became important actors (with voice and vote) in its governing board.

[3] At the administrative level, the CAF distinguished itself for the expediency and the flexibility with which it handled its operations. This derived from the organizational autonomy given to the CAF's management to run its business. The CAF's board of directors met only twice a year, and

As Clifton et al. (2018) indicate, the CAF emerged in a second wave of RDB in the late 1960s, which distinguished it from those of the first wave: including the African Development Bank (AfDB), Asian Development Bank (ADB), and the Latin American IADB (see Chapter 1, this volume). The CAF's objectives did not include Continental development. More importantly, emulation of the IBRD, which served as template for the establishment of first-wave RDB, was limited in the Corporation's foundation. Not only did this mean that the CAF had a regionally defined mandate within which to build its operations that contributed towards integration, but that it escaped the governance structure and ethos of Bretton Woods institutions. This, in turn, meant that the CAF avoided being nudged by a small, influential, dominant group of wealthier industrialized countries which, acting as majoritarian shareholders in other RDB, proved to be less successful in attaining strengthened governance processes, that is, achieving increased transparency, representation, inclusiveness, accountability, and responsiveness to country and civil society (Gomez and Atun 2013).

Regarding the composition of the CAF's portfolio investments, the Corporation attempted to fulfil its mandate, following the integrationist nature of the regional agreement that was its *raison d'être*. Between 1970 and 1981, the operations targeted an ample spectrum of projects, including: industrial development, particularly of intermediate and capital goods, agricultural modernization emphasizing import substitution, scientific and technological research and cooperation, trade support, and the upgrading of transport, communications, and commercialization infrastructures, such as storing and packaging (Camacho 1973). Within such a varied range of options, the CAF's declared preferences focused on industrial ventures, and binational or multinational businesses.

In line with the above, the first loans the CAF advanced for project execution were destined to finance the construction of a network of warehouses for rice in Bolivia, and the development of a fishing complex for tropical tuna in Ecuador. The combined operations amounted to USD 1.8 million, representing forty per cent of total approved loans in 1971. Similarly, the following year it approved USD three million for the construction of a bridge in the state of Zulia (Venezuela) to facilitate road connections with Colombia. This single loan accounted for thirty per cent of total investments in project executions in 1972, or twenty-six per cent of all approved operations.

The financing provided by the CAF in these early years was exemplary in terms of the precision with which it, on the one hand, substantiated the Corporation's mandate to support integration amongst members, and on the other, reflected the privileged status accorded to the more backward economies within the Group. As

oversight was light. This, in turn, resulted from the above-mentioned structure of ownership. See Humphrey (2012) for a detailed review of the consequences of ownership variations upon management amongst MDB.

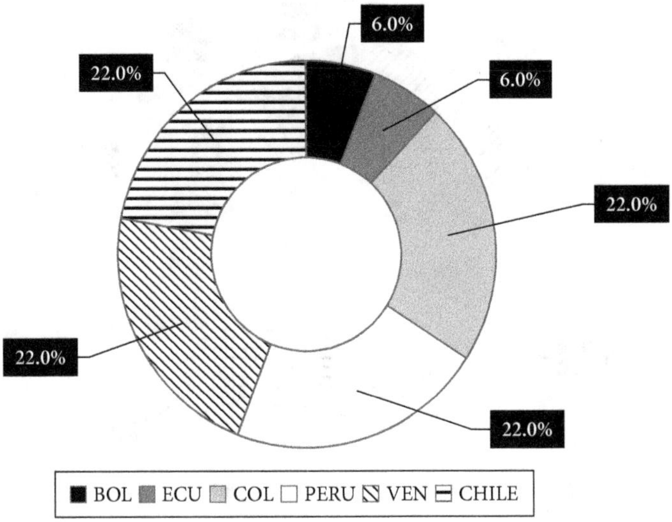

Figure 7.1 Shareholders' subscribed capital (December 1970) (% shares)
Source: CAF (1973).

intended in its constitutive charter, Bolivia and Ecuador became founding members and subscribed the same number and amount of A-Series shares as other founding countries (USD one million each). Regarding B-Series shares, however, Colombia, Peru, Chile and Venezuela subscribed nine times as many, so that of the total paid-in capital of the nascent Corporation, Bolivia and Ecuador, accounted for 6 per cent each, or USD 1.5 million, whilst each other shareholder held 22 per cent, or USD 4.5 million (see Figure 7.1).

Despite the asymmetries amongst shareholders in terms of the value of each other's contributions, voting powers were equal, meaning that Bolivia and Ecuador exerted the same powers as did the rest.[4] As Figure 7.2 shows, by December 1976, and prior to Chile's withdrawal, paid-in capital shares remained very similar to the situation in 1970. Slight differences between the less-developed members can be explained by Ecuador's due unpaid contribution, worth USD 0.8 million. Leaving this aside, Bolivia and Ecuador were by then expected to hold 10 per cent of all shares combined. That these small countries had their voices heard, and were being privileged by the CAF, is beyond dispute, as one contrasts the aforementioned capital contributions with the distribution of credit approvals by country over the same period of time. Figure 7.3 shows, that Bolivia received 28.6 per cent of the CAF's long-term loan approvals, that is, resources for the execution of projects; whilst Ecuador obtained 22 per cent. Combined, the

[4] The CAF's executive committee, which decided over the approval of active and passive credit operations, investments, and any other operation within the reach of the Corporation's mandate, was composed of six directors, one for each country, in representation of A- and B-Series shares.

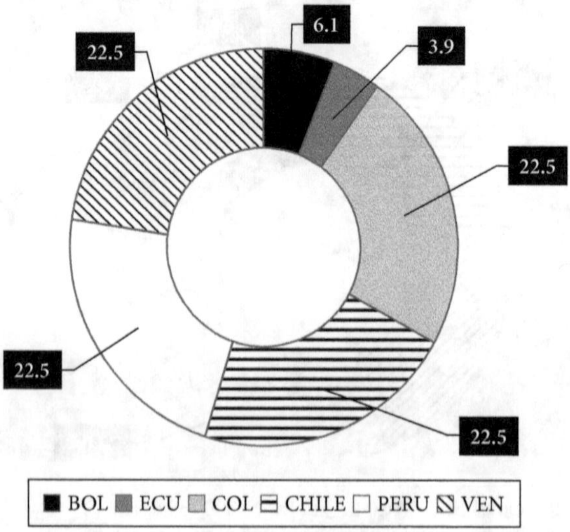

Figure 7.2 Paid-in capital (December 1976) (% shares)
Source: CAF (1976).

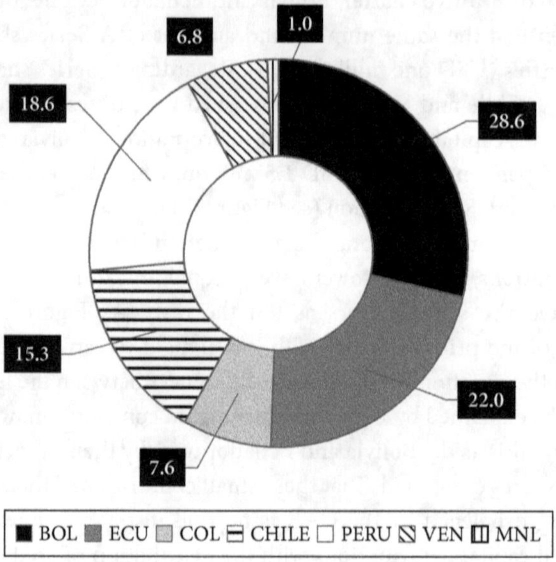

Figure 7.3 Credit distribution by country: long-term approvals (1971–6) (% shares)
Note: **Excludes SAFICO operations.**
Source: CAF (1976).

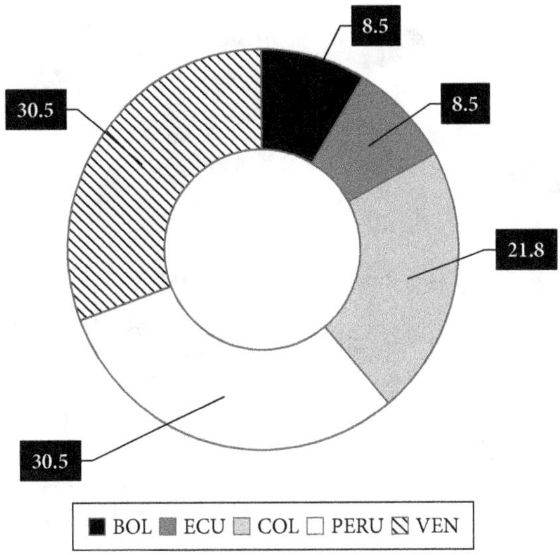

Figure 7.4 Paid-in capital (December 1981) (% shares)
Source: CAF (1981).

less-developed countries of the AG, participating as minority shareholders (see Figure 7.4), reaped more than half of all long-term resources. This amounted to almost five times their contributions. Colombia and Venezuela received the lowest shares, 7.6 per cent and 6.8 per cent, respectively, whilst Peru and Chile were closer to taking out what they put in.

On 12 August 1977, the CAF's directorate approved Chile's withdrawal, and decided to acquire its shares (paid and due). Chile's A-Series were purchased in equal parts by other country members—increasing the subscribed amount from USD 1 million to USD 1.2 million each. The buying of B-Series shares, which represented a larger financial effort (worth USD 52.5 million over five years), were paid in equal portions by Colombia, Peru, and Venezuela (28 per cent each), whereas Bolivia and Ecuador paid out the rest (8 per cent each). Preferential treatment to the latter countries also continued to reflect in the distribution of credit advanced by the Corporation, as can be seen from Figure 7.5. Ecuador was particularly favoured, obtaining 30 per cent of all loans committed for the execution of projects between 1977 and 1981.

Regarding lending terms, the CAF's long-term loans clearly dominated the portfolio between 1972 and 1981, with 72.5 per cent of all approved loans. Short-term credit, consisting mainly of trade financing, accounted for 25.3 per cent; whilst the remaining resources were channelled towards working capital, pre-investment studies, technical assistance, and share subscriptions. In 1973, a mechanism was created to finance trade between the AG countries for the purpose of strengthening the process of integration via the expansion and

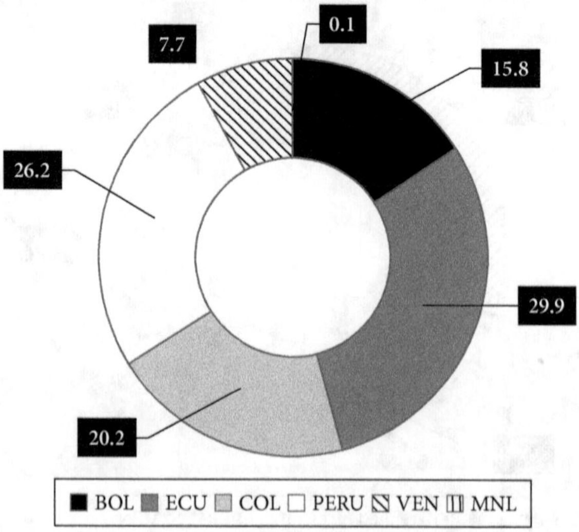

Figure 7.5 Credit distribution by country: long-term approvals (1977–81) (% shares)
Source: CAF (1981).

diversification of exports. The initiative, Sistema de Financiamiento del Comercio Andino (SAFICO), included the alignment of incentives for exporters, a system of export promotion, and a programme of joint actions for such promotion (CAF 1973). This line of business would take on greater importance in the near future, as will be seen below.

The CAF's own finances encountered formidable challenges during the 1970s and early 1980s. Contrary to initial expectations, fundraising from international institutions like the WB and the IADB, as well as from international capital markets, proved elusive. No evidence has been found in the Corporation's official 'Memories' or annual reports to suggest that the CAF preferred alternative sources of funding in order to avoid donor conditionality and equity control. As noted above, part of the thrust with which the CAF had been conceived contained political elements seeking greater economic autonomy and independence for the AG countries, which presumably were also intended in the financial sphere. Although it would be easy to exaggerate the importance of this sought-after independence in the business of the CAF, the fact is that at the time, the structural adjustment lending which came to dominate the Bank's policy advice was still in the making (Webb 2000).

Relative success at fundraising, instead, came from tapping bilateral aid agencies from industrialized countries, such as the US Agency for International Development (USAID) and the Canadian International Development Agency (CIDA). A more important role was played, however, by credit lines and loans with 'strings attached' from official export-credit agencies, such as the

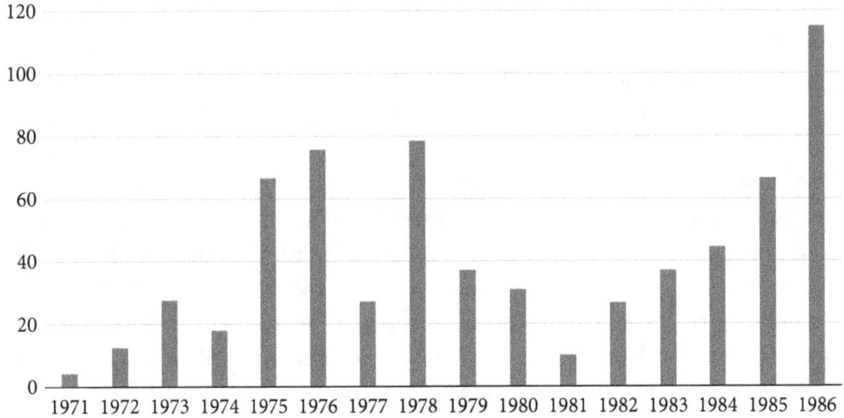

Figure 7.6 Total approved loans (1972–86) (in USD 1971 millions)
Source: CAF, *Annual Reports* (various years).

export-import banks of Japan and the US, the Banco Exterior de España, and the German National Development Bank (NDB), KFW (Kreditanstalt für Wiederaufbau). Equally important were loans obtained from international private banks: a syndicated operation for USD 50 million obtained in 1977, and a series of loans for USD 10 million advanced by the Bank of America. Although funding from these sources was substantial by the CAF standards, the Corporation inevitably had to delve deep into the pockets of its own members. According to Humphrey (2012: 67), by 1980, two-thirds of the USD 397 million raised originated from within the region, and only a third came from outside.

The CAF faced more than fundraising challenges by the late 1970s. Lending commitments had fallen more than 50 per cent in real terms from 1978 to 1979 and 1980, as approved loans plunged from USD 78 million to USD 37 million, and USD 31 million, respectively (Figure 7.6). The situation reached bottom when the Corporation approved only USD 10 million in 1981, which was less than it had committed to a decade earlier. Though recovery would ensue later on, by 1985 its total approved loans still did not match the levels of 1976. The problem was compounded by high-rate incidences of (medium- and long-term) loan withdrawals and unused balances. Between 1976 and 1980, the combination of these two averaged 37.4 per cent of the Corporation's approved loans. SAFICO's operations also started to stagnate in real terms by 1979, and had contracted by more than 25 per cent by 1982 for all member countries, with the exception of Bolivia (CAF 1982, 2000a). Diminishing values of approved operations and declining rates of disbursements led the Corporation almost to operational paralysis during the early 1980s (CAF 2000a).[5]

[5] See the review of the 1976–81 period by CAF's executive president, Julio Sanjinés (CAF 1982, 2000: n.p.).

Finally, the CAF also confronted tensions regarding the destination of its resources. Its mandate made support for industry a priority. Its activities remained formally oriented to serve the wider objectives set by the Cartagena Agreement, of which programming advanced industrialization was particularly significant. Directing loans to industrial enterprises was proving increasingly difficult. According to Julio Sanjinés, the CAF's executive president (1976–81), it was evident that a new orientation had to be defined for both the credit and the developmental policies of the Corporation (CAF 2000b). Scarcity of investment opportunities in industry forced a concentration of efforts and resources in fewer and bigger projects in other areas, such as a USD 38 million operation with the state-owned Colombian Petroleum Company, and another USD 20 million credit for the construction of an oil pipeline in Peru.

To summarize, during the late 1970s and early 1980s, the CAF underwent trying times. These difficulties were due to fundraising hardships, declining credit commitments, relatively higher rates of loan withdrawals and unused balances, as well as a widespread shortage of opportunities for investment in the sectors which the CAF's mandate dictated. Various factors explain the Corporation's problems. First, the emerging and irreversible structural pattern of deindustrialization that spread not only through the Andean countries but through most of Latin America since the mid-1970s. Due to currency over-valuation, import-substituting industrialization exhaustion, and 'Dutch disease', industrial output started to decline relative to other economic sectors, which meant that the CAF—following its mandate—was compelled to play against the market, financing projects and businesses in a sector whose returns exhibited de-escalating prospects. Second, shifts in the trade and industrial policies of governments from within the AG disaligned the Corporation's mission with the changing macroeconomic and development strategies of the countries implementing them. Third, the delayed schedules of the AG's trade liberalization and industrial programming—which according to Sanjinés, constituted the schemes from which 'all the projects that the Corporation served came from' (CAF 2000: n.p.)—undermined the fulfilment of the CAF's mandate. Fourth, Chile's withdrawal contributed further to the Corporation's problems. With the arrival of Pinochet to power, dissent over the treatment that the Group's Agreement provided to foreign direct investment led to Chile's departure from the Group in 1976, and from the CAF the following year. Finally, the interest rate hikes that occurred in industrialized market economies from 1979 tightened monetary policy and raised the federal fund rate, driving up the costs of capital for developing country financial institutions, such as the CAF, thus stemming the inflows of capital.

4. Transition years: crisis and recovery (1982–91)

Within the context of the Latin American Debt Crisis that erupted in 1982, and the 'Lost Decade' that followed, the CAF executive directors realized the agency had to alter its *modus operandi* if it were to survive. The Corporation's directorate approved a new operations policy in July 1983 by which it broadened the range of fields for the financing of projects. These included physical infrastructure integration, agrarian and industrial development, support for the industrial production of capital goods and for the conservation of renewable natural resources. Strictly speaking, these were not entirely new areas—bar the last one. What shifted was emphasis. From then on, the CAF could seek out projects which did not directly exhibit integration content, but that ultimately had the potential to foster closer integration. Concerning physical infrastructure, for instance, the CAF could select national level ventures, which formed part of networks with multinational scope. Similarly, in the cases of services and production in general, the Corporation could support projects that contributed to the development of the national economy, resulting in the strengthening of the capacity for integration in that particular good- or service-line. In short, the new operational policy provided the Corporation with the opportunity to invest in the economic development of individual member countries. In doing so, the new policy removed the shackles of integration that were said to have constrained the CAF's growth, conferring upon the Corporation greater autonomy and independence (CAF 2000b).

Relaxing the restrictions the CAF previously had on its allocation of resources and effectively opening the door to a regional world of opportunities for development investment, only tackled half of the problem. The other half were resources. With access to international capital markets still a relatively distant prospect, and lending by private banks from industrialized countries bounded after 1982, the options for external funding were few and far between. Co-financing arrangements with entities, such as the WB and the IADB, where the CAF acted as both the junior and the local partner, turned into a form of sustaining the Corporation's presence and activities through hard times. Schemes like these worked out particularly well, according to the newly appointed executive president, José Cárdenas (1981–6), in the modernization of small- and medium-sized enterprises and in agribusinesses. The CAF also continued cooperation agreements for technical assistance and pre-investment studies with international entities, such as the World Food Organisation and the International Fund for Agricultural Development. With official agencies including the US Fund for Commerce and Development, the CAF operated as financial administrator. These initiatives notwithstanding, the bulk of the effort to finance the CAF activities fell to the member state governments.

From 1982 to 1984, loans and obligations acquired by the CAF decreased from USD 112 million to USD 63.8.7 million (in nominal terms). Another key source of funding, short-term financial bonds, had also fallen. In real terms, bonds would only exceed their 1981 levels nearly a decade later. With contracting external resources, capital contributions from shareholders were called in. The AG national governments responded. Paid-in capital increased from USD 89 million to USD 145 million during the 1982–6 *lustrum*, and its authorized capital was raised to USD 1 billion, with USD 200 million in callable capital. As debt plunged and equity climbed, the Corporation's leverage ratio altered. The D/E ratio, which reached 1.96 in 1982, declined to 0.86 in 1986.

The 1982-4 years were a period of transition for the Corporation. First, the relatively low volume of the CAF's operations meant the impact of its activities on the Andean national economies was modest. Second, obliged by external constraints to rely on its own resources during trying times, the CAF looked inward and redefined its goals within the framework that the AG Agreement permitted. Albeit with a modified mandate, the Corporation still lacked the financial wherewithal to materialize the aspirations of the new course it had charted. Yet given the subsequent rapid growth that ensued, the 1982-4 period can be seen as a springboard towards better times.

And better times did arrive. To begin with, the CAF's lending commitments in real terms (constant 1982 USD) grew at an annual average rate of 40 per cent between 1986 and 1991—from USD 233 million to USD 970 million. Levels of both unused balances and loan withdrawals declined (Humphrey 2012) and the business being carried out was increasingly profitable. The rate of return-on-equity (RoE) nearly doubled, jumping from 3.5 per cent and 3.9 per cent in 1981-2 to an average of 6.9 per cent for 1986-91, with very small variations in year-to-year results. Finally, the overall impact of the Corporation's lending activities in the region started to show. All credit advanced by the CAF to members of the AG amounted to 0.52 per cent of the credit advanced by the entire financial sectors of these countries to their economies combined—which represented more than a fivefold rise from preceding years.

These improved figures resulted from several factors at play. As the Debt Crisis deepened, adjustments and structural reforms delineating a new economic model for Latin America started to be consolidated. Andean countries, at times because of a coercive policy transmission engineered from IFIs through loan conditionalities, and at others, thanks to the internal initiatives of reformist and/or recently redemocratized governments, implemented or accelerated broad development strategies, and macroeconomic policy frameworks that privileged the re-insertion of their countries into the world economy. The new model entailed freer markets, financial deregulation, trade liberalization, secure property rights and incentives to attract foreign investment, a larger role for the private sector, and a diminishing remit for the state in economic and financial affairs.

Though some of the tenets and practices pervading the individual members of the Group eventually filtered through the CAF, the Corporation's essentially unaltered ownership and governing structures—and probably its low profile—rendered it relatively immune to the type of coercive reforms that other RDB, such as the IADB underwent as the result of US-led shareholder activism (Babb 2018). Unlike the IADB, the CAF continued lending without policy-based conditionalities aimed at advancing the market-oriented restructurings, which Washington privileged as economic solutions for Latin America.

Further research notwithstanding, it is plausible to sustain that direct pressure upon the CAF by the US and/or IFIs to modify its credit policies remained largely absent. The CAF, however, had to align itself with the politics of the AG regarding integration, which in turn, affected its lending activities. Indeed, the politics of AG countries did shift in the 1980s and 1990s. From a strategy based on import substitution or closed regionalism (with governments coordinating economic policy and regional development plans) directing production towards the intra-regional market, towards open regionalism—that is, interdependence stemming from special, preferential agreements, and that arising from market signals produced by trade liberalization (ECLAC 1994; Reinert et al. 2009; Eder 2019). Concrete changes were evident at the national level. In Peru, for example, Belaunde's second presidential term (1980–5) came to pursue 'one of the region's most committed neoliberal reform strategies of the period' (Chwieroth 2010: 43); a transformation which was later continued and deepened by the equally pro-market administrations led by Fujimori (2000–10). In Venezuela, with varying degrees of tolerance by the affected populations, both the Perez and Caldera presidencies implemented 'neoliberal packages' from 1989 to 1999 (Levine and Crisp 1999: 417). Lastly, in Colombia, market-oriented reforms were initiated by the Barco (1986–90) and Gaviria (1990–4) administrations, deepened under Pastrana's presidency (1994–8), as the country negotiated with the IMF, and continued with Uribe's two consecutive presidential terms (2002–10) (Gray 2014).

The Quito Protocol signed in May 1987 brought substantial modifications to the founding agreement of the AG, signalling a new direction. Recognizing the problems and the remaining options for the integration process, the sectoral programming of industrialization was substituted with one of industrial complementation, led by private entrepreneurship so as to infuse this policy with competitive efficiency (CAF 1991). The Quito Protocol also procured a more favourable legal environment for foreign investors altering the AG's common legal regime in place since 1969. Following summits in Cartagena and the Galapagos in 1989, the CAF's directives broadened further its fields of action, including productivity-enhancement schemes, support for biotechnology, assistance to Andean multinational corporations, the development of small- and medium-sized enterprises, and, more generally, investment promotion. The CAF was also expected to contribute to the improvement of the Group's economic and financial articulation with the world, and in particular, with Latin America. To comply with these objectives, the Corporation's paid-in capital was increased from USD 200 million in 1987 to USD 413 million in 1991.

As the CAF attempted to meet the requirements of the new agreements and targets, on the one hand, it accommodated its activities to a still adverse economic

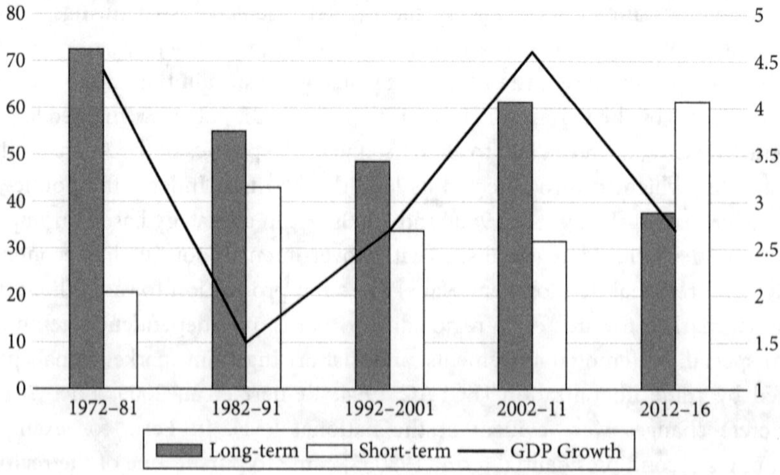

Figure 7.7 AG's GDP average annual growth and loan distribution by terms (1971-2016) (% shares)

Source: CAF, *Annual Reports* (various years; 1972 includes 1971).

climate, on the other, noticeable changes occurred in its operations. One of these changes revealed an essential type of investment, contingent on the economic performance of country shareholders. Following Mazzucato and Pena's (2016) argument about NDB acting to correct market failure, and their classification of investment types and roles for these institutions, the CAF played an identifiable countercyclical role in times of economic slowdown, as seen in Figure 7.7. In the decades where the rate of GDP growth for the AG had been relatively high, such as the 1972-81 and the 2002-11 periods—4.4 per cent and 4.6 per cent, respectively—the share of its long-term loans exhibited correspondingly high shares of total loans—72.5 per cent and 61.2 per cent—whereas its short-term lending was kept at relatively low levels—21.7 per cent and 31.6 per cent. Responsively, as GDP growth rates slackened, the distribution of the CAF's total approved loans shifted, short-term loans doubling to 43 per cent during 1982-91 (the 'Lost Decade'), and doubling again to 61.4 per cent in the 2012-16 period (the Great Recession). The CAF supplied countercyclical finance in the form of short-term credit, mainly trade finance, in times of hardship. Long-term financing for project execution yielded to more pressing needs focused upon exports and imports. To the extent to which the CAF was central in providing countercyclical finance at times of badly needed liquidity, the Corporation facilitated a type of investment quasi-intrinsic to RDB.

For similar reasons—that is, the problems commercial banks encountered obtaining confirmations for lines of credit intended for imports of inputs, spare parts, equipment, and machinery—the CAF created the Mechanism of Confirmation and Financing of Credit Lines and Imports (MECOFIN) in 1987.

The growth in this type of credit was steep, rising from USD 4.4 million in 1987 to USD 221.3 million by 1991. Supply factors also help to explain the surge, of which particular importance was the build-up of an intermediary network of private commercial banks with which the CAF worked together to advance resources. Agreements with more than 160 financial institutions across the Andean region and beyond led to the handing of resources worth more than USD 1 billion by 1991.

The allocation of loans by economic sector was subject to significant changes. In line with the directives set in the Quito Protocol and the Galapagos Summit, emphasis started to shift away from industrial firms (see Figure 7.8). This activity, which had received resources representing 86 per cent of all loans for the execution of projects in the previous decade, saw its share cut by half in the 1982-91 period. Such change amounted to a tectonic movement in the history of the CAF and the AG, for regional industrial integration had been the main initiative under-girding the formation of the Group, and the CAF had been created to finance it. Instead, long-term lending towards physical infrastructure (primarily on transport and communications) reached 25 per cent, and that for mining, 13 per cent. Agricultural ventures grew rapidly during 1982-6 as well, rising to 21 per cent of the total, but afterwards declining to 2 per cent in 1987-91. Other investments, including tourist projects, emerged as increasingly important recipients of funds, taking up to 6.5 per cent of all long-term allocations.

On the other side of the balance sheet, paid-in capital from shareholders continued to finance the bulk of operations, with 41 per cent of all resources (see Figure 7.8). The heavy lifting with regard to external financing in this period (1987-91), however, was carried out once again by developed countries exporting

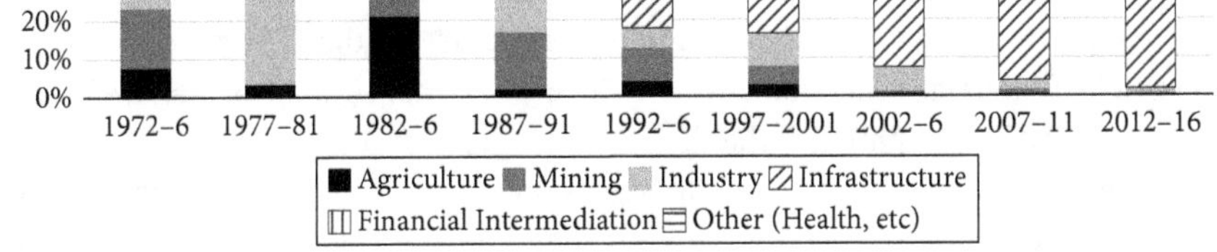

Figure 7.8 Long-term loans distribution by economic sector (1971-2016) (% shares)

Notes: For the years 1971-2008, the histograms represent long-terms loans approved for project execution—excluding SAFICO and MECOFIN operations. For 2009-16 data from total portfolio. Observations derived from annual reports do not permit the complete construction of any one of the two series.

Source: CAF, *Annual Reports* (various years; 1972 includes 1971).

credit, while official agencies and private international banks also provided credit, though to a lesser extent. Loans and obligations with these entities accounted for another 22.2 per cent. Lines of credit by the EX-IM Banks of Japan (Nihon Yushutsunyū Ginkō) and the US added up to more than USD 50 million in 1989 and 1990. Unsurprisingly, these funds came with strings attached. These resources were to be used to purchase goods and services from creditor countries, including machinery and equipment for a big oil project in Peru. Similar operations were conducted with Banco do Brasil, KFW from Germany, and the French Credit Lyonnais amongst others, reaching in total nearly USD 150 million, which in 1990 accounted for more than 50 per cent of the CAF's total liabilities. However, some of the funds obtained through this mechanism were untied, specifically those originating in the German Investment and Development Corporation (Deutsche Investitions und Entwicklungsgesellschaft (DEG)), the IADB, and the Netherlands Development Finance Company (Nederlandse Financierings-Maatschappij voor Ontwikkelingslanden N.V (FMO)).

In general, bonds played a smaller role than in previous years. Compared to the 1982–6 period, the relative contribution of the CAF debt issued nearly halved, from 20.8 per cent to 11.1 per cent. Of serious importance for the future, however, was a smaller transaction (USD 15 million) celebrated in the 'samurai' market in 1991. The CAF's first long-term bond placement in Japan signified entry into global capital markets. This represented a major achievement for a financial institution owned and managed by five sovereign developing countries for which, individually, access to such markets in equivalent terms remained a distant prospect. This successful emission was a watershed, leading the way towards an unprecedented source of reliable and relatively inexpensive capital for years to come. Until 1987, all of the CAF's bonds were periodically subscribed by the AG member state central banks (CAF 1991: 53).

Notwithstanding the diversification of the Corporation's financing resources, its leverage did not change significantly in these years. The D/E ratio rose only modestly, from 1 in 1987 to 1.37 in 1991. Higher ratios had been attained earlier, and much greater ratios would be achieved later. Both rising net income and stronger reserves build-up pushed the equity coefficients upwards.

As seen in Figure 7.9, the fundamental structure of the CAF's shareholding persisted. Bolivia and Ecuador, which since the establishment of the CAF had been treated preferentially thanks to their less-developed country status, remained so, contributing nearly a fourth of the share funded by Colombia, Peru, and Venezuela—the former 7.7 per cent each and the latter 27.1 per cent each. However, noticeable changes also occurred. As mentioned above, Mexico's entry represented the first non-Andean country to join the CAF, with 2.9 per cent of the full paid-in capital (C-series share); whilst a total of nineteen private banks that subscribed USD 950.000 accounted for a modest 0.2 per cent of all contributions. Unlike Mexico, the private banks obtained voting-power representation at

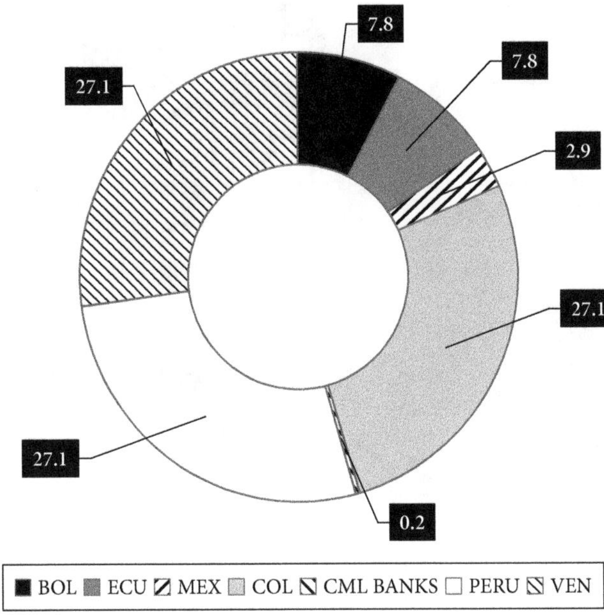

Figure 7.9 Paid-in capital (December 1991) (% shares)
Source: CAF (1991).

the governing board. Opening up the ownership structure of the CAF beyond the founding members of the AG was a major decision, with long-lasting effects, as will be seen below.

The allocation of credit by country during the 1982–91 period was led, again, by Ecuador, which obtaining 27 per cent of all long-term loans received nearly four times as much as its capital contributions (see Figure 7.10). Peru came a close second, with 26 per cent. This is interesting because Peru had not been singled out as a 'less-developed country' within the AG, yet as Table 7.1 shows, by 1985 it had fallen behind Ecuador in GDP per capita. Bolivia, which was llocated 18.4 per cent of long-term loans, received more than double the resources it committed. Colombia and Venezuela continued to be net contributors (see Figure 7.10).

To summarize this section, the 1987–91 period was one of recovery, growth, and change for the CAF. Its lending commitments grew rapidly at a time of macroeconomic challenges and structural reforms. The Corporation's loan portfolio saw a relative reduction in long-term lending for industrial development and the growth of short-term operations for regional trade. Further, the less-developed national economies of the AG continued to enjoy preferential treatment in long-term credit allocation. Lastly, increases in the collection of funds continued to rely to a large extent on past sources—that is, internal capital, export credit, investment banks, and official agencies from developed countries.

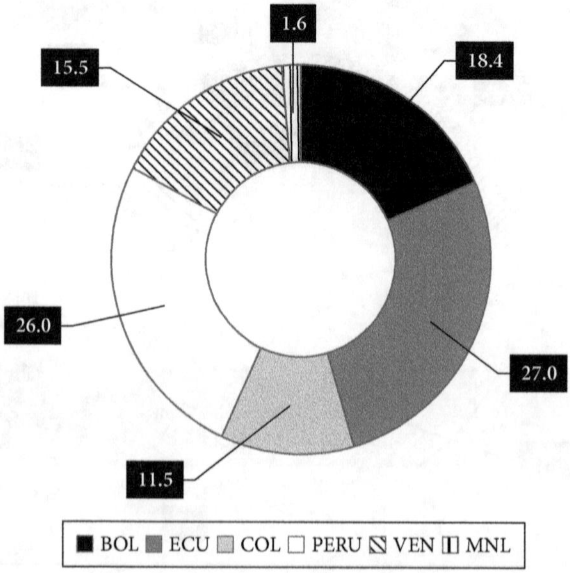

Figure 7.10 Credit distribution by country: long-term approvals (1982–91) (% shares)
Source: CAF, *Annual Reports* (various years).

5. Consolidation and expansion: from regional to Continental (1992–2016)

The CAF transformed from a modest RDB financing sluggish industrial integration and trade amongst the AG into Latin America's main development bank. From 1992 onwards, the Corporation consolidated on at least four fronts, which have stamped upon it a set of defining characteristics. First, the CAF went global, expanding membership from its five founding members plus Mexico (which had joined in 1990 as an associated member), and Chile (which returned in 1992 as an associated member) to seventeen—advancing increasingly significant volumes of loans to the newer non-founding shareholding countries. Second, the CAF prioritized physical infrastructure development over support for industrial manufacturing. Third, though to a lesser extent than in previous periods, the Corporation continued to give preferential treatment to Bolivia and Ecuador. Finally, the CAF gained permanent access to long-term financing in international capital markets.

The possibility of enlarging the number of shareholding countries was explored in the early 1990s, when the CAF directorate decided to deepen relations with Latin America in an attempt to procure further Continental unity and cooperation in economic and financial affairs. The list of new entries started with Trinidad and Tobago (1992), followed by Brazil (1995), Panama and Paraguay (1997), Jamaica

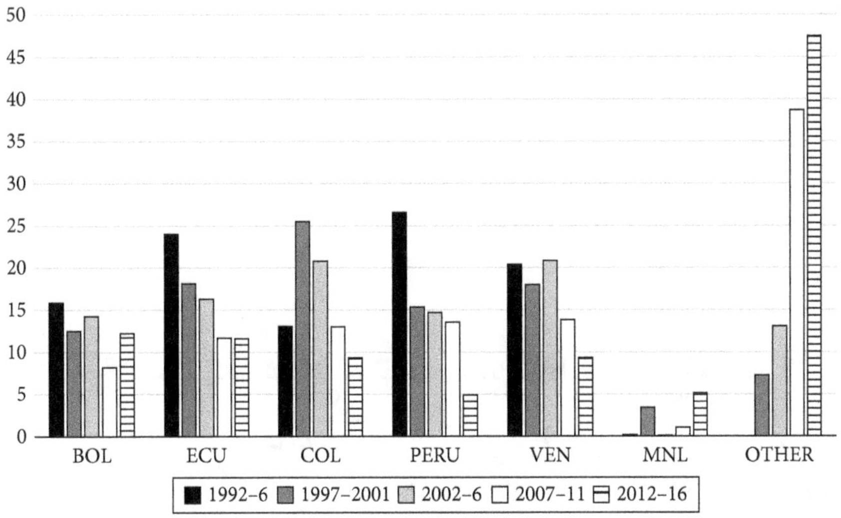

Figure 7.11 Credit distribution by country: long-term approvals (1992-2016) (% shares)

Source: CAF (1993, 1995, and 1996; data are from total portfolio).

(1999), Argentina and Uruguay (2001), Costa Rica and Spain (2002), the Dominican Republic (2004), Portugal (2009), and, finally, Barbados (2015).

The CAF's founding members have received a declining relative share of long-term loans during the last ten to fifteen years (Figure 7.11). Bolivia and Ecuador—whose privileged status as the lesser-developed countries in the AG had ensured larger than average allocations in the early years of the Corporation—have been relative 'losers' with the enlargement process. From obtaining more than half of the CAF's credit during the 1972–81 decade, Bolivia and Ecuador received 35 per cent of loans in the 1992-2001 period, and 23 per cent from 2001 to 2016. Ecuador has obtained larger allocations than Bolivia throughout. Colombia's and Peru's shares also fell, from 14 per cent and 21 per cent in the 1990s, to an average of 11 per cent from 2002 to 2016. Venezuela's share of long-term loans also fell, though it did with a lag—starting to decline in the 2007–11 interval. The share of the new country shareholders has correspondingly jumped from an average of 7 per cent during the 1990s to 47.5 per cent in 2012–16; reaching in certain years, such as 2013 and 2014, more than 50 per cent of all lending commitments, and in 2016 nearly two-thirds of the total. Of the non-founding country shareholders, Brazil obtained the largest share of all approved loans over the last decade (16 per cent), followed by Argentina (8 per cent), Uruguay (4.5 per cent), Panama (2.2 per cent), and Mexico (1.3 per cent).

Despite the relative decline in their share of allocations, Bolivia and Ecuador, as late of 2016, continued to figure as net the CAF recipients. As Figure 7.12

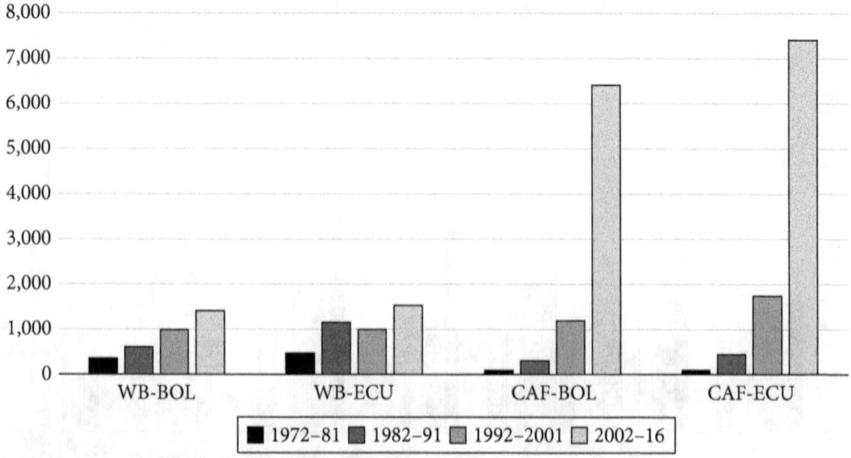

Figure 7.12 World Bank and CAF lending: Bolivia and Ecuador (1972-2016) (in USD millions)

Sources: CAF, *Annual Reports* (various years) and World Bank (2019a).

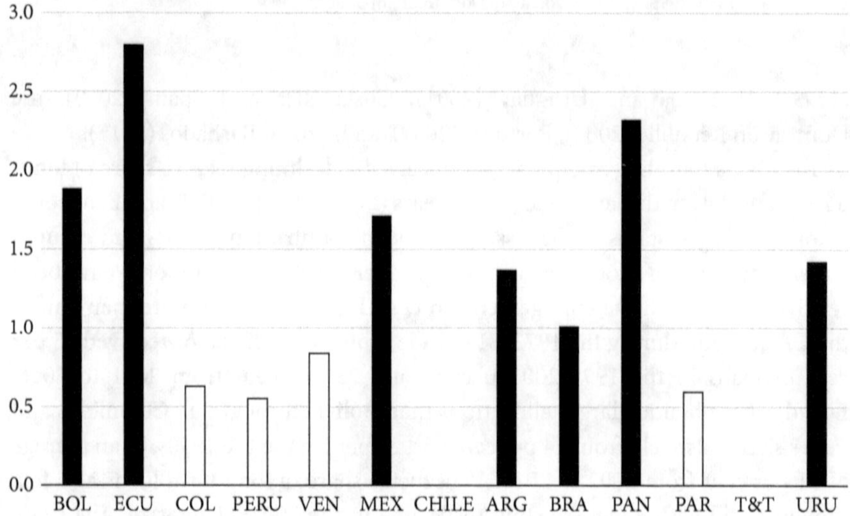

Figure 7.13 Paid-in-capital-to-portfolio ratio (2016)

Source: CAF, *Annual Reports* (various years).

shows, and as captured by the paid-in-capital-to-portfolio ratio, Ecuador was the most favoured amongst all of the CAF's shareholder countries, obtaining 2.8 times the resources it contributed to the Corporation. Bolivia ranked in third place, only behind Panama, with a ratio of 1.9. As net contributors, the founding members of Colombia, Peru, and Venezuela were the only countries exhibiting ratios below 1—along with Paraguay (see Figure 7.13).

The CAF reformed its corporate governance in the 2000s to accommodate its chosen role as Latin America's development bank. Currently, eleven countries represent the A-Series shareholders of the Corporation in the directorate, each entitled to one representative. Founding members, which currently are also B-Series shareholders each elect a second representative. Private banks, which are only B-Class shareholders, are collectively represented by one director. Other countries, in their role as C-Series shareholders, are represented by four directors. The CAF's maintenance throughout its history of equal voting representation regardless of shareholding participation—that is, one director: one vote—means that its founding members no longer hold a majority of votes. Whether or not the preferential treatment of Bolivia and Ecuador—through the fifty years of the CAF's operations, and as demonstrated in this chapter—has been a matter of solid institutional design or simple default, must be the subject of further research.

Focus on the relative allocations to Bolivia and Ecuador may obscure assessments revealing the sheer relevance, in absolute terms, of the Corporation's development finance in recent years. During the last twenty-five years, the CAF's lending approvals to these two less-developed countries have dwarfed those extended by the WB. From 1992 to 2016, they received a total of USD 16.7 billion from the CAF, compared to USD 4.9 billion from the WB. That the CAF's long-term lending to these two countries outstripped the loans advanced by the WB during the 1990s is very interesting, because both these countries implemented neoliberal policies and fiscal austerity at the behest of IFIs, such as the WB. Thus, that at the height of the neoliberal era, Bolivia and Ecuador obtained development finance from the CAF worth far more than that offered by the WB, and yet the governments of these two countries chose to maintain their borrowing from the latter should lead to a serious re-examination of the motivations held by national governments to pursue business with IFIs, and the concomitant conditionalities imposed in terms of structural reforms. Clearly, there were alternatives to WB loans with conditionalities which—as in the cases of Bolivia and Ecuador—were chosen. The CAF lending represented, during the neoliberal 1990s, an important conditionality-free source of financing for both these countries.

Regarding the CAF's pattern of investments, the changes have been profound. During the 1990s, and under Enrique Garcia's long presidency (1991-2016), the CAF redirected the bulk of resources to long-term loans (Figure 7.7). These types of loans increased gradually from representing 48 per cent of all loans in 1992-2001 to 61.2 per cent in 2002-11. In line with the Corporation's focus on the development of the region's infrastructure, in particular, of roads, electricity, and natural gas, as well as telecommunications and fluvial integration, the proportion of loans flowing to industrial ventures declined drastically from nearly 50 per cent in 1987-91 to 5 per cent in 1992-6, and to 1.4 per cent in 2012-16. Conversely, the share of resources directed to infrastructure projects rose dramatically from

22 per cent in 1987-91 to 49 per cent in 1992-2001, to its current heights of more than 60 per cent. As investments in infrastructure surged, those in sectors receiving already relatively small shares in the early 1990s have practically disappeared, as has been the case with agriculture and mining ventures. 'Other' loans advanced to commercial and development banking, health, as well as to community projects, tourism and public administration reform, have been allocated growing shares, accounting for approximately 25 per cent of all long-term loans in the last decade. As evidenced by the rise in this line of lending, the CAF has expanded the scope of its lending in private businesses further than in infrastructure development and economic/financial integration, to include environmental and social protection, capital-market development, and institutional building in both private and public spheres.

The most important aspect in the development of the CAF during the last two and a half decades—and the one under-girding its expanding geographical reach and increasing financial weight in the league of MDB and RDB—has been its successful positioning in international capital markets. As stated by Garcia himself: 'it was a must to have investment grade rating' (Humphrey 2012: 74). This occurred in 1993, when the CAF obtained the prized status (Baa3/BBB) from the three internationally renowned credit rating agencies: Standard & Poor's, Moody's Investor Service, and IBCA (now Fitch Ratings). Since 1993, the Corporation has maintained and improved its ratings on thirteen occasions, making it the issuer with the highest (safest) risk marks in Latin America (Figure 7.14).

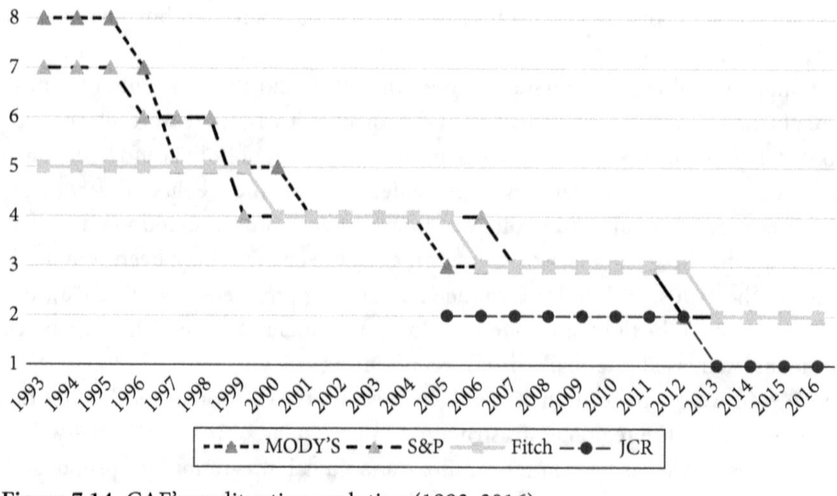

Figure 7.14 CAF's credit rating evolution (1993-2016)

Note: 1 = Aa2/AA, 2 = Aa3/AA–, 3 = A1/A+, 4 = A2/A, 5 = A3/A–, 6 = Baa1/BBB+, 7 = Baa2/BBB, 8 = Baa3/BBB.

Source: CAF, *Annual Report* (various years; 1998, 2010, 2016).

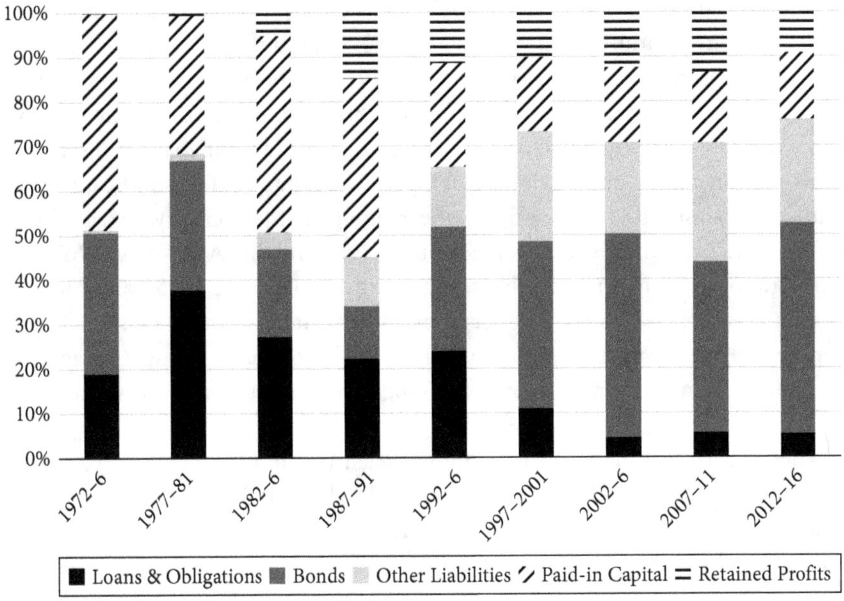

Figure 7.15 Evolution of funding sources (1992–2016) (% shares)
Source: CAF, *Annual Reports* (various years).

Achieving investment-grade status has brought the CAF handsome rewards, transforming its financial outlook and permitting it to grow solidly. From 1993 onwards, the CAF started issuing medium- and long-term bonds and commercial papers, placing them successfully in Asian, European, and North American capital markets. The shift in the Corporation's financing conditions is demonstrated clearly in Figure 7.15, as the share of paid-in capital, which had been historically the most important source of funding, yielded to bonds, which have since the mid-1990s accounted for about 40 to 45 per cent of all resources. Similarly, loans and obligations, which accounted for another significant share of financing—around 25 per cent in the 1980s—have diminished to an average of 5 per cent since 2002. Not only has this changing composition meant better financing conditions for the CAF—that is, relatively more inexpensive terms—but it has also obviously meant they have been able to tap funding from extra-regional sources. According to the CAF, by the early 2000s more than 90 per cent of its funding sources lay beyond the AG (CAF 2001).

Access to international capital markets allowed it to increase significantly its lending activities. Approved loans climbed from USD 2.1 billion in 1992 to USD 12.4 billion in 2016. This expansion has turned the CAF into Latin America's top development bank (in terms of development-finance lending), ahead of both the WB and the IADB (Gallagher and Myers 2015). Accordingly, the sustainable debt-led growth maintained by the CAF in the last two decades has mirrored its financial indicators.

The Corporation's leverage increased considerably as its D/E ratio moved upwards from around 1 to 1.2 in the early 1990s to around 4 in the 2000s, and 5 in the 2012–16 period. The risk-bearing-capital (RBC) ratio also followed an upward pattern with similar timings, practically doubling from 1.1–1.3 to 2.5–2.7, and more recently reaching nearly a 3:1 relation in its outstanding loans and the sum of its paid-in capital and retained earnings. The evolution of this indicator is no outlier amongst MDB operating in the region; on the contrary, according to Prada (2012), the CAF has converged with the WB and the IADB. As for RoE, the Corporation exhibited respectable results in the 1990s and early 2000s, fluctuating between approximately 6 per cent and 8 per cent, peaking at close to 10 per cent in 2007, just before the unfolding of the international financial crisis and the Great Recession, when it consequently plunging to historically low levels at below 2 per cent.

The recent Continental geographic outreach of the CAF combined with its large investments geared to development render difficult the Corporation's classification as an RDB. The CAF is today arriving at a role that entities such as the AfDB, the IADB, and the ADB targeted more than half a century ago. Further, the entry of Brazil as an A-class shareholder in 1995 signals the CAF's awareness and embracing of multi-polarity. The permanence of Venezuela despite its withdrawal from the AG in 2011 also demonstrates the CAF's multi-polarity. And yet, the fact that Chavez's Venezuela promoted the creation of a developmental bank for South America (Bansur),[6] as well as a parallel government-managed trade scheme—the Bolivarian Alternative for Latin America and the Caribbean (ALBA)—which included Bolivia and Ecuador amongst others, also indicate that the CAF and the AG were competitors and key actors in this multi-polarity.

In sum, the CAF's transformation over the last twenty-five years has been remarkable: from a modest RDB financing the AG to Latin America's main development bank. The CAF has progressed from advancing Sub-regional late-industrialization and trade to supporting Continental infrastructure projects, public administration reform, capital market promotion, and social and environmental protection, as well as trade. At the core of this process lay the Corporation's strategy, pursued since the early 1990s, of tapping resources from international capital markets. Under the watchful discipline exercised by the credit rating agencies from industrialized countries, the CAF has placed billions of US dollars in medium- and long-term bonds, allowing it to attain leverage ratios (previously unheard of for the Corporation), in a financially sound and sustainable manner (see Figure 7.16). Thanks to this strategy, the CAF entered the twenty-first century as a competitive RDB at the Continental level in a multi-polarity context.

[6] Chavez called for the liquidation of CAF and the abandonment of the IABD, yet none of his initiatives found an echo amongst Union of South American Nations (UNASUR) members (Giacalone 2013: 141–3).

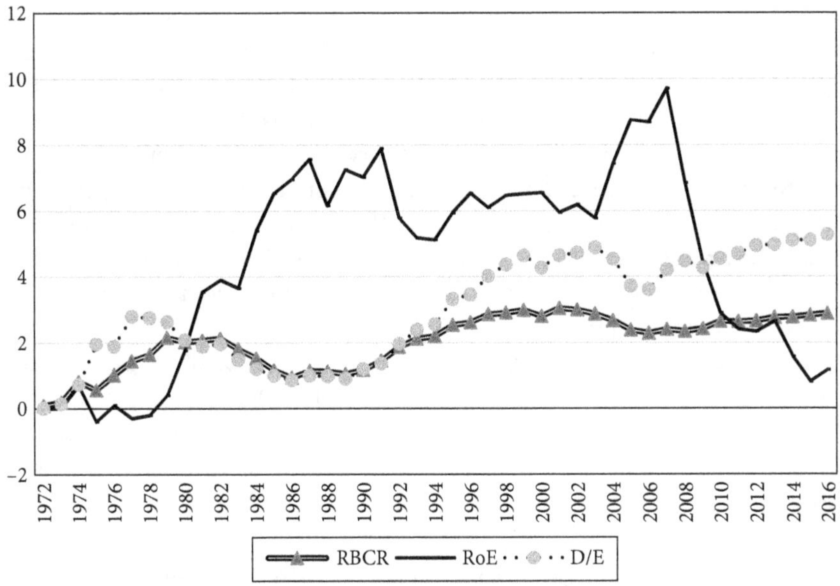

Figure 7.16 Financial indicators (1972–2016) (RBC, RoE, and D/E ratios)
Source: CAF, *Annual Reports* (various years).

6. Conclusions

In taking a long-run perspective of the CAF from its conception in the late 1960s to the present, this chapter offers a new approach to Latin America's (financially) most important RDB today, and also one of the world's most distinctive. On a global scale, the CAF stood out for decades as an RDB whose capital structure featured developing countries only, meaning it operated without donor-industrialized, first-world national governments dominating its lending policies, or attaching policy-based conditionalities to its loans. Though in terms of its core objectives—namely, promoting the economic integration of the members of the AG and guaranteeing their development sustainably—the CAF has resembled other RDB, such as the EIB and CARIBEI, the above-mentioned shareholding structure rendered it unique in the world until the recent foundation of the AIIB in 2014.

This chapter also develops a novel periodization when tracing and characterizing the historical evolution of the CAF. This is rooted in its pattern of loan allocations and the changing sources of its funding. Three distinctive phases have been identified. The phase of the early years of the 1970s details how the CAF's lending portfolio closely followed its mandate—first by prioritizing developmental loans for Bolivia and Ecuador; and, second, by supporting projects with clear integrationist content with a bias towards industrial investment. This period is followed by a long and challenging transition (1981–92) in the aftermath of the Debt Crisis, in which the CAF experienced a worrisome decline in the volume of operations as a result of difficulties finding external financing, on the one hand, and problems identifying investable projects fitting its mandate, on the other. A relaxation of the mandate's constraints opened a new range of opportunities for investment, which in tandem with an alleviation on the funding side, permitted the CAF to survive and to rebalance its portfolio towards non-industrial investments. During these years of transition, the CAF's share of short-term loans directed at financing trade operations for the first time exceeded its lending to long-term productive projects.

The last phase, examining the consolidation and expansion of the CAF, focuses on the transformation of this RBD into Latin America's main development bank. The CAF's Continental ascendancy is described as encompassing three core features. The first was permanent access to long-term funding via the tapping of resources in international capital markets after attaining investment-grade status in 1993. The second was the geographical expansion of the CAF, as it grew from six to seventeen members during the 1992–2016 period. The third core feature was the growth and consolidation of its investment portfolio in physical infrastructure projects, accompanied—albeit to a lesser degree—by lending targeted at supporting public administration reform, capital market promotion, and social protection.

Acknowledgements

The author acknowledges financial support for this project from COLCIENCIAS and the University of los Andes where he was a postdoctoral research fellow at the Department of Political Science. Excellent research assistance was provided by Gustavo Adolfo Rivero. The author also wishes to thank the editors and three anonymous referees, as well as colleagues at the Economics, International Trade and Social Policy Seminar led by Professor Jaime Tenjo at Universidad Jorge Tadeo Lozano for helpful comments and suggestions. Finally; thanks to Rebeca Vidal, Principal Executive at the Financial & Productive Development Department, and Nayive Armas, Executive at CAF's Information Services.

References

Abel, C. and Palacios, M. (1991). 'Colombia since 1958'. In Leslie Bethell (ed.), *The Cambridge History of Latin America*. Cambridge: Cambridge University Press, pp. 629–86.

Adelman, Jeremy. (2010). 'International finance and political legitimacy: a Latin American view of the Global Shock'. In Niall Ferguson, Charles S. Maier, Erez

Manela, and Daniel J. Sargent (eds.), *The Shock of the Global: The 1970s in Perspective*. London: Harvard University Press, ch. 6.

Babb, Sarah. (2018). 'The Inter-American Development Bank and the Washington Consensus'. Paper delivered at the World Economic History Congress, Cambridge, MA.

CAF (Andean Development Corporation) (1973). *Convenio constitutivo de la Corporación Andina de Fomento*. Caracas: Editorial La Corporación.

CAF (1982). *Memoria y Estados Financieros*. Caracas: Editorial La Corporación.

CAF (Andean Development Corporation) (1990). *Informe anual Corporación Andina de Fomento*. Caracas: Editorial Arte.

CAF (Andean Development Corporation) (1991). *Annual Report*. Caracas: Editorial Arte.

CAF (Andean Development Corporation) (1993). *Informe anual Corporación Andina de Fomento*. Caracas: Editorial Arte.

CAF (Andean Development Corporation) (1994). *Informe anual Corporación Andina de Fomento*. Caracas: Editorial Arte.

CAF (Andean Development Corporation) (1995). *Informe anual Corporación Andina de Fomento*. Caracas: Editorial Arte.

CAF (Andean Development Corporation) (1996). *Informe anual Corporación Andina de Fomento*. Caracas: Editorial Arte.

CAF (Andean Development Corporation) (1997). *Informe anual Corporación Andina de Fomento*. Caracas: Editorial Arte.

CAF (Andean Development Corporation) (1999). *Informe anual Corporación Andina de Fomento*. Caracas: Editorial Arte.

CAF (Andean Development Corporation) (2000a). *Informe anual Corporación Andina de Fomento*. Caracas: Editorial Arte.

CAF (Andean Development Corporation) (2000b). *La historia en el tiempo. Corporación Andina de Fomento 30 aniversario*. Bogotá: Villegas Editores.

CAF (Andean Development Corporation) (2001). *Informe anual Corporación Andina de Fomento*. Caracas: Editorial Arte.

CAF (Andean Development Corporation) (2003). *Informe anual Corporación Andina de Fomento*. Caracas: Editorial Arte.

CAF (Andean Development Corporation) (2004). *Informe anual Corporación Andina de Fomento*. Caracas: Editorial Arte.

CAF (Andean Development Corporation) (2005). *Informe anual Corporación Andina de Fomento*. Caracas: Editorial Arte.

CAF (Andean Development Corporation) (2006). *Informe anual Corporación Andina de Fomento*. Caracas: Editorial Arte.

CAF (Andean Development Corporation) (2008). *Informe anual Corporación Andina de Fomento*. Caracas: Editorial Arte.

CAF (Andean Development Corporation) (2019). *Informe Anual*. Caracas: CAF.

Cai, K. (2010). *The Politics of Economic Regionalism: Explaining Regional Economic Integration in East Asia*. London: Palgrave Macmillan.

Camacho, E. (1973). 'El papel de la Corporación Andina de Fomento en el proceso de integración subregional'. In Carlos Amaya (ed.), *Pacto Andino. Su historia, su desarrollo, su futuro*. Bogota: Gloca.

Chwieroth, J. (2010). 'Shrinking the state: neoliberal economists and social spending in Latin America'. In Rawi Abdelal, Mark Blyth, and Craig Parsons (eds.), *Constructing the International Economy*. New York: Cornell University Press, pp. 23–47.

Clifton, J., Díaz-Fuentes, D., and Gómez, A.L. (2018). 'The European Investment Bank: development, integration, investment?', *Journal of Common Market Studies*, 56(4): 733–50.

ECLAC (Economic Commission for Latin America) (1994). *Open Regionalism in Latin America and the Caribbean: Economic Integration as a Contribution to Changing Production Patterns with Social Equity*. Santiago: ECLAC.

Eder, J. (2019). ′Integración regioinal y políticas de industrialización en América Latina: la historia de un amor conflictivo′, *Revista de estudios sociales*, 68: 38–50.

Eichengreen, B. (2010). *The European Economy since 1945*. Princeton: Princeton University Press.

El-Agraa, A.M. and Hojman, D.E. (1988). 'The Andean pact'. In A.M. El-Agraa (ed.), *International Economic Integration*. London:. Palgrave Macmillan.

Ewell, J. (1992). 'Venezuela since 1930'. In Leslie Bethell (ed.), *The Cambridge History of Latin America*, Volume 8. Cambridge: Cambridge University Press, pp. 727–90.

Fajardo, L.E. (2003). 'From the alliance for progress to the Plan Colombia: a retrospective look at US Aid to Colombia'. LSE Crisis State Programme Working Paper Series No. 28.

Ffrench-Davis, R., Muñoz, O., and Palma, J.G. (1998). 'The Latin American economies, 1950–1990'. In L. Bethell (ed.), *Latin America: Economy and Society since 1930*. Cambridge: Cambridge University Press.

Freedman, L. (1998). 'The confrontation of the superpowers, 1945–1998'. In Michael Howard and Roger Louis (eds.), *The Oxford History of the Twentieth Century*. Oxford and New York: Oxford University Press.

Gallagher, K. and Myers, M. (2015). *China-Latin America Database*. Washington, DC: Inter-American Dialogue.

Giacalone, R. (2013). 'Venezuela en UNASUR: integración regional y discurso político', *Desafios*, 25(1): 129–63.

Godoy, H. (1965). 'Actitudes frente a la integración'. In Romulo Almeida et al. (eds.), *La integración latinoamericana. Situación y Perspectivas*. Buenos Aires: INTAL, pp. 14–56.

Gomez, E.J. and Atun, R. (2013). 'Emergence of multilateral proto-institutions in global health and new approaches to governance: analysis using path dependency and institutional theory', *Global Health*, 9(1): 18. Available online at: https://dash.harvard.edu/bitstream/handle/1/11717540/3724587.pdf?sequence=1&isAllowed=y

Gray, V.J. (2014). 'Colombia: unfading glory and furrows of pain'. In Howard J. Wiarda and Harvey F. Kline (eds.), *Latin American Politics and Development*. Boulder, CO: Westview Press, ch. 9.

Griffith-Jones, S., Griffith-Jones, D., and Hetova, D. (2008). 'Enhancing the role of regional development banks', *United Nations Conference on Trade and Development*. New York, Geneva: United Nations.

Humphrey, C. (2012). 'The business of development: borrowers, shareholders, and the reshaping of multilateral development lending'. PhD thesis, The London School of Economics and Political Science (LSE).

Humphrey, C. (2014). 'The politics of loan pricing in multilateral development banks', *Review of International Political Economy*, 21(3): 611–39.

Humphrey, C. (2015). 'Are credit rating agencies limiting the operational capacity of Multilateral Development Banks?' *Policy Paper for the Group of 24*. Washington, DC: G24.

IADB (Inter-American Development Bank). (2019). *Annual Report 2019: The Year in Review*. Washington, DC: IADB.

Lawrence, M.A. (2010). 'Containing globalism: the United States and the developing world in the 1970s'. In N. Ferguson, C.S. Maier, E. Manela, and D.J. Sargent (eds.), *The Shock of the Global: The 1970s in Perspective*. London: Harvard University Press, ch. 12.

Levine, D. and Crisp, B. (1999). 'Venezuela: the character, crisis and possible future of democracy'. In Larry Diamond, Jonathan Hartlyn, Juan J. Linz, and Seymour Martin Lipset (eds.), *Democracy in Developing Countries: Latin America*. Boulder, CO: Lynne Rienner Publishers.

Levinson, J. and de Onis, J. (1970). *The Alliance that Lost its Way*. Chicago: Quadrangle Books.

Mazzucato, M. and Penna, C. 'Beyond market failures: the market creating and shaping roles of state investment banks', *Journal of Economic Policy Reform*, 19(4): 305–26.

McPherson, A. (ed.) (2006). 'Antiyanquismo: nascent scholarship, ancient sentiments'. In *Anti-Americanism in Latin America and the Caribbean*. New York: Berghahn Books.

Prada, F. (2012). 'World Bank, Inter-American Development Bank, and Subregional development banks in Latin America: dynamics of a system of multilateral development banks'. ADBI Working Paper Series No. 380, September.

Randall, S. (1992). *Colombia and the United States: Hegemony and Interdependence*. Athens and London: University of Georgia Press.

Reinert, K.A. and Rajan, R.S. (2009). *The Princeton Encyclopedia of the World Economy*. Princeton: Princeton University Press.

Rivas, D. (2006). 'Patriotism and petroleum: anti-Americanism in Venezuela from Gómez to Chávez'. In Alan McPherson (ed.), *Anti-Americanism in Latin America and the Caribbean*. New York and Oxford: Berghahn Books.

Rivera, S. (2014). *Latin American Unification: A History of Political and Economic Integration Efforts*. Jefferson: McFarland & Company Publishers.

Rubio Vega, V. (2015). 'The Andean Development Corporation (CAF): continuity, scope and role in regional long-term development lending'. Available online at: http://www.academia.edu/3497796/The_Andean_Development_Corporation_CAF_Continuity_Scope_and_Role_in_Regional_Long-Term_Development_Lending

Ruiz Lara, J. (1999). 'La Integración en América Latina: antecedentes del Acuerdo de Cartagena y el desarrollo y perspectivas de la integración regional'. In Otto Morales Benítez (ed.), *Aportes al Periodismo, Clientelismo y Corrupción, Modernización del Estado, Pacto Andino*. Bogotá: Universidad Central.

Sagasti, F.R. (2002). *La banca multilateral de desarrollo en América Latina*. Santiago de Chile: Naciones Unidas.

Salgado, G. (1970). *Ecuador y la integración económica de América Latina*. Buenos Aires: INTAL.

Sanz, F. (2009). 'Carlos Lleras y la integración de América Latina'. In Carlos Lleras Restrepo (ed.), *Comercio Internacional*. Bogotá: Fundación Universidad de Bogotá Jorge Tadeo Lozano.

Seatzu, F. (2014). 'The subregional development banks and the expansion of socio-economic growth in Latin America: Current issues and future prospects', *Anuario Brasileiro de Direito Internacional*, 9(1). Available online at: http://centrodireitointernacional.com.br/publicacoes/anuario-brasileiro-de-direito-internacional.

Shadlen, K.C. (2007). 'Debt, finance and the IMF: three decades of debt crises in Latin America', *South America, Central America and the Caribbean 2004: Regional Surveys of the World*, 12th ed. London: Routledge.

Taffet, J.F. (2006). 'The making of an economic anti-American: Eduardo Frei and Chile during the 1960s'. In Alan McPherson (ed.), *Anti-Americanism in Latin America and the Caribbean*. New York: Berghahn Books, ch. 4.

Villamizar, J.C. (2013). *Pensamiento económico en Colombia. Construcción de un saber, 1948–1970*. Bogotá: Editorial Universidad El Rosario.

Walker, T. (1970). 'El papel de la democracia cristiana en la integración de América Latina', *Foro internacional*, 11(1): 77–91.

Webb, R. (2000). 'The influence of international financial institutions on ISI'. In Enrique Cárdenas, José Antonio Ocampo, and Rosemary Thorp (eds.), *An Economic History of Twentieth-Century Latin America: Industrialization and the State in Latin America*. London: Palgrave Macmillan.

Werz, N. (1990). 'State, oil and capital accumulation in Venezuela'. In Christian Anglade and Carlos Fortin (eds.), *The State and Capital Accumulation in Latin America*. Vol. 2. Basingstoke: Macmillan.

Wise, C. (2003). *Reinventing the State: Economic Strategy and Institutional Change in Peru*. Ann Arbor: University of Michigan Press.

World Bank (2019). 'World Bank group finances: IBRD/IDA summary'. Available online at: https://financesapp.worldbank.org/en/summaries/ibrd-ida/#ibrd-len/countries=EC/sort=board_approval_date-asc/ (accessed 7 November 2019).

World Bank (2019). 'The World Bank data (GDP growth annual %)'. Available online at: https://data.worldbank.org/indicator/NY.GDP.MKTP.KD.ZG?end=2018&start=1961&view=chart (accessed 24 November 2019).

Zúñiga Quevedo, J. (2003). *La contribución de la Corporación Andina de Fomento al desarrollo de la Comunidad Andina de Naciones*. Madrid: Editorial Universidad Autónoma de Madrid.

8

The European Bank for Reconstruction and Development

Constructing the Periphery of the European Political Economy

Stuart Shields

1. Introduction

Of all the regional development banks (RDB) addressed in this volume, the one that has been paid least attention in the academic literature to date is the European Bank for Reconstruction and Development (EBRD). To begin to remedy this oversight, this chapter explores the major role of the EBRD in the transition from Soviet state socialism to capitalist liberal democracy in Eastern Central Europe. The EBRD was set up during the early stages of post-communist transition at rapid speed by the governments of the West. It was formally established on 29 May 1990 and was operational less than a year later, on 15 April 1991 (Shihata and Attali 1990; Weber 1994; Bronstone 1999). Contrast this with its Latin American or Asian equivalents, the Inter-American Development Bank (IADB) and the Asian Development Bank (ADB) which took fifty years to establish as other chapters show (see Barjot and Lanthier, Chapter 4, this volume). As the contributions in this volume illustrate, there is a relative dearth of recent literature on the RDB with a few notable exceptions (Park and Strand 2016). Compare this to the more well-known multilateral development agencies, such as the World Bank, underlining the importance of this volume.

The EBRD stands out even more in this regard. This is a development institution long ignored in International Relations/International Political Economy (IR/IPE) discussions of the politics of development or the area studies literature on Eastern Central Europe. There is some discussion of how the institution was set up in the late 1980s and early 1990s (Weber 1994; Bronstone 1999), the occasional commentary on its legal competencies (Vuylsteke 1995) and its activities as part of broader regionalisation in Eastern Central Europe (Smith 2002). The current research that exists on this institution has analysed the gendered dimensions of the EBRD policy formulations (Shields and Wallin 2015), explored the indicators

Stuart Shields, *The European Bank for Reconstruction and Development: Constructing the Periphery of the European Political Economy* In: *Regional Development Banks in the World Economy.* Edited by: Judith Clifton, Daniel Díaz-Fuentes, and David Howarth, Oxford University Press (2021).
DOI: 10.1093/oso/9780198861089.003.0008

adopted to evaluate country progress in transition (Myant and Drahokoupil 2012), and assessed the policy impact of the annual Transition Reports (Shields 2019). Despite the meagre literature on the EBRD, the institution itself produces an enormous amount of grey literature, and material and data on transition.

The scant scholarly attention paid to the EBRD is a strange anomaly given that the Bank is the largest single investor in the region, 9.4 billion euro in 2015 alone (EBRD 2015), and the way that it explicitly develops parallelism with the strategic thinking in other international financial institutions (IFI) particularly since the 'global financial crisis'. The EBRD plays a crucial role in the parallel and overlapping forms of post-crisis governance (Shields 2019) in Europe and beyond. It situates itself as a crucial provider of transition knowledge and expertise for Eastern Central Europe and beyond, increasingly involved in parts of Western Europe, the Middle East, and North Africa. However, the EBRD sits uncomfortably alongside many of the other RDB addressed in this volume for two reasons. First that the EBRD has an unalloyed democratic mandate. The EBRD's founding constitutional document commits it to: 'foster the transition towards open-market economies and to promote private and entrepreneurial initiative in the Central and Eastern European countries committed to and applying the principles of multiparty democracy, pluralism, and market economies' (EBRD 1990–2013, Article 1).

As the EBRD's president recently noted, 'we are committed to a particular economic and political model' (Chakrabarti 2019). The second reason is that the EBRD is part development bank, but probably more merchant bank. I use the term merchant bank to indicate the EBRD's commitment to private commercial activities. This lends the EBRD a greater freedom of operation than many of the other existing RDB. While it is similar to the other multilateral development banks and RDB its mission is to boost development rather than necessarily to return a profit, but the EBRD is unique in making loans and investments based on commercial criteria to exclusively cultivate private sector development.

Perhaps a brief comparison with the European Investment Bank (EIB) is instructive. The EIB is a development institution that encourages economic integration from its broad mandate on development (Clifton et al. 2018). The EBRD in comparison has the much narrower double mandate of development as promoting privatization and the democracy promotion. While the EIB focuses on low-level investment risks (Mertens and Thiemann 2019; Clifton et al. 2017) the EBRD has always engaged in much higher risk-taking capacity (Vuylsteke 1995). One way this manifests is in its low level of public sector lending: 40 per cent of total EIB lending is to the public sector compared to 2 per cent of the EBRD (Piroska and Podvršič 2019).

Given the importance of this difference, that the EBRD is not a development bank in the way that we might traditionally think of such institutions, the chapter sets out to explore what the implications of this might be in the context of two of the major themes that structure this edited volume: market promotion and regional integration. The chapter does this by outlining briefly the significance of the historical context of the constitutive moment when the EBRD was established (see also Roper, Chapter 10, this volume). The chapter then utilizes these broad heuristics to analyse the social and intellectual context of transition amid the four policy shifts in the EBRD at various critical historical junctures: (1) initial market construction; (2) institutional shock therapy; (3) the promotion of neoliberal competitiveness; and then (4) post-crisis re-invigoration; before offering some reflections on the EBRD as RDB within the wider framing of the principal agent problem.

2. Historical context: the origins and mandate of the EBRD

The priority areas for EBRD operations were clearly laid out in the institution's founding constitution. Article 1 of the constitution indicates that the EBRD's priorities will be: 'developing the financial sector through technical assistance to governments and bank officials, supporting the creation of new financial actors; developing infrastructure in telecommunications, transport, energy, and environment; conversion of the military industry; general privatization and restructuring; and supporting small and medium-sized enterprises (SMEs)' (EBRD 1990–2013, Article 1). These overlap considerably with the International Monetary Fund (IMF) and World Bank, but the EBRD had three distinct tasks: an explicit commitment to democratic transformation; a clearly defined emphasis on private sector development; and a strategic role as the first pan-European institution linking the Eastern Central Europe states to the West.[1] The EBRD is not reticent, explaining that its mandate poses a major challenge: 'to create a new economic framework, while simultaneously changing the political system, behaviour, and even the attitudes of the people involved, without creating intolerable social conditions which could seriously endanger their societies and threaten those nearby' (EBRD 1991: 23).

In the discussions leading up to the establishment of the EBRD, two potential models emerged regarding the future through these interactions, what Adrian Smith (2002) calls the 'maximalist' and 'minimalist' models. Here is potential evidence of how IFI experience the principal-agent problem contrasting the extended chain of delegation between the two models.

The 'maximalist' model, supported largely by the French and German governments, envisaged the absorption of all aid programmes (including Phare, the European Union's (EU) pre-accession instrument preparing applicants from

[1] Sixty per cent of committed loans, guarantees, and equity investments shall be provided to the private sector. A commercial branch of the Bank, lending at market interest rates, controls this part of the business. The remaining 40 per cent to the state sector is mainly for infrastructure projects and is carried out by a development branch at concessionary rates.

Eastern Central Europe for membership) into the new financial institution. As Roper (Chapter 10, this volume) shows, the initial plan developed by the French and German governments had been to develop a consciously 'European' institution in orientation that would not involve the United States (US). The 'minimalist' model, supported by many other Western European governments, but especially the United Kingdom (UK) and US preferred the option of a new institution collaborating with other aid programmes and US involvement. The Anglo-American option essentially emasculated Franco-German commitment to large infrastructural projects and replaced it with a post-communist transition driven by private foreign capital and that maintained US interests (Smith 2002: 650; Ivanova 2007: 350).[2] The contested leadership reflects complications associated with principal-agent problems and more recently the potential *rapprochement* with the EIB.

Two points are important to note for now and will be developed throughout the rest of the chapter. First, that the founding process of the EBRD represents a consolidation of neoliberal thinking about the appropriate future route for post-communist transition to take. Second, in light of later developments explored in this chapter, the four shifts in policy represent policy and intellectual closure around what constitutes the limits of the possible in legitimate government intervention in Eastern Central Europe. As noted above, there is a neoliberal policy orientation as regards how the EBRD operates. In practice, this means that the development and merchant bank roles came into tension at the birth of the institution, when issues emerged related to the amount of capital it should hold, the Bank's location, decision-making and control, scope and objectives, and, not least, its personnel (Jakobeit 1992). The principal-agent problem emerges here too given the EBRD has relationships with clients and member states. Alongside that, the EBRD has sovereign shareholders who do not receive dividends and investments are geo-politically limited to the region.

A further example, in contrast to the other development banks, the EBRD has no 'soft'-loan option, it only lends at market rates. The concessionary soft-loan option is unique to public rather than private sector banks and another distinction to be made between the EBRD and other RDB in this volume. Instead, the EBRD is extremely secretive about loan interest rates (Ben-Artzi 2016: 89). EBRD investments need to be financially sound.[3] This positions the EBRD at the forefront of contemporary development thinking, with the bourgeoning ideational and material impact of private actors in other parts of the world implying

[2] At the time, French president Mitterand, announced that 'Poland, Hungary, the Soviet Union and, in his historic leading role, Mr. Gorbachev, need to be helped (…) What can Europe do? (…) Why not set up a Bank for Europe which, like the European Investment Bank, would finance major projects and have on its Board of Directors the twelve European countries. Not to mention the others, such as Poland and Hungary, and why not the Soviet Union and yet others?' (European Community 1989: 149).

[3] See Reisen (2015) on excess demand for multilateral soft loans.

that development can be left to the private sector without public investment (Carroll and Jarvis 2015). The EBRD has focused on private sector investment, co-financing projects, making sure that these investments promote a particular form of transition.

Second, the EBRD aims at engaging policy-makers and influencing policy debates. Alongside navigating its own macroeconomic forecasting and risk management, it assists economists and policy-makers in the region with macroeconomic analysis and economic forecasting. It provides what itself terms 'thought leadership' inside and outside of the EBRD on economic issues related to the Bank's work in its countries of operation (EBRD 2015: 1). Governments in the region and IFIs have come to rely on the specialized knowledge produced by the EBRD. A canon of appropriate 'transitology', the stylized application of the Washington (and indeed post-Washington) Consensus has emerged in academic and policy circles, re-affirmed by the EBRD. The remainder of the section reflects on the membership and financing of the EBRD.

The EBRD membership includes countries from North America, Africa, Asia, and Australia (EBRD 2020). The US is the biggest shareholder. India recently joined as a member in July 2018, making sixty-nine countries and the two European institutions, the EIB and the EU. The shareholders made a capital contribution which forms the EBRD's core funding. Full details of capital subscription can be found also on the same page of the EBRD's website as above. The member states are also countries of operation, mostly across the traditional regional focus of the EBRD in Central Europe, Southern Europe and the Mediterranean, Central Asia, but most recently the Middle East and North Africa (MENA). The board of directors, is responsible for the direction of the general operations and policies. The president is elected by the board of governors and is the legal representative of the EBRD.

By the end of September 2018, the EBRD had 29.7 billion euro subscribed capital, 57 per cent of that shareholding is Group of Seven (G7) and 84 per cent is Organisation for European Co-operation and Development (OECD). Rather than financing loans, the Bank's capital is used to borrow relatively cheaply in the capital markets. It has a low-risk rating (Standard and Poor's AAA, Moody's Aaa). In comparison to the other RDB, more than 20 per cent of the EBRD's capital is paid-in, compared to an average of 5.8 per cent for other global or regional triple-A rated institutions with callable capital, such as the IBRD, the ADB, the IADB, the African Development Bank (AfDB), and the EIB (Dumała 2018). Alongside its banking activities, the EBRD produces a number of reports, benchmarking riteria, rankings, law and regulation evaluations, and indicators of regulatory progress. There are three that are significant: the EBRD Annual Report, the Transition Report, and Progress in Transition (for a review of their efficacy, see Shields 2019). While there is a commitment to transparency with the publication if such material there is also illustration of principal-agent problems as IFI like the EBRD gain more competencies over members and countries of operation due to the asymmetry of information and the highly technical discourse the EBRD utilizes. Further still, in 1994 the EBRD transition report introduced the transition indicators database that 'provide an understanding of how, why and by what means transition policies have related to economic growth and social development' (Dumała 2018). The indicators emerged from the Chief Economist's Office, at the time run by John Flemming and then later by Nicholas Stern.[4] It is this data base that has come to be so crucial to analysts, academics, and policy-makers (Myant and Drahokoupil 2012).

The transition indicators are an important disciplining tool. They collect a number of indicators and variables and score between 1 and 4+ in two main areas: institutional reforms and infrastructure reforms. A score of 1 implies the absence of appropriate institutional change and indicates the country is some considerable distance from the criteria that encompass the market economy. A score of 4+ would match an advanced, industrialized economy. The EBRD indicators have been subject to criticism and alternatives exist. Campos and Horvath (2012) address a number of potential problems with the indicators including the lack of information on which variables are included in the indices, how they are aggregated, unclear mixes of policy inputs and outcomes, and ultimately the deeply problematic reference point of what constitutes a market economy, functioning or otherwise. Nevertheless, the Transition Indicators dominate most economics analysis of the region. As we might expect, non-economistic and qualitative assessments of the indicators find much to criticize (Hamm et al. 2012).

That said, the crucial point of the indicators is that, 'In this way the EBRD created a discursive standard as a benchmark of transition, which meant countries' progress could be compared with one another and over time' (Shields 2019: 15). Mobilizing large amounts of capital becomes much easier if the EBRD imprimatur is in place. The EBRD uses its political legitimacy to counteract private sector concerns about risk. As the EBRD's operational response describes reforms 'constitute [...] an enabling environment' and are imperative to attracting capital and expanding private sector activity (EBRD 2012: 30). The chapter now turns to how that is operationalized across the four shifts in its policy discourse.

[4] To give some sense of their significance, Flemming was an economist at Oriel and Nuffield Colleges. He edited the high-ranking *Economic Journal*, was an economic adviser and director at the Bank of England prior to appointment as chief economist at the EBRD in 1991. This early period at the EBRD is often remarked upon because of the unprecedented difficulties of the transition itself, but also problematic approaches to the management of the institution itself (see Bronstone 1999). Stern has a similar career trajectory holding academic economist posts at Oxford, Warwick, and LSE. From 1994 until 1999 he was the chief economist and special counsellor to the president of the EBRD. He went on to be chief economist and senior vice-president at the World Bank, second permanent secretary at the UK Treasury, and, more recently, he conducted significant international reviews on climate change and development published as the *Stern Review*.

3. Shift 1: the construction of the post-communist market

Having sketched the emergence of the EBRD in section 2, the chapter turns to the first of the four shifts in policy and discourse within the EBRD that offer ideological coherence, legitimacy, and technical solutions to the perceived 'problems' of communism and post-communism. This section thinks about how the EBRD was instrumental in a first phase of transition based on the construction of the market. Bearing in mind that Eastern Central Europe is a part of the world where ostensibly the market did not exist during the preceding Soviet-type system. The necessity for Western intervention was part of the capitalist 'triumphalism' so prevalent at the time that at best caused mistakes to be made concerning the required speed of post-communist transition and the desirable functions of the state in that transformation. This remains part of the discursive toolkit associated with efforts for contemporary neoliberal market building. As Piroska and Podvrsic (2019) explain, the EBRD's focus on privatization at the expense of the democratic mandate weakens the capacity of governments to pursue alternative policy options in Eastern Central Europe.

As noted above, the role of the EBRD was to encourage private sector development through the now classic formulation of privatization, liberalization, deregulation, and to act as a pan-European institution that linked 'East' and 'West' following the dissolution of Council for Mutual Economic Assistance (COMECON).

Crucially, though, the EBRD is mandated to facilitate democratic political change.[5] Despite the double mandate and the democratic transition component of the transition indicators the EBRD has almost exclusively invested in the economy. In this way the EBRD is no different to the other RDB. There is an express link between lending and investment operations and political rights in the countries of operation on the other. The EBRD plays a crucial role to mobilize private sector investment by leveraging its unique position as part-RDB, part-merchant bank. As then chief economist of the EBRD, John Flemming noted, the EBRD 'is very much "a creature of its time", in that its inception reflected the euphoria that greeted the downfall of the totalitarian regimes in Europe' (Council of Europe 1993: 118). From its inception, the EBRD concentrated on developing the private sector in the region through technical assistance; supporting the creation of new financial actors; developing infrastructure; conversion of the military

[5] Recall that the first article in the EBRD constitution immediately acknowledged this poses a major challenge: 'to create a new economic framework, while simultaneously changing the political system, behaviour, and even the attitudes of the people involved, without creating intolerable social conditions which could seriously endanger their societies and threaten those nearby' (EBRD 1991, 23). CEE Bankwatch asserts that the EBRD 'has never measured the results of its lending in development terms like poverty reduction, gender equality or employment gains, or assessed its contribution to the Millennium Development goals [...] *It has always been assumed that the development of the private sector is good for everyone* (emphasis added)' (CEE Bankwatch 2011, 6).

industry sector; general privatization and restructuring; and supporting SMEs (TACIS 1996). Sixty per cent of the EBRD loans and investments are directed towards the private sector, and the annual report gives details each year of the proportion between public and private sectors.[6] As noted above the commercial branch of the Bank, lending at market interest rates, controls this part of the business. The remaining 40 per cent to the state sector is intended for infrastructure projects and is carried out by the development bank component of the EBRD at concessionary rates as set out in the constitution.[7]

The obvious point of comparison given the discussions throughout the volume about the constitutive moment of the RDB in question is that this is not a second Marshall Plan (Ivanova 2007). As Adam Bronstone (1999) notes, the zeal of Anglo-American politicians resulted in a post-communist transition driven by private foreign capital, cuts in state spending, liberalization of trade, and privatization to restore macroeconomic stability, or, put differently, the construction of the market. This was an opportunity for the assertion of neoliberalism, confirming the victory of neoliberalism over its sclerotic state socialist competitor and the EBRD simultaneously represents an illustration of this and also a perpetration of the ongoing consolidation of the appropriate policy route for transition to take. This represents a closure around what constituted legitimate policy intervention in the region not as a spontaneous process but as a constant stream of ideological and material forces to synthesize a long-term framework for political and economic interests in the region. The first wave of neoliberal transition mapped out the parameters of the reform debate for the first half of the 1990s. Furthermore, it reveals the degree to which the neoliberal context had been pre-configured as the only rational course of action.

Briefly then, what was this set of the EBRD policy interventions? In its own words, since 1991 the EBRD has invested over 100 billion euro in thousands of projects across its countries of operation. It has helped to narrow infrastructure gaps and improve the quality of services delivered by local authorities. It has promoted the development of environmentally friendly energy to fuel expanding economies and worked to reduce energy waste and pollution. It has played a key role in supporting the growth of SMEs that are so crucial to job creation and helped ensure more equality of opportunity across societies.

In an abstract sense, what this initial positioning of the EBRD market construction enabled was a stylized, linear form of transition. Neoclassical economics

[6] See EBRD (2018) for the most recent details.

[7] During this first period of EBRD operations, the EBRD entered into twenty-nine projects committing only 626 million euro. In 1993, the number of projects increased to sixty-six, and the amount committed was over 1.5 billion euro. However, this sum was a small amount of the actual capital available to the Bank. A substantial amount of capital went to the Visegrad states, as they had the most developed private sectors in which the EBRD could invest. By 1998, 80 per cent of total financing went to the private sector compared to 76 per cent in 1997.

became the intellectual framework for the EBRD's social engineering and endorsed the pragmatic one-dimensional Washington Consensus mainstream toolkit to transition. Neoliberal shock therapy came to dominate policy advice. Change should be accomplished concurrently as the 'losers' in transition would experience the costs quicker than the 'winners' would experience success. As key protagonists in the policy process, Jeffrey Sachs' metaphor cropped up aplenty in EBRD discussions, you cannot jump a chasm in two leaps (Bermeo and Pontusson 2012). The EBRD plays a crucial role in articulating the permissive 'international' context for post-communist transition. As Bohle's still incisive intervention avers, imagine what policy prescription would have been concocted for Eastern Central Europe should transition have occurred in the late 1950s rather than the late 1980s? Bohle shows how 'apart from obvious crisis situations, market-oriented structural reforms or radical macroeconomic stabilisation were typically absent from the policy reform packages' of the embedded liberal period (Bohle 2000: 242). As her increasingly prescient analysis claims, 'a major change has occurred in the organisation of private economic activities, the state and the global order. The shift from national development strategies to internationalising neoliberal reforms goes hand-in-hand with the internationalisation of private capital' (Bohle 2000: 244).

This first wave of EBRD policy framed the parameters of reform in Eastern Central Europe for the first half of the 1990s. The EBRD interpreted what constituted effective reform as only a highly liberalized and privatized market rather the varied forms of socio-economic arrangement in the West. Liberalization and privatization are ends in themselves in the transition indicators. This continued until the mid-2000s when the EBRD's *Life in Transition* survey revealed that the impact of these and subsequent policy shifts ignored their impact on the ground (EBRD 2007). Stuckler et al. (2009) record the increased mortality, higher rates of alcoholism, suicide, and cardiac illness, which they link to deteriorating health conditions as a result of mass privatization. While it is difficult to develop clear causal links, the EBRD did shift policy advice as section 4 shows. It might also be worth noting that the EBRD has moved to a more inclusive understanding of transition that is more closely aligned with the Sustainable Development Goals (SDGs). The new strategy ensures that 'anyone regardless of their gender, place of birth, socio-economic environment, age or other circumstances has full and fair access to labour markets, finance and entrepreneurship and, more generally, economic opportunity' (EBRD 2017), though this resonates more clearly with the social innovation discourse the chapter engages with below.

According to the EBRD then there is only one rational course of action for the governments of the region. To develop the historicizing point made in section 2, it is important to remember that this is also all wrapped up in a normative discourse of staunch pro-Western anti-communism. What the EBRD offers for countries in transition is not just a clear set of definitions and strategic goals but crucially also the expertise to achieve this. The Bank continues to offer this in the contemporary period with operations expanded to the MENA, a point developed in the final section 7 of the chapter (EBRD 2013). When it becomes clear that the chasm cannot be jumped in one leap, that as Ellerman (2009) notes, a bridge is needed, the EBRD shifts focus from the construction of the market to getting the 'right' institutions in place. Section 4 turns to this.

4. Shift 2: getting the correct institutions in place

In section 3, the chapter outlined the initial market construction framework that the EBRD helped to develop and apply in the transition countries. One outcome of this was a sharp fall in output as the 'new' private sector failed to compensate and close the gap on the declining state-owned sector. The initial transition shock and the subsequent recession affected the entire population of the region. This has come to be known as the 'transition recession', and was exacerbated by the collapse of intra-COMECON trade and state-led economic planning and activities (Rapacki & Blazyca 2001). Figure 8.1 shows the longer term impact of the recession in terms of average income per capita as a percentage of the G7 average.

If one key aim of the EBRD had been to replace COMECON then its impact was considerable, as the original coordinating mechanisms of Soviet planning disappeared almost overnight to be replaced by the market. The frenetic socio-economic impact of reforms marked the early transition process. As section 3 indicated, this period was often framed as a debate between rival approaches to policy change: a radical shock therapy approach to fully and quickly open their

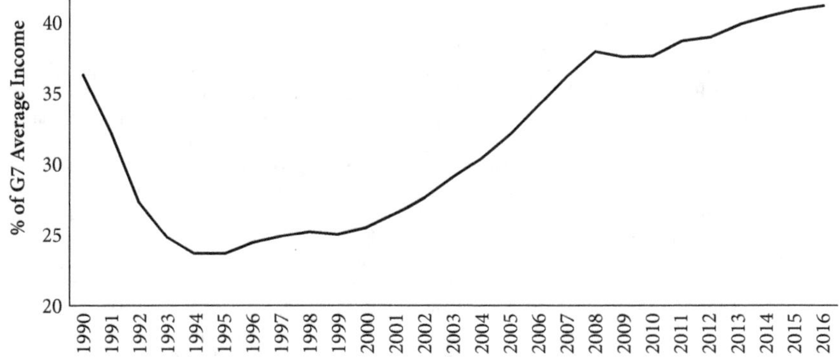

Figure 8.1 Average income per capita in Eastern Central Europe and Central Asia as percentage of G7 average

Source: Georgiev et al. (2017: 2).

economies (Murrell 1995), contrasted with slower reforms delayed by domestic political impediments. The debates also reflect the broader shift in development strategy to institution-building agenda of the post-Washington Consensus. The shock therapy associated with the initial market construction period failed and gradualist policies for privatization and the reconstruction of institutions succeeded far better. This remains an ongoing debate since the emergence of China, the 'global financial crisis', and ongoing reforms across the MENA.[8]

Having witnessed the 'failure' of initial moves towards the construction of the market economy in Eastern Central Europe, the EBRD recognized the necessity to complement the first phase of reforms with the development of institutions and behaviours that supported the functioning of markets and private enterprise to reinforce their efforts at resolving the principal-agent problem. Reforms on the ground were not always consonant with the EBRD policy advice. These second wave addresses deeper institutional reforms such as corporate governance, competition policy, and the reform of financial institutions, or as the EBRD put it in the transition reports, following 'the functioning of the state and the behaviour of its officials, including the issues of corruption and personal safety: the regulatory and legal framework and its effectiveness; the structure and functioning of enterprises in particular their market orientation; financial institutions; and political and social institutions including the democratic process, the freedom of the press, and a social safety net' (EBRD 1998: 2).

When this institutionalizing turn also 'failed' the EBRD moved to re-invigorate the common sense of transition with a renewed commitment to competitiveness as the chapter shows in section 5. For now, though, the chapter focuses on this second shift in policy focus.[9]

This second phase aimed to complete the transition and repair the wrong turns taken in the initial construction of the market economy that had so clearly manifested in the 'transition recession' as noted above. The first phase of market

[8] The EBRD has intervened to revise the debate on the transition recession since the mid-2000s. See for example Falcetti et al. (2006) in an EBRD working paper and later journal article that claims that 'not only are the official statistics highly inaccurate, but they were also systematically biased downwards in the first few years, with the result that the severity of the transition recession was exaggerated' Falcetti et al. 2005: 5). Not only that but, there is a 'robust, positive influence of reforms in one period on subsequent growth across transition economies. This is reassuring to those who have promoted the virtues of reforms; it also serves as a warning of the dangers that arise when 'reform fatigue' sets in, as it appears to have done in parts of the region' (Falcetti et al. 2005: 20).

[9] I draw on Paul Cammack's work here who indicates how the institutional shift begins in the 1980s but it is not fully developed until the 1990s. In combination with Ben Fine on economics imperialism and Guy Standing's critique of Stiglitz it illustrates that there's a shift in thinking coterminous with Stiglitz at the World Bank that: 'represents a "deep" neoliberalism, in contrast to the "shallow" neoliberalism reflected in the idea of a minimal state, and a commitment to deregulation without simultaneous attention to the reshaping of social relations and institutions to make markets competitive' (Cammack 2004: 192). There's so much personnel and intellectual exchange between the institutions that it is difficult to prise apart where the shift came from. For example, Nicholas Stern, chief economist at the EBRD replaces Stiglitz at the World Bank.

construction had presented a set of misguided signposts for the region. The EBRD came to recognize that, 'the next period of the transition [following market construction] must be led by high-quality investment [...] with the right kind of institutions, leadership and partnership, the private markets in these countries can deliver the quality investment which is necessary for successful economic growth' (EBRD 1995: 8).

This appreciation that the hurdles around investment and the restructuring of infrastructure were under-estimated is evident elsewhere among IFI. For example, Clifton et al. (2011: 662–4) analyse the longer term shifts in policy paradigms related to infrastructure. Links between corporate governance and national governance were increasingly the focus at the EBRD. The policy shift aimed to open up oligarchic and exclusive political-economic institutional frameworks and practices to competitive environment. As the EBRD's 2002 transition report review of the late 1990s business environment asserted, vested interests had 'captured' the state. Using the payments made available to them as a result of partial liberalization, insider privatization and the wealth acquired from poorly protected property rights, these vested interests used their economic power to prevent improvements in governance that would have threatened their privileged position (EBRD 2002: 30).

Hellmann et al. (2003) argued that corruption thrives where states are too weak to control their own bureaucrats, to protect property and contract rights, and to provide the institutions that underpin an effective rule of law. This (re-) assertion of regulatory stability is also linked to changes among other multilateral and RDB, especially the prominent World Bank discussions of the enabling state (World Bank 1997), or the debate between Stiglitz and Dabrowski, Gomulka, and Rostowski (see Dabrowski et al. 2001; Stiglitz and Ellerman 2001).[10]

In a number of discussions that emerged across the EBRD transition reports, annual report s, and in benchmarking reviews with the Council of Europe what eventually came to be known as the 'lessons' of the first decade of transition was that economic crime, corruption, and disregard for the rule of law remained powerful threats to the success of the whole transition. Horst Kohler, the EBRD president from September 1998 to April 2000, warned of the threats of weak state institutions, flawed investments, and hampered growth. Kohler advised that the EBRD needed to be more involved in setting up regulatory frameworks, 'We have to be aware that the transition is a much longer process than we had thought'

[10] The EBRD participates in a wider set of discussions concerning recognition and recasting of neoliberalism. Eastern Central Europe is a unique opportunity to test economic ideas out. Eastern Central Europe is the laboratory experiment (see Bockman and Eyal's (2002) work that also links the neoliberal experiment to Cold War connections between 'Western' and 'Eastern' economists) and note how this precedes similar changes in the multilateral development banks where these discussions are happening across multiple institutions, but how it is almost a decade earlier in Eastern Central Europe—the original Dabrowski et al. conference paper is first circulated in 1999 and appears as a working paper in 2000.

(EBRD 1998: 2). One solution was the promotion of further cooperation, which intensified parallelism.

The shift occurred at the EBRD in the mid-1990s with some subtle appreciation for possible different transition paths (Havrylyshyn 2006) but appropriate decisive implementation of reforms was not about to be superseded by history, geography, and culture. Poor levels of growth came from weak state institutions, flawed investment climates, and individual appropriate behaviours (EBRD 1999: 6). With the second policy shift the EBRD transition reports pointed to the harm done by vested interests and rent-seeking in preventing the completion of transition, that 'building institutions that support markets and private enterprise remains a fundamental challenge of transition, but establishing the appropriate laws and regulations is not sufficient' (EBRD 1999: 9). The perceived risk is corruption and vested interests discarding 'the social institutions that facilitate markets and private enterprise: the countries of [Eastern Central Europe] have shown themselves determined to create new democratic market economies. The linkage between the political, economic and social components of the changes have become increasingly clear. A market economy requires an adequate legal and democratic political framework to foster the spirit of enterprise, individual rights and institutional stability necessary for sound investment' (EBRD 1991: 26).

The need to open up key sectors of the economy to competition (coal, ship building, and the steel industry), as well as to promote entrepreneurship and remove existing distortions in the labour market impeded the supply and development of quality human capital.

Having witnessed the failure of initial moves towards the construction of the market the necessity to complement liberalization and privatization with the development of institutions and behaviours that supported the functioning of markets and private enterprise was recognized (EBRD 1999: v). In effect, this abandoned shock therapy and in its place developed a form of institutional shock therapy more easily presented to the populations of Eastern Central Europe. The shift establishes the EBRD as the key source for 'transitological knowledge' in Eastern Central Europe apace with the specific institutional mechanisms needed to lodge firmly the legitimate neoliberal formulations of the market economy in the region. Or as Cammack puts it in reference to the wider IFI project, this is the shift from shallow neoliberalism to deep interventionism with three components. First, interventions that affect the dynamics of the political process; second, irreversibilities distinguished from shallow reform interventions; and, third, a deep disturbance that aimed at the fundamental transformation of society and institutions. This is the 'uncompromising commitment to embedding the social and institutional relations that enforce capitalist competition, thereby seeking to ensure that the systemic imperatives of capitalism work [... reflecting] less a shallow neoliberalism of deregulation and more a deep neoliberalism of fundamental social transformation' (Cammack 2004: 209). Despite the shift in strategy, 'progress' continued to be protracted and the EBRD eventually moved to re-invigorate transition policy paradigms again with a renewed commitment to competitiveness as section 5 examines.

5. Shift 3: the promotion of neoliberal competitiveness

Each previous shift in the EBRD policy discourse has been both an internal re-alignment as well as one motivated by change in the external environment. The third is no different. Competitiveness is driving the imperative of competition by the interplay of structure and even very small scale agency (Nunn 2019). Such imperatives are frequently anticipated and promoted ahead of material pressures which might necessitate this (Hay and Rosamond 2002). The promotion of competitiveness is best understood as part of an effort to restore stable patterns of accumulation that subordinate and intensify ever more aspects of life to the disciplines of neoliberalism. Though in institutions like the EBRD competitiveness remains of primary concern, closely tailored to the constitutive foundations of the market as a socio-economic system (Cammack 2006).

At the EBRD the 1999 transition report review of a decade of transition is pivotal, identifying the first two waves of policy that this chapter has explored above. The 1999 report is important as it prefigures an imminent third shift in the EBRD policy discourse that intones the centrality of competitiveness to transition. For the EBRD the 1999 report foreshadows how competitiveness must become 'embodied in the social norms, practices, and behaviours of both government and the private sector—institutions need social capital and social foundations. The experiences of the first ten years of transition point to the ways in which both formal institutions can be built on firm foundations and social capital accumulated. Of particular importance are: (i) the experiences of liberalization and privatization; (ii) the demands for good governance from entrepreneurs and civil society; and (iii) the forces of competition' (EBRD 1999: 9).

The logic should be clear. If the construction of the market and then positioning of the correct institutions is insufficient for efficacious transition then alternative means for this outcome must necessarily be uncovered. The stalling of state-led neoliberal reforms in Eastern Central Europe needed other responses. Competitiveness became the under-girding of economic and of social policy. The EBRD's solution was to sharpen its attention to the population of Eastern Central Europe. If the forces unleashed by privatization and liberalization are insufficient, if the redrawn state institutions are insufficient, then it is the population itself that needs to be 'transformed' not just property rights, corporate governance, or labour market regulation.

Put bluntly, once market construction and the right institutions were in place, it is the capabilities of a population that need to be addressed next. Or as Nunn

(2019: 4; emphasis added) asserts, 'in a system where competitiveness [becomes] a wired-in characteristic, many efforts to adapt to the system at lower scales (such as states, regions, cities, neighbourhoods, and *ultimately households and individuals*) must inevitably fail'. In 1999 the EBRD adopted the 'Moving Transition Forward' operational strategy which reflects on early formulations of the key aspects of what will become the competitiveness agenda: 'primary responsibility lies with the countries of the region themselves, and they are urged to foster investment, entrepreneurial and market skills and build popular support for them, while the [IFIs] and the international community will play a crucial supporting role' (EBRD 1999).

The competitiveness agenda aimed to build better entrepreneurs, extended the importance of labour market reforms to configure the flexible labour force, or what Carroll has called 'deep marketisation' (Carroll 2012; Clifton and Díaz-Fuentes 2014; Carroll et al. 2019; Cammack 2019; Gerard and Johnston 2019). Households and individuals become the ultimate recipient of coping with competition and the risks associated with failure (Peck 2010). Labour markets are a key area of the EBRD's interventions, especially in terms of their role in promoting competitiveness (Krstic and Sanfey 2012).

As with the previous shifts in discourse, similar reformulations of appropriate policy were taking shape elsewhere. While there was continued commitment to technocratic and institutionally oriented reforms, new modalities of reform emerged, fostering, expanding, and deepening competitive social relations and, concomitantly, patterns of accumulation in a manner that relies less on working through the state as a site of reform and more on the cultivation of market activity. In this, rather as an aside, market activity is used to promote state transformation (Carroll 2012).

What this ultimately constitutes is a form of micro-level social engineering that takes the state-led initiatives of the first policy discourse, that is, shock therapy; the second, the installation of the correct institutions and recalibrates them to be internalized by the wider population of the region, or as the EBRD more euphemistically puts it—the key challenge confronted is changing attitudes. Stern, former chief economist at the EBRD suggests rather more bluntly that any coherent plan to 'fight poverty' requires a strategy for development and 'most aspects of empowering people involve changing attitudes and behaviours [...] As social scientists, we should be trying to understand better just how these changes take place' (Stern 2003: 292–3). This has expressed itself in number of interesting ways at the EBRD centred on changing attitudes that enhance the legitimacy and functioning of the market economy. One important shared characteristic of the region is lower life satisfaction than counterparts in countries of similar income levels that have not experienced transition, the so-called 'transition happiness gap' (Guriev and Melnikov 2017). There have been increased efforts 'to [close] the "happiness gap" especially between East and West through continued economic growth, more macroeconomic stability and more inclusive institutions' (EBRD 2016: 11).

The solution identified was a set of policies and ideas guided by a commitment to the discursive construction of a neoliberal agenda for competitiveness. Labour market reform was an essential component of this strategy, and its principal objective, as elsewhere, the creation of a 'flexible' labour force. It is not surprising that the EBRD promoted competitiveness; recall that the 1990 agreement establishing the EBRD declared that its purpose was 'to promote private and entrepreneurial initiative' in Eastern Central Europe (EBRD 1990–2013). From the late 1990s the EBRD urged governments to adopt and maintain a commitment to sound fiscal policy, good governance, and a disciplined workforce to attract foreign investment affirmed in the 1999 medium-term strategy plan. Political and economic competition is vital to pressure government to provide essential public goods and to encourage firms to restructure and innovate rather than to rely primarily on state support. The process of competition is therefore central to the development of institutions that are able to support markets and private enterprise (EBRD 1999: v).

Sara Wallin's (2018) work shows how this pressure takes the form of advocating for welfare reform. In the period commensurate with the first shift of market construction, the EBRD argued for welfare that enabled individuals to participate in markets. With the turn to the promotion of competitiveness, Wallin underscores how the EBRD sought restraints on public expenditure but enthusiastically supported the construction of markets *within* informal welfare provision. The EBRD's argument is that limits on state contributions and raising the pension age disciplines workers and promotes economic growth (Shields and Wallin 2015: 107).

For the EBRD such recommendations centre on how to mobilize large amounts of capital in the region. Ultimately, the EBRD achieves this in a twofold manner: first as an investor and second as an advisor. Or indeed the even better option of both so as to develop skills training, encourage entrepreneurship, and enable access to finance and the services that enhance economic development. It is worth noting that the EBRD has extended its reach to include gender equality policy as a means of achieving other objectives of economic growth and competitiveness (Shields and Wallin 2015). This has subsequently developed into the social inclusion strategy launched in 2017 (EBRD 2017).

These three shifts in the EBRD policy discourse around transition have configured a specific type of post-communist transition since 1989. Nunn (2019: 5) contends that 'policy experts, consultants, "policy pedlars" and international organisations take on a key role in the transfer of policy models' and each shift has attempted to consolidated earlier phases of reform. In the EBRD's case, first the state's withdrawal from the economy was emphasized; then, second, the role of the state as regulatory overseer for the economy was paramount; and, third, the competitiveness imperative eventually mandates that the only route out of previous policy failures is to further embed and internalize competitiveness (Nunn 2019: 6). This is not convergence around a universal set of policies but endless adaptation at the national to the very local levels. In section 6, the chapter begins to think about how the global financial crisis and the Eurozone crisis have pushed further developments in policy reformulations at the EBRD.

6. Shift 4: social innovation, crisis, and beyond

Each of these temporal shifts in policy discourse at the EBRD have ultimately served to intensify the neoliberal restructuring of European social relations.[11] The most recent manifestation of a similar shift has emerged since the so-called global financial crisis and the Eurozone crisis. The EBRD remains relatively absent from analysis of the two crises. However this is Eastern Central Europe's RDB and the institution itself has intervened extensively both during and since the crisis (Berglof 2015). The subsequent policy response to the Eurozone crisis was mobilized by the EBRD in the shape of the Vienna Initiative or more formally the European Bank Coordination Initiative (Howarth and Quaglia 2015; Shields 2019). In this final substantive section, the chapter outlines the emergence of the latest policy discourse at the EBRD. Inspired by responses to the crises, the chapter frames this as a commitment to social innovation. The section spends little time discussing the actual crises but instead focuses on the implications of the crises, articulating the EBRD's shift to social innovation and how this was institutionalized in parallel with other institutions in the form of the Vienna Initiative.

The Vienna Initiative was coordinated by the EBRD, EIB, and other IFI to prevent the Eastern Central European financial crisis escalating. Across the region, foreign banks had come to dominate total banking assets with foreign subsidiaries owning over 80 per cent; even more in some cases (Epstein 2014: 848). With the imminent threat of financial disaster and of foreign banks vacating their funds to their parent states, the Vienna Initiative coordinated bank home and host states so that the major multinational banks limited their withdrawals from Eastern Central Europe. The EBRD made crucial interventions in the European political economy to prevent the escalation of the global financial crisis. In doing so they help prevent the contagion of the banking crisis spreading through what Epstein (2014) notes was the expected response of 'cut and run'. Rather than being an example of an alternative policy option to the existing neoliberal mainstream, as the then EBRD chief economist suggested, this was also an opportunity to prevent reform backsliding, an opportunity for further neoliberalization.

Eastern Central Europe has been the most affected of all emerging markets by the long downturn since the global financial crisis then exacerbated by the

[11] This was primarily focused on the transition countries but the subtext to much of this chapter's analysis is that the construction of markets configured along neoliberal lines in Eastern Central Europe has also had an effect to discipline workers in Western Europe.

Eurozone crisis. The region's historical integration into existing European political and economic structures after Soviet collapse contributed a certain vulnerability of Eastern Central Europe to the global financial crisis (Becker et al. 2010; Walter 2016). The emerging financial markets in Eastern Central Europe were unique opportunities for finance capital with credit markets for portfolio and foreign direct investment in a region largely devoid of such means (Karwowski and Stockhammer 2017). These events have been a crucial point of policy intervention for the EBRD.

The EBRD began to emphasize the external origins of the crisis arguing that the region's financial integration into the European banking system acted as a buffer by reducing the reversal of capital flows associated with previous crises (EBRD 2009; Shields 2019). The global financial and Eurozone crises offered a number of opportunities for the renewal of neoliberalism. As then chief economist, Erik Berglof, forewarned in the 2008 annual report,

> Finding and financing worthwhile projects will be more difficult in a region affected by the crisis and a reduction of FDI flows. At the same time, the crisis brings opportunities to accelerate change and to support the structural reforms required to foster transition and take advantage. (EBRD 2008: 21)

The EBRD will be closely involved in the process, or in their own terminology they will be the 'catalyst' (EBRD 2008: 21). The new policies of post-crisis development will necessitate continued commitment to active market construction. By 2010, Berglof was bracing the region and policy-makers to not lose their nerve 'complacency would threaten not only recovery, but also long-term economic growth. There can be no return to the region's pre-crisis dynamism without new reform' (EBRD 2010: iv).

The new reforms have taken the shape of social innovation and have come to be associated with 'New Public Management' and an ambiguous relationship with neoliberalism (for an excellent review, see Fougere et al. 2017). Social innovation is narrowly framed in market terms (Jessop et al. 2013) as the appropriate reaction to the global financial crisis, it is an apolitical pragmatic set of solutions to post-crisis problems focused on 'driving a new type of society in which the provision of social welfare is less the responsibility of the state and more a matter of enterprising individuals and organisations' (Fougere et al. 2017: 821). This should not sound too unfamiliar when considered across the three discursive shifts in the EBRD.

The social policy responses to the crisis enthusiastically promoted by the EBRD and other institutions become far more focused on the individual and non-state institutions rather than the more traditional placement of responsibility on the state to intervene. By 2009 the EBRD was steering discussions along with other IFI to identify the hindrances to a return to growth and entrepreneurial vitality in

Eastern Central Europe (EC/OECD/EBRD 2009). Consulting this documentation, reveals how most recommendations focused on reforms associated with innovation systems that foster regional business clusters, SMEs, and entrepreneurship. There is a clear connection with the preceding shifts in policy at the EBRD. This is framed in parallel cases across the EU, for example as a way to rescue the wider European compatibleness project to restore creativity and flexibility to the European political economy. The EBRD has a wealth of experience to draw on having been here before. 'It is well equipped to support the ongoing and uneven transition process further, reforms will constitute [...] an enabling environment' (EBRD 2012: 30). One of the EBRD's roles has been to extend such technical aspects into parts of the world where in many respects such activities have been absent. This exacerbates the potential principal-agent problem for EBRD members and countries of operation when decision-making is concealed behind closed doors.

One way to promote this enabling environment has been the EBRD's role in facilitating the parallelism across other institutions. This may be relatively informal for the EBRD normally, but in the wake of the crisis this is embodied in the Vienna Initiatives the outcome of institutional attempts at 'coordinated crisis management' by the EBRD, private sector actors (mainly banks), other IFI and EU institutions. The Vienna Initiative of 2009 implemented a set of initiatives to minimize systemic risk in Eastern Central Europe and in banks' home countries, and then the 2011 iteration that came to be known as Vienna 2.0 attempted to revitalize sustainable growth with a shift towards domestic funding for finance in Eastern Central Europe, and establish a seemingly permanent emergency response to crisis in the region. Or as Berglof, EBRD chief economist, volunteers, 'what can be done to design institutions and procedures to facilitate coordination where existing formal frameworks fail' (Berglof 2012: 437). The Vienna Initiative emerged when several bank groups with a strong presence in the region wrote a letter to the European Commission, the EIB, and the EBRD, thus 'exposing the governance vacuum at the heart of the pan-European financial system: the lack of an ultimate guardian for the interdependent, pan-European financial system' (Pistor 2011: 17). The Vienna Initiative shows how the EBRD as agent seeks to extend its competencies.

As Berglof's account reveals, the EBRD (alongside the Austrian Ministry of Finance) organized a number of workshops and brainstorming sessions devoted to stakeholders and ensured cooperation with the EIB to provide resources to pan-European bank groups to prevent a major capital retrenchment in Eastern Central Europe. The plan signalled IFI commitment to address the regional components of the crisis not just distinct national ones (EBRD, EIB, and World Bank 2011). The wider strategic promise to reinforce neoliberal policy is also clear: most countries are demonstrating continuing commitment to market reforms and democratic processes. 'A crisis can lead to reversals, but can also create new opportunities in healthier and stronger systems'. The EBRD is committed to being the catalyst in this process (EBRD 2008: 21).

The immediate outcomes of the Vienna Initiative included host country commitments to provide liquidity and deposit insurance to subsidiaries of foreign bank groups, no ring-fencing of assets and that the use of bailout funds should not be restricted. The initiative included funding for European bank groups to remain involved in specific regional countries. The EBRD and EIB would monitor regional developments while the banks agreed not to disengage from Eastern Central Europe and make public such commitments. Does this indicate an emerging next iteration of EBRD policy?

The joint IFI brought 25 billion euro of investment to the financial sectors of Eastern Central Europe from 2010 (EBRD 2009) shifting focus to domestic production and finance in the region. This is a permanent emergency response to crisis in Eastern Central Europe. The EBRD has utilized the crisis as an opportunity to renew commitment to reforms, the EBRD did not waste the opportunity of the crisis to nurture further shifts in policy (Shields 2019). The shift in strategy is necessitated as by 2013 the EBRD was concerned that Eastern Central Europe faced being 'stuck in transition' rather than in crisis. The focus of crisis-related reform offered a potential mechanism to escape being stuck. Neoliberal policy responses have won the day, and these responses partly go beyond crisis management to a broader fulfilment of the neoliberal project, 'The legacy of the crisis so far looks like being a move towards a smaller state and more unequal society' (Myant et al 2013: 408). At the EBRD, the focus of the 2013 transition report uncovers how policy can address any potential immobility to ensure future sustainable growth. As per the earlier shifts in discourse, opportunities for reform have opened up despite the difficulties of the current period. There will be difficult and protracted market-sustaining reforms (competition policy, governance, and restructuring) to surmount perceived threats of delayed reform (EBRD 2010).

7. Conclusion

This chapter started from the ambitious proposition of exploring the role played by the EBRD in Eastern Central Europe's post-communist transition. Despite this wide-scoped contribution to discussions of RDB activities in the global political economy, the EBRD remains an institution long overlooked in the academic literature. Part of that is explained by one of the key motifs running through this chapter: that the EBRD has an explicitly democratic political mandate, not just economic. Parallel to this motif is the Bank's dual role both as RDB and, crucially, as merchant bank, which frames a very specific type of engagement with what constitutes appropriate forms of development (both in terms of the financial contribution it makes to Eastern Central Europe but also the knowledge produced). The EBRD has been transparent regarding data since its establishment, in contrast to the EIB, which is key to the EBRD's ambition to be the knowledge bank for transition.

In terms of the principal-agent problem, the EBRD is an interesting case. RDB do not necessarily share the preferences of their member states. This is exacerbated in the EBRD with its dual identity as RDB and private merchant bank. The EBRD management is even further removed from the principal control of the population agents in its region of operation. See for example the grassroots activism of organizations like Bankwatch.

The chapter analysed the development of the EBRD advice and focus along four broad policy discourse shifts. These were: the initial construction of the market; the configuration of the correct institutions; the promotion of competitiveness; and then finally the post-crisis turn to social innovation. Each shift has been an attempt at re-invigorating reforms as the previous shift at best stuttered and at worst failed. The last three decades have represented a frenetic period in Eastern Central Europe, and the EBRD has contributed much to financial development and policy dialogue in the region. The Bank will continue to be significant because the global financial crisis, the Eurozone crisis, and the populist threat to democratic legitimacy in parts of Eastern Central Europe call out for an institution that has a specific position on the incoherent responses of policy-makers to allay such challenges, and to partially coordinate these responses. The EBRD is uniquely positioned to respond to developments in the European periphery, and, with the added potential of more formal coordination with the EIB, the next wave of policy responses will be crucial to the problems of the European political economy. Whether or not the current policy formulation of hegemonic neoliberalism will be able to ameliorate these problems is a question for further reflection.

References

Becker, J., Jäger, J. Leubolt, B., and Weissenbacher, R. (2010). 'Peripheral financialization and vulnerability to crisis: a regulationist perspective', *Competition and Change*, 14(2): 225–47.

Ben-Artzi, R. (2016). *Regional Development Banks in Comparison: Banking Strategies versus Development Goals*. Cambridge: Cambridge University Press.

Berglof, E. (2012). 'Filling the gaps—the Vienna Initiative and the role of the international financial institutions in crisis management and resolution'. In F. Allen, M. Aoki, J. P. Fitoussi, N. Kiyotaki, R. Gordon, and J. Stiglitz (eds.), *The Global Macro Economy and Finance*. Basingstoke: Palgrave Macmillan, pp. 211–23.

Berglof, E. (2015). 'New structural economics meets European transition', *Journal of Economic Policy Reform*, 18(2): 114–30.

Bermeo, N. and Pontusson, J. (2012). *Coping with Crisis: Government Reactions to the Great Recession*. New York: Russell Sage Foundation.

Bockman, J. and Eyal, G. (2002). 'Eastern Europe as a laboratory for economic knowledge: the transnational roots of neoliberalism', *American Journal of Sociology*, 108(2): 310–52.

Bohle, D. (2000). 'Internationalisation: an issue neglected in the path-dependency approach to post-communist transformation'. In M. Dobry (ed.), *Democratic and Capitalist Transitions in Eastern Europe: Lessons for the Social Sciences*. Dordrecht, NL: Springer, pp. 235–61.

Bronstone, A. (1999). *The European Bank for Reconstruction and Development: The Building of a Bank for East Central Europe*. Manchester: Manchester University Press.

Cammack, P. (2004). 'What the World Bank means by poverty reduction, and why it matters', *New Political Economy*, 9(2): 189–211.

Cammack, P. (2006). 'The politics of global competitiveness', Papers in the Politics of Global Competitiveness, No. 1, Institute for Global Studies, Manchester Metropolitan University, e-space Open Access Repository.

Cammack, P. (2019). 'The OECD and the world market: antecedents of deep marketization', *Globalizations*, 16(6): 804–18.

Campos, N. and Horváth, R. (2012). 'On the reversability of structural reforms', *Economics Letters*, 117(1): 217–19.

Carroll, T. (2012). 'Working on, through and around the state: the deep marketisation of development in the Asia-Pacific', *Journal of Contemporary Asia*, 42(3): 378–404.

Carroll, T. and Jarvis, D.S.L. (2015). 'The new politics of development: citizens, civil society, and the evolution of neoliberal development policy', *Globalizations*, 12(3): 281–304.

Carroll, T., Clifton, J., and Jarvis, D.S.L. (2019). 'Power, leverage and marketization: the diffusion of neoliberalism from North to South and back again', *Globalizations*, 16(6): 771–77.

CEE (Central and Eastern Europe) Bankwatch (2011). *Are We Nearly There Yet? Dilemmas of Transition after 20 Years of the EBRD's Operations*. Prague: CEE Bankwatch.

Chakrabarti, S. (2019). 'Europe and the future of development finance'. Speech at Kreditanstalt für Wiederaufbau, 14 January. Available online at: www.ebrd.com/news/speeches/europe-and-the-future-of-development-finance.html

Clifton, J. and Díaz-Fuentes, D. (2014). 'The OECD and "The Rest": analyzing the limits of policy transfer', *Journal of Comparative Policy Analysis: Research and Practice*, 16(3): 249–65.

Clifton, J., Lanthier, P., and Schröter, H. (2011). 'Regulating and deregulating the public utilities 1830–2010', *Business History*, 53(5): 659–72.

Clifton, J., Díaz-Fuentes, D., and Gómez, A.L. (2017). 'The European Investment Bank: a new database (1958–2012)'. MPRA Paper No. 78173.

Clifton, J., Díaz-Fuentes, D., and Gómez, A. L. (2018). 'The European Investment Bank: development, integration, investment?', *Journal of Common Market Studies*, 56(4): 733–50.

Council of Europe (1993). 'Report on the European Bank for Reconstruction and Development—achievements, activities and priorities'. Doc. 6861 1403–3/6/93-2-E. Available online at: http://assembly.coe.int/nw/xml/XRef/X2H-Xref-View HTML.asp?FileID=7214&lang=EN

Dabrowski, M., Gomulka, S., and Rostowski, J. (2001). 'Whence reform? A critique of the Stiglitz perspective', *Journal of Policy Reform*, 4(4): 291–324.

Dumała, H. (2018). 'Support of economic transition of Eastern European countries by the European Bank for Reconstruction and Development', *Facta Simonidis*, 11(1): 139–60.

EBRD (European Bank for Reconstruction and Development) (1990–2013). *Basic Documents of the EBRD*. London: EBRD.

EBRD (European Bank for Reconstruction and Development) (1991). *A Changing Europe: Annual Review and Financial Report*. London: EBRD.

EBRD (European Bank for Reconstruction and Development) (1995). *Transition Report 1995: Investment and Enterprise Development*. London: EBRD.

EBRD (European Bank for Reconstruction and Development) (1998). *Transition Report 1998: Financial Sector in Transition*. London: EBRD.

EBRD (European Bank for Reconstruction and Development) (1999). *Annual Report 1999*. London: EBRD.

EBRD (European Bank for Reconstruction and Development) (2002). *Transition Report 2002*. London: EBRD.

EBRD (European Bank for Reconstruction and Development) (2007). *Life in Transition: A Survey of People's Experiences and Attitudes*. London: EBRD.

EBRD (European Bank for Reconstruction and Development) (2008). *Annual Report 2008*. London: EBRD.

EBRD (European Bank for Reconstruction and Development) (2009). *Transition Report 2009: Transition in Crisis*. London: EBRD.

EBRD (European Bank for Reconstruction and Development) (2010). *Annual Report 2010: Securing the Recovery*. London: EBRD.

EBRD (European Bank for Reconstruction and Development) (2012). *Transition Report 2012: Integration across Borders*. London: EBRD.

EBRD (European Bank for Reconstruction and Development) (2013). *Guide to EBRD Financing*. London: EBRD.

EBRD (European Bank for Reconstruction and Development) (2015). *Annual Report 2015*. London: EBRD.

EBRD (European Bank for Reconstruction and Development) (2016). *Strategy for the Promotion of Gender Equality 2016–2020*. London: EBRD.

EBRD (European Bank for Reconstruction and Development) (2017). *Regional Economic Prospects in EBRD Countries of Operations*. May. London: EBRD.

EBRD (European Bank for Reconstruction and Development) (2018). *EBRD Annual Review*. London: EBRD. Available online at: https://2018.ar-ebrd.com/

EBRD (European Bank for Reconstruction and Development) (2020). *EBRD Shareholders and Board of Governors*. London: EBRD. Available online at: https://www.ebrd.com/shareholders-and-board-of-governors.html

EBRD (European Bank for Reconstruction and Development), EIB (European Investment Bank) and World Bank (2011). *Final Report on the Joint IFI Action Plan*. London EBRD.

Epstein, R. (2014). 'When do foreign banks "cut and run"? Evidence from West European bailouts and East European markets', *Review of International Political Economy*, 21(4): 847–77.

European Commission (1998). *Establishing a Phare/EBRD Bangkok Facility Programme DGIA/EN/51/98*. Brussels: European Commission.

EC/OECD/EBRD (European Commission / Organisation for European Co-operation and Development / European Bank for Reconstruction and Development) (2009). *SME Policy Index, Progress in Implementation of the European Charter for Small Enterprises*. Paris: OECD.

Ellerman, D. (2009). *Helping People Help Themselves: From the World Bank to an Alternative Philosophy of Development Assistance - Evolving Values for a Capitalist World*. Ann Arbor: University of Michigan Press.

European Community (1989). *Official Journal of the European Community L 377*, 25 December. Brussels: EC.

Falcetti, E., Lysenko, T., and Sanfey, P. (2006). 'Reforms and growth in transition: Re-examining the evidence', *Journal of Comparative Economics*, 34(3): 421–45.

Fougère, M., Segercrantz, B., and Seeck, H. (2017). 'A critical reading of the European Union's social innovation policy discourse: (re)legitimizing neoliberalism', *Organization*, 24(6): 819–43.

Georgiev, Y., Nagy-Mohacsi, P., and Plekhanov, A. (2017). 'Structural reform and productivity growth in emerging Europe and Central Asia', *ADB Economics Working Paper Series* 523, Asian Development Bank.

Gerard, K. and Johnston, M. (2019). 'Explaining microfinance's resilience: the case of microfinance in Australia', *Globalizations*, 16(6): 876–93.

Guriev, S. and Melnikov, N. (2017). 'Happiness convergence in transition countries'. EBRD Working Paper No. 204.

Hamm, P., King, L., and Stuckler, D. (2012). 'Mass privatization, state capacity, and economic growth in post-communist countries', *American Sociological Review*, 77(2): 295–324.

Havrylyshyn, O. (2006). *Divergent Paths in Post-Communist Transformation*. Basingstoke: Palgrave Macmillan.

Hay, C. and Rosamond, B. (2002). 'Globalization, European integration and the discursive construction of economic imperatives', *Journal of European Public Policy*, 9(2): 147–67.

Hellman, J.S., Jones, G., and Kaufmann, D. (2003). 'Seize the state, seize the day: state capture and influence in transition economies', *Journal of Comparative Economics*, 31(4): 751–73.

Howarth, D. and Quaglia, L. (2015). 'The political economy of the euro area's sovereign debt crisis: introduction to the special issue of the *Review of International Political Economy*', *Review of International Political Economy*, 22: 457–84.

Ivanova, M.N. (2007). 'Why there was no "Marshall Plan" for Eastern Europe and why this still matters', *Journal of Contemporary European Studies*, 15(3): 345–76.

Jakobeit, C. (1992). 'The EBRD: redundant, or an important actor in the transformation of Eastern Europe?'. *Intereconomics*, 27(3): 119–23.

Jessop, B., Moulaert, F., Hulgård, L., and Hamdouch, A. (2013). 'Social innovation research: a new stage in innovation analysis?' In F. Moulaert, D. Macallum, A. Mehmood and A. Hamdouch (eds.), *International Handbook on Social Innovation: Collective Action, Social Learning and Transdisciplinary Research*. London: Edward Elgar Publishing, pp. 110–30.

Karwowski, E. and Stockhammer, E. (2017). 'Financialisation in emerging economies: a systematic overview and comparison with Anglo-Saxon economies', *Economic and Political Studies*, 5(1): 60–86.

Krstic, G. and Sanfey, P. (2012). 'Earnings inequality and the informal economy: evidence from Serbia'. EBRD Working Paper No. 114.

Mertens, D. and Thiemann, M. (2019). 'Building a hidden investment state? The European Investment Bank, national development banks and European economic governance', *Journal of European Public Policy*, 26(1): 23–43.

Murrell, P. (1995). 'The transition according to Cambridge, Mass', *Journal of Economic Literature*, 33(1): 164–78.

Myant, M. and Drahokoupil, J. (2012). 'International integration, varieties of capitalism and resilience to crisis in transition economies', *Europe-Asia Studies*, 64(1): 1–33.

Myant, M., Drahokoupil, J., and Ivan Lesay, I. (2013). 'The political economy of crisis management in East–Central European countries', *Europe-Asia Studies*, 65(3): 383–410.

Nunn, A. (2019). 'Neoliberalization, fast policy transfer and the management of labour market services'. *Review of International Political Economy*. doi.org/10.1080/09692290.2019.1625424

Park, S. and Strand, J.R. (2016). *Global Economic Governance and the Development Practices of the Multilateral Development Banks*. London: Routledge.

Peck, Jamie (2010). *Constructions of Neoliberal Reason*. Oxford: Oxford University Press.

Piroska, D. and Podvršič, A. (2019). 'New European banking governance and crisis of democracy: bank restructuring and privatization in Slovenia', *New Political Economy*. DOI: 10.1080/13563467.2019.1669548 1–15.

Pistor, K. (2011). 'Governing interdependent financial systems: lessons from the Vienna Initiative'. Columbia Law and Economics Working Paper No. 396, Columbia University School of Law.

Rapacki, R. and Blazyca, G. (2001). *Poland into the New Millennium, Economies and Societies in Transition.* Cheltenham: Edward Elgar.

Reisen, H. (2015). 'Will the AIIB and the NDB help reform multilateral development banking?'. *Global Policy*, 6(3): 297–304.

Shields, S. (2019). 'Defining, censuring, and resolving: the EBRD, collective organic intellectuals and the global financial crisis in Eastern Central Europe', *Globalizations*, 16(6): 819–37.

Shields, S. and Wallin, S. (2015). 'The European Bank for Reconstruction and Development's gender action plan and the gendered political economy of post-communist transition', *Globalizations*, 12(3): 383–99.

Shihata, I. and Attali, J. (1991). *The European Bank for Reconstruction and Development: A Comparative Analysis of the Constituent Agreement.* Nijhoff: Brill.

Smith, A. (2002). 'Imagining geographies of the "new Europe": geo-economic power and the new European architecture of integration', *Political Geography*, 21(5): 647–70.

Stern, N. (2003). 'Development as a process of change: toward a dynamic public economics', *Proceedings of the British Academy*, 121: 277–99.

Stiglitz, J. and Ellerman, D. (2001). 'Not poles apart: "whither reform?" and "whence reform?"', *Journal of Policy Reform*, 4(4): 325–38.

Stuckler, D., King, L., and McKee, M. (2009). 'Mass privatisation and the post-communist mortality crisis: a cross-national analysis', *The Lancet*, 373(9661): 399–407.

TACIS (Technical Assistance to the Commonwealth of Independent States) (1996). 'TACIS summary of indicative programmes 1993–1995'. EU Commission Working Document. Available online at: http://aei.pitt.edu/36324/

Vuylsteke, C. (1995). 'The EBRD: its mandate, instruments, challenges and responses', *MOCT-MOST: Economic Policy in Transitional Economies*, 5(2): 129–55.

Wallin, S. (2018). 'Gender mainstreaming at the European Bank for Reconstruction and Development'. In Juanita Elias and Adrienne Roberts (eds.), *Handbook on the International Political Economy of Gender*. London: Edward Elgar.

Walter, S. (2016). 'Crisis politics in Europe: why austerity is easier to implement in some countries than in others', *Comparative Political Studies*, 49(7): 841–73.

Weber, S. (1994). 'Origins of the European Bank for Reconstruction and Development', *International Organization*, 48: 1–38.

World Bank (1997). *World Development Report: The State in the Changing World.* New York: Oxford University Press.

9

The Asian Infrastructure Investment Bank

Its Birth, Mandates, and Infrastructure Financing

Jiajun Xu

1. Introduction

The hegemonic power transition from the United States (US) to China has manifested itself in the creation of the Asian Infrastructure Investment Bank (AIIB) under Chinese leadership. The AIIB is a unique regional development bank (RDB), because it is the first time that nations, both rich and poor, have embraced an initiative from an ascending power *without* the participation of the incumbent hegemon—the US. Hence, the AIIB may have the potential to exert a substantial influence upon the US-led international hegemonic system after the Second World War. The present chapter addresses three questions: Why did China initiate the AIIB outside the US-centred international development financing system? What is the likely evolution of the AIIB's mandate? And to what extent the AIIB's infrastructure financing differs from that of the Asian Development Bank (ADB)?

To tackle the first question, this chapter deploys Hirschman's 'Exit-Voice' analytical framework to unveil China's decision to set up the AIIB. It hypothesizes that the ascending power will opt for exit if it fails to gain influence commensurate with its rising economic status within the existing hegemonic system. Empirical evidence largely supports this hypothesis, but also enriches it by showing that China has deployed a 'two-leg' strategy instead of an either-or (exit or voice) one: China has set up new institutions while vying for influence within the US-dominated multilateral development banks (MDB).

For the remaining two research questions that direct this chapter, the AIIB is too young to subject its mandates or operations to empirical testing. Thus, the chapter relies on comparative analyses to gain fresh insights. The AIIB fosters sustainable economic development and improving infrastructure connectivity in Asia by investing in infrastructure and other productive sectors. While the AIIB's mandate might adapt to emerging demands over time, the Bank is likely to focus on infrastructure financing for the foreseeable future for two reasons. First, significant collective action would be necessary to modify the well-focused official mandate of the AIIB. Second, the AIIB was set up to redress the problem of the

Jiajun Xu, *The Asian Infrastructure Investment Bank: Its Birth, Mandates, and Infrastructure Financing* In: *Regional Development Banks in the World Economy*. Edited by: Judith Clifton, Daniel Díaz-Fuentes, and David Howarth, Oxford University Press (2021). © Oxford University Press. DOI: 10.1093/oso/9780198861089.003.0009

proliferating development agenda in the existing MDB and RDB at the expense of infrastructure financing. The AIIB's official mandate puts equal emphasis on sustainable economic development and regional cooperation. In practice, so far the AIIB have primarily invested in single-country infrastructure projects instead of multi-country ones. Compared with infrastructure financing at the well-established ADB, the AIIB has a much greater potential for enlarging its operations among a more diverse group of clients than the ADB and, furthermore, the AIIB has already demonstrated that it is more likely to undertake environmentally and socially riskier projects than the ADB.

The rest of the chapter will proceed as follows. Section 2 reviews the existing literature on the AIIB specifically and RDB in general that is relevant to the research questions posed above. Next, in section 3, the chapter examines briefly the geo-political and economic situation in which the AIIB was established. Section 4 explores why the AIIB was set up, while section 5 examines the original mandate of the AIIB and its likely evolution. Section 6 compares the AIIB's infrastructure financing with that of the ADB. And section 7 summarizes the key findings.

2. State of the art

The AIIB has been in the spotlight as the topic of lively debates in media and policy circles. The often public debates have concentrated on China's geo-political ambitions and their potential negative impact upon the so-called international best practice in multilateral development financing. It has been argued that the AIIB represents a challenge to the US-dominated economic world order (European Political Strategy Centre 2015; Hakans and Hynes 2017) and that the AIIB may offer loans with fewer strings attached and downgrade standards of transparency and accountability (Qing 2015). Yet rigorous academic research is relatively scant,[1] as the AIIB is such a young institution in comparison to most of the RDB examined in this volume and to the World Bank.

Most of the existing academic research examining the AIIB has concentrated on the question of why China established the Bank. Chow (2016) argues that the primary reason was China's limited role in the US-dominated World Bank and International Monetary Fund (IMF) and the dim prospects to exercise an expanded role in the near future. He further contends that China will use the AIIB to pursue its own national interests such as internationalizing the Chinese currency (RMB) and mitigating excessive domestic industrial over-capacity, as the US has used the World Bank to advance its own interests. Ikenberry and Lim

[1] For pilot efforts, see Gu (2017a, 2017b, 2017c, 2018, 2019), Radavoi and Bian (2018), Zhao, Gou, and Li (2019), Gransow and Price (2019).

(2017) maintain that aside from specific pecuniary and development motivations, China initiated the AIIB for potential 'counter-hegemonic' purposes that are constrained by multilateralism, international financial markets, and the broader challenge of competitive order building. Wan (2016) compares the AIIB's institutional design with that of the World Bank and the ADB to assess the strategic significance of the AIIB in advancing China's East Asian International Order. This work builds on previous studies on RDB which argue that they can help to mitigate power asymmetry between rich and poor countries; that developing countries called for the establishment of RDB to redress the deficiencies of the World Bank (White 1972); and that the structure of national power capabilities affects the operation of RDB (Krasner 1981). In short, the efforts of developing countries in vying for influence has been an important underlying factor regarding the creation of RDB in the past.

3. Background of the birth of the AIIB

The birth of the AIIB reflects the ongoing hegemonic transition from the US to China. China was previously a capital importer and aid recipient in a US-centred international monetary and financial system. Yet the four decades of robust economic growth after the reform and opening up in the late 1970s have enabled China to emerge as an increasingly important provider of development financing, including foreign aid, equity investments, and long-term loans. This status of capital-provider is strongly backed up by China's huge foreign exchange reserves—over USD 3 trillion in 2016. However, China's large foreign reserves denominated in US dollars have carried the risk of dramatic depreciation due to the central role of the US currency in the international monetary system. Hence, the Chinese government has moved to investing its foreign exchange reserves in real assets that generate a reliable flow of returns over the coming decades. One recent example is the China-Africa Fund for Industrial Cooperation (CAFIC) with the initial share capital of USD 10 billion—80 per cent from foreign reserves and 20 per cent from China's Ex-Im Bank.

The AIIB was the brainchild of the Chinese government, and was first proposed by the Chinese president, Xi Jinping, and premier, Li Keqiang, during their respective visits to South-East Asian countries in October 2013. One year later, on 21 October 2014, twenty-one Asian countries signed a memorandum of understanding (MOU) to establish the AIIB with the authorized capital of USD 100 billion and with Beijing elected as the future headquarters.[2] After the accession of the United Kingdom was officially announced in March 2015, a significant

[2] The MOU on establishing the AIIB was signed in Beijing (AIIB 2015a; Xinhua News Agency 2014a).

number of additional national governments moved to join the AIIB, reaching a total of fifty-seven prospective founding members by June 2015.[3] Once its Articles of Agreement entered into force on 25 December 2015, the AIIB opened its doors on 16 January 2016 aimed at pioneering the 'Lean, Clean and Green' mode of operating—lean, with a small efficient management team and highly skilled staff; clean, an ethical organization with no tolerance for corruption; and green, an institution that is built on respect for the environment.[4]

The AIIB's membership has already rapidly expanded to seventy-one as of the end of October 2019, exceeding that of the ADB. The membership includes forty-four regional members and twenty-seven non-regional members. It is worth noting that six prospective regional members and eighteen prospective non-regional members plan to join the AIIB. The AIIB has attracted the accession of most major advanced economies except the US and Japan. Compared to the ADB, the AIIB has attracted far more country members from outside the region, which is testimony to the AIIB's strategic importance for countries even outside Asia. This importance is clear especially given the fact that the AIIB, unlike most established RDB,[5] sticks to the principle of universal procurement and universal recruitment that does not grant any tangible club goods to non-regional members.

4. Why the AIIB was established

What has motivated China to initiate the AIIB—an 'exit' option in Hirschman's (1970) terminology—outside the US-led international development financing system established after Second World War?

Overcoming market failures in infrastructure financing

The official answer from the Chinese government is that given the vast infrastructure financing gap in developing countries in general and developing Asia in particular, development banks are well-positioned to provide long-term finance and mitigate the infrastructural deficit.[6] An emerging consensus among scholars and practitioners is that filling the infrastructure financing gap is pivotal to economic growth and poverty reduction (Czernich et al. 2011; Calderón and Servén 2014; Ismail and Mahyideen 2015). The ADB estimates that developing Asia will require an investment of USD 26 trillion from 2016 to 2030, or USD 1.7 trillion per year,

[3] AIIB (2015b). [4] AIIB (2015c, 2019a).

[5] For instance, the ADB's procurement policy stipulates that only bidders from member countries are eligible to bid for projects financed by loans or grants from its OCR- or ADB-administered funds (ADB 2017).

[6] MoF of the PRC (2015).

if the region is to maintain its growth momentum, alleviate poverty, and respond to climate change (ADB 2017).[7] Development banks are established to advance the objective of public policies (such as building basic infrastructure with positive externalities) rather than profit maximization as commercial banks do. Commercial banks and private capital markets are often associated with short-ermism and risk aversion so that they are unwilling or unable to provide long-term and high-risk infrastructure financing. This kind of market failure is particularly acute in developing countries where risks are misperceived and financial markets are under-developed.

National and international fiscal resources are often too limited to redress such market failures and fill the infrastructure gap. Official international and national development assistance is too piecemeal with the bulk directed to social sectors. From 2011 to 2015, Development Assistance Committee (DAC) donors mainly from the Organisation of European Co-operation and Development (OECD) countries provided an annual average of USD 122 billion of Official Development Assistance (ODA) to developing countries, accounting for 0.3 per cent of the donor countries' gross national income (GNI). Yet only 17 per cent of this amount was invested in economic infrastructure, whereas a majority of ODA (nearly two-fifths) was concentrated in the areas of social infrastructure such as education, health, and government and civil society. As for domestic resource mobilization, many developing countries have very limited fiscal resources.

Entrenched disparity between economic capacity and policy influence in the existing MDB

While the infrastructure deficit may be a primary motivation behind China's decision to establish the AIIB, this factor alone is insufficient in explaining why China did not invest all of its surplus capital in the existing MDB. A close look at the internal governance of the existing MDB reveals that voting power reform has lagged far behind shifts in relative economic capacity, thus discouraging an ascendant China from investing within the US-centred MDB. The pre-emptive rights principle—no country can gain more voting power unless all member countries agree—has further entrenched the status quo, worsening the disparity between voting power and economic capacity. In the case of the World Bank, the US resists selective capital increases which run the risk of diluting US voting power and even depriving it of 'veto power' privilege. Other economic powers in relative decline in Europe and North America are also reluctant to relinquish their

[7] An earlier study estimated that between 2010 and 2020, Asia would need to invest approximately USD 8 trillion in overall national infrastructure or about USD 750 billion per year during the eleven-year period (ADB and ADBI 2009).

voting power, as they often view the ranking in World Bank voting power as a manifestation of their international status. Despite the recent voice reform at the World Bank, Vestergaard and Wade (2013, 2015) show that it was too piecemeal and slow to redress the disparity between voting power and economic capacity. In the case of the ADB, Japan and the US have dominated the governance with a voting power of 12.798 per cent and 12.710 per cent, respectively, whereas China only has a voting power of 5.459 per cent, despite the fact that China overtook Japan as the world's second largest economy in 2010. Hence, as declining powers are reluctant to relinquish their voting powers in the traditional MDB, the rigid governance system creates little incentive for an ascending China to increase its financial support within the US-led international development financing system.

Despite China's limited voice in the established institutions, as setting up a brand new MDB or RDB entails huge upfront costs and uncertainties, the Chinese government may have good reason to take the initial step to seek to influence the existing MDB and RDB before establishing a new one. In rationalist terms, China had to weigh up the benefits of influencing the existing MDB and RDB against the cost of establishing a new one. Delving deeper into the Chinese government's decision-making process, Xu (2017) discovers that the government initially took a stakeholder approach and chose the 'voice' option prior to setting up new MDB. In 2007, the Chinese government decided to become a new donor to the World Bank's soft-loan window—International Development Association (IDA)—to vie for influence from within, because the Chinese government was concerned as to its de facto status as 'a quasi-donor without rights' in the Bank that it decided to buy 'voice' opportunities. On the one hand, traditional IDA donors had taken advantage of negotiating how to 'replenish' IDA to capture de facto decision-making power at the World Bank, bypassing the board of executive directors and marginalizing the voice of both IDA recipients and International Bank for Reconstruction and Development (IBRD) borrowers. On the other hand, China and other IBRD borrowers reluctantly made indirect financial contributions to IDA via IBRD net income transfers that were urged by rich donor countries. In short, before venturing to establish a new RDB, the Chinese government attempted to seek more influence from within.

However, this effort to increase influence within the existing MDB was frustrated, leading the Chinese government ultimately to decide to adopt a 'two-leg' approach by both initiating new MDB and simultaneously shaping the existing ones. In order to persuade the Chinese government to forgo the pursuit of the outside option, the US administration promised to cede more influence to China and other emerging economies in the Bretton Woods Institutions. However, the pace was too slow and the scale too piecemeal. By way of example, in the wake of the recent global financial crisis, Group of Twenty leaders agreed in 2010 that individual IMF quotas and voting rights needed to better reflect Fund members' standing in the world economy. The quota and governance reforms were then approved by the IMF's board of governors in December 2010. The reforms required the acceptance by the membership—with an 85 per cent majority of the total voting power—which in many cases involved parliamentary approval. This granted the US Congress—the largest shareholder—a de facto veto power and the US Congress dragged its feet on agreeing to the reforms for five years. It was not until the Chinese government successfully initiated the AIIB—and succeeded in even bringing on board US allies such as the United Kingdom—that the US Congress ultimately approved the IMF reforms, in December 2015.[8] In summary, the frustration of the Chinese government with its progress in gaining influence in the existing MDB encouraged it to initiate new international development finance institution in order to put competitive pressures upon the existing ones.

Thus, the birth of the AIIB results primarily from the entrenched disparity between economic capacity and policy influence in the existing MDB where rising economic powers failed to strengthen their position. Establishing the AIIB is a key element in the Chinese government's 'two-leg' stakeholder approach to reforming the international development financing system—that is, establishing new RDB while participating in the existing ones to vie for more influence.

5. The AIIB's original mandate and its potential evolution

According to its articles of agreement (AoA), the purpose of the AIIB is similar to other RDB with a focus upon both development and regional integration. It is to:

> (i) foster sustainable economic development, create wealth and improve infrastructure connectivity in Asia by investing in infrastructure and other productive sectors; and (ii) promote regional cooperation and partnership in addressing development challenges by working in close collaboration with other multilateral and bilateral development institutions. (AIIB 2015d: ch. I, Article 1.1)

In comparison with the existing MDB and RDB, the AIIB has a much clearer sectoral focus. Unlike the World Bank and most of the existing RDB that touch nearly every sector that is important to fighting poverty, the AIIB gives prominence to infrastructure and other productive sectors—a more direct focus upon stimulating economic growth and thus alleviating poverty in the long run. Such an emphasis on infrastructure financing can help the AIIB to fill a niche in that most existing MDB, including the World Bank, have reduced their support for infrastructure since the 1990s. By way of example, the bulk of the World Bank's lending falls into the category of social sectors and public administration, whereas infrastructure only accounts for about one-third (see Figure 9.1).

[8] IMF (2015).

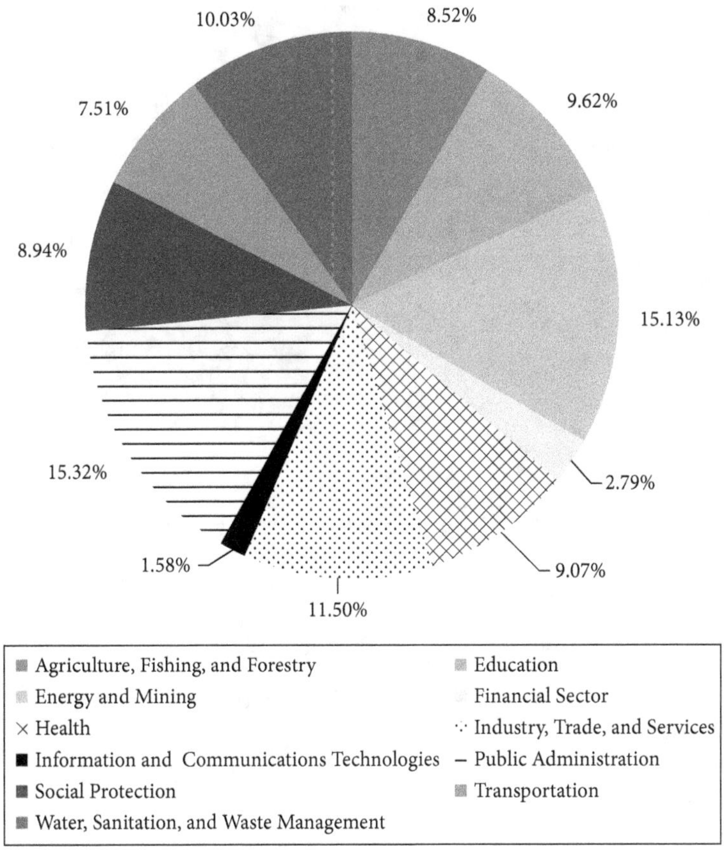

Figure 9.1 World Bank: sectoral distribution of loans (2018)
Source: World Bank (2018: 82, 86).

A close look at the sectoral distribution (b) of RDB reveals that the ADB, African Development Bank, and Inter-American Development Bank (IADB) have also diversified their operation into multiple sectors including health, education, and public sector management despite the recent increase in infrastructure financing (see Figures 9.2, 9.3, and 9.4). This further emphasizes the relatively unique mandate of the AIIB.

Will the mandate of the AIIB expand to include additional sectoral priorities in the future? The development of MDB and RDB over time reflects the preferences of their shareholders and/or because of the more proactive initiatives of the banks' management. Sometimes adaptation is necessary and desirable because development banks may accomplish their original mandates and would fall into oblivion without revised objectives. For example, the IBRD—the parent institution of the World Bank—was initially set up to focus primarily on reconstructing Western Europe and Japan after the Second World War, thus meeting US geo-strategic

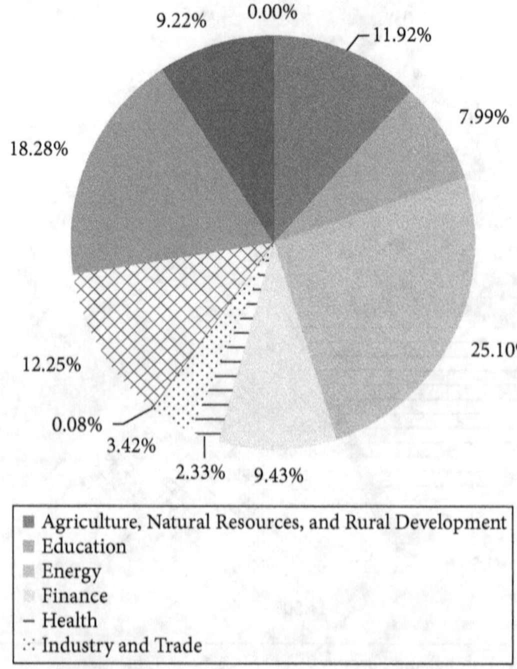

Figure 9.2 Asian Development Bank: sectoral distribution of loans (2018)
Source: ADB (2018, appendix 6).

objectives. Following reconstruction, the IBRD shifted its primary focus to economic development of developing countries. Later on, the World Bank went a step further by establishing the IDA that provided interest-free loans to low-income countries, too poor to borrow at the IBRD's near-market rate. Yet, on other occasions, the expansion of the original mandate may fall into the trap of mission creep. This can result in overlapping mandates with other international institutions and the dilution of operational focus. For instance, a European executive director once commented that the World Bank was 'the victim of its own success'—as key shareholders recognized the efficiency of the Bank's management, they were inclined to add additional functions resulting in the dilution of the Bank's focus and moving away from its core competencies.[9] Given the limited resources available, the proliferating policy agenda resulted in shrinking World Bank funding for infrastructure and yawning financing gaps. To address this problem, the Chinese government garnered the support of a range of national governments to initiate a specialized development bank with the primary focus on infrastructure financing.

[9] Interview with the World Bank's executive director, Washington, DC, May 2012.

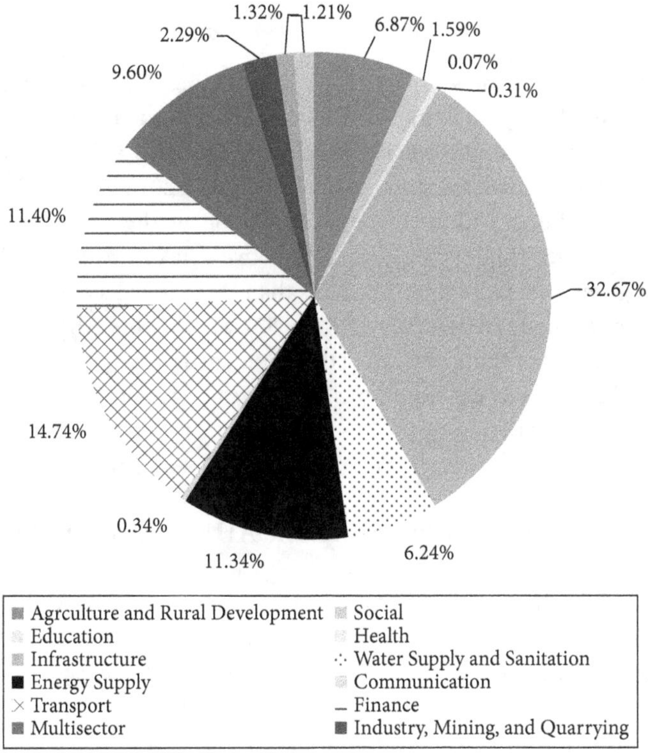

Figure 9.3 African Development Bank Group: sectoral distribution of loans (2018)
Source: African Development Bank (2018: 49).

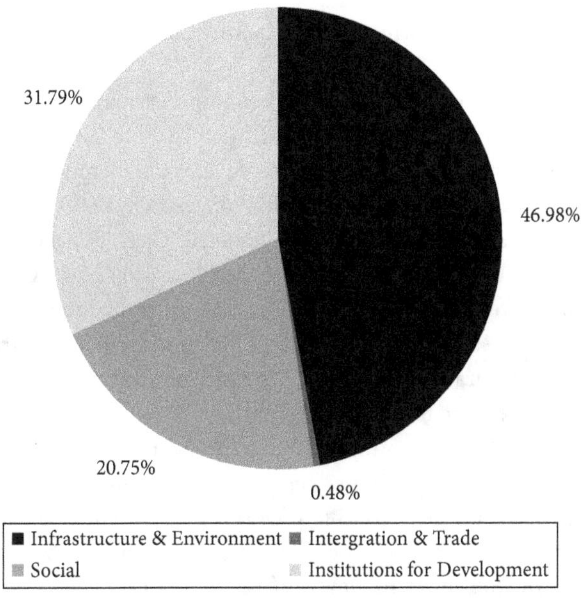

Figure 9.4 Inter-American Development Bank: sectoral distribution of loans (2018)
Source: Inter-American Development Bank (2018: 6).

While the AIIB's mandate might evolve over time, there is good reason to believe that the AIIB will continue to focus on infrastructure financing in the foreseeable future. First, the official mandate of the AIIB is highly focused, as compared with the broad mandate of the IBRD (IBRD 2012, Article 1). The AIIB Agreement may be amended only by a resolution of the board of governors approved by a super-majority vote—an affirmative vote of two-thirds of the total number of governors, representing not less than three-fourths of the total voting power of the members (AIIB 2015d, Article 53). Second, the AIIB was set up to redress the problem of the proliferating development agenda in the existing MDB and RDB, which offered the lesson to shareholders that nothing is prioritized if everything is the priority.

6. Infrastructure financing: the AIIB versus the ADB

This section will compare the infrastructure financing of the AIIB with that of the ADB. It starts with a brief comparison between the AIIB's mandate, membership, and governance and those of the ADB. It then compares the capital stock, financial instruments, and lending eligibility of the two RDB, examines the size and sectoral distribution of their infrastructure financing, explores their environmental and social safeguards, and finally makes a tentative evaluation of their project performance.

Mandate, membership, and governance

Founded in 1966, the ADB aims to 'foster economic growth and co-operation in the region of Asia and the Far East...and to contribute to the acceleration of the process of economic development of the developing member countries in the region, collectively and individually' (ADB 1965, Article 1). Compared with the ADB, the AIIB's mandate is much more focused. Over the past five decades, the ADB's membership has expanded from thirty-one to sixty-eight. Among the current members, forty-nine are regional members and nineteen non-regional members. Figure 9.5 shows that the accession of new members to the ADB year by year has been very gradual. This stands in sharp contrast with the rapid expansion of the AIIB's membership as outlined above.

As for the distribution of voting power at the ADB as of 31 December 2018, regional members provide 63.390 per cent of its capital and have 65.040 per cent of total voting power, whereas non-regional members provide 36.610 per cent of its capital and possess 34.960 per cent of the votes. Japan and the US are the largest shareholders with the voting power of 12.756 per cent each (ADB 2018: 64). To protect the Asian influence in key decisions in the organization, it is stipulated

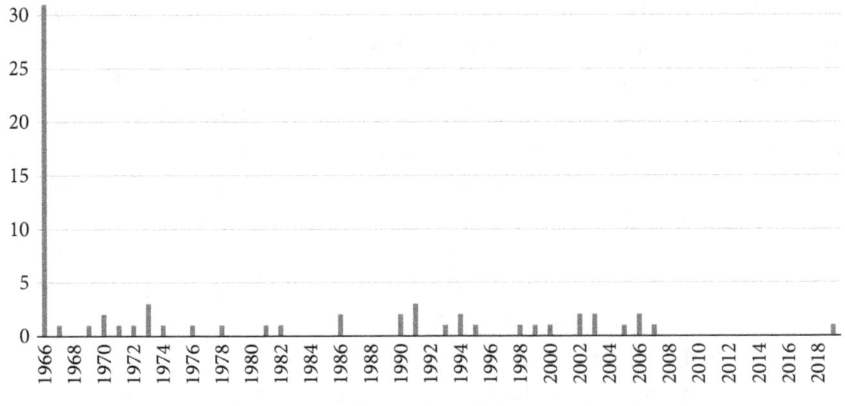

Figure 9.5 Asian Development Bank: number of new members by year
Source: ADB (2019a).

in the ADB Charter that regional members must always hold at least 60 per cent of the capital stock. Non-regional members, therefore, may never hold more than 40 per cent of the authorized stock.

Compared with the structure of voting power at the ADB, the AIIB gives more prominence to regional members than non-regional members, and grants more weight to developing economies than advanced economies. It is set down in the AIIB's AoA that non-regional members hold no more than 25 per cent of the Bank's capital stock compared with 40 per cent in the case of the ADB.[10] As of October 2019, regional members provide 76.3691 per cent of its capital accounting for 73.9671 per cent of its total voting power, whereas non-regional members provide 23.6309 per cent of its capital and enjoy 26.0329 per cent of the voting power (AIIB 2019b). Meanwhile, the AIIB adopts a gross domestic product-(GDP) based share formula to decide a member's capital subscription (AIIB 2015d, Article 5). Hence, the AIIB formula is 'pro-development,' since developing countries including China generally perform better in GDP than by other measures (Gu 2017a).

In MDB and RDB, veto power plays a pivotal role as it grants certain members tremendous power to prevent governance reforms or policy changes from occurring. Both the ADB and the AIIB require a super-majority vote—an affirmative vote of two-thirds of the total number of governors, representing not less than three-fourths of the total voting power of the members in order to decide on important issues. This means that any member whose voting power is greater than 25 per cent will be able to exercise veto power. In the case of the ADB, Japan

[10] While the board of governors by a super-majority vote may decide the percentage of capital stock held by regional members be reduced below 75 per cent, there should be a minimum of 70 per cent regional shareholding (AIIB 2015d, Article 5, and Explanatory Notes regarding Article 5, paragraphs two and three).

and the US collectively possess over 25 per cent of total voting power, which means that if they work together they can block reforms that they perceive to be to the detriment of their interests or values. In the case of the AIIB, China as the largest shareholder subscribes 30.7940 per cent of the AIIB's authorized capital and possesses 26.5664 per cent of the Bank's total voting power as of October 2019. China has veto power over important issues, like decisions on the size of the board of directors, the election of the president, as well as the amendment of the AoA.

In terms of governance, a distinction between the AIIB and the ADB is that the former has a non-resident board of directors whereas the latter has a resident one similar to the existing MDB. The AIIB executive directors meet on a roughly quarterly basis to approve the Bank's strategy, annual plan, and budget; establish policies; take decisions concerning Bank operations; supervise management and operations of the Bank; and establish an oversight mechanism (AIIB 2019c). By contrast, the ADB executive directors are resident at the headquarters and meet more frequently.[11] There are pros and cons of having a resident board at the MDB. On the one hand, a resident board may be inclined to exert undue political influence upon the Bank's operations at the expense of the Bank's professional independence. A resident board may be tempted to exercise excessive micro-management in the Bank's daily operations, leaving little room for strategy setting. Research shows that the AIIB's non-resident board system contributes to fair procurement compared with traditional MDB where the resident executive directors tend to maximize the business interest of their own countries (Gu 2018). Such tendency for micro-management also raises a deeper issue of accountability: if projects turn out to be unviable, who is responsible for the decision-making—executive directors or the bank management? On the other hand, international organizations may become unfaithful 'agents' without the appropriate oversight by the 'principals', that is, the member countries. Bank management may pursue narrow organizational interests to the detriment of its shareholders and clients. One way to solve the potential conflicts between Bank management and shareholders was to establish the Complaints-Resolution, Evaluation and Integrity Unit which reports directly to the AIIB's board of directors. Yet if principals (or shareholders) have conflicting goals, the agent (or Bank management) may enjoy greater discretion if multiple shareholders have conflicting goals. In the case of the AIIB, the number of its membership expanded from fifty-seven to seventy-one with potential divergent interests among shareholders. One potential conflict is the distribution of loans between regional members and non-regional members. Currently the AIIB has invested in non-regional countries such as Egypt. Non-regional members may put pressure

[11] Moreover, the ADB has to pay USD 243,942 for each executive director and USD 208,570 for each alternate executive director annually (ADB 2016, Organizational Information, Appendix 10).

on a greater number of loans outside Asia. Another potential conflict may be about environmental and social safeguards. While the Chinese government proclaims that it is important to set up high-quality environmental and social standards, it criticizes some of the existing environment and social safeguard policies at the MDB saying they are are 'bureaucratic, unrealistic and irrelevant' so that reforms are needed to 'reduce operation cost and increase efficiency' (Xinhua News Agency 2014b). A third potential conflict among shareholders is about policy conditionality. China's official development finance is characterized as having no political strings attached. By contrast, traditional RDB tend to deploy their financial leverage to achieve policy changes in borrowing countries. As argued by Kavvadia in Chapter 12 of this volume, the AIIB advocates few conditionalites in its financing operations. Hence, it is important to strike a balance between sufficient oversight by the board and professional autonomy of the bank management. In summary, in comparison with the ADB, the AIIB has a much clearer focus on infrastructure financing with a rapidly growing membership and a non-resident board, whose governance gives more weight to regional members and developing countries.

Capital stock, financial instruments, and lending eligibility

The original authorized capital stock of the ADB was USD 1 billion in 1966, equally divided into USD 500 million paid-in shares and USD 500 million callable shares. The authorized capital of the AIIB in 2016 was USD 100 billion, with USD 20 billion as paid-in capital and USD 80 billion as callable capital. According the AoA of the ADB and the AIIB, the authorized capital stock may be increased by the board of governors by a vote of two-thirds of the total number of governors, representing not less than three-fourths of the total voting power of the members (ADB 1965, Article 4.3; AIIB 2015d, Article 4.3). As of 31 December 2018, the ADB's authorized and subscribed capital amounted to USD 147.965 billion, of which only USD 7.029 billion was paid-in (ADB 2018: 9).

At the ADB, there are two primary sources of funding: ordinary capital resources (OCR) and special funds resources. To finance its OCR lending operations, the ADB issues debt securities in the international and domestic capital markets. Other funding sources for paid-in capital, retained earnings (reserves), and proceeds from debt issuance (ADB 2019b). By contrast, special funds resources often rely on donations from donor countries. One example is the Asian Development Fund (ADF). Established in 1974, the ADF initially provided loans on concessional terms and then offered grants in 2005.[12] ADF resources

[12] Beginning 2017, with ADB's concessional lending financed from its OCR, the ADF has become a grant-only operation (ADB 2019c).

come mainly from contributions of the ADB's rich member countries, which are mobilized under periodic replenishments and net income transfers from OCR.

Similar to the ADB, the AIIB is legally entitled to use both OCR and special funds resources. Even though the AIIB currently does not manage any trust fund or special fund, the AoA allows the AIIB to 'establish and administer funds held in trust for other parties, provided such trust funds are designed to serve the purpose and come within the functions of the Bank' (AIIB 2015d, Article 16.7). These funds need to be under a trust fund framework that shall have been approved by the board of governors. Like the ADB, the AIIB's AoA stipulates that the ordinary resources and the special funds resources 'shall at all times and in all respects be held, used, committed, invested or otherwise disposed of entirely separately from each other' and that the financial statements 'shall show the ordinary operations and special operations separately' (AIIB 2015d, Article 10.2).

Regarding financial instruments, both the ADB and the AIIB can deploy a wide range of options including loans, equity investment, guarantee, special funds, technical assistance, and co-financing. The ADB has continuously updated the menu of financial products: in 1983, it introduced a direct equity investment in the private sector; in 1986, it began direct lending to private sector enterprises without the benefit of any government guarantees; in 2005, it initiated local currency loans for sovereign borrowers to help address the potential mismatch of borrowing in foreign currency and earning income in local currency; and, in 2006, it started lending without sovereign guarantees to public sector borrowers such as state-owned enterprises or municipalities (McCawley 2017: 10). A nuanced difference is that the AIIB's AoA allows the flexibility for innovating financial instruments in the future without requiring the modification of the charter. The AoA allows the Bank to make other types of financing which may be determined by the board of governors by a special majority vote (AIIB 2015d, Article 11.2 (vi)).

With regard to the lending eligibility, the ADB employs a classification system for its developing member countries (DMCs) to determine their access to ordinary capital resource loans and their eligibility to receive concessional assistance from the ADF. OCR loans are generally made to DMCs that have attained a higher level of economic development, whereas the ADF's clients are primarily low-income countries and/or DMCs with moderate to high risk of debt distress. As countries move up the ladder into the high-income status, they graduate from the ADB and are no longer eligible for ADB financing.

By comparison, the AIIB does not use the threshold of GDP per capita to decide its lending eligibility while it is willing to give special regard to the needs of less developed members in the region (AIIB 2015d, Article 2 (ii)).

Instead, the AIIB may provide or facilitate financing to 'any member, or any agency, instrumentality or political sub-division thereof, or any entity or enterprise operating in the territory of a member, as well as to international or regional agencies or entities concerned with economic development of the region' (AIIB 2015d, Article 11.1). This innovative criterion is based on the assumption that countries, both rich and poor, need public finance to solve infrastructural bottlenecks. It also was adopted to address unprecedented risks that private sectors or capital markets are unable or unwilling to take.

Finally, a substantial difference between the AIIB and the ADB concerns their operational ceilings: the AIIB has much more lending capacity than the ADB. At the ADB, the total amount outstanding of loans, equity investments, guarantees, and other types of financing provided by the Bank in its ordinary operations shall not exceed its unimpaired subscribed capital, reserves, and retained earnings included in its ordinary resources (ADB 1965, Article 12.1). Despite the similar preceding provision, the AIIB allows that the board of governors may by a supermajority vote determine at any time that the limitation may be increased up to 250 per cent of the Bank's unimpaired subscribed capital, reserves, and retained earnings included in its ordinary resources. The board's judgement needs to be based on the Bank's financial position and financial standing (AIIB 2015d, Article 12.1). In case of equity investment, the AIIB allows that the amount of the Bank's disbursed equity investments can be as big as an amount corresponding to its total unimpaired paid-in subscribed capital and general reserves (AIIB 2015d, Article 12.2), whereas the ADB requires that the total amount invested shall not exceed 10 per cent of the aggregate amount of the unimpaired paid-in capital stock of the Bank actually paid up at any given time together with the reserves and surplus included in its OCR (ADB 1965, Article 12.3). In addition, the ADB has imposed a ceiling on currency-specific lending, that is, the total amount of principal outstanding and payable to the Bank in a specific currency shall not at any time exceed the total amount of the principal of outstanding borrowings by the Bank that are payable in the same currency (ADB 1965, Article 12.2).

To sum up, the AIIB allows for much greater operational capital in both lending and equity investment than the ADB. Moreover, the AIIB does not make lending eligibility conditional upon the client's income level having potentially more flexible financial instruments. These key factors enable the AIIB to have a much greater potential for enlarging its operations among a more diverse group of clients than the ADB.

Size and sectoral distribution of infrastructure financing

Infrastructural financing—for transport, power, telecommunications, water supply, and other urban infrastructure and services—accounts for a substantial share of the ADB's total operations. In 2018, the ADB provided total financing of USD 21.82 billion, among which USD 11.74 billion is infrastructure financing (53.79 per cent). Infrastructure financing includes energy, transport, information and communication technology (ICT), water supply, and other municipal infrastructure and services. From 2016 to 2018, the three-year average total financing amounted to USD 18.39 billion, 57.8 per cent of which (USD 10.62 billion) was devoted to infrastructure financing. Taking co-financing into account, in 2018 total ADB operations reached USD 35.82 billion, of which 49.8 per cent was invested in infrastructure. Regarding the ADB's infrastructure financing instruments, loans were the primary channel complemented by equity investments, guarantees, grants, and so on.[13]

To kick-start the operation in an efficient manner, the AIIB has effectively established partnerships with the existing international financial institutions (IFI) including the ADB, IBRD, International Financial Corporation (IFC), European Bank for Reconstruction and Development (EBRD), and European Investment Bank (EIB). The AIIB strengthened its efforts to deepen the partnership with a growing number of IFI and RDB. In May 2017, the AIIB signed a MOU with the IADB and Inter-American Investment Corporation (IIC) to foster knowledge exchange, policy coordination, and the co-financing of infrastructure projects in their respective member countries (AIIB 2017).

As a start-up institution, the AIIB approved loans of eight projects worth USD 1.13 billion in the first year in operation. Together with co-financing, the AIIB's total operations as of October 2019 reached USD 30.48 billion with the leverage ratio of over 3:1. As of October 2019, the AIIB has approved forty-nine infrastructure projects since it came into operation in January 2016. The regional coverage is diverse, spanning from South Asia to South-East Asia and from Central Asia to Western Asia. It covers seventeen countries including twelve projects in India, five projects in Bangladesh and Indonesia respectively, three projects in Pakistan and Turkey respectively, two projects in China, Egypt, Oman, Sri Lanka, and Tajikistan respectively, and one project in Azerbaijan, Cambodia, Georgia, Lao, Myanmar, Nepal, and Philippines respectively. While very few projects have been invested in enhancing infrastructure connectivity across countries, the AIIB has made efforts to foster the Asian climate bond market and develop debt capital markets for infrastructure with a strong environmental, social, and governance standards. In terms of the size of financing, the AIIB has invested USD 9.45 billion in total ranging from USD 20 million to USD 600 million in a single project.

Apart from the forty-nine approved projects, there were twenty-nine proposed projects in the pipeline at the AIIB by October 2019. Regarding the sub-sectoral distribution, nine projects focus on energy, seven transport, six water, four urban, one finance, rural, and multi-sector respectively. As for the geographical coverage, five projects were located in Bangladesh, four in Nepal, three in each of Pakistan and Uzbekistan, two in Turkey and multi-country level, and one in

[13] The first direct equity investment was introduced to the Republic of Korea in 1983. The first non-sovereign loan was introduced to Pakistan in 1986. See McCawley (2017).

China, Georgia, Indonesia, Maldives, Russian Federation, Sri Lankan, and Tajikistan respectively. All projects were expected to be put forward for the board consideration in 2019, and most of them had obtained the concept approval. Together with co-financing, the total project value of the proposed projects amounts to USD 11.58 billion.

By the end of 2018, the AIIB accounted for more than half of the ADB's infrastructure financing. But a straightforward comparison of the size is problematic, as the ADB is a well-established institution with over fifty years' experience. As of 31 December 2018, the ADB had 3,381 authorized salaried staff in total, among which 1,514 were located in the headquarters, Manila, Philippines. The remaining officials were found in three representative offices (Europe, Japan, and North America) and thirty-one field offices in South Asia, Central and West Asia, East Asia, South-East Asia, and the Pacific. By comparison, the AIIB is a much younger and smaller institution. To date, the AIIB has no subsidiaries. However, the Bank may establish subsidiary entities with the approval of the board of governors by a special majority vote—an affirmative vote of a majority of the total number of governors, representing not less than a majority of the total voting power of the members. To put it in a historical perspective, in the first four years of the ADB's operations (from 1967 to 1970) total loans only amounted to USD 648 million, or an annual average of USD 160 million. Figure 9.6 shows that the ADB's operations initially experienced steady but modest growth from the 1960s to the 1980s, then reached a peak during the Asian financial crisis in 1997 after a dip in the mid-1990s, followed by a rapid expansion from 2004.

Despite the modest size of the AIIB's infrastructure financing in its early stage, (Reisen 2015) predicts that the combined loan portfolios (*c.*USD 230 billion) of

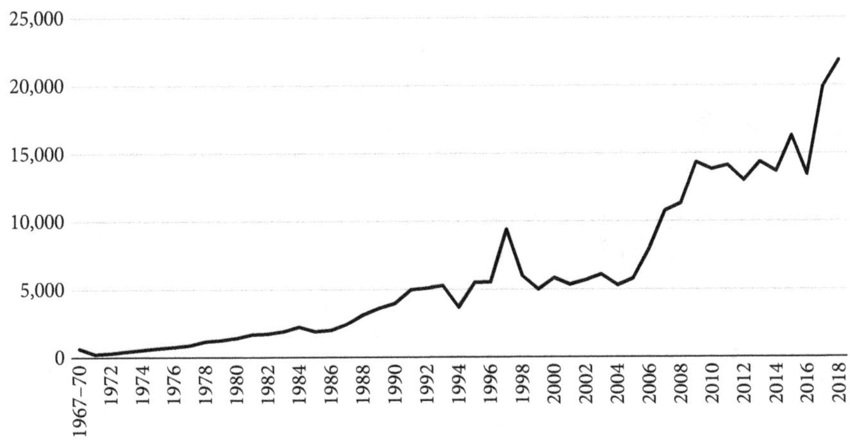

Figure 9.6 Total ADB operations (in USD millions)

Note: The figures here do not include co-financing; current prices.

Source: ADB (1967–2018).

the AIIB and the New Development Bank would equal the combined loan portfolios of the ADB and IBRD.

Regarding sectoral distribution, energy, transport, and ICT have received the bulk of the ADB's infrastructure financing. Figure 9.7 shows that after fluctuations in the late 2000s infrastructure financing accounted for over 60 per cent of the ADB's total operations from the early 2010s onwards. On average from 2004 to 2018, transport and ICT accounted for 45.37 per cent of total infrastructure financing,[14] energy 39.94 per cent, and water supply and other municipal infrastructure and services 14.69 per cent.

By comparison, the AIIB primarily invests in infrastructure projects. As of October 2019, all forty-nine approved projects belong to the broad category of infrastructure in line with the core mandate of the AIIB, with fifteen projects in the sub-sector of energy, ten in transport, six in water, four in multi-sector, two in urban development, and one in telecommunications and digital infrastructure respectively. In terms of the size of the projects, energy accounts for 27.91 per cent

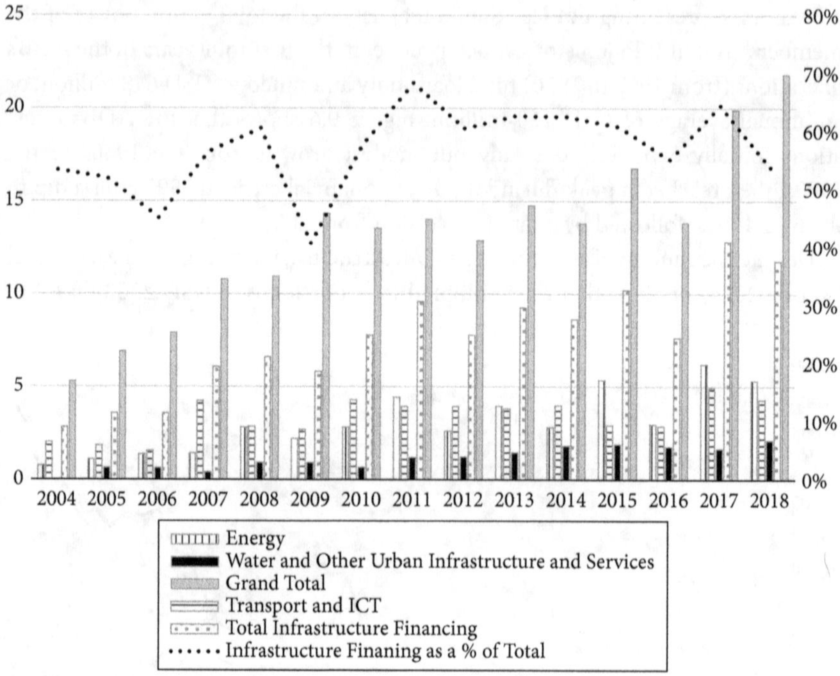

Figure 9.7 Sectoral distribution of ADB's operations
Source: ADB (2004–18).

[14] At the ADB's project classification system, transportation and ICT was split into two separate categories in 2014 with the bulk falling into the category of transportation. From 2014 to 2015, 139 transportation projects were approved whose total project value accounts for 97 per cent, whereas ten ICT projects accounting for the remaining 3 per cent.

of the AIIB's total financing, transport 24.37 per cent, water 14.40 per cent, urban 4.41 per cent, telecommunications 2.53 per cent, and digital infrastructure 0.37 per cent.

To sum up, while the current financing provided by the ADB was about twice the size of the AIIB in 2018, the AIIB's operation has witnessed rapid growth in the past four years and is likely to keep the momentum in the near future. Although the bulk of the ADB's operations concentrates on infrastructure financing, in the first years of its operation, the AIIB devoted all its resources to infrastructural investments with a salient focus on energy and transport.

Environmental and Social Framework

To mitigate any negative environmental and social impact of its operation, the ADB progressively developed and extended its environmental and social safeguard policies and procedures from the early 1980s. Later on, the ADB adopted the Involuntary Resettlement Safeguards in 1995, Indigenous Peoples Safeguards in 1998 and Environment Policy in 2002. Yet it turns out that these safeguard policies, albeit well-intentioned, were less effective than expected. According to the ADB's Independent Evaluation Department (IED), the Environment Policy was based on an ineffective 'one size fits all' approach, had an over-emphasis on procedural compliance without enough attention paid to results delivery, and created 'a perverse incentive' for ADB lending decisions to be actively directed to avoiding financing projects that might trigger environmental procedures (IED 2006a). The over-emphasis upon procedural compliance at the expense of result orientation and capacity building has also been pointed out in the IED's evaluation of the Involuntary Resettlement Safeguards (IED 2006b) and Indigenous Peoples Safeguards (IED 2007). To redress the limitations of the original environmental and social safeguards, the ADB released the 'Safeguard Policy Statement' (SPS) in 2009 that had built upon the three previous safeguard policies and brought them into one single policy to enhance consistency and coherence. The SPS came into operation on 20 January 2010 (ADB 2009).

To dispel the suspicion that the AIIB would not implement environmental and social safeguard policies resulting in racing to the bottom among the MDB and RDB,[15] the AIIB released the draft document of its environmental and social safeguard policies in September 2015. After consultations, the AIIB finalized the Environmental and Social Framework in February 2016 (AIIB 2016a). Compared with the existing environmental and social safeguard policies at the MDB and

[15] For concerns about the AIIB's environmental and social safeguards, see Lean Alfred Santos (2015) and Bill Laurance (2016).

RDB, the AIIB places more emphasis on the 'leading' role of the client in integrating consideration of environmental and social risks and impact into the projects. In line with this principle, the AIIB emphasized the importance of strengthening country and corporate systems.

Both the AIIB and the ADB adopt a similar classification system to reflect the significance of a project's potential environmental and social impact. Category A means that projects are likely to have significant adverse environmental and social impact that is irreversible, cumulative, diverse, or unprecedented. Category B indicates that projects have a limited number of potentially adverse environmental and social impact that are not unprecedented and hardly irreversible or cumulative. Category C means that projects are likely to have minimal or no adverse environmental and social impact. Finally, a proposed project is classified as Category FI, if its financing structure involves the provision of funds to or through a financial intermediary (FI) for the project. The Bank requires the FI client, through the implementation of appropriate environmental and social policies and procedures, to screen and categorize sub-projects as Category A, B, or C, review, conduct due diligence on, and monitor the environmental and social risks and impact associated with the Bank-financed sub-projects in line with the Bank's Environmental and Social Policy.

A close look at the ADB's ratings of environmental and social safeguards reveals that the ADB tends to primarily invest in medium-risk projects. Among 5,132 sovereign infrastructure projects (including multi-sector ones) from 2005 onwards—as of 19 January 2019—the ADB provides the information on the ratings of environmental safeguards for 2,182 projects (about 42.52 per cent). Among these rated projects, 310 projects (14.21 per cent) were classified as Category A—high risk; 1,233 projects (56.51 per cent) were assigned to Category B—medium risk; 561 project (25.71 per cent) fell into Category C—low risk; and 78 projects (3.57 per cent) were in Category FI and FI-C.

By comparison, the AIIB had invested in higher risk projects than the ADB. Among the forty-nine approved infrastructure projects, each was evaluated to gauge their potential impact upon the environment and society. Sixteen projects (33 per cent) were classified as Category A. Twenty-two projects (45 per cent) were assigned to Category B. No project fell into Category C, which means that no project is likely to have minimal or no adverse environmental and social impact. Eight projects (16 per cent) belonged to Category FI, as their financing structure involved the provision of funds to or through an FI.[16] Among the twenty-nine proposed projects, there is one project that is classified as Category A environmentally, while as Category C socially. As regards the rest of the twenty-eight proposed projects, fourteen projects (50 per cent) were classified

[16] The remaining three projects (6 per cent) are not applicable to the Environmental, Social and Governance (ESG) Framework.

as Category A, eleven projects (39 per cent) were assigned to Category B, and the three remaining projects (11 per cent) fell into Category FI. The above analysis shows that the AIIB has not shied away from potentially risky infrastructure projects, which may help to fill the gap left by the existing MDB and RDB, and, even, the ADB. Yet it is still too early to evaluate the effectiveness of the AIIB's environmental and social safeguard policies on the ground. In summary, both AIIB and ADB have adopted rigorous environment and social safeguard policies, and the AIIB tends to undertake environmentally and socially riskier projects than the ADB.

Project performance

The ADB set up the IED that independently and systematically evaluates ADB policies, strategies, operations, and special concerns that relate to organizational and operational effectiveness. The IED relied on project completion reports, project validation reports, and project performance evaluation reports up to December 2016 to evaluate the performance of up to 1750 projects from 1968 to 2015.[17] Among these evaluated projects, 726 belonged to the broad category of infrastructure including energy, transport, ICT, water, and other urban infrastructure services. The overall rating results are as follows: about 4 per cent was unsuccessful, nearly 21 per cent less than successful, and the remaining three-quarters were generally successful. To ensure the effective and independent evaluation of its operations, the AIIB established the Compliance, Effectiveness and Integrity (CEI) Unit, renamed to the Complaints-Resolution, Evaluation and Integrity Unit now, whose mandate includes monitoring and evaluating the Bank's portfolio, ensuring policy compliance, and overseeing internal and external grievance procedures. In April 2016, Mr Hamid Sharif—the former country director for the People's Republic of China at the ADB, was appointed as the first CEI director general. The position reports to the Bank's board of directors (AIIB 2016b). In summary, both the ADB and the AIIB put in place independent evaluation units to monitor and evaluate the banks' operations. The independent evaluation of the ADB's infrastructural projects indicates that most are generally successful although a quarter of projects failed to reach the objective. It is still too early to evaluate the AIIB's operations.

[17] Note: In 2000, the rating system was changed from three categories (generally successful, less than successful / partly successful, and unsuccessful) to four categories (highly successful, successful, less than successful, and unsuccessful). Since there is no one-to-one correspondence between the three category system and the current four category system, the rating of generally successful (GS) has been retained for projects rated before 2000. As of 1 May 2012, IED changed the previous rating category of 'partly successful' to 'less than successful' to clarify that such a category indicates 'below the line' performance.

7. Conclusion

The chapter has tackled three key questions: why the AIIB was established; what is the likely evolution of the AIIB's mandate; and how to compare the AIIB's infrastructure financing with that of the ADB. The main findings are as follows. First, China undertook the leadership to establish the AIIB, not only because the existing US-led MDB and RDB—notably the World Bank—failed to provide sufficient infrastructure financing, but also, more importantly, China was impatient with the slow progress in the governance reform of the existing MDB and RDB. Hence, China adopted a 'two-leg' stakeholder strategy to vie for influence from both within and outside the US-led international development financing system.

Second, in comparison with the mandate of the World Bank, the AIIB has a much clearer sectoral and regional focus. The Bank is mandated to foster sustainable economic development and to improve infrastructure connectivity in Asia by investing in infrastructure and other productive sectors. The core mandate of the AIIB is unlikely to shift in the foreseeable future, notably because the Bank was set up to redress the problem of the proliferating development agenda in the existing MDB. Furthermore, modifying the mandate requires a difficult-to-obtain super-majority vote. The AIIB puts equal emphasis on sustainable economic development and regional integration; despite efforts to foster regional partnerships to development climate bond market and debt capital markets with high environment, social, and governance standards, a majority of infrastructure projects have so far focused on single countries.

Finally, this chapter has compared the nascent infrastructure financing of the AIIB with that of the well-established ADB. First, the AIIB has a much clearer focus on infrastructure financing with a rapidly growing membership and a non-resident board, whose governance gives more weight to regional members and developing countries in comparison with the ADB. Second, the AIIB has a much greater potential for enlarging its operations among a more diverse group of clients than the ADB as its operational ceilings are much less stringent than those of the ADB. Third, despite the modest size of the AIIB's operations to date compared with the ADB, it is predicted that the AIIB's operation will witness rapid growth in the near future. Although the bulk of the ADB's operations concentrates on infrastructure financing, the AIIB has devoted all its resources to infrastructural investments with a salient focus on energy during the first stage of its operation. Fourth, both the AIIB and the ADB have adopted rigorous environment and social safeguard policies, while the AIIB has undertaken environmentally and socially riskier projects than the ADB. Finally, both the AIIB and the ADB have put in place an independent evaluation unit to monitor and evaluate the Bank's operations. The independent evaluation of the ADB's infrastructural projects indicates that most have been generally successful although a quarter of projects have failed to reach their objective. It is still too early to evaluate the AIIB's operations.

References

ADB (Asian Development Bank) (1965). *Agreement Establishing the Asian Development Bank (ADB Charter)*. Manila: ADB.

ADB (Asian Development Bank) (2009). 'Safeguard policy statement', June. Available online at: https://www.adb.org/documents/safeguard-policy-statement?ref=site/safeguards/publications

ADB (Asian Development Bank) (1967–2018). *Annual Report*. Manila: ADB.

ADB (Asian Development Bank) (2017). *ADB Procurement Policy: Goods, Works, Nonconsulting and Consulting Services*. Manila: ADB.

ADB (Asian Development Bank) (2018). *Annual Report*. Manila, Philippines: Publication Stock No. FLS190058.

ADB (Asian Development Bank) (2019a). *Members*. Manila: ADB. Available online at: https://www.adb.org/about/members

ADB (Asian Development Bank) (2019b). *Ordinary Capital Resources*. Manila: ADB. Available online at: https://www.adb.org/site/funds/ocr

ADB (Asian Development Bank) (2019c). *Asian Development Fund (ADF)*. Manila: ADB. Available online at: https://www.adb.org/site/funds/adf

ADB (Asian Development Bank) and ADBI (Asian Development Bank Institute) (2009). *Infrastructure for a Seamless Asia*. Tokyo: Asian Development Bank Institute.

AIIB (Asian Infrastructure Investment Bank) (2015a). *The Memorandum of Understanding on Establishing the Asian Infrastructure Investment Bank (AIIB)*. Signed in Beijing, April 8. Beijing: AIIB. Available online at: https://www.aiib.org/en/news-events/news/2015/20150408_004.html

AIIB (2015b). *50 Countries Sign the Articles of Agreement for the Asian Infrastructure Investment Bank*, 29 June. Beijing: AIIB. Available online at: https://www.aiib.org/en/news-events/news/2015/20150629_001.html

AIIB (2015c). *AIIB's Charter Enters into Force on 25 December 2015*, 16 January. Beijing: AIIB. Available online at: https://www.aiib.org/en/news-events/news/2016/20160116_001.html

AIIB (2015d). *Articles of Agreement*. Beijing: AIIB.

AIIB (2016a). *Environmental and Social Framework*. February. Beijing: AIIB. Available online at: https://www.aiib.org/en/policies-strategies/framework-agreements/environmental-social-framework.html

AIIB (2016b). 'Mr. Hamid Sharif appointed as Director General of the Compliance, Effectiveness and Integrity Unit', 14 April. Available online at: https://www.aiib.org/en/news-events/news/2016/20160414_001.html

AIIB (2017). *The Asian Infrastructure Investment Bank and the IDB Group Expand Ties*, 16 May. Beijing: AIIB. Available online at: https://www.aiib.org/en/news-events/news/2017/20170516_001.html

AIIB (2019a). *About AIIB*. Beijing: AIIB. Available online at: https://www.aiib.org/en/about-aiib/index.html

AIIB (2019b). *Members and Prospective Members of the Bank*. Beijing: AIIB. Available online at: https://www.aiib.org/en/about-aiib/governance/members-of-bank/index.html

AIIB (2019c). *AIIB Governance: Board of Directors*. Beijing: AIIB. Available online at: https://www.aiib.org/en/about-aiib/governance/board-directors/index.html

Alfred Santos, L. (2015). 'AIIB releases draft environmental and social safeguards, opens consultations', *Devex*, 16 September. Available online at: https://www.devex.com/news/aiib-releases-draft-environmental-and-social-safeguards-opens-consultations-86924

African Development Bank (2018). *Annual Report*. Abidjan, Côte d'Ivoire.

Calderón, C. and Servén, L. (2014). 'Infrastructure, growth, and inequality: an overview'. The World Bank Policy Research Working Paper No. 7034.

Chow, D.C.K. (2016). 'Why China established the Asia Infrastructure Investment Bank', *Vanderbilt Journal of Transnational Law*, 49(1255): 1255–98.

Czernich, N., Falck, O., Kretschmer, T., and Woessmann, L. (2011). 'Broadband infrastructure and economic growth', *The Economic Journal*, 121(552): 505–32.

European Political Strategy Centre (2015). *The Asian Infrastructure Investment Bank: A New Multilateral Financial Institution or a Vehicle for China's Geostrategic Goals*, Issue 1.

Gransow, B. and Price, S. (2019). 'Social risk management at AIIB—Chinese or international characteristics?', *Journal of Chinese Political Science*, 24(2): 289–311.

Gu, B. (2017a). 'Chinese multilateralism in the AIIB', *Journal of International Economic Law*, 20(1): 137–58.

Gu, B. (2017b). 'MDBs' accountability mechanism: a perspective of AIIB', *Journal of World Trade*, 51(3): 409–23.

Gu, B. (2017c). 'Developing MDBs' dispute settlement systems: a perspective of Asian Infrastructure Investment Bank', *Hong Kong Law Journal*, 47(3): 871–98.

Gu, B. (2018). 'Procurement of Asian Infrastructure Investment Bank: five legal issues', *Asian Journal of WTO & International Health Law and Policy*, 13(1): 233–67.

Gu, B. (2019). *The Law and Governance of the Asian Infrastructure Investment Bank*. London: Wolters Kluwer.

Hakans, E. and Hynes, P. (2017). 'China's challenge to the world economic order', *Global Research*, 17 January.

Hirschman, A.O. (1970). *Exit, Voice, and Loyalty: Responses to Decline in Firms, Organizations, and States*. Cambridge, MA: Harvard University Press.

IBRD (International Bank for Reconstruction and Development) (2012). *Articles of Agreement*. Washington, DC: IBRD.

IED (ADB's Independent Evaluation Department) (2006a). *Special Evaluation Study of Environmental Safeguards*, September. Manila: ADB. Available online at: https://www.adb.org/documents/environmental-safeguards

IED (ADB's Independent Evaluation Department) (2006b). *Special Evaluation Study on Involuntary Resettlement Safeguards*, September. Manila: ADB. Available online at: https://www.adb.org/documents/involuntary-resettlement-safeguards

IED (ADB's Independent Evaluation Department) (2007). 'Indigenous peoples safeguards', February. Available online at: https://www.adb.org/documents/indigenous-peoples-safeguards

Ikenberry, G.J. and Lim, D.J. (2017). 'China's emerging institutional statecraft: the Asian Infrastructure Investment Bank and the prospects for counter-hegemony'. *Project on International Order and Strategy*. New York: Brookings Institution.

IMF (International Monetary Fund) (2015). 'IMF managing director Christine Lagarde welcomes US Congressional approval of the 2010 quota and governance reforms, 18 December. Available online at: https://www.imf.org/en/News/Articles/2015/09/14/01/49/pr15573

Inter-American Development Bank (IADB) (2018) *Annual Report*. Washington, DC: The IDB Knowledge, Innovation and Communication Sector, IADB.

Ismail, N.W. and Mahyideen, J.M. (2015). 'The impact of infrastructure on trade and economic growth in selected economies in Asia'. ADBI Working Paper Series No. 553.

Krasner, S.D. (1981). 'Power structures and regional development banks', *International Organization*, 35(2): 303–28.

Laurance, B. (2016). 'Will new mega-banks force a "race to the bottom" for the environment?', 4 April. Available online at: http://alert-conservation.org/issues-research-highlights/2016/4/2/will-new-mega-banks-force-a-race-to-the-bottom-for-the-environment

McCawley, P. (2017). *Banking on the Future of Asia and the Pacific: 50 Years of the Asian Development Bank*. Manila: ADB.

MoF of the PRC (Ministry of Finance of the People's Republic of China) (2015). 'Minister Jiwei Lou comments on the establishment of the AIIB at the press conference' [in Chinese]. Available online at: http://www.mof.gov.cn/zhengwuxinxi/zhengcejiedu/2015zcjd/201512/t20151225_1632389.htm

Qing, K.G. (2015). 'China's AIIB to offer loans with fewer strings attached'. Reuters, 1 September. Available online at: http://www.reuters.com/article/us-aiib-china-loans-idUSKCN0R14UB20150901

Radavoi, C.N. and Bian, Y. (2018). 'The Asian Infrastructure Investment Bank's environmental and social policies: a critical discourse analysis', *Journal of International and Comparative Social Policy*, 34(1): 1–18.

Reisen, H. (2015). 'Will the AIIB and the NDB help reform multilateral development banking?', *Global Policy*, 6(3): 297–304.

Vestergaard, J. and Wade, R.H. (2013). 'Protecting power: how Western states retain the dominant voice in the World Bank's governance', *World Development*, 46(June): 153–64.

Vestergaard, J. and Wade, R.H. (2015). 'Still in the woods: gridlock in the IMF and the World Bank puts multilateralism at risk', *Global Policy*, 6(1): 1–12.

Wan, M. (2016). *The Asian Infrastructure Investment Bank: The Construction of Power and the Struggle for the East Asian International Order. The Political Economy of East Asia*. New York: Palgrave Macmillan.

White, J. (1972). *Regional Development Banks*. New York: Praeger Publishers.

World Bank (2018). *Annual Report*. Washington, DC: World Bank Publications.

Xinhua News Agency (2014a). '21 Asian countries sign MOU on establishing Asian Infrastructure Investment Bank', 24 October. Available online at: http://news.xinhuanet.com/english/business/2014–10/24/c_133740149.htm

Xinhua News Agency (2014b). 'AIIB to set up high-standard, feasible safeguard policies', 24 October. Available online at: http://europe.chinadaily.com.cn/business/2014–10/24/content_18799036.htm

Xu, J. (2017). *Beyond US Hegemony in International Development: The Contest for Influence at the World Bank*. Cambridge: Cambridge University Press.

Zhao, J., Gou, Y., and Li, W. (2019). 'A new model of multilateral development bank: a comparative study of road projects by the AIIB and ADB', *Journal of Chinese Political Science*, 24(2): 267–88.

PART TWO

COMPARATIVE AND POLICY ANALYSIS

10

Considerations in the Initial Design of Regional Development Banks

A Comparison of the Inter-American Development Bank and the European Bank for Reconstruction and Development

Steven D. Roper

1. Introduction

While much has been written about the origins, the lending policies and the economic and political impact of the World Bank (IBRD) and the International Monetary Fund (IMF), only recently has there been a focus on regional development banks (RDB), such as the work contained in this volume. Since the 1960s, a RDB have been created. The Inter-American Development Bank (IADB) was the first RDB, established in 1959, and its mission and banking structure has served as a model for several of the RDB that followed, including the African Development Bank (AfDB, 1964), the Asian Development Bank (ADB, 1966) and the Caribbean Development Bank (CDB, 1969).[1] Although the IBRD provides more total development loans in the world than any other international financial institution (IFI), RDB can actually provide more finance than the IBRD for their specific regions and for specific member countries. For example, many smaller countries, particularly in Latin America, have come to rely on the IADB for a large percentage of their financial assistance, which has outpaced the assistance provided by the IBRD. It is through these RDB that countries that do not command the attention of the IBRD or IMF get the needed international financing to engage in development projects and strengthen their economy (for example the IADB lent over USD 14 billion in 2018 to member countries).[2]

While there are differences among all RDB, the recently formed European Bank for Reconstruction and Development (EBRD) diverges considerably from

[1] Technically, the CDB is a Sub-regional RDB with ties to the IADB.
[2] This amount was the second highest total in the history of the IADB, see https://www.iadb.org/en/news/idb-reached-one-highest-lending-levels-its-history.

Steven D. Roper, *Considerations in the Initial Design of Regional Development Banks: A Comparison of the Inter-American Development Bank and the European Bank for Reconstruction and Development* In: *Regional Development Banks in the World Economy.* Edited by: Judith Clifton, Daniel Díaz-Fuentes, and David Howarth, Oxford University Press (2021).
 DOI: 10.1093/oso/9780198861089.003.0010

the model of the IADB. The fact that the IADB and the EBRD are so distinct is somewhat surprising given that both banks serve regions that have undergone dramatic economic and political change. In this chapter, I seek to understand and account for the differences between the IADB and the EBRD by understanding the early design features of both banks. I examine the interests of member countries, especially the United States (US), as well as the regional political environment and broader international factors that account for the creation of these RDB.

What is striking about the literature on RDB is how little attention has focused on their origins and lending practices. Aside from the series published by Lynne Rienner[3] in the mid-1990s, there has been scant attention paid to RDB. That said, over the last decade, the literature that has emerged tends to focus either on technical, financial issues (Bland and Kilby 2012; Korfker 2012) or more contemporary concerns over transparency and funding impact (Gray 2014; Shield and Wallin 2015). This chapter examines the origins, the lending policies, and the RDB relationship with the IBRD from a comparative perspective focusing on the IADB and the EBRD. Generally, the historical works that have been written tend to focus on single case studies rather than explore similarities and differences among RDB.[4] By comparing these two IFI in terms of the broader political considerations in which they were formed, we develop a greater understanding of the diversity and the similarity of RDB. This chapter argues that the international environment and regional competition among states played a substantial role in the initial development of each of these banks which in turn has fundamentally influenced the nature of lending and types of projects supported (see Figure 10.1).

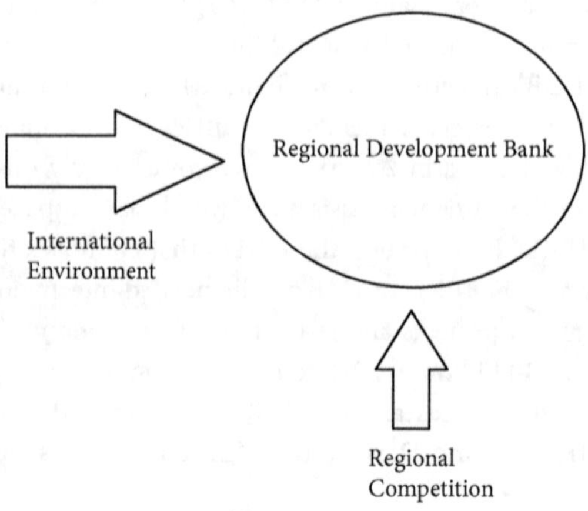

Figure 10.1 Factors that influenced initial design of the IADB and the EBRD

[3] The series entitled 'The Multilateral Development Banks' produced five volumes devoted to RDB.
[4] Culpeper's (1997) volume in the Rienner series stands out as an exceptionally broad-based comparative analysis of RDB.

2. Origins, membership, and structure

Institutions such as the IADB and the EBRD are not only a result of bargaining among member states but also reflect the concerns of the international system. While the IADB was created during the height of the Cold War, the EBRD has often been referred to as the first 'post-cold war international institution' (Easton and Rorer 1991: 527) and as such reflects particular concerns that were thrust upon European and Western countries immediately after the collapse of the Berlin Wall in November 1989 (see Shields in Chapter 8, this volume). The international system in 1990 and 1991 was still in flux following the collapse of communism in East Europe, reunification of Germany, and the continuing presence of the Soviet Union until August 1991. It is not surprising, therefore, that the early debates over the EBRD reflect the ambiguity that was present in the international system. What is striking is that while the international system was quite different when the IADB was created in 1959, the concerns and influence of the US were similar in both cases.

The differences in the external environment (specifically the Cold War) in which the institutions were created helps explain the differences in membership, structure, and lending policies. Cold War politics were an important aspect of the initiation of both the IADB (regarding Cuba) and the EBRD (the dismantling of East European communist regimes). Steven Weber (1994) argues that the Cold War, US hegemony, and the relationship of state and various inter-governmental organizations should be viewed within the context of an institutional environment in which Cold War politics is one feature. While international institutions and states were primary actors involved in the creation of the IADB and the EBRD, there are stark differences in the relative importance of certain actors and their international concerns that had a pronounced influence on the design of these institutions. This section explains some of the principle differences between these two institutions including the debate over the conception of the RDB, structure, and membership composition of the institution.

IADB origins

As discussed by López and Rougier in Chapter 2, this volume, the idea of a Latin American RDB pre-dates the Cold War period, going back to the nineteenth century. At the First Inter-American Conference held in 1889–90, participants discussed how to strengthen banking links between the US and Latin American countries (Dell 1972). However, the US Congress opposed the creation of an institution that it viewed as establishing 'spheres of influence'[5] and would involve

[5] There was a concern that the Europeans would view this as an opportunity to create their own spheres of influence, which the US opposed.

governments in activities that were considered more natural within the scope of the private banking community. During the next sixty years, this dominant economic and worldview continued to influence any discussion concerning the creation of a Latin American RDB (Tussie 1995).

The end of the Second World War brought about the creation of several IFI to deal with global economic issues, including the IMF and the IBRD. In Latin America, the expectation was that these institutions would provide financial support to the region. However, it soon became evident in the discussions at the Bretton Woods Conference that the initial focus of these institutions would be the reconstruction of Europe. Starting in 1948, Latin American governments began pressing their case for a lending agency that would specialize in providing loans and increasing the flow of financial resources to the region. A 1954 report by the Economic Commission for Latin America (ECLAC)[6] pointed out that from 1950 to 1953, the annual net flow of resources into Latin America had averaged around USD 422 million; however, only USD 79 million had been made available by the IBRD and other IFI for development projects. The group of ECLAC experts urged for the creation of an RDB. Even though they acknowledged that the activities envisioned for this new RDB (a focus on industrial, agricultural, and mining credits) could be provided by existing IFI, they argued that these IFI would have to change their structure and priorities since they had not previously been engaged in these lending activities.[7] In addition, these experts believed that one of the problems with IFI was their lack of specialization and knowledge of local conditions. In addition, they felt that this new RDB would provide additional personnel to process loans and provide technical assistance in the preparation of projects that was lacking in other IFI and increase the potential for regional development and integration through regional project financing (Mikesell 1955).

At a ministerial level conference in Brazil at the end of 1954, Latin American countries passed a resolution (with the abstention of the US and Peru) calling on economists and members of ECLAC to make a specific proposal for the creation of the bank to the Organization of American States (OAS). The 'Santiago Draft' of 1955 envisioned the new RDB's primary objective as the promotion of economic development of the member countries by investing in the creation or expansion of enterprises, operations, and services whether public, private, or mixed. Although the US was not involved in the discussions leading to the Santiago

[6] The Economic Commission for Latin America (ECLA; the Spanish acronym is CEPAL), was established by Economic and Social Council resolution 106(VI) of 25 February 1948. The scope of the Commission's work was later broadened to include the countries of the Caribbean, and by resolution 1984/67 of 27 July 1984, the Economic Council decided to change its name to the Economic Commission for Latin America and the Caribbean (ECLAC; the Spanish acronym, CEPAL, remains unchanged).

[7] The IMF and the IBRD had been in existence for fewer than ten years and were still developing ways in which to accomplish their missions.

Draft, Latin American countries assigned one-third of the subscribed capital of the new Bank to the US with the remainder provided by Latin American countries. In this way, much like the IMF, the US controls important votes which require a majority of total voting power (Kwakwa 2017). Quotas would be determined based on IMF subscriptions. The voting structure would resemble that of the IMF and the IBRD, but no member would hold more than one-third of the total voting power.

Interestingly, when the Santiago Draft was circulated for consideration and comment, only nine countries in principle approved the Draft—two gave conditional support,[8] and three (including the US) conveyed opposition. Seven countries did not even reply. However, the US reversed its position in 1958 when a visit by Vice-President Richard Nixon to the region raised awareness of the political, social, and economic unrest in the region. Finally, Cold War concerns of the potential expansion of communism into an unstable Latin America led the US to support the idea of closer economic ties through a bank.[9] In many Latin American countries, Vice-President Nixon was confronted with demonstrations motivated by the perceived neglect of the US government and the poor economic conditions in the region. Juscelino Kubitschek, president of Brazil, called on President Dwight Eisenhower to jointly re-evaluate the Pan American relationship with the aim of strengthening the ties between the countries on the continent. President Eisenhower responded to this call and sent Secretary of State John Foster Dulles to negotiate an agreement.

The negotiating committee began work in January 1959, completing the proposal in April (Scheman 1997). The agreement entered into force on 30 December 1959. The agreement establishing the IADB states that 'the purpose of the Bank shall be to contribute to the acceleration of the process of economic and social development of the regional developing member countries, individually and collectively' (IADB 1959, Article I.1). Unlike the EBRD's agreement which will be discussed below, there were no political demands for democratization in the region. Cold War concerns seemed to have tilted the balance towards an emphasis in fighting the potential expansion of communism into the region. In addition, even though loans could be provided both to public and private entities without government guarantees, the IADB has largely focused on public financing, and thus supporting governmental entities in Latin America. The first meeting of the board of governors was held in February 1960 when the president and the first board of executive directors were elected. The Bank officially began operating in October 1960 and made its first loan in February 1961.

[8] These countries made suggestions to modify certain sections of the Santiago Draft.

[9] Cuba's revolution was in 1959.

EBRD origins

The actual origins of the EBRD pre-date the fall of the Berlin Wall; thus, it is the last Cold War institution designed for a post-Cold War environment. Unlike in the Latin American case, lenders took the initiative in advocating for what eventually became the EBRD in a speech delivered by President François Mitterrand to the European Parliament on 25 October 1989. Mitterrand (1989: 79) argued that 'Poland, Hungary, the Soviet Union…need to be helped. Why not set up a Bank for Europe, which, like the European Investment Bank, would finance major projects and have on its Board of Directors the twelve European countries.' In November, the French proposed a 'Bank for Europe' that would coordinate European Union (EU)[10] project development in East Europe. While the British were especially hostile to the notion of an East European RDB and the West Germans were at best ambivalent, it was agreed at the European Council's December Strasbourg meeting to begin negotiations over the creation of the newly named EBRD. This agreement reflected the desire of the US to create an economic mechanism which reflected its political goals of securing democracy in former communist countries (a goal aligned with France). As part of the framework of the negotiations, two principles were agreed to at the Strasbourg meeting. First, the EBRD would complement rather than supplant the IMF and the IBRD. Mitterrand's special advisor on these negotiations, Jacques Attali, who became the first head of the EBRD had proposed a 'maximalist' conception of the EBRD in which the Bank would be the lead development agency in East Europe (Weber 1994). However, it was clear at Strasbourg that several countries, including future member, the US, would never agree to create an East European RDB that would serve as an alternative to existing IFI. The second principle agreed to was to open the negotiations and membership to all Group of Twenty-Four (G24) countries including the US and Japan. While the Bank was to retain a 'European character', countries such as Britain insisted that the US be invited to the negotiations as a counterbalance to Continental European countries. Even within Continental Europe, there was a division on the importance of the EBRD as French support was based on the need to contain unilateral actions by Germany to support individual post-communist countries (Weber 1994: 9).

As an indication of French influence in the process, the negotiations began in Paris in January 1990, and Attali was named the chair of the first constitutive conference. All twelve EU countries, ten other European countries, ten non-European countries,[11] eight recipient countries, and a representative from the EU and the European Investment Bank (EIB) attended the meetings. The most fundamental

[10] While EBRD negotiations and operations began under 'the European Community', for purposes of simplicity, I have decided to use 'the European Union' throughout the chapter.

[11] The list of non-European countries includes developing countries such as Egypt and Morocco.

issue discussed at the conference concerned the nature of EBRD lending. In the Latin American case, IADB lending focused on the public sector; however, the US and Britain maintained that the EBRD should only provide financial support to the private sector. The US was concerned that any financial assistance to the state would ultimately 'amount to subsiding failing socialism' (Menkveld 1991: 61). While countries such as France did not object to private sector lending, they wanted the EBRD to have the flexibility to lend to the public sector. The Soviet delegation in particular was concerned with the emphasis on the private sector given that a law on property had not yet been passed and therefore private property was still technically illegal in the country.

At the March 1990 constitutive conference, the US and France agreed to a provision in which at least 60 per cent of EBRD financial assistance would be directed to the private sector with the remaining 40 per cent or less available to the public sector. The state sector would later be defined in the EBRD agreement as that part of the economy that includes 'national and local Governments, their agencies, and enterprises owned or controlled by any of them' (EBRD 1990, Article 11.3 [iiia]). Therefore unlike the IADB, the EBRD primarily funds non-state institutions and enterprises and thus is more similar to the International Financial Corporation (IFC)[12] than other RDB. This reflected US interests in 'bailing in' private lenders to reduce the burden on official state lending.

In addition to debating lending policies, several participants to the constitutive conferences insisted that the EBRD's agreement include explicit language linking economic reform to democracy and human rights as communism was collapsing. This human rights discourse was embraced by all members of the G24 as democratization efforts in countries such as Bulgaria and Romania in 1990 were just beginning. For the US, in particular, the concern was to tie economic assistance to EBRD member borrowers within a more general view of the role of economic development aid (Weber 1994: 21). The Soviet delegation was concerned about linking access to finance with a commitment to multiparty democracy, but in the end, Article 1 of the agreement clearly states that the purpose of the Bank is to promote private initiative in those countries 'committed to and applying the principles of multiparty democracy, pluralism and market economics' (EBRD 1990, Article 1). While Birch (1988: 257) argues that RDB come into existence in order to 'free development finance from the appearance of political considerations', the EBRD not only sought to promote a specific form of economic policy-making but also a specific form of governance. Indeed, the agreement provides that the board of directors is responsible for overseeing the actual implementation of democratic and economic policies (Menkveld 1991).

[12] The IFC was founded in 1956 as part of the World Bank Group and provides financial assistance to the private sector. Although the IFC coordinates its activities with other World Bank Group institutions, it operates independently and is financed independently.

One of the unusual features of the EBRD negotiations was the relatively quick period of time that it took the contracting parties to sign the Bank's agreement. As events in East Europe were moving quickly, countries such as the US and France forged a consensus with Britain and German to create the EBRD in order not to lose political momentum during the transition to democracy in East Europe (Weber 1994: 12). Both informal and formal negotiations took less than five months and by March 1991, the agreement came into effect and the EBRD inauguration in London occurred the following month. For Latin America, one could argue that the IADB was fifty years in the making, and Cold War concerns provided the final impetus for its creation. There are a few reasons why the EBRD negotiations occurred so quickly. First, events in Eastern Europe dictated the pace of negotiations. President Mitterrand's initial speech occurred the month before the fall of the Berlin Wall. Between that speech and the inauguration of the Bank, almost every Eastern European country had elections and many governments were pursuing policies of privatization. The pace of changes, reforms, and possible backsliding created in an environment in which the US and European countries felt compelled to move quickly. Second, the statutes and working experience of the IBRD and RDB, including the IADB, meant that negotiators were aware of the issues involved in creating a new RDB.

IADB structure

The IADB was, until the founding of the EBRD, the only regional bank whose headquarters was not in a borrowing member country (BMC). The IADB's headquarters are located in Washington, DC. The board of governors is composed of one governor and an alternate governor appointed by each of the forty-six member countries. Governors are usually ministers of finance, presidents of central banks, or other officials. The board holds an annual meeting to review the Bank's operations and to make major policy decisions; however, it delegates many of its powers to the board of executive directors.

The IADB's fourteen-member board of executive directors is responsible for conducting the operations of the Bank. Board members are elected or appointed to three-year terms by the board of governors. The executive directors for the US and Canada represent their own countries, but all other executive directors represent groups of countries. Split voting is not allowed within the different groups, so each group must reach a compromise and put forth a single vote by its designated director. The board is in charge of establishing the institution's operational policies, approving project proposals submitted by the president of the Bank, determining interest rates for Bank loans, authorizing borrowings in the capital markets, and approving the Bank's administrative budget.

The president of the IADB, who is elected by the board of governors to a five-year term, conducts the day-to-day business of the institution along with the executive vice-president. The president of the Bank always comes from a BMC; thus he or she is a Latin American. The president presides over meetings of the board of executive directors but has no vote except to break a tie. The executive vice-president has always been a US citizen. Since its founding, the Bank's leadership has been very stable. There have only been four presidents: Felipe Herrera (1960–70), Antonio Ortiz Mena (1970–87), Enrique Iglesias (1988–2005), and Luis Alberto Moreno (2005–present).

One of the issues that Latin American countries paid special attention to was the staffing of the Bank. Based on the experience of the Marshall Plan, there was a sense that local participation in the management of a development institution would provide countries a greater stake in the success of the institution, with a clearer understanding of regional and country-specific needs. Therefore, there is an IADB country office in every BMC to channel technical assistance and enhance project supervision.

The resources provided by the member countries to finance the Bank's operation are structured into two separate windows, the ordinary capital resources (hard window) and the Fund for Special Operations (FSO; soft window). Ordinary capital resources include capital paid by the member countries, funds borrowed in capital markets and loan repayments. The FSO depends exclusively on government contributions, except for some income derived from liquid investments and interest payments. In addition to the resources available through the IADB, BMC have access to assistance from the Inter-American Investment Corporation (IAIC) and the Multilateral Investment Fund (MIF) which form part of the IADB Group.[13]

EBRD structure

The EBRD and the IABD share a similar structure (Shihata 1990). Like the IADB, the EBRD's headquarters are located in a non-borrowing member countries (NBMC; Britain), and the Bank has field offices in every BMC. In addition, both banks have a three-tier structure (president and staff, board of governors, and board of directors). For both banks, the board of directors is responsible for conducting day-to-day operations. In the case of the EBRD, there are twenty-three directors. Britain, France, Italy, Germany, Japan, the US, the EU, and the EIB have their own director while the rest of the members are grouped into constituencies. As noted by Shields in Chapter 8, this volume, one indication of the relative

[13] The IAIC and the MIF were created to provide financing for private sector projects without government guarantees.

influence of NBMC and BMC involves the selection of the president. In an NBMC-dominated institution such as the EBRD, the president comes from a European donor country.[14]

Initially, the structure of the EBRD included two separate banking divisions based on the dual mandate of both private and public financing. The merchant banking division was headed by the EBRD's senior vice-president[15] and was in charge of loans to the private sector. The development banking division, while technically equal to the merchant side, was involved in more traditional development-based (i.e., public sector) loans. These two different banking divisions reflected the early choice to allocate a minimum of 60 per cent of financing to the private sector. By the mid-1990s, it became apparent that this structure encouraged competition between the two banking divisions and placed the development division at a disadvantage. Therefore, the decision was taken to merge these two divisions into a single banking division with seven policy and country regional sub-divisions.[16]

IADB membership

One of the reasons for the creation of the IADB in 1959 was to strengthen the Pan American alliance, and therefore initially only members of the OAS were eligible for membership. IADB member states were divided into BMCs and NBMC. Initially, the US was the sole NBMC. Later, an amendment to the agreement in 1972 allowed Canada, which was not even a member of the OAS, to become an NBMC of the IADB. Later, nineteen other countries joined the Bank as NBMCs in the 1970s and 1980s. One of the main reasons for the expansion of NBMC has been the stipulation that goods and services for IADB projects can only be provided by businesses from IADB member countries. These contracts number in the thousands each year and provide a strong incentive for countries to join the IADB (Tussie 1995). Today the Bank has forty-eight members (the newest member is China in 2009).

The IADB provides financial assistance to BMC from Latin America and the Caribbean. In these countries, a number of entities can borrow directly from the Bank, including national, provincial, state and municipal governments, autonomous public institutions, and civil society organizations that have a government guarantee. Interestingly, four independent Sub-regional organizations which are not members of the IADB and do not have voting powers (the Andean Development

[14] Since 1991, the EBRD has had six presidents (far more than the IADB given its shorter history).

[15] As Upton (2000) notes, the vice-president of the EBRD is nominated by the US.

[16] President Jacques de Larosière (1993–8) instituted this change to also strengthen the EBRD's focus on individual countries.

Corporation, the Central American Bank for Economic Integration, the River Plate Basin Financial Development Fund, and the Caribbean Development Bank) are also eligible to borrow from the Bank for projects in their member countries.

Voting rights are determined by the number of shares in ordinary capital stock of the Bank held by a member country. The IADB structure was designed to give BMC more voting power than NBMC in order to offset the power that industrialized countries have in other IFI established at Bretton Woods. Even though NBMC dominate other IFI, the IADB was created by the impetus of Latin American countries which were able to take advantage on Cold War concerns to propose a favourable voting power structure. There were examples in the 1970s and early 1980s in which the IADB lent to members states (such as Allende's Chile and Nicaragua under control of the *Sandinistas*) that had a domestic and foreign policy opposed by the US. In 1994, the Articles of Agreement were amended to stipulate that the voting power of the BMC could not fall below 50.0005 per cent. In 2017, the US held 30 per cent of the votes while other NBMC held just under 20 per cent of the votes. Among the BMC, Argentina and Brazil each hold approximately 11 per cent of the voting power.

Until the Seventh Replenishment[17] in 1989, decisions by the board of executive directors on ordinary capital loans required a simple majority vote. Decisions concerning concessional loans from the FSO require a two-thirds majority. However, management in the Bank avoided the submission of loan applications that did not have US support. During the Seventh Replenishment negotiations, the US sought a change in the Articles of Agreement to secure an effective veto power over the operations of the Bank. The new voting structure allows a single director to delay the consideration of a loan for one month, and after this period two or more directors can delay a loan an additional two months. Therefore, the US director can delay the consideration of a loan for up to three months with the support of one or more additional directors. Indeed Babb (Chapter 11, this volume) argues that the Baker Plan during the Reagan administration effectively brought the IADB under US control and incorporated the Bank into the Washington Consensus. In this way, the IADB eventually became part of the Regan administration's Cold War policies in which multilateral banks were used for political purposes.

EBRD membership

By May 1990, the forty participants[18] to the constitutive conferences had agreed to the basic principles of the EBRD including the division of voting power. The

[17] The last replenishment took place in 2010 when the Bank increased its capital by USD 70 billion, its largest expansion of resources.

[18] Since 1990, the number of shareholders has increased to sixty-five.

decision to designate the Soviet Union as a recipient country was a hotly debated issue. All EU member states, including Britain, agreed that the Soviet Union should be invited to participate. However, because the Soviet Union did not embrace the core political and economic goals of the EBRD, the US urged that the Soviets be excluded or at least only given observer status with no lending rights (Bronstone 1999). A compromise solution was found in which the Soviet Union was granted full membership; however, to placate the Bush administration, the Soviets were only allowed to borrow up to the amount it paid into the Bank in hard currency. The other membership dispute involved the inclusion of the EIB as a shareholder. The US was concerned that the membership of a pro-public sector institution would 'send the wrong signals to the political and business leaders of the CEECs' (Bronstone 1999: 32). The EIB was eventually admitted as a full member, and therefore the EBRD is the only RDB in which intergovernmental organizations (IGOs) can become full members.

As with other RDB and the IBRD, the number of shares determines voting rights. Because the EBRD was to be a 'European' RDB, the French felt that European countries had to have majority voting power. Thus, EU member states, the EU, and the EIB jointly control 51 per cent of the voting shares. The US is the single largest shareholder with France, Great Britain, and Germany, and Italy and Japan next, all having the same voting share. While many votes only require a simple majority, decisions regarding the use of loans by BMC require a super-majority of 85 per cent.[19] Even with the addition of several new members after the break-up of the Soviet Union, donor or creditor countries still control majority voting in the EBRD. Post-Cold War concerns, as well as the European initiative for creating the bank help account for the NBMC control of the EBRD. Also while the EBRD initially included a much more diverse NBMC profile than the IADB, NBMC did not join the EBRD in order to benefit from special membership procurement policies as in the IADB. The EBRD does not permit contracts and tenders to include a preference for member businesses.

3. Lending policies and practice

In this section, I examine how the charters and the mandates of the IADB and the EBRD have influenced their lending practices. While there are lending differences among all the RDB (particularly in the case of the EBRD), these differences have narrowed over time. It is important to recall that with the broad mandate, the IADB has focused on public financing. On the other hand, the initial EBRD agreement provided for a maximum of 40 per cent for public financing, and it allowed private sector assistance in excess of the 60 per cent.

[19] Even though the US is the single largest shareholder, Upton (2000) argues that the US influence in the EBRD is considerably less than in the IADB.

IADB lending policies

During its first three decades of existence, the IADB concentrated on project lending. In the 1960s, 40 per cent of IADB lending went to the agriculture, industry, and mining sectors. Infrastructure (e.g., electric power, transportation, and communications) received close to 30 per cent. Social development projects involving water supply and sewerage systems, urban development and housing, and education accounted for nearly 25 per cent (Tussie 1995). By the 1970s, the IADB also began making programme loans which targeted not only specific projects but also encouraged the creation of institutions to implement projects and deliver services. At the Fifth Replenishment of 1981, the Bank established a target of 50 per cent lending to programmes that would benefit low-income groups. However during the debt crisis of the 1980s, the Bank began to provide balance-of-payments assistance (so-called 'policy lending' normally associated with the IMF). The IADB has also become the major source of technical assistance for the region.

In order to guide access to resources from the Bank, the BMC are grouped into four categories, known as Groups A, B, C, and D[20] according to their level of development.[21] The IADB's largest borrowers have been the largest economies in the region. Approximately 70 per cent of the Bank's disbursed loans have gone to Brazil, Mexico, Argentina, Colombia, Chile, and Peru which together account for about 85 per cent of the region's gross domestic product (GDP). However on a *per capita* basis, the Bank has lent more to the smaller and poorer BMC.

The Bank's impact as a development institution has been more significant for the smaller and poorer BMC. These BMC have been more dependent on official development assistance and have had greater manpower constraints than larger BMC. They have generally needed more guidance from the IABD and have absorbed relatively larger amounts of lending and staff time (Bland and Kilby 2012). Changes in lending policies have also allowed favourable treatment for smaller BMC in the relative share of funds granted by the Bank for the total cost of a project. The share of total costs financed by the Bank is 50 per cent for Group A countries, 60 per cent for Group B countries, 70 per cent for Group C countries, and 80 per cent for Group D countries. In addition, the share of total costs that would be funded by the IADB can be supplemented by an additional 10 per cent for projects that provide at least 50 per cent of their benefits to

[20] Group A is comprised of Argentina, Brazil, Mexico, and Venezuela. Group B is comprised of Chile, Colombia, and Peru. Group C consists of the Bahamas, Barbados, Costa Rica, Jamaica, Panama, Suriname, Trinidad and Tobago, and Uruguay. Group D is composed of the poorest, least-developed BMC: Belize, Bolivia, the Dominican Republic, Ecuador, El Salvador, Guatemala, Guyana, Haiti, Honduras, Nicaragua, Paraguay.

[21] Nine indicators were used as measurements of development: gross domestic product (GDP), GDP per capita, population, annual rate of population growth, share of investment in GDP, rate of growth of per capita GDP, life expectancy at birth, infant mortality rates, and literacy rates.

Table 10.1 IADB annual loans and guarantees authorized (1961–2001)

	Total
1961–1971	4.8
1972–1981	15.2
1982–1991	31.8
1992	6.1
1993	6
1994	5.3
1995	7.2
1996	6.7
1997	6
1998	10
1999	9.4
2000	5.2
2001	7.8
2002	4.1
2003	6.2
2004	5.4
2005	6.7
2006	5.7
2007	8.5
2008	11
2009	15.2
2010	12.1
2011	10.4
2012	10.8
2013	13.3
2014	12.6
2015	10.4

[a] *Source*: IADB *Annual Reports* (1961–2015); IADB *Information Statements* (1961–2015).

low-income groups. Annual lending has grown dramatically from USD 294 million approved in 1961 to almost USD 10.4 billion in 2015. From its inception until 2015, loans have reached almost USD 250 billion (see Table 10.1). The IADB has become the most important lender to Latin American countries, surpassing the financial assistance provided by the IBRD to the region.

EBRD lending policies

During its first two and a half years of operation, the EBRD was repeatedly criticized for the slow disbursement of its loans and the rather modest amount of lending that occurred. For example during the 1991-2 period, the EBRD entered into twenty-nine projects committing only ECU 626 million. In 1993, the number of projects did increase substantially to sixty-six, and the amount that was committed was over ECU 1.5 billion. However, this sum was a small amount of the actual paid-in capital available to the Bank. Another concern about the early lending practices of the EBRD was the substantial amount of capital that went to the Visegrád countries (Wyles 1994). From 1991 to 1993, 46 per cent of 95 signed projects were with the Czech Republic, Hungary, and Poland. However, these countries (like the largest Latin American countries) had the most developed private sector in which the EBRD could invest. The EBRD funds up to 35 per cent of the total project costs for either a Greenfield project[22] or an established company.

Under President Jacques de Larosière, the number of projects and committed capital increased greatly. After his re-organization of the Bank, the processing and dispersal of loans was streamlined and there was greater attention paid to finding partners in small- and medium-sized enterprises (SMEs). For example between 1998 and 1999, 300 projects were signed and the Bank committed ECU 4.5 billion. By 1998, 80 per cent of total financing went to the private sector compared to 76 per cent in 1997. Of the 300 projects approved between 1998 and 1999, approximately 12 per cent were signed with the Czech Republic, Hungary, and Poland showing that while these three countries still enjoyed substantial access to capital, the Bank's country portfolio had substantially changed. For example during the period of 1998-9, approximately 13 per cent of signed projects were with Russia.

The composition of member state borrowing has dramatically changed over the past fifteen years demonstrating a shift away from core European member lending. For example in 2015, the three countries that received the greatest amount of EBRD investment included Turkey followed by Egypt and Kazakhstan. The other change in the EBRD's lending reflected an increasing ability to target SME and other private sector businesses for investment. During its early years, the majority of EBRD financing was in the form of loans. However since 1996, the share of projects financed strictly through loans has declined. Since 2000, several projects were financed as guarantees or the issuing of senior debt. In addition, the number of SME and micro and small enterprise (MSE) loans has dramatically increased. To consolidate its work, the EBRD in 2014 launched the Small Business Initiative focused on sustaining growth of SMEs. Unlike other RDB, including the IABD, the EBRD does not have a soft window.[23]

4. Relations with other IFI

All RDB are concerned with establishing a division of labour between themselves and other IFI, particularly the IBRD. RDB do not want to be seen as duplicating the tasks of the IBRD and thus rendering themselves superfluous. On the other

[22] A Greenfield project must be a completely new business or enterprise.

[23] A soft window provides credits or concessional loans below the prevailing market rate and is considered different than a hard window's market rate loans. Fundamentally, these windows reflect the differences between a development and banking emphasis.

hand, RDB have increasingly worked with the IBRD to co-finance projects. Cooperation between RDBs and the IBRD is often promoted in order to ensure efficiency in projects. The question is how do RDB balance the concern between duplicating efforts and promoting cooperation? This section examines the relationship between RDB and the IBRD and other IFI, noting areas of cooperation and competition.

IADB relations with the IBRD

The IADB Articles of Agreement specify that 'the Bank shall cooperate as far as possible with national and international institutions and with private sources supplying investment capital' (IADB 1959, section 2.b). However, it does not specify how this cooperation will take place. In the beginning of the IADB's operation, the relationship with the IBRD was more competitive than cooperative. To help diffuse this competition, informal sectoral agreements were worked out to guide operations. For example in the area of education, the IADB focused on loans in higher education and the IBRD focused on secondary education loans. An initial division of labour also emerged whereby the IBRD concentrated on large-scale loans, such as those required for infrastructure projects, while the IADB focused on smaller projects. However by the end of the 1960s, this division had eroded as the IBRD entered into social and poverty reduction projects, and the IADB began large-scale funding of infrastructure projects.

Coordination between the IADB and the IBRD increased after the Seventh Replenishment of 1989. Prior to 1990, both institutions had only about three to four joint operations per year. After the Seventh Replenishment, this number substantially increased. Coordination, however, has taken place without a formal memorandum of understanding (since both institutions are headquartered in Washington, DC). The IADB has had less leverage in the larger BMC which have access to alternative financial sources. In these countries, the IABD has accepted the focus of the IMF and the IBRD on policy programmes involving exchange rate, trade policy, and other price issues (Iglesias 1992). The IADB attempts to avoid providing conflicting advice or stipulating conflicting conditions in these areas policy areas. However, relations with the IBRD tend to be more competitive regarding smaller BMC. The IADB lends to smaller BMC at a rate two to three times that of the IBRD. For many of these smaller borrowers, the Bank is the main IFI. Programming differences between the IADB and IBRD are more likely to occur in these cases. The IADB's relationship with the IBRD is unique. Since 1991, the IADB has surpassed the IBRD in lending to the region. Perhaps because of its leadership in the region, the IADB co-finances more projects with the IBRD than any other RDB.

EBRD relations with the IBRD and other IFI

Because of its emphasis on the private sector, the EBRD was not as concerned about duplicating IBRD efforts. Indeed, in the EBRD's agreement, Article 2.2, states that the EBRD will work in close cooperation with the IMF, the IBRD, and the IFC. In July 1990, an IBRD official noted that because of the EBRD's emphasis on the private sector, the IBRD would focus its lending in the public and the social sectors (Fidler 1990). For example in 1994, finance and business investments were approximately 40 per cent of the Bank's total sector activity compared to only 7.5 per cent for the IBRD (Culpeper 1997: 117). Therefore, the EBRD was not concerned about competition from the IBRD, but it was concerned about establishing a separate mandate from the IFC. One of the means by which the EBRD has attempted to distinguish itself from the IFC is to promote finance for SME which is typically not the focus of the IFC. In terms of the IFC, EBRD loan commitments have been substantially greater. While the EBRD is not the lead IFI in the region (compared to the IADB in Latin America), it is the lead IFI in private sector loans. Besides the competition between RDB and the IBRD, there is also the issue of competition between the various RDB. The EBRD and the ADB include several of the same member states (principally from Central Asia as well as the Caucuses). In order to coordinate lending activity in Central Asia, the two banks entered into a formal agreement in which the EBRD would be considered the lead IFI in the private and financial sectors, and the ADB would be the lead institution in social sectors (Culpeper 1997).

5. Conclusions

This chapter examined the differences and, in many cases, the similarities between the IADB and the EBRD. Given the importance of these institutions in their respective regions, particularly the IADB, it is surprising how little attention has been paid to these institutions specifically and the role of RDB generally. Most of the literature on IFI has tended to focus on the IBRD and IMF as the leading financial institutions in the world. However, RDB are increasingly playing important roles in the respective regions. Even though their structures are similar, the mandates of IADB and EBRD are quite different, leading to distinct lending pattern and lending policies. While the IADB focuses on social development and poverty reduction loans (broadly defined), the EBRD's focus has been on private sector development. The EBRD's focus on the private sector not only differentiates it from the IADB but also the IBRD and even to a certain extent the IFC. This gives it a niche to fill in the area of IFI.

The influence of BMC and NBMC in the creation of these banks can help explain some of the differences between the IADB and the EBRD. There is a distinction between two different types of RDB: those controlled by creditors (e.g., the EBRD) and those controlled by borrowers (e.g., the IADB). In the case of Latin America, when BMC take the initiative in creating an RDB, it would appear that their control over the bank's policies is more pronounced. Even though the US was a critical actor in the negotiations for the creation of the IADB, BMC were able to retain voting control over the bank, as well as designate its president (albeit the influence of the US increased dramatically by the end of the 1980s under the Baker Plan). In the case of the EBRD, the initiative in the creation of this IFI from the outset came from NBMC, particularly France with the active participation of the US, which ultimately lead to an RDB controlled and presided over by NBMC.

The international environment in which the discussions took place also provides a picture of how politics play an important role in developing IFI. Concerns over the spread of communism in Latin America in the 1950s led to the creation of a bank where democratic efforts were not as important as is the case with the EBRD in the 1990s. The collapse of the Soviet Union led NBMC to pay special attention to democratization and citizen's rights. These concerns were not expressed in the 1950s, where the discussions of an IFI for Latin America were not constrained by whether democracy and human rights were being respected in the region. Preventing the spread of communism was perhaps a much more important factor. In the case of the EBRD, intense regional and international competition among key players such as the US, France, and Germany led to initial decisions concerning the scope and breadth of lending and political considerations in the promotion of economic development. Indeed, the EBRD has been referred to as a 'political bank' (Weber 1994) in which lending decisions, early in its tenure, were based more on political necessity than economic analysis. As many BMCs democratized and underwent several successful democratic elections, the political considerations became less important and economic development became firmly the basis for lending decision-making. This comparison between the IADB and the EBRD illustrates the importance of the international environment a in the initial creation of regional banks but also shows how that environment as well as changes in country conditions influences lending decisions.

References

Birch, M.H. (1988). 'Institution building: multilateral development banks and State-Owned Enterprises', *World Development*, 16: 255–70.

Bland, E. and Kilby, C. (2012). 'Informal influence in the Inter-American Development Bank'. Villanova School of Business Economics. Working Paper No. 22.

Bronstone, A. (1999). *The European Bank for Reconstruction and Development: The Building of a Bank for East Central Europe*. Manchester: Manchester University Press.

Culpepper, R. (1997). *Titans or Behemoths?* Boulder, CO: Lynne Rienner.

Dell, S. (1972). *The Inter-American Development Bank: A Study in Development Financing*. New York: Praeger.

Easton, M. and Rorer, K. (1991). 'Recent developments – the European bank for reconstruction and development', *Harvard International Law Journal*, 32: 527–49.

EBRD (European Bank for Reconstruction and Development) (1990). *Agreement Establishing the European Bank for Reconstruction and Development*. London: EBRD.

Fidler, S. (1990). 'World Bank to play a smaller role in the long term', *Financial Times*, 6 July: 2.

Gray, C. (2014). 'Finding out what works: tracking results in the Inter-American Development Bank', *Journal of Development Effectiveness*, 6: 480–9.

IADB (Inter-American Development Bank) (1959). *Agreement Establishing the Inter-American Development Bank*. Washington, DC: IADB.

IADB (Inter-American Development Bank) (1961–2015a). *Annual Reports*. Washington, DC: IADB.

IADB (Inter-American Development Bank) (1961–2015b). *Information Statements*. Washington, DC: IADB.

Iglesias, E.V. (1992). *Reflections on Economic Development: Toward a New Latin American Consensus*. Washington, DC: Inter-American Development Bank.

Korfker, F. (2012). 'Reflection on private-sector evaluation in the European Bank for Reconstruction and Development: 1991-2010', *Evaluation*, 19: 85–96.

Kwakwa, E. (2017). *Globalization and International Organizations*. New York: Routledge.

Menkveld, P.A. (1991). *Origin and Role of the European Bank for Reconstruction and Development*. London: Graham & Troutman.

Mikesell, R.F. (1955). *Foreign Investments in Latin America*. Washington, DC: Pan American Union.

Mitterrand, F. (1989). *Bulletin of the European Community 10:80*. In Paul A. Menkveld (ed.), *Origin and Role of the European Bank for Reconstruction and Development*. London: Graham & Troutman, 1991, pp. 25–6.

Scheman, L.R. (1997). 'Banking and growth: the role of the Inter-American Development Bank', *Journal of Interamerican Studies and World Affairs*, 39: 85–100.

Shields, S. and Wallin, S. (2015). 'The European Bank for Reconstruction and Development's gender action plan and the gendered political economy of post-communist transition', *Globalizations*, 12: 383–99.

Shihata, I.F.I. (1990). 'The role of the European Bank for Reconstruction and Development in the promotion and financing of investment in Central and Eastern Europe: a legal analysis', *ICSID Review*, 5: 207–31.

Tussie, D. (1995). *The Inter-American Development Bank*. Boulder, CO: Lynne Rienner.

Upton, B. (2000). *The Multilateral Development Banks: Improving US Leadership*. Westport, CT: Prager.

Weber, S. (1994). 'Reconstruction and development', *International Organization*, 48: 1–38.

Wyles, J. (1994). 'Europe's development banks: banks building Europe', *Europe*, 334: 10–2.

11

The Inter-American Development Bank and the Washington Consensus

Shareholder Activism and the Taming of a Reluctant Partner

Sarah Babb

1. Introduction

At the end of the 1980s, the term 'Washington Consensus' was coined to describe a set of market-liberalizing policy reforms that were being disseminated to developing countries by international organizations (Williamson 1990). The organizations usually associated with the term were the World Bank and the International Monetary Fund (IMF), which became famous, or infamous, for conditioning their loans on the adoption of reforms, including trade liberalization, privatization, and deregulation.

Yet there was also a third international organization in the consensus. Located less than a mile from the World Bank and IMF in downtown Washington, DC, the regional Inter-American Development Bank (IADB) similarly began to engage in market-liberalizing policy conditionality in the 1980s. Unlike the World Bank and IMF, which took up the Washington Consensus with gusto, the IADB was a far more reluctant partner: both its borrowing members and its Latin American-dominated management had strong reservations about having the organization take up this role (Tussie 1995).

How was the IADB brought into the Washington Consensus? In this chapter, I trace how the United States (US) Treasury engineered the major shift in the Bank's policy and formal structure through negotiations over donor contributions to its financial resources. This story illustrates how a powerful donor government such as the US may sometimes behave as an 'activist shareholder'—using its control over resources to bargain with management for organizational change (Gillan and Starks 2007). The governments that contribute the bulk of the resources to the development banks do so because they believe that their contributions will yield valuable returns. Yet in contrast to 'shareholder value' in private firms, which can be assessed in dollars and cents, international donors can use

Sarah Babb, *The Inter-American Development Bank and the Washington Consensus: Shareholder Activism and the Taming of a Reluctant Partner* In: *Regional Development Banks in the World Economy.* Edited by: Judith Clifton, Daniel Díaz-Fuentes, and David Howarth, Oxford University Press (2021).
DOI: 10.1093/oso/9780198861089.003.0011

foreign aid to pursue a range of incommensurable goals (Fiss and Zajac 2004; Lancaster 2007).

The IADB's initiation into the Washington Consensus resulted from a historic and durable shift in US policy-makers' conception of shareholder value, from one in which the banks were worthy of support because of their ability to promote US security and diplomatic goals, to one that valued the Banks' ability to change national economic policies. US shareholder activism not only brought the development banks into alignment with Washington's agenda, but also into alignment with one another, making them into powerful promoters of a free-market revolution across the developing world.

2. The development banks and donor control

Like other international organizations, the multilateral development banks (MDBs) derive legitimacy from appearing independent from powerful states. As one state department official explained to the US Congress in 1973,

> The [multilateral development] banks...enjoy an impartial and objective observer status due to their multinational membership... The receptivity of borrowing countries to suggestions from the multilateral institutions is great: questions of sensitive national pride are minimized when recommendations come from a prestigious international financial institution rather than from any single bilateral aid donor. (US Congress 1973: 11; Casey testimony in US House)

Nevertheless, the states that contribute the most to financing these institutions have always sought to preserve some measure of control over how their money is spent. This is reflected in the weighted voting shares of the World Bank and regional development banks (RDBs), in traditional mechanisms for selecting top management for these institutions, and in their geographical location. The compromise between the need for legitimacy and the desire for control is manifested in a disproportionate but nevertheless imperfect influence of donors in these institutions. For example, the US cannot unilaterally approve a loan in the World Bank, although it can veto one of which it disapproves. In the IADB, the US on its own cannot veto regular loans, but it can veto subsidized loans to the poorest countries in the bank's Fund for Special Operations.

There are occasions, however, when donors can effect major changes within these organizations. Periodically, donors engage in negotiations around increasing a bank's capital resources (known as a general capital increase), or the replenishment of a bank's concessional window offering subsidized loans or grants to low-income borrowers (such as the International Development Association in the World Bank, or the Fund for Special Operations in the IADB). These moments constitute critical junctures at which donors can use their control over the purse strings to negotiate significant changes from the status quo (Kappagoda 1995: 39; Kapur et al. 1997: 1145). These present opportunities for leading donors to behave as activist shareholders.

Throughout the second half of the twentieth century, the US stood out as by far the most influential shareholder in the World Bank and RDBs (Sanford 1982). This influence derived in part from its comparatively large share in contributions (although these declined over time). American leadership in multilateral forums such as the Group of Five (G5) gave the US unmatched influence with other donor governments, and this was magnified by the unusual structure of the US policy-making process. In contrast to countries with parliamentary systems, where multilateral negotiations are carried out by unitary governments, in the US, it is only the executive branch that is included in the bargain; Congress may refuse to go along with the multilateral agreements the executive reaches with other governments (Lancaster 2007). Although this dynamic imposes constraints on the executive, it can also be used to its advantage: the US can tell other parties that if its position is not adopted, Congress will fail to ratify the agreement and appropriate the requisite funds (Kappagoda 1995; Kapur et al. 1997).

It is well known that the US has often used its leverage during negotiations around the banks' replenishments and general capital increases. However, there have been few detailed accounts of how US shareholder activism in the banks has played out in practice. This is because negotiations among donors, between donors and management, and between donors and borrowing governments mostly occur in a 'black box' that is unamenable to scrutiny by outsiders. For example, there is no public record of negotiations among G5 finance ministers, or of the informal discussions that occur between MDB management and the US Treasury.

To shed light into the story of how the IADB was brought into the Washington Consensus, I draw on a variety of sources, two of which are particularly important. First, I examine the annual testimonies presented by the US Treasury to Congress to justify ongoing US financing for the MDBs, as well as the Congressional discussions that followed these testimonies. In these annual hearings, the executive branch shares with Congress its rationale for why the US should fund these institutions—it explicitly promotes particular conceptions of shareholder value. These hearings therefore provide a relatively reliable record of US initiatives towards the banks.[1] Second, I delve into internal documents from the Office for the Assistant Secretary for International Affairs of the US Treasury,

[1] Official statements of the US Treasury to Congress are a matter of public record; inaccuracies, if discovered, can be potentially embarrassing. Members of Congress have a strong interest in getting accurate information from the Treasury, and have a number of ways to investigate the validity of Treasury statements they believe to be false or misleading, including the research of their own staff, the Congressional Research Service, and the Government Accountability Office (GAO).

recently declassified and available at the National Archive in response to multiple requests that I filed through the Freedom of Information Act.

3. The IADB and the US in historical perspective

Until the 1980s, US support of the IADB and other development banks was informed by a range of objectives, from the promotion of economic development to the generation of procurement contracts for US firms. Overall, however, they were dominated by a conception of shareholder value that emphasized US security objectives. Economic development, it was believed, was good for containing communism; moreover, US support for the banks served as a diplomatic 'symbol of US commitment to Third World development' (US Congress 1980: 26 (Blumenthal testimony in US House)).

The US was the IADB's leading donor at its founding in 1959, and the Bank was conveniently located in Washington, DC. Yet American influence in the Bank was, while strong, counterbalanced by the force of its Latin American members. The Bank was founded in response to overwhelming demand from Latin American governments at a time when the US was increasingly preoccupied with addressing political and social unrest in its own back yard (White 1972). In contrast to the shareholder-dominated World Bank and Asian Development Bank (ADB), the IADB granted a majority voting share to its developing country members. By tradition, the head of the IADB was a Latin American, and Latin Americans occupied many key management positions. According to one observer, the head 'appeared to see itself as the spokesman of Latin America rather than as a mediator between the northern and southern continents' (White 1972: 140).

Compared to the World Bank, which was famous for delegating decisions to management, the IADB had a very active board of directors. Armed with a majority share, Latin American board members occasionally even over-ruled the objections of the US. For example, the IADB provided a loan to the Chile during the Marxist presidency of Salvador Allende in the early 1970s (Sanford 1982). This contrasted starkly with the World Bank, which discreetly stopped lending to Chile during this period (Ascher 1990).

In spite of such objectionable behaviour, for many years the US continued to be a generous and remarkably forgiving shareholder (White 1972; Tussie 1995). Yet as time passed, the foundations of this support began to weaken. There was a growing sense on Capitol Hill that the US had been spending a lot on foreign aid, but had little to show for it (Gwin 1997). Many in Congress began to suggest that US contributions to multilateral banks were tantamount to taking money from beleaguered American taxpayers to subsidize third world elites and bloated multilateral bureaucracies. Most critical of all were Congressional conservatives, who resented support for third world governments with socialist leanings, or that spoke against the US in the United Nations. The controversial IADB loan to the Allende government in Chile was one example. Throughout the 1970s, Congress expressed its displeasure by refusing to appropriate the funds the Treasury had requested to meet US commitments to the IADB and other development banks. When the Reagan administration took office in early 1981, support for these banks on Capitol Hill had reached an all-time low (Babb 2009).

The Reagan years brought about a marked shift in the attitude of the US executive to the MDBs. There were quite a few in the new administration who shared Congressional Republicans' scepticism towards these institutions. Overall, the first Reagan administration's (1981-5) position towards the IADB and other banks could best be described as 'disciplinary', oriented towards holding down US contributions, pushing the banks to use their resources more efficiently, and blocking them from making objectionable project loans (Babb 2009).

In the IADB, however, this discipline was met with resistance from the Bank's historically independent borrowing members. In early 1983, over the objections of the US, the IADB approved a USD 30 million loan to the Soviet-tilting Sandinista government of Nicaragua with the purpose of revitalizing its fishing industry. Later that year, the administration successfully opposed another Nicaragua loan, this time from the Bank's concessional lending window, in which the US could exercise a veto (Farnsworth 1983). In 1985, a third Nicaragua IADB loan was kept from coming to a vote by a personal letter from Secretary of State George Schultz to the IADB's president, Antonio Ortíz Mena (De Young 1985).

4. The rise of the Washington Consensus

During the early 1980s, the political climate in Washington was rendering the traditional conception of shareholder value obsolete. It was no longer compelling to say that the banks served as a symbol of US commitment to third world aspirations. However, during Reagan's first term, no alternative vision of shareholder value arose to take the place of the older conception (Babb 2009).

It was ultimately events in the international economy that would help solidify a new view of shareholder value. During the prior decade, the Bretton Woods system had collapsed, and developing country governments had been wracked by supply shocks and balance-of-payments crises. Many borrowed from international banks. With the rise in global interest rates after 1979, these debt burdens became unsustainable. In 1982, the Mexican government became the first to announce that it would no longer be able to service its debts. Over the next few years, the US partnered the IMF to prevent governments from defaulting, but were unsuccessful in resolving the debt crisis.

On 8 October 1985, at the annual meetings of the World Bank and IMF in Seoul, South Korea, US Treasury Secretary James A. Baker III proposed a bold new approach to the third world debt crisis, the so-called 'Program of Sustained Growth', soon known simply as 'The Baker Plan'. The plan proposed a novel role for three international financial institutions: the World Bank, the IMF, and the IADB. Rather than working independently, as in prior decades, these three institutions would be charged with collaborating closely to offer loans that were conditioned on the adoption of market-liberalizing policies.

As it was announced in Seoul, Baker's plan was made up of three related elements. First, debtor countries needed to adopt 'comprehensive macro-economic and structural policies supported by the international financial institutions, to promote growth and balance of payments adjustment, and to reduce inflation'. Second, Baker called for 'a continued central role for the IMF, in conjunction with increased and more effective structural adjustment lending by the MDBs, both in support of the adoption by principal debtors of market-orientated policies for growth'. And third, Baker proposed 'increased lending by the private banks in support of comprehensive economic adjustment programs' (Montagnon 1985).

One of the most novel aspects of the Baker Plan was that it unambiguously endorsed getting the multilateral banks involved in policy-based loans. Traditionally, the banks had specialized almost exclusively in making loans for tangible projects, such as bridges and dams (although the IADB was known for promoting more socially oriented projects). In the late 1970s, the Bank had launched a 'structural adjustment facility', which offered loans for balance-of-payments support, rather than projects, and in exchange for policy reforms (Kapur et al. 1997). Lending for policy reform had long been practiced by the IMF, but had been limited to fiscal and monetary conditions, such as cutting deficits and reducing the money supply, aimed narrowly at stamping out inflation and promoting currency stability (Babb 2007). In contrast, World Bank structural adjustment loans were aimed at changing the underlying structure of national economies. Yet until the mid-1980s they made up a relatively small proportion of World Bank loans.

The Baker Plan proposed not only expanding the World Bank's structural adjustment lending, but also getting the IMF and the IADB involved. In line with this reasoning, both the World Bank and the IADB were expected to expand their lending in fast disbursing structural and sectoral adjustment loans. These loans would be conditioned on market-liberalizing policies, including 'growth oriented tax reform', 'improvement of the environment for both domestic and foreign direct investment', 'trade liberalization and the rationalization of import regimes', and 'the privatization of burdensome and inefficient public enterprises' (US Congress 1986: 595 (Baker testimony in US House). This policy agenda would soon become known as the 'Washington Consensus'.

The new role for the World Bank and IADB was based on a new conception of shareholder value. The worth of the banks was no longer seen as lying in their promotion of US security. Rather, the banks were best directed towards promoting US global economic and financial objectives. This meant that a key role for the banks was to encourage countries to pursue particular economic policies. For, as Baker explained to the Congressional sub-committees in the Spring of 1986: 'Absent *appropriate economic policies*, no amount of money—whether derived from external borrowing, foreign aid, or domestic monetary expansion—will produce sustained growth (emphasis added)' (US Congress 1986: 595 (Baker testimony in US House)).

5. Leveraging the seventh replenishment

The Baker Plan implied a major re-orientation of the activities of the IADB, which—in contrast to the World Bank—had little experience with policy-conditional loans. Moreover, the Baker Plan was predicated on two additional changes to the bank, both of them significant. First, to effectively promote policy reforms, the IADB would need to develop 'country strategies'—plans for reforming national economies—and orient their loans to fit with these strategies. Second, the Baker Plan required the IMF, World Bank, and IADB to engage in 'coordinated lending', to prevent the conditionality of one from being undercut by loans from another. Significantly, this was not envisaged as a collaboration among equals: the IMF—which was also being encouraged to use its conditional lending to promote free-market reforms—would be the senior partner. For its part, the IADB would be expected to work under the supervision of the World Bank (US Congress 1986: 594-600 (Baker testimony in US House)).

The IADB had been given advance notice of the turmoil to come. More than six months earlier, in March 1985, US Deputy Treasury Secretary David Mulford explained at the IADB's annual board meeting that the administration wanted the bank to 'thoroughly analyze the policies of its borrowers and, where necessary, encourage reform before committing its resources', and 'improve its policy coordination and cooperation with other international lenders' (Mulford 1985a). Mulford elaborated on his meaning in a private letter to newly appointed USAID Director Peter McPherson in September. 'There are fundamental problems with the way the IADB does business', he wrote. 'The Bank's reticence in practicing policy conditionality, its willingness to consider projects which violate even its own policies, its lack of policy coordination with other donors, and its inadequate encouragement of private sector development—these all limit the IADB's effectiveness as a development bank for the key Latin American and Caribbean region' (Mulford 1985b).

To overcome the IADB's expected resistance to the Baker Plan, the Treasury planned to use the negotiations over the bank's seventh replenishment and general capital increase. This strategy was laid out in an internal memo briefing Mulford for a meeting with IADB President Antonio Ortiz Mena on 1 November 1985. Mulford was advised to be candid with Ortiz Mena about the consequences of failure to comply. 'Secretary Baker has asked me to make clear we expect your support on all aspects', it read. 'In absence of such support, we are prepared to withhold support for IADB replenishment, even if it means interruption of some duration in IADB lending'. On the other hand, compliance would be amply rewarded: 'If US plan is implemented, we are prepared to consider substantial replenishment of IADB resources which would make IADB an extremely significant player in all Latin American countries, especially major debtors' (Conrow 1985: 1).

The thirteen-page long memo went into considerable detail regarding the changes that the US Treasury was proposing. 'We want the IADB to introduce a program of well defined, well targeted, fast disbursing non-project [policy-conditional] loans', it explained. 'Project lending would continue but within a context of country programs with appropriate conditionality' (Conrow 1985, Tab A). To become an effective lender for market-liberalizing reforms, the IADB would need to reform its own policies, organization, and decision-making rules. It would have to commit to preparing country strategies, to be reviewed annually by its executive board. And rather than lending independently, the IADB would be required to follow the World Bank's lead: '[a]ny borrower would be presumptively eligible for an IADB structural adjustment loan if it had and was in compliance with a World Bank structural adjustment or sector loan' (Conrow 1985: 1).

Aligning with the Baker Plan would also require the IADB to undergo significant organizational restructuring. The briefing noted that '[a]s currently organized, IADB has no internal entity that is strong enough to insist upon quality/conditionality'. To remedy this, the Treasury was wanted the bank to create a new department by merging its Economic and Social Development (DES) and Plans and Programs (DPL) departments. This new department would 'play a lead role so that projects are integrated and consistent with overall country strategies' (Conrow 1985: 3). In order to make these organizational changes work, the memo asked that the new department be led by 'a qualified American, Canadian, or non-regional'. The Treasury also wanted such individuals to fill other key positions in the IADB, including (among others) Senior Deputy Manager in the Operations Department, one new Operation Division Chief position, and the Deputy Manager of Human Resources (Conrow 1985: 4).

The IADB would also need to reform its governing structure to award greater control to donor governments. Under the current structure 'while the US has enormous influence, the actual [voting] structure of the IADB gives control to the recipient countries rather than to the donors. This is in complete contrast to the

World Bank and IMF' (Conrow 1985: 4). The IADB's Articles of Agreement would need to be modified so that loans needed a sixty-five per cent majority for approval, which would 'give the US combined with one other chair a veto over decisions in the Executive Board' (Conrow 1985, Tab A). At the time, the US controlled only 34.5 per cent of the votes. This meant that it was possible for a simple majority to approve a loan over the objections of the US, as had occurred with the Nicaragua loan in 1983.

6. The taming of the IADB

Ortiz Mena's response to this message was equivocal. 'Ortiz Mena indicated he wants the Bank to be an active participant and acknowledged that the Bank must move to require conditionality', reported Mulford in a memo to Secretary Baker the following week. Yet Mulford also acknowledged that 'the scope of the changes we seek is broader and deeper than those presently envisaged by Ortiz Mena and the Latins', and that 'we should expect a long and difficult negotiation'. At the IADB President's suggestion, Treasury scheduled a joint meeting in January 1986 with Ortiz Mena and representatives from Mexico, Argentina, Venezuela, and Brazil. These 'key Latin debtors' were among those most likely to be impacted by Baker Plan conditionality, and also were among the IADB's most powerful borrowing members (Mulford 1985c: 1).

We do not have a record of what was said at this meeting. However, circumstantial evidence suggests that it did not go well. Upon initiating negotiations for the IADB's seventh replenishment and general capital increase in the Spring of 1986, IADB President Antonio Ortiz Mena stated unequivocally that 'the IADB will remain a project lending institution' (Friedland 1986).

The US was adamant in its demands, and two years later the negotiations had not yielded an agreement. That year, the US announced that it was temporarily suspending its contributions to the IADB—including the funds it had promised for the earlier replenishment—due to the stalled negotiations. Agreement had been reached that twenty-five per cent of the bank's resources would be earmarked for sectoral adjustment loans aimed at reforms such as trade liberalization and privatization, under the supervision of the more experienced World Bank (Pine 1987). Non-Latin Americans had been appointed to key management posts.

Nevertheless, the proposal to change the bank's voting structure remained a sticking point with the IADB's larger Latin American members, particularly Mexico, Brazil, Argentina and Venezuela, as well as many among its mostly Latin American staff. As one IADB official angrily remarked to the *Washington Post,* 'The US Treasury is acting like the 20th-century equivalent of the British colonial office' (Rowen 1987). However, Baker saw the matter quite differently. As he explained to the House Appropriations Committee in 1987, 'we think it is not unreasonable to suggest that the countries which furnish the most money should have the most say in where that money goes' (US Congress 1987: 520 (Baker testimony in US House)).

On 17 December 1987, IADB President Antonio Ortiz Mena, announced his resignation, clearly in part because of his failure to negotiate a mutually acceptable agreement with the US. It would fall to Ortiz Mena's successor, Enrique Iglesias, to come up with a way out of the impasse. Adopting a conciliatory tone, in December 1988, Iglesias proposed a restructuring of the bank that cut around 125 people from the staff of 1,700 as a response to US concerns that the IADB was over-staffed (Farnsworth 1988). Only two months later, the recently inaugurated George H.W. Bush administration announced that it was dropping its demand for the 65 per cent approval threshold, accepting instead a compromise that would give the U.S. Executive Director a means of delaying (but not halting) loans (Fidler 1989). With the deadlock thus broken, donors proceeded to approve a USD 26.5 billion increase in IADB resources. From that point forward, the IADB would be much more responsive to US-led policy initiatives.

There is no evidence of other major donors opposing the US in its efforts to bring the IADB to heel. In general, the Baker Plan seems to have strong support among other wealthy industrialized countries. As Baker himself put it to Congress, he was 'encouraged by international consensus which has emerged on the critical importance of MDB support for reducing structural rigidities, strengthening incentives for the private sector, reducing the size of government, and improving the investment environment' (US Congress 1986: 665 (Baker testimony in US House)). Other shareholder governments allowed the Americans to put negotiations over IADB resources on hold until the bank complied to the US Treasury's satisfaction.

7. Conclusion

This chapter has shown how the IADB was reluctantly inducted into the Washington Consensus through US-led shareholder activism. Threatened with dwindling resources, the bank's spirited management and borrowing members were forced into retreat, and the bank was thoroughly transformed in only a few short years. The bank's voting rules were altered to give greater weight to the donor governments; its management became less Latin American; and its operations became fully aligned with the goals of the Baker Plan. By the time John Williamson made his famous observations in 1989, the IADB was a full-fledged participant in the Washington Consensus.

The IADB was not the only RDB to be brought into the Washington Consensus in this way. Like the IADB, the African Development Bank (AfDB) was persuaded to adopt policy-based lending as part of its fourth general capital increase, concluded in 1986. Also like the IADB, the AfDB was required to alter its voting rules to give the US and other donors greater formal influence, and to work as a junior partner to the World Bank. For its part, the Asian Development Bank (ADB) was brought into the consensus several years later through quiet negotiations between the US and Japan, the ADB's other leading donor (Babb 2009: 136-41).

What all these episodes had in common was a particular conception of shareholder value, in which the banks were useful as promoters of 'appropriate policies'—an economic rather than a security objective of the US government. US shareholder activism in the development banks and the IMF harnessed these organizations to a common purpose, facilitating the liberalization of economies across the developing world in the 1980s and 1990s. As time passed, this conception endured, even as the content of what constituted appropriate policies evolved from the Washington Consensus to the 'augmented Washington Consensus' and beyond.

References

Ascher, W. (1990). 'The World Bank and US Control'. In M.P. Karns and K.A. Mingst (eds.), *The United States and Multilateral Institutions: Patterns of Changing Instrumentality and Influence*. Boston, MA: Unwin Hyman, pp. 115–39.

Babb, S. (2007). 'Embeddedness, inflation, and international regimes: the IMF in the early postwar period', *American Journal of Sociology*, 113(1): 128–64.

Babb, S.L. (2009). *Behind the Development Banks: Washington Politics, World Poverty, and the Wealth of Nations*. Chicago: University of Chicago Press.

Conrow, J. (Deputy Assistant Secretary) (1985). 'Memo to Assistant Secretary Mulford', 3 September 1985. Box 1. Record ID: HS1-99113253. Office of Multilateral Development Bank Subject File Correspondence, Office of the Assistant Secretary for International Affairs, Record Group 56, National Archives, College Park, MD.

De Young, K. (1985). 'Shultz intervenes on loan'. *Washington Post*, 3 August: A1.

Farnsworth, Clyde H. (1983). 'US blocks bank loan for Nicaragua roads', *New York Times*, 30 June: D1.

Farnsworth, C.H. (1988). 'Restructuring planned by Latin Aid Bank', *New York Times*, 20 December: D20.

Fidler, S. (1989). 'US drops demand to veto loans by Inter-American Bank', *Financial Times*, 13 February: D6.

Fiss, P.C. and Zajac, E.J. (2004). 'The diffusion of ideas over contested terrain: the (non)adoption of a shareholder value orientation among German firms', *Administrative Science Quarterly*, 49(4): 501–34.

Friedland, J. (1986). 'Dispute expected over lending at Inter-American Bank meeting', *American Banker*, 24 March: 2.

Gillan, S.L. and Starks, L.T. (2007). 'The evolution of shareholder activism in the United States', *Journal of Applied Corporate Finance*, 19(1): 55–73.

Gwin, C. (1997). 'U.S. relations with the World Bank, 1945–1992'. In D. Kapur, J.P. Lewis, and W. Richard (eds.). *The World Bank: Its First Half Century.* Volume 2: *Perspectives.* Washington, DC: Brookings Institution Press, pp. 195–274.

Kappagoda, N. (1995). *The Multilateral Development Banks.* Volume 2: *The Asian Development Bank.* Boulder, CO: Lynne Rienner.

Kapur, D., Lewis, J., and Webb, R.C. (1997). *The World Bank: Its First Half Century.* Washington, DC: Brookings Institution.

Lancaster, C. (2007). *Foreign Aid: Diplomacy, Development, Domestic Politics.* Chicago: University of Chicago Press.

Montagnon, P. (1985). 'Baker's third world debt plan', *Financial Times*, 10 September: 4.

Mulford, D.C. (1985a). 'Address to the third plenary session of the twenty-sixth annual meeting of the board of governors of the Inter-American Development Bank'. *Proceedings of the Twenty-Sixth Annual Meeting of the Board of Governors.* Washington, DC: Inter-American Development Bank, pp. 121–5.

Mulford, D.C. (1985b). 'Letter to Peter McPherson', 3 September. Box 1, Record ID: HS1-99113253. Office of Multilateral Development Bank Subject File Correspondence, Office of the Assistant Secretary for International Affairs, Record Group 56, National Archives, College Park, MD.

Mulford, D.C. (1985c). 'Memo to Secretary of Treasury James A. Baker, III', 6 December. Box 1, Record ID: HS1-99113253, Office of Multilateral Development Banks Subject File Correspondence, Office of the Assistant Secretary for International Affairs, Record Group 56, National Archives, College Park, MD.

Pine, A. (1987). 'US faces showdown over bid to gain power to override loans at the IADB', *Wall Street Journal*, 20 March.

Rowen, H. (1987). 'US and Canada seeking veto power on IDB loans', *Washington Post*, 18 March: F1.

Sanford, J.E. (1982). *US Foreign Policy and Multilateral Development Banks.* Boulder, CO: Westview Press.

Tussie, D. (1995). *The Multilateral Development Banks.* Volume 4: *The Inter-American Development Bank.* Boulder, CO: Lynne Rienner.

US Congress (1973). *Foreign Assistance and Related Agencies Appropriations for 1974. Hearings before a Subcommittee of the Committee on Appropriations, House of Representatives.* House of Representatives, Committee on Appropriations, Subcommittee on Foreign Operations and Related Agencies, 93rd Congress, 1st Session. Washington, DC: US Govt. Printing Office.

US Congress (1980). *Foreign Assistance and Related Programs Appropriations for 1981: Hearings before a Subcommittee of the Committee on Appropriations, House of Representatives.* House of Representatives, Committee on Appropriations, Subcommittee on Foreign Operations and Related Agencies, 96th Congress, 2nd Session. Washington, DC: US Govt. Printing Office.

US Congress (1986). *Foreign Assistance and Related Programs Appropriations for 1987: Hearings before a Subcommittee of the Committee on Appropriations, House of Representatives.* House of Representatives, 99th Congress, 2nd Session. Washington, DC: US Govt. Printing Office.

US Congress (1987). *Foreign Assistance and Related Programs Appropriations for 1988: Hearings before a Subcommittee of the Committee on Appropriations, House of Representatives.* House of Representatives, 100th Congress, 1st Session. Washington, DC: US Govt. Publishing Office.

White, J.A. (1972). *Regional Development Banks: The Asian, African, and Inter-American Development Banks.* New York: Praeger Publishers.

Williamson, J. (1990). 'What Washington means by policy reform'. In J. Williamson (ed.), *Latin American Adjustment: How Much Has Happened?*. Washington, DC: Peterson Institute for International Economics, pp. 5–20.

12

The European Investment Bank and the Asian Infrastructure Investment Bank

Incumbents and Challengers in the Field of Regional Development Banking

Helen Kavvadia

1. Introduction

The 'reorientation' of the world, paraphrasing and borrowing Andre Gunder Frank's title (Frank 1998), and the Asian return to centre stage of global power in a period of a new multi-polar world order, casts doubts on the prevailing global economic governance system. Its reverberation across the multilateral development banks (MDB) and regional development banks (RDB) has renewed interest in them (Xu et al. 2015; Güven 2017; Brunsden and Khan 2018; Shields 2019). Reflecting on the past seventy-five years since the Bretton Woods conference, it becomes evident that major geo-political challenges have triggered the creation of new MDB and RDB, while economic crises and global challenges triggered only re-adjustments of the objectives and functioning of existing ones. A number of significant economic and financial crises—including the abolishment of the gold standard, the oil crises, the introduction of the euro, and climate change—failed to result in the creation of new banks, provoking rather a review of their objectives and slight re-adjustments of their modus operandi. RDB can be seen as instruments for international coordinated action to tackle both major geo-political and economic challenges. This chapter examines two RDB: the European Investment Bank (EIB) as one of the oldest from the first generation which is in the process of re-adjusting its activities in response to major challenges; and the Asian Infrastructural Investment Bank (AIIB), which is one of the newest, from the third generation of RDB, and still in the process of formulating its role to tackle these challenges.

The EIB, the primary financing arm of the European Union (EU) since its foundation in 1957, has developed to become the world's largest development bank, increasingly solicited within the EU as an anticyclical mechanism (Marzinotto 2011; Griffith-Jones et al. 2012; Federico 2019; Griffith-Jones and Naqvi 2019) for

Helen Kavvadia, *The European Investment Bank and the Asian Infrastructure Investment Bank: Incumbents and Challengers in the Field of Regional Development Banking* In: *Regional Development Banks in the World Economy.* Edited by: Judith Clifton, Daniel Díaz-Fuentes, and David Howarth, Oxford University Press (2021). © Oxford University Press.
DOI: 10.1093/oso/9780198861089.003.0012

promoting recovery and growth in the aftermath of the recent economic crises, as well as an economic diplomacy instrument with its operations stretching progressively across the world (EIB 2019). In contrast, the AIIB was created only five years ago, in 2015, as a South-South RDB for furthering economic and social development in Asia mainly through infrastructure financing. The AIIB has already achieved the second largest global membership behind the World Bank (WB), while expanding its remit to other geographical and sectoral areas.

Against this backdrop, both institutions have increasingly been the focal point of academic interest, with scholarly work remaining, however, limited—especially given the political and economic importance of the two RDB. Academic work on the EIB remains predominantly centred on the bank's financing activity (Coppolaro 2010; Fedele et al. 2010; Marzinotto 2011; Griffith-Jones and Tyson 2013; Clifton et al. 2014; Pistoia 2014; Anghel et al. 2016; Clifton et al. 2018; Federico 2019; Griffith-Jones and Naqvi 2019; Liebe and Howarth 2019). As a Chinese government initiative, the AIIB attracts above all the interest of international relations scholars (Xu et al. 2015; Hakans and Hynes 2016; Larionova and Shelepov 2016; Wan 2016; Xu 2017; Gao and Quayle 2018; Gutner 2018; Bustillo et al. 2018; Shelepov 2018; Chuang 2019), while a number of other studies focus on the bank's governance (Xu 2017; Bin 2018; Ransdell 2019), legal issues (Bin 2018), and decision-making (Lim and Mako 2015). Furthermore, existing works analyse different facets of the two RDB, without, however, embedding them in the banks' organizational fundamentals.

This chapter attempts to complement existing scholarly work by taking a holistic and contextual view of these two RDB. It addresses the following questions: How are the business fundamentals of the EIB and AIIB organized so as to fulfil their broader objectives? How are they 'equipped' to meet the requested increased objectives and face the current and future challenges? What role do these two institutions play in the RDB field? And what are their future prospects in this field?

In attempting to answer these questions this chapter follows a synthetic approach by initially investigating each RDB individually as an organizational entity and subsequently as an actor in the field of RDB. In order to analyse the EIB and AIIB as organizations, this chapter employs a novel mechanism developed by the author with recourse to Business Models. Business Models constitute powerful tools for describing, understanding, and analysing organizations, through the visual 'articulation' of their business fundamentals. Business Models are considered as conceptual maps of the strategic choices and operating implications of organizations.

Furthermore, the representational nature of Business Models facilitates the comparison between organizations. In this case the comparison of the EIB and the AIIB, as examples of a well-established and a very recent RDB, offers insights as to whether the AIIB shows path-dependency from Bretton Woods traditions followed by all RDB to date or whether it constitutes a RDB paradigm innovator, as claimed by the AIIB itself (AIIB 2017), and as reflected in certain academic views (Xu et al. 2015; Xu 2017).

Business Models are, however, not in the public domain. Mentions of EIB's Business Model have usually been short verbal references linking it to its triple-A credit rating (EIB 2011, 2012; Maystadt 2010; Szymczak 2010; Camdessus 2010), substituted recently by the term 'EIB's financial model' (Hoyer 2019). Statements on the AIIB's Business Model are even rarer and more amorphous (Bundesfinanzministerium 2019). The Business Models of the two RDB have therefore been determined by 'embroidering' the author's Business Model archetype by using exclusively official publicly available information, including statutes, annual reports, and policy papers. The archetype used is a 'hybrid' model based on existing academic proposals (Johnson et al. 2008) elaborated with additional elements from the work of Shafer et al. (2005). In order to fit supranational, public, non-profit seeking organizations, the Business Model archetype for RDB is comprised of four basic elements which, through their interrelationship, create and deliver value: strategic choices, value capture, value creation, and value network.

Business Models are prime examples of a Parmenidean ontological line of thought, dealing with organizations and their functions. They depict how functions are grouped according to similarities and differences and how these categories relate to each other within a hierarchy. They go, therefore, beyond a mere taxonomy, enabling the understanding of how an organization formulates its remit and subsequently puts it into practice in an interplay with its environment. They are useful tools to assess whether and how RDB are endowed to meet evolving objectives assigned in order to meet new challenges. Analysed subsequently through a Popperian approach, by viewing RDB policies and practices as trial solutions to the prevailing economic and social problems, an examination of Business Models allows the investigation of how the business fundamentals of the EIB and AIIB enable them to fulfil their remits. Given their shared geographical and sectoral objectives, and often in interaction, the two banks are not isolated individual actors, but members of the entire RDB sector. In order to analyse their role with regard to their interrelationship as part of the 'collective dynamics' in the sector, this study also draws on economic sociology and in particular the Theory of Fields (Fligstein and McAdam 2012).

The Theory of Fields constitutes a suitable conceptual framework for analysing banks and their interaction within the RDB sector, as it deals with actors, including organizations, and their actions taking place within organizational groups. In order to highlight both the structuring of the field and the role of the actors, this organized terrain of action, considered the 'basic structural building block of political and organisational life in the economy, civil society, and the state' (Fligstein 2011: 3), is named a Strategic Action Field. Strategic Action Fields include actors, who 'undertake actions that take into account what others are doing [thereby having a role] in the production and transformation of the field' (Fligstein 2015: 242). Strategic Action Fields change, in the sense of a real transformation (construction and ending), as a result of 'the unintended consequence of exogenous shocks to the field' (Fligstein 2015: 248), instigated by their environment, or other influential Strategic Action Fields, rather than being the 'result of internal processes' (Fligstein 2011: 19). Change is however, ubiquitous also within systems, albeit non-transformative. Actors through agency, 'framing and entrepreneurship' (Fligstein 2011: 7), operate in the field in a perpetual process of collective dynamics, provoking the field's oscillation across a spectrum of stability and re-adjustment. Mobilized by threats and opportunities, actors seek in the Strategic Action Field arena 'to fashion and maintain order' while 'competing for material and status-rewards' (Fligstein 2011: 5), given that 'fields imply that something is at stake and can be won or lost' (Fligstein 2015: 238). In other words, stability is sought through change, given that 'even under generally stable conditions, actors are engaged in a constant set of adjustments that introduce incremental change into constructed social worlds' (Fligstein 2011: 7). In their striving to maintain stability, actors share the 'roles of incumbents, challengers and often governance units' (Fligstein 2011: 13) exercising coercion, competition, cooperation, or some combination of them, especially during episodes of contention. Thereby 'incumbents worry daily about how to maintain their advantage, and challengers search for and seek to exploit any "cracks" they discern in the system' (Fligstein and McAdam 2012: 97).

Business Models appear a natural and logical extension of the Theory of Fields and vice versa. We can examine Business Models in the study of individual entities as constituent actors of fields and we can use the Theory of Fields to analyse inter-entity relations as well as the sector as a whole. The common ground of the Business Models approach and the Theory of Fields and their 'binding gist' is their shared view of institutions. Both understand institutions as a system of interdependent activities which enable through framing and agency the creation of value and the appropriate share of that value, which transcend institutional boundaries through interactions and outcomes influencing the environment in which they operate. In this sense, they can be both considered as conceptual maps of actors and actions.

The conception and use of this synthetic approach constitutes this chapter's main scientific contribution. Furthermore, it is the first comparative study of the EIB and AIIB, as well as the first empirical application of the Theory of Fields to the RDB sector.

This chapter is organized as follows. Section 2 presents the current EIB Business Model benchmarking it against EIB's countercyclical activity during the crisis-ridden period of the late 2000's. Section 3 showcases the AIIB's Business Model, analysing it against the backdrop of the major infrastructure, economic, and social needs in its region, while also evaluating the degree to which it fits the existing RDB paradigm. Section 4, applies the Theory of Fields to assess the role of the EIB and AIIB in the RDB sector, and offers a perspective on the field's future development. The concluding section 5 briefly summarizes the main findings on the EIB and AIIB as well as their role in the RDB arena, arguing the following. First, contrary to academic views and self-claims, the AIIB is expected to play along with the EIB the role of an incumbent rather than a challenger. Second, the field of RDB is currently demonstrating a smooth progression without contention effects, despite AIIB's ascendance. Third, the RDB sector's future major change and restructuring in the short-term will be mainly shaped by proxy actions of other players in the field, such as state and supranational actors, as well as other RDB, leading to the creation of a new European RDB, dedicated to development outside the EU.

2. EIB: multifaceted and privileged? A model that cannot be copied?

EIB's current Business Model, presented in Figure 12.1, is the product of a revision brought about amid the economic crisis in 2010, building on its previous Business Model in use since 1999. The latter was the result of the first Business Model major change since the EIB's creation in 1957. It bolstered the EIB in the run up to the euro, allowing it to maintain its relevance and lending levels. Through an inherent flexibility, this Business Model enabled the EIB to develop a multifocal activity (Clifton et al. 2014, 2018), serving an increased number of EU policy objectives by adding human capital and innovation, while balancing out results across a wider range of sectors and types of activity. Self-proclaimed thereafter as a 'policy-bank', and keeping its product mix mainly focused on lending, the EIB increased its leverage through structured finance and risk capital, provided in a small scale through its own operations—up to one billion euros for small and medium-sized enterprise (SME) under the Amsterdam Special Action Programme initiated in 1997, and the European Investment Fund (EIF), the EIB's venture capital subsidiary, as well as through an upgrading of its role through a more coherent intra-group finance. Although the main changes aimed at the quantitative target of maintaining and even increasing EIB activity, they were introduced by qualitative changes privileging softer value creating aspects of its Business Model. They allowed the EIB to gain a profile as a private sector financier through risk capital and structured finance operations, while maintaining its position as a prime source of funding for infrastructure. The latter was achieved by encouraging the private sector participation in previously public sector type of projects in the form of Public-Private Partnerships (Liebe and Howarth 2019), and by privileging its early involvement in project development playing a catalyst, as well as advisory role in financial and technical aspects. For these changes the EIB counted on the strength of its value capture and value network sides of its

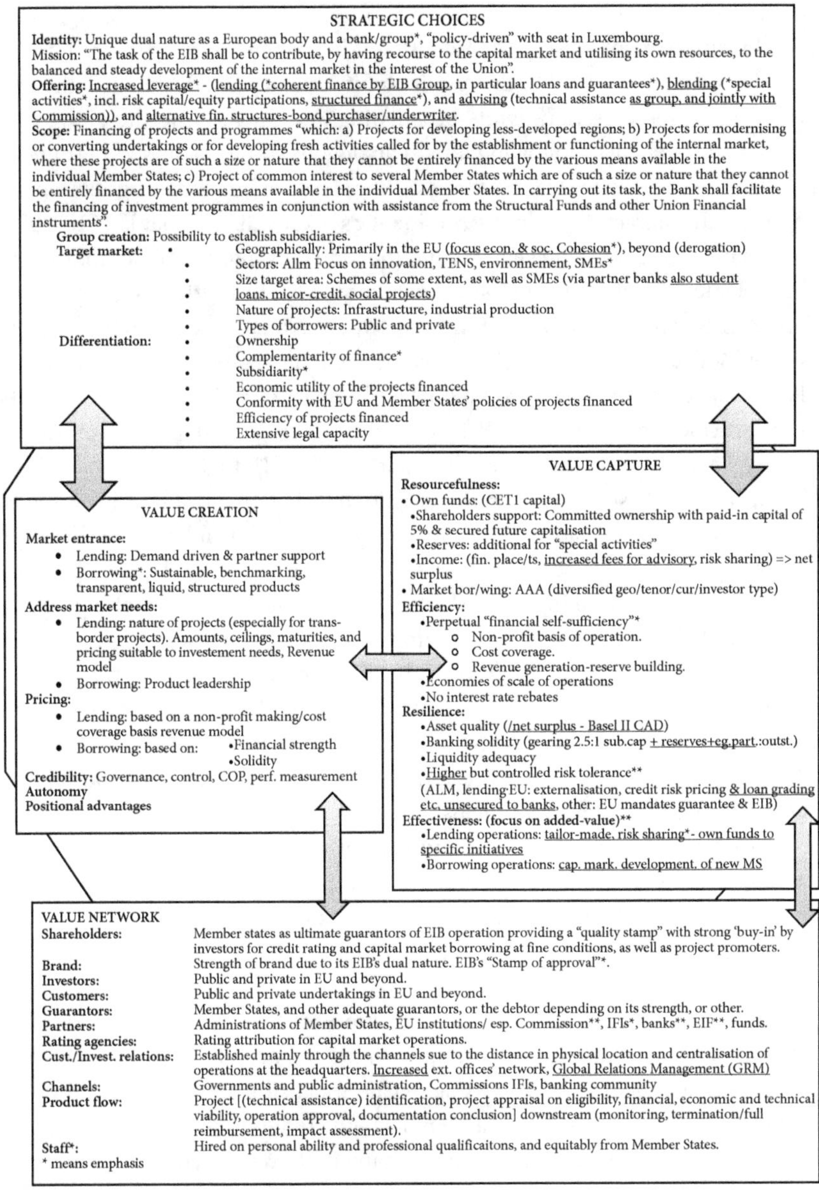

Figure 12.1 European Investment Bank 2010 Business Model

Source: Author's own elaboration drawn from EIB public documents.

Business Model, which enabled a safe increase in leverage, on the one hand, and the extension of its client base and project portfolio through synergies with the RDB and banking sectors on the other.

Despite being successful—as recognized in successive European Council meetings, by allowing the EIB to navigate safely the introduction of the euro, the bank's

1999 Business Model had to be revised again in 2010, as the EU was caught in a trap of low investment, despite abundant liquidity, when the international financial crisis broke out in 2008. In the revision of its Business Model in 2010, the EIB followed the same direction, while broadening and intensifying the above features by further changes following a path analogous to Lindblom's (1959) incrementalism, for a further strengthening of its relevance by increasing its impact, being recently characterized by its president as a 'crowding-in bank' (EIB 2019: 12). The latter has been achieved through the judicious interplay of all four interlocking elements of its Business Model, which in 2010 institutionalized the three pillars of EIB activity, partly previously tested on a smaller scale under its 1999 Business Model, as mentioned above. Its three pillars, namely lending, blending, and advising led to the increased volume and impact of EIB lending, through its higher contribution to investments, by providing leverage, better costed products, and early stage support. The three pillars allowed the EIB to develop a mix of five different lines of business and banking, enjoying thereby flexibility in terms of resources and cost allocation. These banking types are wholesale banking for SME financing, development banking for financing in non-EU countries, for-profit banking for risk-taking and risk-sharing operations, policy banking for the financing of EU priority projects, and service banking for advisory services.

Additionally, the three pillars allowed the EIB to play three distinct roles and to proceed with three significant developments. First, as a policy-taker in an increased politicisation process (Mertens and Thiemann 2019b), the EIB was enabled to prove itself once more as a useful EU policy implementation tool by pushing stronger for smart and inclusive growth, the EU's prime policy goals. It thus proved again its relevance, gaining further political support from member states, as exemplified in its 10 billion euros capital increase in 2012, and raising its profile anew. The EIB pursued these goals by prioritizing lending in the new areas set out in the strategic choices element of its Business Model, deemed conducive for achieving these goals, namely human capital, research and development, climate-change mitigation, and innovation. As these activity areas entailed greater risks, the EIB developed new appropriate financial products. Despite the EIB's increased appetite for risk, its aggregate intrinsic risk remained, however, rather low, allowing the bank to maintain its high credit rating. This can be attributed to the EIB's value capture strength, namely its resourcefulness, efficiency, resilience, and effectiveness, which are based on key EIB features of its ownership, area and mode of operation as well as expertise. These features include: the bank's extensive shareholder support in recognition of its policy implementation role, as evidenced by its successive increases in capital and the metrics of its 2016 and 2017 risk-management reports; its strained yet satisfactory capital adequacy due to its high-quality assets—with impaired loans at 0.3 per cent of its gross loans in 2017; its low-risk operating environment, as European loans were 95 per cent of its outstanding loans in 2017; its diverse loan portfolio; its extensive liquidity policy, which foresees a twelve-month buffer, further strengthened by the EIB's access to the European Central Bank (ECB)'s liquidity facilities, which are quite unique for an RDB—with the exception of the Banque Ouest-Africaine de Developpement; its prudent risk-management, enhanced by its preferred creditor status, a feature not disposed by all RDB—exemplified best in the normal reimbursement of Greek loans during capital controls after 2015; and its high-quality assets due to its rigorous due diligence, pinpointing in turn its expertise to anticipate risk, as a strong risk-management tool. The latter leads to the second distinct role of the EIB as an institutional entrepreneur (Lachmann 1986), which relies on its value network for actively creating and exploiting policy windows and opportunities, when promoting its catalyst contribution and advisory role. To do so, the bank hinges on its experienced and highly qualified staff that through the 'quality shield' provided after rigorous project appraisals, inducts commercial banks and other investors to 'crowd in', given that a good number of risk elements, even beyond the usual concern of commercial bankers, are properly assessed, including financial risks, market, economic, environmental, and technological risks. Additionally, the EIB intensified its cooperation with its extensive and well-cultivated partner network with other MDB, RDB, national development banks (NDB) and other financial institutions. This type of cooperation has been often laid out in the form of memoranda of understanding (MoU). This role is on a win-win basis and brings strategic and operational benefits to the EIB as well as to its counterparts. At a strategic level the EIB and cooperating public financial institutions affirm their relevance by actively seeking the efficient use of public funding. At the operational level, all network partners can increase their client base, reduce operating costs by sharing project appraisal tasks, decrease project risks, and consequently improve asset quality. Highlighted and intensified recently, crowding-in is a historic feature, given the EIB's statutory conception as a complementary source of finance, with its funding limited generally to 50 per cent of aggregate project costs. This funding limit allows other financiers to partake in deals, enabling the EIB's symbiosis with other financing institutions, while serving additionally as a project provider mechanism for the EIB, given that investment scheme proposals are often coming from the partner institutions, when seeking to share expertise and risks. This symbiotic relationship allowed the EIB to operate for some forty years until its first Business Model revision in 1999 without any active client solicitation mechanism. Established in 1999, such a mechanism was made to stand out more prominently in the Business Model revision of 2010, whereby customer and investor relations have been privileged through increased direct contact in the form of active promotional efforts, inter alia road-shows and national and regional conferences. Various communication efforts and deliberate endeavours have also been implemented to create a system of global relations management, as well as a worldwide office network—reaching forty-five in 2017 from seventeen in 2006. The institutionalization of the blending of the EIB loans with the EU grants increased the prominence of the EIB's agenda-setting role. The EIB cooperated and coordinated with the European Commission in terms of policy implementation primarily but policy formation also, through its lobbying efforts. The EIB worked together with the Commission under a variety of mandates in relation to funding inside and outside the EU, such as the New Community Instrument and the financing to third countries as the Union's economic diplomacy instrument respectively, for an efficient and effective coordination of the EU's investment funding. The EIB is the only RDB privileged to have a sister organization such as the Commission with which to cooperate in terms of policy and operational support. Under various mandates, the EIB has been provided with EU funding and guarantees, while the Commission has relied on the EIB for its appraisal process for channelling funds to appropriate projects. This cooperation was accentuated, officially institutionalized and extended in 2010. As a result, EIB's penetration increased by the provision of reduced funding cost, by blending EIB resources at market rates with Commission grants at zero cost for project promoters—having a similar effect to interest rate subsidies at net present value, as grants are paid upfront and not over the term of the loan. Additionally, the institutionalization of the EIB-Commission closer cooperation has been exemplified through various joint initiatives—in support of SME and micro-enterprises (JEREMIE), urban-social development (JESSICA), and technical assistance (JASPERS). These initiatives enlarged EIB's customer base—with 530 new assignments in 2018 (EIB 2019), off-balance sheet operations and income from mandates as well as from various management and advisory roles, while enriching the Commission's technical skills.

An amplified form of blending constituted the springboard for the EIB's increased activity in support of the EU's countercrisis efforts for recovery and growth through the creation of the European Fund for Strategic Investments (EFSI), created within the framework of the Juncker Investment Plan in 2015 (EIB 2016).[1] Apart from granting higher lending volumes, the EFSI also foresaw increased risk-taking and risk-sharing, focusing on particular projects in 'strategic infrastructure, education, research, development, and innovation (RDI), renewable energy and resource efficiency, as well as support for smaller enterprises, including SME and Midcaps' (EIB 2016: 1). The EIB's increased risks under the EFSI—representing some 17 per cent of its total lending in 2016 and some 3 per cent of its total outstanding loans, are partly though covered by European funds. Loans under the EFSI benefit from a guarantee from the EU,

[1] Established in 2015 by the Commission in cooperation with the EIB in order to bolster the economy through the mobilization of private financing for strategic investments, EFSI comprised a guarantee of 16 billion euros from the EU budget plus 5 billion euros from the EIB's own capital, with the aim of triggering investment to the sum of 315 billion euros. It has been extended in July 2018, and the so-called EFSI 2.0 contains an extra 10 billion euros of guarantees and pledges to reach a new target of 500 billion euros in investment by the end of 2020.

representing 25 per cent of the total amount of loans provided, while the equity and mezzanine instruments are also guaranteed by the EU. The EIB will continue to play a lead role, albeit smaller, in InvestEU, the successor to the Juncker Plan, foreseeing a further increased guarantee of 38 billion euros from the EU budget, targeted to mobilize 650 billion euros of investment to ensure that the EU remains 'social, green and competitive' (EIB 2019: 1). For serving the latter, and in association with the EU 'Green Deal' the EIB has become 'a climate bank' in 2019.

3. AIIB: path-dependent evolution or paradigm shift?

The AIIB's current Business Model, presented in Figure 12.2, is its establishing one, as the bank is the most recent addition to the existing constellation of RDB, seventy-five years after the Bretton Woods conference. It is therefore natural that its set-up reflects the currently prevailing politico-economic conditions. Does the creation of the AIIB represent a paradigm shift or should it be seen in terms of a path-dependent evolution of existing peer examples? With the objective of aligning members' policy preferences for instance, the AIIB disposes the traditional RDB three-tier political governance structure, superposed on its technocratic structure, resulting in a high and multilayered organizational pyramid of an old-style bureaucracy in terms of organizational theory. It follows also the EIB's example of a non-resident board (Larionova and Shelepov 2016). Furthermore, the AIIB conforms to the existing paradigm in other respects: it has a focus upon regional development; it invests in both public and private sectors; it presupposes the complementarity of its financing, hinting even at subsidiarity, in the sense that AIIB finance should be provided only when appropriate funding cannot be secured from other sources; projects financed have to conform with the recipient states' policies; and its full legal personality and capacity, including relevant immunities, follow the legal status of other RDB. What principally differentiates the AIIB from its peers are its objectives, which are

> to (i) foster sustainable economic development, create wealth, and improve infrastructure connectivity in Asia by investing in infrastructure and other productive sectors and (ii) promote regional cooperation and partnership in addressing development challenges by working in close collaboration with other multilateral and bilateral development institutions.
>
> (AIIB 2015, Articles of Agreement, Article 1)

There are two points of interest for understanding its nature. The first is wealth creation and development. This appears as a logical jump, since development is a prerequisite for wealth, especially for a good number of low-income countries in

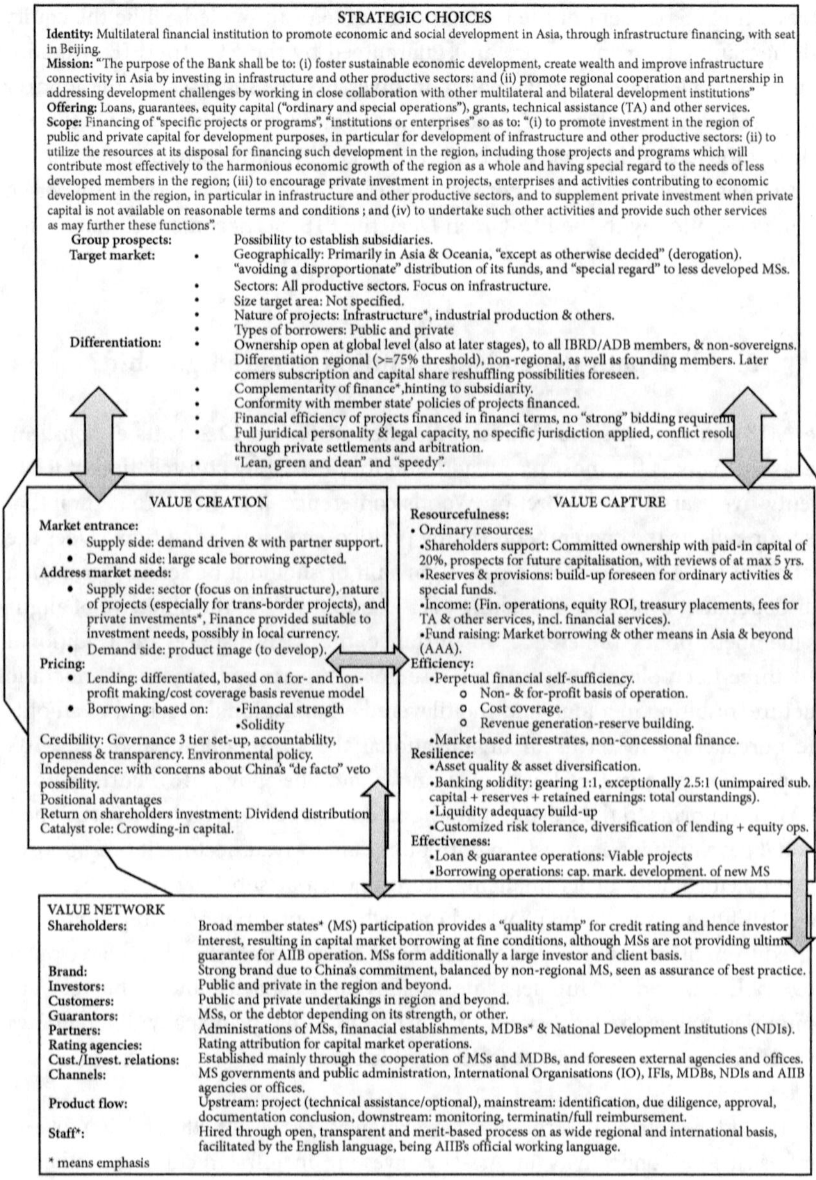

Figure 12.2 Asian Infrastructure Investment Bank's Business Model
Source: Author's own elaboration drawn from AIIB public documents.

the AIIB's region of concern, for which the AIIB makes special provisions in its Articles of Agreement, by ensuring them both shareholding and a balanced share of its funding in their favour. The AIIB places emphasis upon infrastructure—of particular interest to these countries, for development rather than wealth creation. Second—unlike other RDB—the AIIB's Articles of Agreement emphasize the importance of cooperation with other RDB and bilateral development institutions. On the first point—the special provisions for lesser developed countries—there is no obvious operational reason for including them in the AIIB's Articles of Agreement. The second, however, could be possibly explained by the AIIB's endeavours to penetrate easier the market and develop quickly its activity, by claiming to be a specialized niche infrastructure financier on the one hand (ADB 2017; Arcus Foundation 2018), and through its synergies with other RDB on the other. In this respect the AIIB has already signed five MoU, including the WB, Asian Development Bank (ADB), European Bank for Reconstruction and Development (EBRD), EIB, and the International Finance Corporation. From the total projects approved of USD 7.94 billion by April 2019, half were co-financed with other RDB. By signing framework agreements or MoU with other RDB, the AIIB exploits their know-how, especially at its start-up phase, while profiting at the same time from its participation in their project pipelines for establishing its own clients. Moreover, through its cooperation with the ADB in particular, the AIIB increases its credibility, by demonstrating synergy and complementarity between these two RDB, with overlapping geographical focus. The AIIB deviates from most existing RDB, also on several other issues, as on its pricing, which is not clearly stated as non-profit-based, even for concessional finance, and on its requirement such funds to be 'on terms and conditions consistent with the purpose and functions' of the bank (AIIB 2015, Articles of Agreement, Article 17.1:1). 'This open-ended language, coupled with repeated Chinese (Government) statements emphasizing the AIIB's profit-minded nature, may presage an aversion to concessional lending' (Ransdell 2019: 7), despite the bank's emphasis on low-income countries. Additionally, AIIB's vague bidding requirements, characterized occasionally as 'universal' (Xu 2017) align with the bank's claim that the AIIB will impose no conditionality and policy application prerogatives to recipient countries. An assessment of AIIB's bidding policy is premature, as the bank's impact on the efficiency/inefficiency of the projects financed has not yet been shaped nor reflected on its Business Model. A further difference between the AIIB and other RDB is the absence of a specific jurisdiction for the settlement of issues other than the AIIB's borrowings. Issues such as lending and staff can only be resolved through arbitration. The eventual repercussions of resolving such issues through arbitration only, cannot be estimated at present. As expected for a multilateral institution, the AIIB's basic legal documentation is comprehensive and detailed in setting out the bank's governance. Being not embedded in a supranational structure, unlike for example the EIB in the EU, the AIIB is fully independent in its decision-making and determination of its Articles of Agreement. The detected broadness of its operating principles can, therefore, be considered purposeful. The arbitration as sole settlement approach is a major differentiating factor from AIIB's peers. This broadness makes the study of the

AIIB Business Model even more compelling, as a means to understand better its operating processes.

Broadness is also evidenced in the AIIB's strategic choice element of its Business Model, which concerns principally its ownership, geographical and sectoral target market, as well as its offering. Despite a claimed Asian focus, the AIIB draws its ownership from around the globe, with all member countries of the World Bank qualifying as potential shareholders, therefore keeping membership possibilities open to a very large number of countries that can join at some point in the future. Although as of 1 January 2019, the AIIB has already reached ninety-three shareholders, future newcomers are still allowed to join in, as foreseen in its capital share reshuffling provisions. There is only one limitation described in its Articles of Agreement, in order to safeguard AIIB's Asian profile: a threshold of 75 per cent of regional membership. In line with its claimed Asian regional character, the AIIB targets Asia, and Oceania—by derogation. However, the bank's funding is available to other areas as evidenced by its recent and planned operations in Africa (starting with Egypt), Latin America, and beyond. Although infrastructure financing is found in the AIIB's name, mission, and scope, its sectoral target market is much broader, encompassing all productive sectors. Matching this, the AIIB's offering is also very broad, ranging from non-concessional 'straight vanilla' loans and guarantees for specific projects or programs to equity participation and concessional finance—including grants and advisory services, such as technical assistance, as well as other services.

The AIIB's offering is so broad that it encompasses five different forms of banking: wholesale banking—large and often repeat lending and guarantee operations; a policy bank in support of international development and poverty elimination; for-profit banking at premium over market rates—equity participation and other forms of risk-sharing with regards to projects; service banking on a fee basis for technical assistance related advisory; and investment banking—for assisting the creation of capital for third parties through underwriting new debts and securities. No other RDB had such a broad offering at its establishment, and none currently has the investment banking element. Of course, the AIIB's name refers to the bank as an 'investment bank'—not as a development bank, although its rationale is to promote economic and social development. The only other major RDB with the term 'investment bank' in its name is the EIB, which however lacks investment banking in its statutes, strategic choices, and activities. The EIB is also the only other RDB that has a similar number of forms of banking under one roof. This was, however, not the case at its establishment, but rather came gradually into effect after two subsequent Business Model revisions—as shown above. As in the case of the EIB, these different banking type activities can remain within the AIIB—assuring its future development through well-diversified market, income, resource, cost, and risk possibilities, thereby giving to the bank a head start compared to its peers. Alternatively, the AIIB, which is still rather a middle-range RDB, as characterized by one of its principal shareholders (Bundesfinanzministerium 2019) could develop into a group of the World Bank-type through spin-offs and the creation of subsidiaries or other institutional forms of a more independent nature, as already foreseen in its Articles of Agreement. This is also similar to the EIB, which evolved and thrived by offering flexibility with the statutory possibility to create specialized subsidiaries since 2007. As shown above, AIIB's Business Model reveals that the bank follows the existing RDB paradigm in several respects.

Currently, the AIIB promotes a growth-enabling environment through projects following three thematic priorities: sustainable infrastructure, cross-border connectivity, and private capital mobilization. In order to build momentum in the early stages of its operations, the AIIB demonstrated institutional entrepreneurship by trying to exploit its positional advantages in Asia with the aim of addressing obvious infrastructure needs. At the same time, the AIIB's leadership sought to develop the bank's value network for enlarged customer relations by increasing its shareholder basis and cooperation with other RDB. For raising investor awareness, the AIIB approached the rating agencies for receiving as early as possible a rating. Prior to any bond issuance, it received in a short time a triple-A, which enabled the bank to test the cost efficiency of its product. In order to ensure a dynamic start of operations, the AIIB assured its expertise by hiring international staff through universal recruitment (Xu 2017), without being limited to nationals of its shareholding countries. Furthermore, during its first years, the AIIB, raised its value creation element by increasing its credibility through public statements of being 'lean, green, and clean' (AIIB 2017; Qingyang 2018). Succumbing to political and public pressures from some of its shareholders and other countries such as the United States (US), as well as non-governmental organizations (NGOs), the AIIB also adopted best-practice procedures on accountability, transparency, and environmental policies to achieve good governance, social and environmental ratings, while stressing its independence from the Chinese government amid vocal concerns expressed by a range of public and private sector actors (Bin 2018). The AIIB's self-proclaimed catalyst role in crowding-in capital resources for the realization of projects has, however, not yet been established. The bank's borrowing side has also not yet been developed, as there were no bond issues floated to date in the capital markets. As the AIIB's value creation element has been developed cautiously, its value capture, counterbalancing Business Model element, has been exceptionally solid in all four of its constituents—namely resourcefulness, efficiency, resilience, and effectiveness. Its USD 100 billion capitalization held by ninety-three countries—with a rather low, compared to its peers, median credit rating of AA- or better—at 28 per cent is compensated by a large 20 per cent paid-in capital portion and expected to reach its full amount of USD 18.9 billion by the end of 2019. Its paid-in capital is very high compared to other RDB, most of which though have built up reserves to counter their lower paid-in capital ratios. The AIIB's banking solidity, with a gearing ratio of 1:1, is also very strong compared to its peers—explained by its paid-in capital share. Its strong value capture element has been decisive for the top Aaa credit rating assigned to the bank on 29 June 2017 by Moody's (Bundesfinanzministerium 2017), followed by a triple-A from Standard and Poor's and Fitch. Nevertheless, as the AIIB enters its development phase, expected by its management to start in 2020, its activity will extend beyond sovereign 'straight vanilla' lending to more risk-carrying products, as contained in its offering. In this case, the AIIB's value capture will have to carry the main burden. The AIIB has though room to manoeuvre through some variable components of the value capture element of its Business Model. With this perspective in mind, the AIIB has already established a comprehensive and proactive risk-management approach, while further flexibility will be provided as reserves and income start to pick up following operations' increase. The AIIB's lending and equity portfolios are estimated to reach USD 45 billion and USD 2.5 billion, respectively, by 2027, while the infrastructure needs, as mentioned above, are forecasted at USD 26 trillion by 2030 (ADB 2017; Bhattacharyay 2010). If, on average and based on a rule of thumb, an AIIB loan represents a third of the aggregate investment cost of the total investment cost, the total investment that can be achieved through its 'straight vanilla' lending action will represent only about 0.01 per cent of the region's total investment needs. To increase its impact, the AIIB would have to use higher leverage products for infrastructure finance. In this case, however—even with a multiplier of fifteen, as used in the EIB's Juncker plan—the AIIB's funding would only contribute 0.08 per cent of total Asian infrastructure investment needs. It is questionable to what extent the AIIB would wish to stretch its leverage to improve its impact and to what extent its value capture element will be able to support such a stretch. Its efficiency, resilience, and effectiveness components can only carry a certain amount of risk. Despite AIIB's sophisticated risk-management policies, which apply 'comprehensive' risk limits covering all areas of operation, including investment, treasury, liquidity risk, and market risk, the bank appears exposed to risk, especially if operations will be highly leveraged. This is mainly due to the predominance of infrastructure financing. This type of project portfolio 'is very sensitive to concentration, credit quality, and tenor' (Chuang 2019: 2). Its resourcefulness will depend on investors' trust, attitudes, capacity, and wish to invest (Wong 2018) in AIIB paper floated in capital markets. Investors will therefore have the ultimate say as to whether the AIIB will divert from a RDB path-dependent evolution and, if so, to what extent the bank will be able to implement a new paradigm based on its broad charter. With predicted funding needs 'in excess of 10 billion dollars per year in the mid-2020s' (Chuang 2019: 2), investors will distinguish the feasible from the wishful and determine whether the AIIB will make the paradigm shift to multilateral banking.

4. The Copernican Principle put to proof

If applied in the RDB Strategic Action Field, the Copernican Principle—epitomized in that a good first approximation of how long something will last is how long it has already lasted, looking to the past RDB stability, one should be able to foresee its future development. As explained, both the EIB and the AIIB operate in the RDB Strategic Action Field. They have important differences but also similarities, including geographically overlapping areas of responsibilities in Asia, Africa, and Latin America. Nevertheless, apart from the analysis of the Business Models of the two organizations, it is worth investigating their interaction within the RDB sector, and the sector's consequent eventual developments. To connect to the third leg of this chapter, and in order to apply the Theory of Fields to the EIB and the AIIB, this section undertakes the following. First, it delineates the boundaries and defines the actors in the Strategic Action Field. Second, this section examines whether the RDB can be seen as forming a Strategic Action Field, identifying basic characteristics of this field under review and providing a brief historical account of its development. This is followed by an analysis of the role of the EIB and the AIIB in the Strategic Action Field. For the purposes of this study, the actors of the Strategic Action Field under review, are understood to comprise all established RDB, and not only those involved in development banking, regardless of their 'generation'. Existing RDB can be viewed as forming a Strategic Action Field, given that they form a network with close ties and interrelationships. Their ties have been strengthened in the end of the 1980s and picked up in the mid-1990s, a period of very competitive capital markets' conditions, due to their integration, liquidity, and enlargement as well as the introduction of the euro. The RDB cooperation can additionally be attributed to the increased complexity of projects and financial mechanisms, requiring specialized know-how for new products and forms of funding, such as inter alia Public-Private Partnerships and Project Bonds. As a consequence, risk had to be shared, as it exacerbated considerably with bigger projects' size, and more complicated finance structures.

The RDB Strategic Action Field has shown a remarkable stability over the last seventy-five years since the Bretton Woods conference, despite two transformations resulting from new actors in 1991 and in 2014-15. Of the three possible bases of stability in Strategic Action Fields—coercion, competition, and cooperation—the latter prevailed in shaping the physiognomy of the RDB field, in spite of a creeping competition (Kavvadia 2018). The cooperation is demonstrated in the proliferation of a series of MoU, signed between and among several of the RDB over the last thirty years and the increasing number of projects co-financed by two or more RDB. Competition is revealed predominantly in the convergence of the operating methods and product mix offered by the various RDB, as witnessed for example in the evolution of the EIB's Business Model since its establishment, and the similarities it has with the incipient Business Model of the AIIB. The diversification of EIB's and other RDB product range in the 2000s with new offerings and the diffusion of financing practices, such as Public-Private Partnerships, Trade Finance Facilities, and risk-sharing products, is mainly driven by the need to cater to a diversifying clientele and to cover a broader range of market areas, so as not to leave any niche areas open to competitors for entering their market segment or gaining profile. The judicious blending of competition and cooperation, in a constant interplay of fine adjustments, predicated on the basis of mutual observation and framing from the part of the actors, has ensured the stability of the Strategic Action Field. The question is whether the RDB field will remain stable in the future.

According to the Theory of Fields, what happens in a Strategic Action Field is a function of the strategic action and the roles that its skilled actors decide to play. As mentioned above, the Theory of Fields distinguishes the actors according to their role in a Strategic Action Field into three categories; incumbents, challengers, and governance units. Given that in the RDB field there is no governance unit overseeing, legitimizing the logic and coordinating external contacts of the field, this chapter concentrates on the two other role types that RDB play in this Strategic Action Field. On the one hand, incumbents are the influential organizations with political and/or material means to have their interests and views reflected, respected, and reproduced overtime in the field, so as to maintain their dominant position. The challengers on the other, are the niche caretaking organizations, who accept the incumbents' predominance and views, often being unable to contest or choosing deliberately not to do so, till they see the appropriate chance.

Building on the insights gained through the analysis of EIB and AIIB above, the EIB appears to be an incumbent in the RDB field for the following reasons. It is a well-established first-generation RDB with over sixty years operating experience. It has developed to the world's largest lender and borrower. As the EU's bank, its shareholders, which are also its major borrowers, are exclusively industrialized countries supporting the bank politically and financially. As a policy bank the EIB has carved out a leading role in promoting EU's normative power at the financial implementation level. The EIB enjoys unique privileges among RDB such as the ECB refinancing facility. Belonging to the EU institutional family, the EIB enjoys joint operations with the Commission, as a sister organization, for joint operations, as seen above. Its flexible, solid, and composite Business Model allows it to adapt easily to prevailing conditions. This allowed EIB's transformation to the world's first international 'Climate Bank' in 2019, affirming its positioning and EU support. As the only RDB operating in industrialized as well as developing countries, the EIB disposes and projects state-of-the-art know-how in financial and technical aspects of project development enjoying therefore positional advantages.

The latter feature seen from a different angle, however, also limits the EIB's incumbent role, attributing to it a secondary challenger hue, as far as development banking is concerned. Development finance is an EIB niche operations area, given that it represents on average only 10 per cent of its annual lending. Moreover, its approach and modus operandi is trans-regional, and hence not necessarily adapted to development prerequisites. In development banking the EIB has therefore a far smaller and disproportionate to its incumbent primary RDB role institutional impact. Its influence in development is rather the result of being the EU economic diplomacy instrument, and stems mainly from EU's clout, rather than the EIB itself.

The AIIB has self-proclaimed its challenger role mainly by advocating its absence of conditionality in its financing operations, which has equally been heralded by a number of scholars. It is a third-generation institution with only three years of operational experience at the time of writing. It is vocal in articulating its difference from the Bretton Woods and Washington Consensus practices, avoiding the imposition of conditionalities in its financing operations. The bank claims to offer niche financing by concentrating on infrastructure lending mainly in Asia. This challenger role is, however, not confirmed by the analysis of its Business Model. Instead, the AIIB plays an incumbent role in the RDB field (Stanzel 2017), mainly due to its exceptionally wide shareholding structure foreshadowing strong political influence. Nevertheless, some of its shareholders such as India are strongly opinionated to alter the world economic governance (Raisina Dialogue 2019) and support AIIB's privileged position in the field, hoping for a future challenger activism. Additionally, its remit foresees a broad geographical and sectoral scope, by no means limited solely to infrastructure and Asia. Its Business Model, although recent, does not deviate substantially from EIB's 2010 Business Model (Bundesministerium 2019). It has had the bulk of its portfolio co-financed with other incumbent RDB, accepting de facto and in a pragmatic way their views, modus operandi and conditions. It has moreover signed several MoU for cooperation with other RDB, accepting also de jure the partners' prevailing views and practices. The major limiting factor for the bank's challenging role stems from capital markets, and the willingness of investors to support a new, if not unorthodox modus operandi in development banking.

The analysis of the two actors in the RDB field in this chapter, shows that the EIB is, as expected, an incumbent. More surprisingly, the AIIB can also be seen as an incumbent despite a prima facie reading as a challenger. Incumbents tend to support the status quo, whereas challengers take 'what the system gives them... awaiting new opportunities to challenge the structure and logic of the system' (Fliegstein 2011: 13). It is worth investigating therefore likely future developments in the RDB field, especially because the above analysis shows that both actors have combined, primary and secondary roles. Both institutions are primarily incumbents, while both also play a secondary role as challengers.

This makes the investigation of what will be the evolution of the RDB field even more important, especially as the challenger role implies the occurrence of an appropriate opportunity, as a *terminus ante quem* for coming forward to contest the status quo. Will one of the two actors play the challenger role and if so when? Having achieved very quickly an incumbent role, the AIIB seems for the moment content in this role. This is exemplified by the growing number of MoU signed with other RDB, and the implied adoption of internal policies reflecting the best-practice status quo, in environmental, transparency, and accountability issues. On the contrary the EIB is, as announced, on the brink of having its niche development banking activity spun off to a new institution dedicated solely to development financing (Brunsden and Khan 2018; Antonowicz-Cyglicka 2019; *Global Capital* 2019). Nevertheless, this cannot be seen as the result and expression of the EIB's challenger role, as the new institution will not necessarily be a wholly owned EIB subsidiary, but rather of combined ownership foreseen to include the EU, EBRD, and possibly other shareholders (*Global Capital* 2019; Antonowicz-Cyglicka 2019; Mertens and Thiemann 2019a). Moreover, the creation of the new RDB institution is a political act, beyond the EIB's reach, to be decided by EU member states, which are the EIB's 'political masters', as well as shareholders. The latter provide directly or through the EU budget, the bulk of resources, which the EIB manages under mandate for development financing under an umbrella guarantee. Unlike other RDB, the EIB is the 'manager' and not the 'owner' of development funds, and in this respect—officially at least—a policy-taker. It is though a backstage policy entrepreneur in steering lending decisions. In doing so, the bank has three considerations: reputational issues; key financial features concerning its liabilities and assets, such as the share of the capital and outstandings to be spun off; and operational necessities. This entrepreneurial role can be revealed and analysed only once the set-up of the new institution is officially announced, and its shareholding, governance, structure, mission, and operating objectives become known. In any case, however, it is clear that the creation of the new RDB will be triggered by factors external to the current RDB field. The decision to create the new bank falls ultimately in the discretion of the EU member states, the EIB's shareholders. The decision is influenced also by the Commission, which has recently criticized openly EIB's role in development (Antonowicz-Cyglicka 2019), as well as other states such as the US and Japan, especially if the EBRD will also participate in the new institution (Brunsden and Khan 2018). The latter two countries have deliberately chosen not to become shareholders of the AIIB. By gaining additional leverage in the region through their participation in the new RDB, these two countries, which are already prominent participants of the ADB, will increase their ability to contain indirectly the AIIB. In a nutshell, the change of the RDB field will be triggered externally, through the creation of a new RDB, which will constitute the episode of contention, for the RDB field's transformation. The new RDB and the geo-political background of its creation, might provide to the AIIB the critical thrust to roll out its challenger views. This is in full concordance with the Theory of Fields, which claims that Strategic Action Fields' transformations are not triggered by internal processes, but are rather the result of episodes of contention originating from other implicated fields. Subsequently, through a ripple effect the original external shock is diffused within the Strategic Action Field. The invasion of a new actor, such as a new RDB, is considered as an episode of salient importance, causing significant turbulence within the field, given a 'shared sense of uncertainty regarding the structure and dominant order of the field' (Fligstein 2011: 21).

With the creation of the new RDB, the EIB will lose its secondary role as challenger remaining a 'mainstream' incumbent, while the AIIB will maintain its challenger role. Will this episode of contention trigger a change in the AIIB role in the RDB field? Episodes of contention are necessary conditions for change in Strategic Action Fields, but not sufficient. Actors have to show additionally the deliberate will to roll out the 'social skills' to gain influence, build new coalitions in the field and impose their views, as well as to demonstrate a normative stance. Further to the analysis of the role of the AIIB in the RDB field above, and considering the eminent timing for the creation of the new RDB, reported for 2020 (*Global Capital* 2019), the AIIB is unlikely to show a challenger activism at this point in time. The signature of an MoU for the establishment of a Multilateral Cooperation Centre for Development Finance in March 2019 (AIIB 2019) at the initiative of the Chinese Ministry of Finance, with the International Fund for Agricultural Development, World Bank, EIB, AIIB, EBRD, and three other RDB demonstrates a Chinese initiative to play an increased role in the RDB field. Given China's lead role in establishing and maintaining a majority shareholding in the AIIB, this new coordinating initiative can in the future serve as a platform for the AIIB to develop its challenger role, by mobilizing actors and building cooperative coalitions for refashioning the structure and logic of the RDB field in order to articulate an alternative vision of development banking. Supported in this activism by purveyors of more proclaimed oppositional logic such as India (Raisina Dialogue 2019), but restricted by other shareholders of a different position, such as the EU countries, the outcome of the prospect remains ambivalent. It is therefore worth researching further 'to what extent China's growing ascent in the realm of global governance is reshaping world's regional and global architectures vis-à-vis financial multilateral cooperation' (Menegazzi 2017: 1). The latter comprises the dilemma of continued stability versus a potential destabilization of the RDB field.

5. Conclusions

Seventy-five years after the Bretton Woods conference, and following two economically tumultuous decades, there is renewed interest in RDB, with the rethinking of established ones and the creation of new banks. With the aim of examining developments in the RDB sector, this chapter analyses the EIB and the AIIB, as well as the RDB field as a whole. For this purpose, a synthetic approach is devised and applied, drawing upon organizational studies and economic sociology to enable a combined micro-macro focus. This approach combines the strength of the Business Model for the study of the two banks and the Theory of Fields as a framework to understand their interaction and the 'collective dynamics' in the RDB field. This approach allows the analysis of the banks and their ways of advancing their interests through framing and agency, consequently shaping their field and wider environment, despite complexities and path-dependencies.

The Business Models of the two actors have been fashioned using an archetype developed by the author to suit RDB. By analysing and categorizing official documentation in the public domain, this archetype Business Model was subsequently refined by adding a further level of detail to its four primary interlocking elements, including strategic choices, value capture, value creation, and value network.

The EIB's Business Model proved sufficiently flexible to meet the demand to operate as a major anticyclical instrument (Griffith-Jones et al. 2012) of the EU in its efforts to respond to the financial crisis and widespread recession of the late 2000s. Moreover, associated with EU's Green Deal in 2019, the EIB was asked to be at the forefront of the climate political agenda. The EIB's position in the EU institutional order appears to be an important source of its strength and differentiates it from its peers. This is due to both its remit to support EU policy objectives and its role supporting primarily projects in its shareholders territory. As a result, the EIB has enjoyed constant and strong shareholder support, as demonstrated in multiple capital increases. The EIB's position as an EU body, and in particular its operational links with the Commission and the ECB, is central to explaining its relative importance among RDB.

The AIIB's incipient Business Model aligns with, but is substantially broader than its peers, coming though closest to the EIB's. Its lending in its first few years has only been a tiny fraction of the vast infrastructure needs of AIIB's target region. If the AIIB is to fulfil its mission, it will have to increase significantly not only this lending, but also its leverage and risk-taking. Without the backing of a supranational entity, and based solely on its own financial strength, the AIIB will be substantially constrained by the capital markets' risk tolerance. The investors' attitudes will determine how much, and in what form, the AIIB will be providing support for investment schemes, by controlling AIIB's funding possibilities through capital markets. Investors will thus distinguish the feasible from the wishful, and will have determining influence over whether the AIIB's operations will involve the self-proclaimed paradigm shift.

Unlike their RDB peers, both the EIB and the AIIB have Business Models that allow them a mix of five different banking types under one roof. They enjoy thereby flexibility in terms of resources, cost, as well as risk allocation, while leaving the possibility of spin-offs and the creation of a World Bank-type of group open to both of them. These banking types, four of which are common to the EIB and the AIIB, comprise: policy banking for the financing of EU priority projects and international development and poverty elimination for EIB and AIIB respectively; wholesale banking for large and repeat operations, in particular lending to smaller businesses in the case of the EIB; for-profit banking at premium over market rates for equity participation and other forms of project risk-sharing; and service banking for technical assistance and advisory services. The AIIB's activities also include investment banking for assisting the creation of capital for third parties through underwriting new debts and securities. Whereas the EIB engages in development banking in non-EU countries. This fifth EIB banking activity will soon be altered to coincide with the departure of Great Britain from the EU and the EIB (UK Government 2018), leading to a major transformation of the its Business Model (Brunsden and Khan 2018; Mertens and Thiemann 2019a). As a result, development banking is expected to spin-off to a new RDB (*Global Capital* 2019). The Commission's criticism of EIB's role in development (Antonowicz-Cyglicka 2019) in late 2019, hints further in this direction.

Using the Theory of Fields for examining the role of the EIB and the AIIB in the field of RDB, this chapter shows that both banks currently play the same type of role, namely acting as incumbents in their primary role and as challengers in their secondary role. The similarity in their roles is revealing for the EIB and surprising for the AIIB. This similarity undermines claims by a number of academics and the AIIB itself regarding the bank's challenger status and paradigm-shifting activism. The similarity is explainable partly through the AIIB's path-dependent Business Model, given that, 'it is better for reputation to fail conventionally than to succeed unconventionally' (Keynes 1936: 158).

The RDB field has been characterized since the Bretton Woods conference by a stable equilibrium, returning always to its path-dependent evolution even after major geo-political changes and financial crises. This smooth progression without contention effects, is also demonstrated currently despite the ascendance of the AIIB as a new major player. Through insights gained by implementing the Theory of Fields framework of analysis, this chapter argues that the creation of the new EIB spin-off development institution instigated by EIB's owner states, and other non-EU countries—and notably the US and Japan—could, depending on its set-up, eventually develop as a way to restrict the AIIB's advance. This future expansion of the new RDB could subsequently trigger the AIIB's challenger role.

References

Anghel, M.G., Anghelache, C., Dumitrescu, D., and Ursache, A. (2016). 'The European initiative for small and medium enterprises', *Revista Româna de Statistica-Supliment*, 6: 49–58.

Antonowicz-Cyglicka, O. (2019). 'European Commission criticises the EIB's role as a development bank'. CEE Bankwatch Network, 11 October. Available online at: https://bankwatch.org/blog/european-commission-criticises-the-eib-s-role-as-a-development-bank

ADB (Asian Development Bank) (2017). 'Meeting Asia's infrastructure needs'. Available online at: https://www.adb.org/sites/default/files/publication/227496/special-report-infrastructure.pdf

AIIB (Asian Infrastructure Investment Bank) (2015). 'Articles of Agreement'. Available online at: https://www.aiib.org/en/about-aiib/basic-documents/articles-of-agreement/index.html

AIIB (Asian Infrastructural Investment Bank) (2017). 'President Jin Liqun, Opening Address, Meeting of the AIIB Board of Governors', 16 June. Available online at: https://www.aiib.org/en/news-events/news/2017/20170616_002.html

AIIB (Asian Infrastructural Investment Bank) (2019). 'Establishment of a Multilateral Cooperation Center for Development Finance', 29 March. Available online at: https://www.aiib.org/en/about-aiib/who-we-are/partnership/_download/collaboration-on-matters.pdf

Arcus Foundation (2018). 'Towards more sustainable infrastructure: challenges and opportunities in ape range states of Africa and Asia'. In Arcus Foundation (ed.), Infrastructure Development and Ape Conservation. Cambridge: Cambridge University Press, pp. 10–39.

Bhattacharyay, B. (2010). 'Estimating demand for infrastructure in energy, transport, telecommunications, water and sanitation in Asia and the Pacific: 2010–2020'. ADBI Working Paper No. 248, September.

Bin, G. (2018). *The Law and Governance of the Asian Infrastructure Investment Bank*. Alphen aan den Rijn: Kluwer Law International B.V.

Bustillo, R., and Andoni, M. (2018). 'China, the EU and multilateralism: the Asian Infrastructure Investment Bank', *Revista Brasileira de Política Internacional*, 61(1): e008. doi: http://dx.doi.org/10.1590/0034–732920180010.

Brunsden, J. and Khan, M. (2018). 'France and Germany call for shake-up of EU development banks', *Financial Times*, 1 October.

Bundesfinanzministerium (2017). 'Zweite Jahrestagung der Asiatischen Infrastruktur-Investitionsbank.Analysen und Berichte', Monatsbericht Juli. Available online at: https://www.bundesfinanzministerium.de/Monatsberichte/2017/07/monatsbericht-07–2017.html

Bundesfinanzministerium (2019). 'Drei Jahre Asiatische Infrastruktur - Investitionsbank: Wichtige Wegmarken erreicht'. Analysen und Berichte, Monatsbericht März. Available online at: https://www.bundesfinanzministerium.de/Monatsberichte/2019/03/Inhalte/Kapitel-3-Analysen/3-4-Drei-Jahre-AIIB.html

Camdessus, M. (2010). 'Report and recommendations of the Steering Committee of "wise persons"'. European Investment Bank's external mandate 2007–13, Mid-Term Review.

Chuang, A. (2019). 'AIIB risk chief on steering China's World Bank rival'. Risk.net 3 January. Available online at: https://www.risk.net/risk-management/6264946/aiib-risk-chief-on-steering-chinas-world-bank-rival

Clifton, J., Díaz-Fuentes, D., and Revuelta, J. (2014). 'Financing utilities: how the role of the European Investment Bank shifted from regional development to making markets', *Utilities Policy*, 29: 63–71.

Clifton, J., Díaz-Fuentes, D., and Gómez, A.L. (2018). 'The European Investment Bank: Development, Integration, Investment?', *Journal of Common Market Studies*, 56(4): 733–50.

Coppolaro, L. (2010). 'Setting up the financing institution of the European Economic Community: the creation of the European Investment Bank (1955–1957)', *Journal of European Integration History*, 15(2): 87–104.

EIB (European Investment Bank) (2011). *Annual Report 2010 Activity Volume*. Available online at: https://www.eib.org/en/publications/annual-report-2010-activity

EIB (European Investment Bank) (2012) *Activity Report 2011*. Available online at: https://www.eib.org/en/publications/activity-report-2011

EIB (European Investment Bank) (2016). *Annual Report on EIB Group Operations inside the EU for 2015: EFSI*. Available online at: https://www.eif.org/news_centre/publications/report_eibgroup_EFSI_3_pillar_assessment_methodology.htm

EIB (European Investment Bank) (2019). 'Agreement on InvestEU confirms EIB Group as central partner for new EU investment programme in 2021-2027'. 21 March. Available online at: https://www.eib.org/en/infocentre/press/releases/all/2019/2019-081-agreement-on-investeu-confirms-eib-group-as-central-partner-for-new-eu-investment-programme-in-2021-2027.htm

Fedele, A., Mantovani, A., and Liucci, F. (2010). 'Credit availability in the crisis: which role for the European Investment Bank Group?'. Working Paper DSE No. 699, University of Bologna.

Federico, L. (2019). 'What has the "Juncker Plan" achieved?'. Presented at the 'Analysing the European Investment Bank' Conference, University of Luxembourg, 10–11 July.

Fligstein, N. (2011). 'A Theory of Fields'. Unpublished manuscript. Oxford University Press. Available online at: https://sociology.berkeley.edu/sites/default/files/faculty/fligstein/Chapter%201%20Theory%20of%20Fields.pdf

Fligstein, N. (2015). 'The Theory of Fields and its application to corporate governance'. Paper presented at 'The Nature of the Modern Corporation' Conference, Seattle University, 26–7 May. Available online at: https://pdfs.semanticscholar.org/ef7b/0a54497fe550524cb786fb5b435b063bbf88.pdf

Fligstein, N. and McAdam, D. (2012). *A Theory of Fields*. New York: Oxford University Press.

Frank, A.G. (1998). *ReORlENT: Global Economy in the Asian Age*. California: University of California Press.

Gao, X., and Quayle, P. (2018). *Asian Infrastructure Investment Bank*. Oxford: Oxford University Press / Max Planck Foundation. Available online at: http://www.iber-global.com/files/2018/OPIL_Asian_Infrastructure_Investment_Bank_AIIB.pdf

Global Capital (2019). 'EIB planning to launch new development bank', *Global Capital*, 8 May. Available online at: https://www.globalcapital.com/article/b1fb0wtd8tpd6l/eib-planning-to-launch-new-development-bank

Griffith-Jones, S. and Naqvi, N. (2019). 'The Juncker Plan (EFSI), InvestEU, and the EIB; assessing achievements and limitations'. Presented at the 'Analysing the EIB' Conference, University of Luxembourg, 10–11 July.

Griffith-Jones, S. and Tyson, J. (2013). 'The EIB and SMEs: key lessons for Latin America and the Caribbean'. *CEPAL—Serie Financiamiento del desarrollo* 236.

Griffith-Jones, S., Kollatz-Ahnen, M., Andersen, L., and Hansen, S. (2012). 'Shifting Europe from Austerity to Growth: a Proposed Investment Programme for 2012-2015'. Policy brief in Foundation for Progressive Studies.

Gutner, T. (2018). 'AIIB: Is the Chinese-led development bank a role model?' Council on Foreign Relations, 25 June. Available online at: https://www.cfr.org/blog/aiib-chinese-led-development-bank-role-model

Güven, A.B. (2017). 'The World Bank and emerging powers: beyond the multipolarity–multilateralism conundrum', *New Political Economy*, 22(5): 496–520.

Hakans, E. and Hynes, P. (2016). 'China's Challenge to the World Economic Order'. ISS Risk Special Report, December. Available online at: http://issrisk.com/wp-content/uploads/2017/01/DOC-20170112-WA000.pdf

Hoyer, W. (2019). 'Speech at the EIB Annual Press Conference', 29 January. Available online at: https://www.eib.org/attachments/general/events/annual-press-conference-2019-werner-hoyer-speech.pdf

Johnson, M., Clayton, W., Christensen, M., and Kagermann, H. (2008). 'Reinventing your business model', *Harvard Business Review*, December.

Kavvadia, H. (2018). *The Special Status of Economic Activities of the Hellenic State and of Greek Citizens in Balkan Countries: Theoretical Approaches and Empirical Perspectives*. Athens: Centre of Vocational Training, Studies, Research and Development.

Keynes, J.M. (1936). *The General Theory of Employment, Interest, and Money*. London: Macmillan. Available online at: http://www.hetwebsite.net/het/texts/keynes/gt/gtcont.htm (accessed 16 October 2018).

Lachmann, L.M. (1986). *The Market as an Economic Process*. Oxford: Basil Blackwell.

Larionova, M. and Shelepov, A.V. (2016). 'Potential role of the NDB and AIIB in the global financial system', December. Available online at: https://www.researchgate.net/publication/314749421_Potential_role_of_the_NDB_and_AIIB_in_the_global_financial_system

Liebe, M. and Howarth, D. (2019). 'The European Investment Bank as Policy Entrepreneur and the Promotion of Public-Private Partnerships', *New Political Economy*. doi: 10.1080/13563467.2019.1586862

Lim, W. and Mako, W.P. (2015). 'AIIB business strategy decisions: what it can do differently to make a difference'. Working Paper 15–04. KDI School of Public Policy and Management, August.

Lindblom, C.E. (1959). 'The science of muddling through', *Public Administration Review*, 19(2): 79–88.

Marzinotto, B. (2011). 'A European fund for economic revival in crisis countries', *Bruegel Policy Contribution No. 2011/01*. Brussels: Bruegel.

Maystadt, P. (2010). 'How can the EIB support the accession into the European Union?'. Zagreb School of Economics and Management, Zagreb, 15 October.

Menegazzi, S. (2017). 'Global economic governance between China and the EU: the case of the AIIB', *Asia Europe Journal*, 15(2): 1–14.

Mertens, D. and Thiemann, M. (2019a). 'The EIB is becoming increasingly politicised'. LSE blog, 20 February. Available online at: https://blogs.lse.ac.uk/brexit/2019/02/20/the-european-investment-bank-is-becoming-increasingly-politicised/

Mertens, D., and Thiemann, M. (2019b). 'The politicisation of the EIB: managing hybridity in European economic governance'. Presented at the 'Analysing the EIB' Conference, University of Luxembourg, 10–11 July.

Pistoia, E. (2014). 'Non-financial concerns in the lending policy of the EIB in context'. In Giorgio Sacerdoti with Pia Acconci, Mara Valenti, and Anna De Luca (eds.), *General Interests of Host States in International Investment Law*. Cambridge: Cambridge University Press, pp. 325–54.

Qingyang, G. (2018). 'Lean, clean and green: a new model of multilateral development bank for building infrastructure in Asia and beyond—an interview with AIIB President Jin Liqun', *Journal of Infrastructure, Policy and Development*, 2(1): 1–10.

Raisina Dialogue (2019). 'Conference report 2019'. 4th Raisina Dialogue, New Delhi, 8–10 January. Available online at: https://www.orfonline.org/wp-content/uploads/2019/07/Book_Raisina2019_Report5_compressed.pdf

Ransdell, J. (2019). 'Institutional innovation by the Asian Infrastructure Investment Bank', *Asian Journal of International Law*, 9(1): 125–52.

Shafer, S.M., Smith, H.J., and Linder, J.C. (2005). 'The power of business models', *Business Horizons*, 48: 199–207.

Shelepov, A.V. (2018). 'The AIIB, multilateral and national development banks: potential for cooperation', December. Available online at: https://www.researchgate.net/publication/324663295_The_AIIB_multilateral_and_national_development_banks_potential_for_cooperation.

Shields, S. (2019). 'Never waste a crisis: The European Bank for Reconstruction and Development, the European Investment Bank, and the European Bank Coordination Initiative as a case of fail forwards neoliberalism'. Presented at the 'Analysing the EIB' Conference, University of Luxembourg, 10–11 July.

Stanzel, A. (2017). 'A German view of the Asian Infrastructure Investment Bank'. European Council on Foreign Relations, 21 April. Available online at: https://www.ecfr.eu/article/commentary_a_german_view_of_the_aiib_7275

Szymczak, P. (2010). 'European Investment Bank: Supporting European objectives in Eastern Europe'. Presented at the 'Southern Caucasus and Russia. Eastern Partnership: Strategy for 2011 and Beyond—PISM International' Conference, Lublin.

UK Government (2018). 'Agreement on the withdrawal of the United Kingdom of Great Britain and Northern Ireland from the European Union and the European Atomic Energy Community'. Endorsed by leaders at a special meeting of the European Council, 25 November.

Wan, M. (2016). *The Asian Infrastructure Investment Bank: The Construction of Power and the Struggle for the East Asian International Order*. New York: Palgrave Macmillan.

Wong, M.C.S. (2018). 'Credit Rating and OBOR Bond Market Development: issues, challenges and possible solutions'. Policy Paper No. 1, Research Centre for Sustainable Hong Kong, January. Available online at: https://www.cityu.edu.hk/cshk/files/PolicyPapers/CSHK%20Policy%20Paper%201.pdf

Xu, J. (2017). 'Asian Infrastructure Investment Bank (AIIB): Its birth, mandates, and infrastructure financing'. In J. Clifton, D. Díaz-Fuentes, and D. Howarth (eds.), *Regional Developments in the World Economy*. Oxford: Oxford University Press.

Xu, J., Humphrey, C., Griffith-Jones, S., Carey, R., and Prizzon, A. (2015). 'Multilateral development banks in the 21st century: three perspectives on China and the Asian Infrastructure Investment Bank'. Overseas Development Institute. Working Paper, December. Available online at: https://www.researchgate.net/publication/305108939_Multilateral_development_banks_in_the_21st_century_Three_perspectives_on_China_and_the_Asian_Infrastructure_Investment_Bank

13

Regional Development Banks and the Promotion of Public-Private Partnerships

The EIB as a Case Study

David Howarth and Moritz Liebe

1. Introduction

Regional development banks (RDB) around the world have actively promoted the use of Public-Private Partnerships (PPPs)—to a greater or lesser extent. Finding precise, comparable data on RDB financing of PPP projects—in total and relative terms—and RDB promotion of PPP usage requires further research. RDB use different definitions of PPP and different systems to measure the share of operational activities devoted to PPPs (World Bank Group 2015).[1] However, for most RDB, the financing of PPP projects has increased significantly over the past two decades and all but the newest RDB—the Asian Infrastructure Investment Bank (AIIB)—list a number of PPP projects on their websites and in publications. The reliance of a number of RDB on leveraged finance—of which PPP is but one example—is a major reason for the increased RDB promotion and use of PPP-financed projects. From a tiny number of countries with PPP projects in the 1990s, by 2015 PPPs were used in 134 countries, contributing 15 to 20 per cent of total global infrastructure investment (World Bank Group 2015).

The role of RDB in the promotion of PPPs matters for several reasons. They represent an introduction of private sector finance into infrastructural projects that are seen by many as within the remit of the public sector and thus opposed on ideological grounds. Moreover, the operation of PPPs is highly controversial and has attracted considerable criticism in both political and academic circles due to, inter alia, hidden costs (Dudkin and Välilä 2005; Saussier et al. 2009), excessive profits to PPP companies (National Audit Office 2007), the problems of monitoring and enforcing contracts (Lonsdale 2005; Lonsdale and Watson 2007), the impact of PPPs on the nature of public service delivery (Hebson et al. 2002), and democratic accountability in PPP projects (Hodge 2006; Asenova and

[1] For one recent attempt to classify different forms PPPs, see Vecchi et al. 2017.

David Howarth and Moritz Liebe, *Regional Development Banks and the Promotion of Public-Private Partnerships: The EIB as a Case Study* In: *Regional Development Banks in the World Economy.* Edited by: Judith Clifton, Daniel Díaz-Fuentes, and David Howarth, Oxford University Press (2021).
DOI: 10.1093/oso/9780198861089.003.0013

Beck 2010; Reeves 2010). For its 2018 report on PPPs in the EU, the European Court of Auditors selected the subtitle 'Widespread shortcomings and limited benefits' (ECA 2018). Thus, if the RDB are active in their promotion of PPPs, this matters politically.

The European Investment Bank (EIB) was at the vanguard of PPP promotion and financing and has been the world's biggest institutional funder of PPP projects for over two decades (World Bank Group 2015)—which explains its selection as a case study in this chapter. Nonetheless, both the European Bank for Reconstruction and Development (EBRD) and the Asian Development Bank (ADB) financed major PPP projects and promoted PPP use in their loan countries from the 1990s (Appendix: interviews 21, 22). Of all the RDB, the EBRD's mandate came closest to sanctioning formally the financing and promotion of PPPs. The EBRD was established to promote the development of market economies in the former communist countries of Central and Eastern Europe. The bank financed its first PPP project in 1993 only two years after it started operations. However, the EBRD's support for PPP projects has been principally in terms of finance: the bank offered little in the way of transaction advice or technical assistance until the mid-2010s, although the bank has provided legal advisory services to some national governments seeking to reform their national legislative framework (Appendix: interviews 21, 22; World Bank Group 2015). The EBRD lacked a specific PPP plan until the mid-2010s. In 2015—in recognition of the bank's lack of strategic capacity on PPPs—the bank established its Infrastructure Project Preparation Facility (IPPF) to, in part, prepare for the operationalization of PPPs and other strategic infrastructure for those countries—currently eight—where PPPs have been financed.[2]

The ADB financed its first public sector project with a PPP component in 1998. Over the next decade ADB loans to the public sector had PPP elements worth approximately USD 20 billion or 20 per cent of total loans to the public sector (World Bank Group 2015: 142). During the 1998 to 2008 period, the PPP elements of ADB loans to the private sector were worth approximately USD 3 billion or 20 per cent of total loans to the private sector (World Bank Group 2015: 142). Given perceived weaknesses in the economic impact of these funded PPP projects, the ADB launched an independent evaluation in 2009 and in 2012 adopted a PPP operational plan (ADB 2012). Following the plan, the ADB moved to integrate PPP activities across the bank's operations and improve advisory technical and legal support for PPP projects. In 2014, the ADB established its own PPP unit—modelled on the EIB's European PPP Expertise Centre (EPEC) from the previous decade—to provide expertise to public and private sector actors at the national level.[3]

[2] https://www.ebrd.com/infrastructure/infrastructure-IPPF.com
[3] https://www.adb.org/site/public-private-partnerships/main

While PPP take up and promotion has been more recent for other RDB and less significant in total and relative terms, several have engaged in active PPP promotion over the past decade. In 2012, the African Development Bank (AfDB) established PPPs as an integral part of the bank's Private Sector Development Strategy (2013–17) (AfDB 2012; Appendix: interviews 19, 23, 27). During the 2010s, the AfDB significantly increased its financing of PPPs—although this only represented a small percentage of total AfDB lending—and provided technical advice for PPP projects. In addition to the provision of funding to PPP projects, the Andean development bank, Corporación Andina de Fomento (CAF), has organized courses on the management of PPPs and information on PPP best practice. The Central American Bank for Economic Integration (CABEI) has promoted PPP usage through funding, courses, and information provision, with the financial assistance and expertise from the World Bank Institute (WBI), the World Bank Group's Public-Private Infrastructure Advisory Facility (PPIAF) and Public-Private-Partnership Legal Resource Centre (PPPLRC).[4] The Inter-American Development Bank (IADB) lacked a formal classification of PPPs—at least to the late 2010s—but estimates place de facto IADB financing of PPP projects at up to 20 per cent of total new IADB lending by the early 2010s (World Bank Group 2015: 147). The most recently created RDB, the AIIB, is actively considering the use of PPPs (Appendix: interview 20). The efforts by MDB and RDB to promote and establish best practice in PPPs are also demonstrated by the joint effort from the EBRD, ADB, AfDB, IADB, the Islamic Development Bank, and the World Bank Group to establish in 2015 the PPP Knowledge Lab. The Lab is an online information repository on PPPs, which was heralded by an EBRD official as 'close to a revolution in information as we could ask for'.[5] The effect of the close cooperation between RDBs is a gradual global convergence on PPP policies (Hodge and Greve 2019).

Given the possibility of other financial mechanisms to enable leveraged finance, what explains this rapid and ubiquitous spread of PPP promotion and use? On the 'demand' side, many national governments around the world are 'not spoiled for choice' on sources of lending/funding—especially given very poor credit ratings—and are thus more receptive to the option of PPP financing than a number of wealthier national governments with less constrained public finances (Appendix: interviews 21, 22, 23, 27). Even in Europe, the take up of PPPs has been particularly pronounced by a number of national governments with severe budgetary and funding difficulties—notably Portugal and Spain. On both the 'supply' and 'demand' side, there are a good number of private sector companies that actively promote PPP usage and offer expertise. One of several is Africa PPP,

[4] https://ppiaf.org, https://ppp.worldbank.org/public-private-partnership/overview/world-bank-group
[5] https://www.worldbank.org/en/news/feature/2016/01/25/ppp-knowledge-lab

which regularly organizes conferences and training sessions on PPP projects in various African locations.[6]

Two additional factors have contributed to this spread, both with a link back to United Kingdom (UK) -based or -origin expertise—one of the major themes of this chapter. The first is the provision of PPP expertise linked to UK government funding. The UK government and a number private sector companies enjoyed first mover advantage on PPPs given their relatively early usage in the country from the late 1980s and then engaged in active promotion of PPPs from the late 1990s under the New Labour government. A special vehicle of PPP promotion was Partnerships UK (PUK; dissolved in 2011), a PPP in its own right in which the UK Treasury held a minority stake. PUK provided not only assistance to interested parties in the UK but actively engaged in public sector capacity-building around the world.[7] Furthermore, the major lobby group promoting the interests of the UK financial sector, TheCityUK—previously known as International Financial Services London—has promoted UK companies with PPP expertise internationally. The UK government (Department for International Development (DFID)) has provided funding for RDB and NDB which directly or indirectly encourages PPP promotion and usage, with the attached provision of UK expertise from both the public and private sectors. UK government funding for the World Bank's PPIAF has provided PPP-related assistance to a number of regional and NDB, including CABEI (Appendix: interviews 25, 26) and the South African Development Bank (Appendix: interviews 23, 24, 26). The UK Treasury and private sector companies—notably from professional services firms such as KPMG—have provided expertise and training for both development bank staff and officials in loan-recipient countries to set up and to manage PPP projects (Appendix: interviews 19, 23, 27).

The second factor contributing to the spread of PPPs is the provision of expertise and the co-financing of projects between multilateral development banks (MDB), RDB, and/or with national development banks (NDB). MDB, RDB, and NDB with a more established track record using and greater expertise on PPPs encourage their use and offer expertise (Appendix: interviews 23, 24, 27). The World Bank Group has expanded its support to PPPs through a wide range of instruments and services offered to RDB, NDB, other national officials, and private sector firms. World Bank Group support to PPPs increased significantly during the 2000s from USD 0.9 billion in 2002 to 2.9 billion in 2012, and from 4 to 7 per cent of total group funding (World Bank Group 2015: XV). Such co-financing involving PPPs has also taken place between the EIB and a number of RDB—including the AfDB (Appendix: interviews 19, 23)—and NDB. The IADB partnered with the more experienced ADB in the organization of PPP-focused

[6] https://africappp.com

[7] https://www.partnershipsuk.org.uk/BusinessSectors/international-sector.asp

training and capacity-building (World Bank Group 2015: 143, 148), while the ADB co-financed PPP projects with the EBRD.

In terms of a principal-agent analysis, most of these RDB can be seen to have acted as agents engaged in slippage given that most—if not all—of their shareholding national governments and loan-recipient countries had limited or no prior experience with and knowledge of PPP financing. This activism can also be seen in both MDB and NDB promotion of PPPs and reinforces wider claims in the literature—on NDB activism, see Mazzucato and Penna (2016) and Moslener et al. (2018). More generally, Gavin and Rodrik (1995) argue that international financial institutions (IFIs) bolster their long-acquired skills in technical and information expertise in order to remain relevant—a claim that this chapter explores with regard to PPPs in particular. The promotion of PPPs should also be seen in terms of RDB operating as agents to move beyond the correction of market failure towards the creation and/or shaping of markets through a particular financing mechanism and with specific market actors (Mazzucato and Penna 2016: 305).

The EIB case study

This chapter focuses on the role of the EIB in the EU's promotion of PPPs. In the late 1980s, PPPs (re-)emerged as a new form of infrastructure procurement in the European context, starting with the Channel (Euro-)Tunnel project. However, procurement through PPPs did not increase significantly in EU member states until a decade later due to promotion efforts by the UK New Labour government. Spain, Ireland, and Portugal were relatively early PPP adopters (Blanc-Brude et al. 2007). From the mid-2000s, France, Germany, Italy, and a number of other member states introduced legal frameworks and institutional arrangements allowing private finance in infrastructure, resulting in the rapid rise of investment through PPPs in these countries (Button 2006). PPPs introduce private capital and participation into areas—for example, school and hospital construction and maintenance—which were predominately in the public realm (Evans and Bowman 2005; English 2005). PPPs became popular with public authorities for a number of reasons, including perceived 'value for money' (Martimont and Pouyet 2008) and the possibility of removing costs from the public ledgers (Koen and van den Noord 2005; Budina et al. 2007, Heald 2003).

Accounts on the scope of PPPs projects in the EU differ but figures from the EIB suggest that by 2010—the peak year by value for new PPP projects in the EU—more than 1,400 PPP projects had been signed corresponding to an estimated capital value of almost 260 billion euros (EIB 2010). Both the number and value of new PPP projects declined from, respectively, peaks in 2006 and 2010. In 2017 and 2018, respectively, the value and number of new transactions were at their lowest since the late 1990s (EIB 2018). The EIB as the EU's main lending body has provided senior debt to PPP-like projects since the late 1980s and is regarded as one of the biggest single lenders to such schemes in Europe (Thomson et al. 2005; Carty and Nemoz 2010; Appendix: interview 8).

In addition to the controversies surrounding the operation of PPPs noted above, this topic matters because the apparent activism of the EIB on PPPs appears to exceed its mandate. Officially, the EIB is a 'policy-driven' bank that contributes funding to a number of EU programmes that are designed by other EU institutions—the Council, Commission, and European Parliament—and the member states.[8] The EIB has no formal role in the design of the policies that direct its lending. EIB officials regularly present their employer as a 'policy-taking' body and not a 'policy-making' body (Appendix: interviews 14, 17). The EIB has described its position towards PPPs as 'one of neutrality between…procurement mechanisms' (Thomson et al. 2005: 15), a position embraced by a number of RDB. At the same time, a number of EIB officials—including former president, Sir Brian Unwin—are on public record for stating that the promotion of PPPs was a priority for the Bank.[9]

This chapter explains why there are good reasons to doubt both the EIB's more general claim about its non-existent policy-making role and its more specific claim about neutrality on PPPs. Preliminary research also demonstrates that number of other MDB, RDB, and NDB actively promote PPPs. We present empirical evidence to show that with regard to the promotion of PPPs, the EIB's role went beyond that of 'policy-taker' and neutral technical advisor to the involved parties—notably the European Commission and recipient governments. The main research question driving this chapter is: how should the EIB's role in PPP promotion best be understood? This chapter demonstrates that with regard to the promotion of PPPs, the supranational activism of the EIB can be explained in terms of the bank's operation as a policy entrepreneur (Kingdon 1995; and in the EU context Cram 1997). We further argue that the entrepreneurial role of the EIB with regard to PPPs relied massively on the presence of, principally, British 'norm entrepreneurs' (Finnemore and Sikkink 1998) who actively promoted the PPP concept and the specific norms that supported it

[8] See, for example, Maystadt (2005): 'The Bank has defined itself as a public policy bank, and seeks to interpret this to the maximum as congruence with EU policy as developed principally by the Commission'.

[9] Sir Brian Unwin, chairman and president of the EIB from 1993 to 1999 noted: 'Setting up Partnerships UK is a positive move which fills a gap in the market. It will increase the flow of soundly structured PFI/PPP deals and complement the growing capacity of the private sector to provide finance for these schemes. The EIB, one of whose priorities is to promote the development of PFI/PPP projects in Europe, is very glad to support this important and innovative initiative by the British Government'. See: http://www.eib.org/en/infocentre/press/releases/all/1999/1999-068-support-for-pfi-partnership.htm

The officials of a number of other EU bodies and national governments working on PPPs have also confirmed the promotion of PPPs as a priority for the EIB (Appendix: interviews 15, 16).

within the EIB.[10] By combining an analysis of the role of the EIB in promoting PPPs with one focused upon the important role of individuals in promoting specific norms with the EIB, this chapter offers a more accurate understanding of EIB activism in the realm of PPP-promotion.

This chapter is organized as follows. Section 2 provides a brief summary of the institutional design and powers of the EIB and the relevant literature that examines EIB and development bank policy activism. Section 3 examines the role of the EIB in the promotion of PPPs through the lens of policy entrepreneurship; whereas section 4 engages with the crucial role played by a small number of EIB officials and persons working for the EIB operating as norm entrepreneurs in the promotion of PPPs. The methodologies employed to undertake the analysis of this chapter include semi-structured elite interviews with twenty-seven RDB, EIB, and European Commission officials and other public and private sector stakeholders who have worked on PPPs. We were unable to interview the norm entrepreneurs themselves. The findings from these interviews have been triangulated with written material from press reports, private sector company documents, official Commission and EIB documents, and articles written by the norm entrepreneurs identified in this chapter and other EIB officials. (See also the Appendix at the end of the chapter.)

2. The EIB as a potential policy-making body

The EIB was established to facilitate balanced growth in the Community notably by lending to less-developed regions and to facilitate and ensure the functioning of the internal market (Treaty on the Functioning of the EU (TFEU) 2008, Article 309; Föcking 2000; Bussière et al. 2008; see Clifton et al. Chapter 5, this volume). Most financing is only permissible under the condition 'that projects are of such a size or nature that they cannot be entirely financed by the various means available in the individual member states' (TFEU 2008, Article 309). The EIB has three statuary bodies which are involved in its decision-making. The board of governors, which is made up of the EU's member state finance ministers, who agree on the general directives of the Bank. They also appoint the members of the board of directors, which formally holds decision-making power for the Bank's operational business. The management committee is responsible for preparing the board of directors' decisions, and for the pre-selection, monitoring, and implementation of

[10] We use the term 'policy entrepreneur' to refer to the efforts of the EIB as an institution to promote PPPs. We use the term 'norm entrepreneur' to refer to the efforts of a small number of EIB officials to promote the use of PPPs within the EIB and in their dealings with the Commission and EU member states. These efforts can be either formal or informal. In some contexts, the difference is moot, especially when the norm entrepreneurs represent the EIB in discussions on PPP with the Commission and member states. However, the efforts of individual officials and the institution can be distinguished in most cases.

projects, which grants the committee de facto a strong informal decision-making power (Robinson 2009: 653). The EIB has an operational independence which was intended to create political and market confidence in its ability to base lending decisions on economic considerations rather than political considerations. However, although the EIB has de jure and de facto autonomy in its financial operations, it lacks both a formal policy-making role and Treaty safeguards from the influence of other EU bodies—which differentiates the Bank from a number of other EU supranational institutions, including the Commission and the European Central Bank (Roslychy and Spanjaard 2002).

From the late 1980s, the EIB faced increasing difficulty in fulfilling its mandates and, thus, in justifying its existence (Bussière et al. 2008). While EIB total loan levels remained high in the 1990s, top EIB officials feared that business opportunities inside the Community were diminishing. Two factors contributed to this concern. First, with the extensive privatization programmes in EU member states, the EIB lost its 'traditional' clientele. Second, as European financial market integration advanced and private finance became more easily available and less expensive, the EIB faced the problem that many projects could obtain finance from elsewhere. Projects that needed support were, on the other hand, more likely to be risky and/or not economically sound and could therefore not qualify for EIB support (Lankowski 1996). In this context, PPPs were a mechanism to promote and diversify EIB lending activities.

Our chapter reinforces the claims of Clifton et al. (2014, 2017, Chapter 5, this volume) who argue that EIB entrepreneurship—a term they do not employ but imply—has been achieved through its lending, through which the EIB shifted from regional development to market-making activities notably in the utilities (infrastructure) sectors—without any direct instruction from the European Commission or EU member states. These authors argue that this shift was informed by national privatization programmes and excess private capital that fuelled questions about the relevance of the EIB and other IFIs. Our chapter takes a different approach and attempts to show the EIB's capacity for entrepreneurship in promoting innovative funding techniques. More generally, our chapter contributes to the growing body of literature that places emphasis upon the role of the EIB in both the fulfilment of EU policy objectives and its own interests (Mertens and Thiemann 2019), even though we do not place emphasis on the EIB's interests per se.

3. The European Investment Bank as PPP policy entrepreneur

The EIB's unofficial promotion of PPPs has resulted in the extension of the bank's policy influence. Applying a principal-agent analysis, the EIB operated as semi-autonomous agent and arguably engaged in 'slippage' by promoting and using a financing mechanism that was used by very few of its EU member state government principals in the 1990s and early 2000s. A number of EIB government shareholders were both opposed to using PPPs at the national level and reluctant to encourage EIB activism on PPPs (Hager 1996; Appendix: interviews 4, 7). Furthermore, the EIB can be seen as having had a decisive role in relation to its other principal—the European Commission—which, with the member states, set the EIB's policy direction. Commission preferences on PPPs were fluid and independent knowledge very limited (see Liebe and Howarth 2020 for further details). Some EU Commissioners promoted PPP usage and the Commission adopted a number of measures to encourage their usage notably to finance Trans-European Networks (TEN) infrastructural projects. However, the Commission relied heavily on EIB expertise and initiatives. On several occasions the PPP industry perceived the European Commission as having a myopic view on PPPs and their potential, and even saw its actions as potentially harmful (Appendix: interview 6, 9, 12). Thus, EIB preferences on PPPs must be seen as having largely developed within the bank: they were not imposed by other EU institutions or by member state governments through the EIB's board of governors.

To shed further light on EIB activism on PPPs, our chapter combines the well-worn approaches of policy entrepreneurship (Kingdon 1995) and norm entrepreneurship—central to the 'life cycle of norms' approach (Finnemore and Sikkink 1998). Our chapter argues that the policy-shaping role of the EIB which officially lacks a policy-making role cannot be understood without analysing the contribution of norm entrepreneurs—individual officials working in the EIB—who both defined and promoted the underlying norms that resulted in the de facto promotion of PPPs by the institutional entrepreneur. Much of the focus of the policy entrepreneurship literature—notably upon 'negotiation skills', the ability to build alliances/coalitions and the possession of 'first mover advantage' (Kaunert 2010: 42)—appears less relevant to the EIB's cautious and officially denied role in policy-making. This chapter nonetheless uses Kingdon's (1995) understanding of policy entrepreneurship and shares his focus upon the role of entrepreneurs in shaping why some policy solutions gain support over equally sound alternatives. Although Kingdon's concept was developed with respect to individuals and in a US context, the features which enable persons to act as policy entrepreneurs can also be applied to institutions like the EIB—excluding the entirely human features such as charisma. (On EU institutions as policy entrepreneurs see, in particular, Cram 1997.)

That an opportunity for change is realized in a 'policy window' depends often on the action of a policy entrepreneur who/which will attempt in the right political context to persuade others that a problem is apparent for which the entrepreneur has a solution at hand. The entrepreneur's role, however, starts well in advance. In expectation of future rewards—Kingdon (1995) mentions 'satisfaction' or material rewards, thus encompassing both ideational and rationalist motives—the entrepreneur will develop and advance a policy solution and is willing to invest his, her, or its own resources for this undertaking. The actor will persistently try to inform and persuade different actors inside and outside of the policy stream of the appeal of the idea. Even though the entrepreneur may not be directly successful, the ground will incrementally be 'softened up'. This allows the entrepreneur to push the solution without much opposition through the 'policy window' when an opportunity arises. Other specific features of successful policy entrepreneurship highlighted by Kingdon (1995) and other scholars also apply to the role of the EIB: notably specialist knowledge and experience which provide authority; an ability to theorize and frame ideas; and good connections. Notably, the policy entrepreneur possesses specialist knowledge about the policy area and can present a good track record of implementing it which gives credibility to its cause. This chapter argues that EIB 'satisfaction' with regard to the promotion of PPPs can best be understood in terms of the promotion of specific norms underlying PPPs by a small number of EIB officials—norm entrepreneurs. The most important underlying norm promoted by these officials focused specifically on the value added of private sector financial techniques to public sector lending activities.

On the promotion of PPPs, the overview in section 1 suggests that the Commission was the most important supranational actor and that the EIB rarely acted on its own but rather proposed measures that had to be approved by either the Commission or the Council and were jointly promoted. However, we argue that on PPPs the EIB played a distinctive role and demonstrated most of the features of a policy entrepreneur over the three decades from the late 1980s. By the 2000s, the EIB had become the single biggest lender for PPP projects in Europe. The PPP portfolio for projects signed in the period 2000–10 comprised 133 PPP projects reaching 24.4 billion euros, which corresponded to roughly 9.4 per cent of all PPP projects set up in the EU over the period (own calculations based on EIB 2010; EPEC 2019). The strong operational engagement of the EIB with PPPs was accompanied with its activity in creating a positive policy environment conducive for PPP uptake.

Creating 'policy windows'

Over the past thirty years, the EIB was regularly present when PPPs were discussed at the European level, engaging in what can be described as 'softening up the ground' (Cram 1997) with the aim of preparing and facilitating 'windows of opportunity'. The Franco-British Eurotunnel Project provided the EIB with the first opportunity to create a 'policy window' for PPPs. The Thatcher government was reluctant to spend any public money on the project either through national or European Community (EC) funds and instead sought EIB funding with a guarantee from private lenders and investors (Bussière et al. 2008, Appendix: interview 13). Years later, EIB officials in the TENs working group recommended the further examination and possible promotion of PPPs, thus creating a second 'policy window'.[11] Following the publication of the TENs working group report in 1997, the EIB engaged more directly in the promotion of PPPs as a possible solution to EU and member state financing. From 1998, the EIB began to discuss the relative usefulness and efficiency of PPPs in its monthly newsletters (EIB 1998a, 1998b). In 2002–3, following a consultation process involving the EIB and a number of member state PPP units, the Commission clarified its support for private participation in implementing its Instrument for Structural Policies for Pre-Accession (ISPA) and future funding through Cohesion and Structural Funds (European Commission 2003; de La Motte and Hall 2003).[12] In its 'Growth Initiative', the Council gave an explicit mandate to the EIB to explore how best to mobilize private financing in research and development and the TENs. The EIB responded by introducing further instruments for financing PPPs (including securitisation) and by 'developing institutional links' with the Commission, member states, and specialist financial institutions (EIB 1998b: 2, 2003b). In the aftermath of the international financial crisis, the Commission and the EIB undertook substantial action to revive lending to PPP projects by announcing plans to facilitate the creation of EU project bonds (the Europe 2020 Project Finance Bond Initiative, European Commission 2011; Appendix: interview 7).

Coalition building

What further enabled the EIB to be influential on PPPs—meeting a core characteristic of policy entrepreneurship—was the wide array of pertinent public and private sector contacts it developed. The EIB was the centre of PPP-related knowledge at the EU level. It had access, due to its operations, to a vast policy network on PPPs which reached across Commission directorates-general, down to national, regional, and local authorities, and to private sector operators (both financial and infrastructural companies). This unique position enabled the EIB to understand the needs of other actors, to define the PPP issue accordingly, and to mobilize a supportive coalition. The versatility of the concept of PPPs enhanced the EIB's ability to speak differently to different audiences. The EIB formed long-term relations in the field because the bank not only engaged in the provision of

[11] In its own reporting on the work of this group, the EIB (1998a: 3) notes that 'A particular emphasis is given by the Bank to support for public-private partnerships (PPPs) for transportation infrastructure projects, in line with the recommendations of the… Group'.

[12] 'The European Commission has a particular interest in promoting and developing PPPs within the framework of the grants that it provides' (European Commission 2003: 7).

finance but also in the regular monitoring of the performance of PPP contracts and constant information exchange (Thomson et al. 2005). The EIB helped to 'prepare the legal and regulatory framework for long-term projects and PPPs, drawing upon the initial experience in one country but with careful adaptation to the requirements of another' (EIB 2003b: Annex 2). Because the EIB was doing deals in all EU member states, it had a unique understanding of the diverse financing problems facing infrastructural projects.

During the early 2000s, with increasing uptake of PPPs in Europe, the EIB established the post of a PPP coordinator in the Project Directorate. The first coordinator was Patrick Boeuf, before he took on the task as head of the French PPP Task Force (MAPPP). His successor was Hugh Goldsmith, a British engineer with Harvard University training in infrastructure market economics. Goldsmith's role was the coordination of PPP activities across sectors, which included risk assessment and policy procedures. He became subsequently the main point of contact for the European Commission and national PPP units with respect to projects (Appendix: interview 4). In 2005 the EIB coordinated a non-public consultation among member state PPP task forces with the aim of formalizing the existing network by creating EPEC (Goldsmith 2005). The consultation on EPEC resulted in eighteen national PPP task forces launching a formal call for the creation of EPEC (European Commission 2005: 6). In 2008, EPEC was launched by the Commission, the EIB, member states, and candidate countries, as an EIB-based and co-funded[13] centre with the official mandate of capacity-building among participating member states and as a forum for information exchange. EPEC was able to provide policy and programme support for the Commission subject to the agreement of the EPEC steering committee—which consisted of both EIB and Commission officials (Bozier et al. 2013). EPEC members were to be national PPP units—that is, public authorities with policy-making capacity on PPPs at the national level. PPP-related knowledge could then be passed from EPEC to the member states through these units (EIB 2008). EPEC was thus explicitly created with the aim of helping to strengthen the capacity of its national public sector members to promote PPPs; a fact also welcomed by the national authorities (Appendix: interviews 2, 16). In addition, EPEC maintained a—now defunct—public sector forum to facilitate information exchange with industry (Appendix: interviews 6, 12). In late 2018, EPEC had thirty-nine national or regional PPP units as members. The EIB maintained its official policy of neutrality on PPPs. However, the creation of EPEC and the imposed requirement that member states create national PPP units should be seen as de facto promotion (Appendix: interview 3).

[13] Until 2013 EPEC was jointly sponsored by the Commission (DG TREN and DG REGIO) and the EIB (Bozier et al. 2013).

Traditionally the EIB maintains strong links with National Promotional Banks via the Club of Institutions of the European Union Specializing in Long-Term Credit (ISLTC) and its successor the European Association of Long Term Investors (ELTI). The cooperation between the Bank and its national counterparts extended also into the promotion and the development of PPPs. Not only acted the EIB and NPBs as joint financiers for PPPs—an example would be the UK's Channel Tunnel Rail Link where both the EIB and Kreditanstalt für Wiederaufbau (KFW) provided the senior debt for the project—but they entered more strategic cooperation with regards to PPPs. For instance, in 2008 the KfW became partner in the Joint Assistance to Support Projects in European Regions (JASPERS)—a joint EIB- and EU-funded initiative providing technical assistance to the new member states (more details on JASPERS below). Another example of the EIB coalition building on PPPs is a joint letter to the European Commission produced with the NPBs of France, Germany, Italy, Poland, Spain, and the EIB to announce their support for the Juncker Plan through activities including the creation of new PPPs for infrastructure projects (BGK et al. 2015, quoted in Mertens and Thiemann 2019: 35).

Exploiting expertise and experience

For both public and private sector actors, the EIB's guidance and additional scrutinizing role were of importance. The trust in the EIB from both the public and the private sector and its broad experience gave the Bank a role of authority and legitimacy for proposing and promoting PPPs (Appendix: interview 12). The expertise of the EIB on PPPs enabled it to generate knowledge and frame ideas. EPEC issued a number of detailed guidance papers, among them an interpretation of Eurostat's accounting rules for PPPs (EPEC 2010) and advice to member states on how to support PPP markets (EPEC 2009, 2011). As a major financier of PPP projects, the EIB had access to detailed data. This placed the EIB in the position of central advisor to the European Commission on PPPs (Appendix: interview 4) and allowed its own team of economic researchers (Economic and Financial Studies (EFS)) to analyse PPPs intensively. This expertise gave the EIB an important information advantage in analysing public investment more generally and the efficacy of PPP programmes policy in particular. The EIB came to possess greater knowledge of PPP financing techniques than both governments and many private sector actors (Appendix: interview 4). The publications of the EIB's economic research department added to the EIB's standing and authority as a leading (if not the leading) source of expertise on PPPs (cf., Riess 2005)—even prior to the establishment of EPEC.

The strategic promotion of PPPs

Despite its official neutrality on the use of PPPs (confirmed in Appendix: interviews 1, 4, 8), EIB official documentation and discourse was dominated by a positive positioning on PPPs. Official EIB communications and publications rarely discussed the (potentially) negative aspects of PPPs. For example, in a memorandum to an inquiry of the UK House of Lords (2010) into PPPs, the EIB made no reference whatsoever to their pitfalls (Great Britain 2010). From the early 1990s, the Bank was sought out by the Council and Commission for advice on how to facilitate European policy programmes. From the late 1990s, the EIB not only helped national authorities to set up PPPs but also actively helped national governments to draft regulatory frameworks to facilitate PPP take-up. In a briefing note to the ECOFIN Council, the EIB (2003, annex 2) stated:

> Firstly, the EIB has worked with the public sector and with the Commission to help prepare the legal and regulatory framework for long-term projects and PPPs, drawing upon the initial experience in one country but with careful adaptation to the requirements of another. Secondly, the EIB has sought to involve itself as early as possible in the tendering and negotiation of individual operations. As well as optimising the operation's financing structure and terms, the EIB's early involvement has served as an important signal to other market partners on the project's creditworthiness and on the basis of EIB's independent technical assessment on its feasibility and viability.[14]

The EIB as a 'rational' policy entrepreneur?

The EIB's move to embrace PPPs and instruments supporting PPPs might also be interpreted as an attempt to free itself from the dilemma created by national privatization programmes and financial market integration, which (as noted above) undermined its traditional raison d'être (Appendix: interview 8). First, PPPs open a new 'clientele' for the Bank because private companies could for the first time approach the EIB for credits through this mechanism, with the precedent of the Eurotunnel Project. Second, the use of PPPs also coincided with the transformation of the EIB into a centre of expertise. PPPs are relatively complex contractual arrangements which require a high degree of due diligence in the project planning stage. However, most national and local public authorities lacked the expertise and resources to scrutinize financial arrangements effectively—creating a de

[14] See also a contribution by an EIB vice-president to the magazine *European Files* (2013: 26–7), http://www.europeanfiles.eu/?portfolio=2013feb (*European files* is an industry-sponsored magazine and sent to EU institutions and governments. It ran issues focused on PPPs in 2008 and 2013).

facto dependence upon the EIB. Third, EIB involvement was welcomed by the private sector as it allowed a company to borrow at favourable rates, while providing a certain safeguard against political risks (Appendix: interview 4). These activities were increasingly emphasized by EIB officials as the Bank's non-financial value-added (EIB 2003a; Thomson et al. 2005; Carty and Nemoz 2010).

In a paper written in 1998 marking the fortieth anniversary of the EIB, Hurst and Perée (1998) reflect on the future of IFIs in the context of continued privatization and the increased use of PPPs. Lending to private companies alters the risk structure for IFI lending operations. In this respect, IFI investment in PPPs could help to assure investors in an underdeveloped regulatory environment:

> When regulatory regimes are immature, there may be some doubt by investors over the way in which regulations will be interpreted in the future. If an IFI is involved in a [PPP] project, this may give considerable comfort to other investors that regulatory decisions taken in the future will be fair and based upon sound criteria. (Hurst and Perée 1998: 20)

Over the years high-ranking EIB officials, on rare occasions, explicitly asserted the Bank's role in not only promoting PPPs but also creating new standards and frameworks for PPPs. Wolfgang Roth (vice-president of the EIB, 1993–2006) at an EIB event in Berlin 2003, announced:

> In the last few months the EIB has shared its pan-European experience with various ministries of the Länder and of the Federal Government in order to encourage the progress of PPPs in Germany. The critical state of the budgets of the Federal Government, the Länder and the municipalities gives good reason to apply new financing models and thereby to bridge gaps in budgets and clear backlogs in investment projects.[15]

In a 2006 briefing, the EIB made a direct connection between EIB value-added and PPPs:

> The EIB plays an important catalytic role in boosting private sector involvement in TENs as demonstrated by the increased support for public private partnerships (PPPs). In 2005, the Bank reaffirmed this focus by hosting successful PPP conferences in Luxembourg and Hungary. In 2005 . . . [i]n the transport sector, finance contracts worth €355 million supported key PPP schemes such the construction of the E18 motorway in southern Finland between Muurla and Lohja.[16]

[15] http://www.eib.org/infocentre/press/releases/all/2003/2003-037-public-private-partnerships-objectives-and-experiences-in-germany-and-europe.htm

[16] http://www.eib.org/attachments/general/events/briefing2006_tens_en.pdf

4. The PPP norm entrepreneurs

While 'rationalist' aims might have contributed to the EIB's entrepreneurial promotion of PPPs, this chapter argues that there is stronger evidence that norms directed this effort. Six officials working for the EIB played a central role developing instruments in support of EIB lending to PPPs and in promoting PPPs.[17] All but one were British—the exception was an Irishman with PPP professional experience in the UK. All had economics and/or business training. Most had both public and private sector work experience and all had considerable experience with and expertise in PPPs. For all, this experience was gained in the UK or by following developments in UK private finance initiative (PFI) markets for the EIB. All were motivated by a strong ideological commitment to the contribution of private sector methods to public sector financing and expressed—at least in their function as employee of or secondee to the EIB—a belief in the potential efficiency gains offered by these methods. Table 13.1 (in the Appendix) summarizes these officials' backgrounds and experience with PPPs and the EIB. Two long-serving EIB officials were the earliest promoters of PPP: Tom Barrett, an Irish official, and Thomas Hackett. Both played a crucial role in transferring knowledge on PPPs developed in the UK to the EIB and promoted PPPs for the efficiency gains they could provide (Hackett and Barrett 1996).

Tom Barrett was advisor for the EIB on the Channel Tunnel deal (Gourvish 2006) and was well-versed in the development of the UK PPP market. During his lengthy career at the EIB he was strongly involved in the development of the TENs. He sat as EIB expert on all relevant TEN working groups. He additionally sat on the European Industry PPP Task Force for the Galileo project. It might also have been Tom Barrett who made government leaders aware of the fact that EIB borrowing did not account against the balance sheet of governments (Holland 2010). During the first wave of UK Labour government-led PFI projects he was the EIB director for UK, Ireland, and the Nordic Countries. His work also secured him a place in the steering committee of PUK (operational from 2000 to 2011) which aimed at knowledge dissemination on PPPs and the promotion of PPPs in UK and abroad. A former British senior EIB official (Appendix: interview 13), noted on Barrett: 'in ministries people change and collected memory disappears, bankers change, different banks take over… but Tom Barrett went on year after year and had a profound knowledge of the British [PPP] scene'. From 2006 onwards, Barrett worked under Thomas Hackett (DG Lending operations in Europe) as Director for 'Action for Growth Instruments'.[18]

[17] This selection of the most important norm entrepreneurs reflects an examination of officials who were visibly involved in EIB financing decisions. Given limited usage of PPP in most other EU member states prior to the 2000s, there was less likelihood that officials originating in those member states would have PPP experience. Given that, in the 1990s and 2000s, PPP usage in the UK was the highest in the EU, programme officers working on lending to the UK—many of which were British—were also most likely to have PPP experience.

[18] http://www.eib.org/attachments/general/bei_info/bei_info122_en.pdf

He was then head of 'Structured Finance' at the EIB. According to several colleagues interviewed, Barrett was the major force behind the creation of EPEC, having pushed for a centre for PPP expertise and information exchange since the early 2000s (Appendix: interview 4; see also Great Britain 2010).

After thirteen years working in private banking, Hackett joined the EIB in 1981 to work on capital markets. From 1994 onwards he was responsible for deals in the UK, from 1999 to 2004 for Greece and Italy, and from 2004 onwards for the Baltic countries. In 1996, Hackett joined with Barrett to publish the first EIB views on PPPs and infrastructure finance in a specialist magazine (Hackett and Barrett 1996). They highlighted explicitly that the UK's PFI model was a major influence on the other PPP/PFI projects in which the EIB was involved. Hackett facilitated the knowledge transfer from the UK Treasury to the EIB because he was responsible for the UK at that time. Subsequently, he became director general of EU Lending Operations. In this position, he was an influential actor in launching the JASPERS. Whereas JASPERS was conceptualized as a demand-led service for the provision of technical assistance to member state governments on larger infrastructure projects in general, the unit was active in providing expertise for PPP projects and how to blend EU funds with PPP arrangements (JASPERS 2016). The unit's work in support of PPPs consisted on the one hand of providing advice, guidance, and project preparation, and on the other hand in launching pilot projects to facilitate learning and knowledge transfer (Smyth 2013).

During the 1990s and 2000s a number of additional officials with a background in banking were hired by the EIB (Bussière et al. 2008). These officials brought in what some current and former EIB officials have referred to as 'Anglo-Saxon financial engineering ideas' (Appendix: interviews 17, 18). One of these officials was Nick Jennett, who had developed considerable PFI-related expertise during his work in the UK for the KPMG auditing firm focused specifically on the implementation of reforms to National Health Service (NHS) Trusts. Jennett joined the EIB specifically to work on investment in UK Health PPPs and the UK education sector. He then moved on to structured finance, which was led by Barrett. In the late 2000s, Jennett took over the job from Goldsmith to lead the EIB's negotiations with the Commission and member states to establish EPEC.[19] On the work of EPEC, Jennett is unabashedly open about its role in the promotion of PPP usage—which he views as positive and a 'model' for investment:

> We have moved on from that debate about whether something should be public or private. I see no contradiction in the public sector defining a service and the standards it expects, and then making use of private sector skills to make sure those service levels are met... Some of the analytical papers that have been produced have helped to move the market forward. Quite often, they have helped officials to make the case for PPP to their political masters in a compelling and

[19] http://www.partnershipsbulletin.com/interviews/view/131

> robust way... Something that is not always fully appreciated is the important role PPPs play in ensuring there is transparency and rigour in all aspects of procurement... They bring a degree of scrutiny that is without comparison.[20]

Jennett argues that the transparency offered by PPP projects would also be important in forcing some EU member states to open their infrastructure to international investors.

Another important pro-PPP, British official working in the EIB is Andy Carty. Carty was seconded to the EIB in 2008, specifically to help build up EPEC as Special Advisor. He had been chief operating officer at the PFI-promoting PUK (1998-2008) and had previously been the chief executive of the Strategic Investment Board Northern Ireland at the UK Treasury. Carty left the EIB in 2013 to work at the newly established planning body Infrastructure UK. The work of these four officials was bolstered more recently, from 2013, by Ed Farquharson another British national with lengthy EIB experience in the UK public and private sectors. Finally, the role of at least one British private sector official should be highlighted. Timothy Stone served from 2003 as external advisor and independent non-executive director on the EIB's board of directors. Stone is widely considered to have been one of the masterminds behind PFI in the UK.[21] A longstanding KPMG official, Stone was also chairman of the IFSL (formerly British Invisibles, now part of TheCityUK), the PPP Export group. To conclude, both documentary evidence—and notably their own writings—and a range of interviewees confirm the activism of these five senior EIB officials and one top EIB advisor in favour of PPPs and the importance of this activism to both the EIB's and the European Commission's promotion of PPPs.

5. Conclusion

The EIB has been at the vanguard of PPP promotion and has been followed by most RDB and many NDB around the world. EIB activism on the promotion of PPPs can best be understood through the lenses of policy and norm entrepreneurship. As an institution, the EIB can be seen as having met most of the core features of a policy entrepreneur with regard to PPP promotion—despite its oft-repeated official insistence that it was neutral on financing methods. It repeatedly created a 'policy window' through which to promote PPPs in different contexts. The EIB developed unrivalled PPP expertise among public bodies globally—with the possible exception of the UK Treasury. The European Commission and the Council called regularly upon the EIB's advice and cooperation on PPPs. The

[20] http://www.partnershipsbulletin.com/interviews/view/131

[21] http://www.independent.co.uk/news/business/analysis-and-features/there-was-a-time-when-you-couldnt-talk-about-nuclear-power-at-dinner-parties-983598.html

establishment of EPEC in 2008 was the institutionalisation of a role which the EIB had already performed in its operational business for over a decade. Thanks to its wide network of private and public sector contacts throughout the EU, the EIB was able to build broad coalitions in favour of PPPs—both informally and officially. There are indications that the EIB operated strategically in its promotion of PPPs. While the EIB was potentially motivated by 'rationalist' institutional goals—regarding which there is some evidence—ideational considerations motivated a small group of British and Irish norm entrepreneurs to promote PPPs. These officials were motivated by an ideological commitment to the contribution of private sector methods to public sector financing and all believed in the potential efficiency gains offered by these methods. Thus, understanding the EIB as a policy entrepreneur in the promotion of PPPs relies in part upon understanding the norm entrepreneurship of a small number of its officials.

It is beyond the scope of this chapter to examine the impact of the Juncker Plan—which involved a marginal increase in total EIB lending from 2014—and the extent to which EIB officials—and specifically our norm entrepreneurs—saw it as an opportunity to promote PPP usage further. During his time at EPEC, Jennett established the Project Bond Credit Enhancement facility which arguably provided the template for the financing arrangements in the Juncker Plan.[22] The plan created a new potential for the expansion of PPPs—but its focus was on leveraged finance. Moreover, EIB lending on PPP projects declined significantly from 2010, while total funding for PPPs in Europe declined from a 2013 peak. While the financial and sovereign debt crises stimulated EIB efforts to continue to promote PPPs—which did not however translate into increased funding for PPPs—our study demonstrates that the EIB was engaged in policy entrepreneurship on PPPs long prior to these crises which cannot therefore be seen as having created a 'critical juncture' that resulted in a significant shift in EIB entrepreneurship on PPPs. It is unclear what the long-term impact of the EIB's efforts to promote PPPs would be. Brexit and the imminent departure of the UK from the EIB narrow the channels through which PPP-related ideas and expertise flowed—even if a number of pro-PPP British officials continue to work in the EIB at least for the time being. We argue that an appreciation of the EIB's PPP promotion efforts over the past three decades in terms of policy and norm entrepreneurship remains important to how we should understand both the role of the EIB as a de facto policy-making EU body but also the Bank's relationship with the Commission and other EU bodies, member states, and a range of other public and private sector actors. The EIB is—compared to other RDB—unique in its status as the official bank of a highly integrated union of sovereign states. Nonetheless, the patterns of EIB activism and policy entrepreneurship—and even agency slippage—outlined in this chapter can be detected in a number of other RDB and merit further analysis.

[22] http://www.partnershipsbulletin.com/interviews/view/131

Appendix 1: list of interviews (anonymized)

1. MEP with PPP-relevant knowledge; 6 September 2011, by telephone
2. Committee of the Regions member; 2 December 2011, Brussels
3. EPSU official; 8 March 2012, Brussels
4. Senior EIB official; 9 March 2012, Brussels
5. EU Commission official, DG Secretariat-General; 13 March 2012, Brussels
6. Former senior official working for Veolia; 27 March 2012, London
7. EU Commission official, DG ECFIN; 5 March 2012, Brussels
8. Senior EIB official; 8 May 2012, Luxembourg
9. The CityUK PPP and Projects Group senior official; 15 June 2012, London
10. Former EU commissioner; 9 July 2012, Brussels
11. Former high-ranking CEEP official; 18 July 2012, Cologne (CEEP is the European Centre of Employers and Enterprises providing Public Services and Services of general interest)
12. Joint interview with representatives of the European Construction Industry Federation (FIEC), 12 August 2013, Brussels
13. Senior British EIB official; 16 January 2014, London
14. Interview with and written feedback from an EIB economist who has worked on PPPs; 13 February 2017, Luxembourg
15. Interview with senior EU Court of Auditors official with professional experience working on PPP issues; 10 November 2017, Luxembourg
16. Interview with UK Treasury official who previously worked on PPP-related topics; 27 April 2018, London
17. Interview with EIB official who has worked on PPPs; 26 October 2018, Luxembourg
18. Interview with EIB official who has worked on PPPs; 6 December 2018, Luxembourg
19. Interview with AfDB official who works on PPPs; 28 June 2019, by Skype (Luxembourg-Abijan)
20. Interview with AIIB official who is informed on PPPs; 4 July 2019, by Skype (Luxembourg-Beijing)
21. Interview with EBRD official who works on PPPs; 24 September 2019, by Skype (Luxembourg-London)
22. Interview with EBRD official who has worked on PPPs; 6 October 2019, by Skype (Luxembourg-London)
23. Interview with former AfDB official who worked on PPPs; 25 October 2019, Luxembourg
24. Interview with South Africa-based consultant who works on PPPs; 18 November, by Skype and email
25. Interview with a CABEI official who has worked on PPPs; 27 November 2019, by Skype (Luxembourg-Tegulcigalpa)
26. Interview with World Bank Group's PPIAF official; 10 January 2019, by Skype and email
27. Interview with Portugal-based consultant who works on PPPs in Portugal and internationally; 16 February 2020, Luxembourg

Appendix 2: Table 13.1:

Table 13.1 The main PPP norm entrepreneurs

	Nation	Education	Public Sector prior to EIB	Private Sector prior to EIB	Years of direct PPP experience	Years working for the EIB
Nick Jennett	UK	Economics/ MBA	Yes	Yes (KPMG)	From mid 1990s, first with KPMG and then with EIB, focused on UK PPP projects in the school and health sector.	From 1998
Tom Barrett	Ireland	Maths/ MBA	n/a	n/a	From late 1980s. Advisor to EIB on the Channel Tunnel deal ('the world expert on Channel Tunnel funding' (interview with former high-ranking EIB official); from 2000, member of steering committee of PUK. Described as a major force behind the creation of EPEC (Great Britain 2010).	From the mid-1980s
Ed Farquharson	UK	Economics/ MBA	Yes	Yes	PUK from 2004 to 2010; led the international work of PUK advising governments on PPP programmes and policies; Head of International Infrastructure UK (six months). Executive Director Private Infrastructure Development Group November 2011 – September 2013	From 2013
Andy Carty	UK	Economics	Yes: Chief Executive Strategic Investment Board, NI, 2000–3; At UK Cabinet office and Treasury from 1995 to 2000.	Yes		From 2008 to 2013 (on secondment)

Continued

Table 13.1 *Continued*

	Nation	Education	Public Sector prior to EIB	Private Sector prior to EIB	Years of direct PPP experience	Years working for the EIB
Thomas Hackett	UK	Economics	No	Yes over a decade in banking	Over twenty	From 1981 to 2010 (moved to the EBRD)
Timothy Stone	UK	Economics/ MBA	No	Yes, considerable: at KPMG from 1995, chairman of its Global Infrastructure and Projects Group and held this position until 2011 and remained in the firm until 2014 as Global Senior Advisor.	UK PFI: over a decade. 'One of the great sages of the PFI' (Independent, 1 November 2008).	From 2003 on the EIB board of directors

Acknowledgement

Some material in this chapter is drawn from Liebe and Howarth (2020).

References

ADB (Asian Development Bank) (2012). *Public-Private Partnership Operational Plan 2012–2020*. Manila: Asian Developmnet Bank. Available online at: https://www.adb.org/sites/default/files/institutional-document/33671/ppp-operational-plan-2012–2020.pdf (accessed 18 December 2020).

AfDB (African Development Bank Group) (2013). Supporting the Transformation of the Private Sector in Africa: Private Sector Development Strategy, 2013–17', July. Available online at: https://www.afdb.org/fileadmin/uploads/afdb/Documents/Policy-Documents/2013-2017_-_Private_Sector_Development_Strategy.pdf (accessed 10 January 2020).

Asenova, D. and Beck, M. (2010). 'Crucial silences: When accountability met PFI and finance capital'. *Critical Perspectives on Accounting*, 21(1): 1–13.

BGK (Bank Gospodarstwa Krajowego) et al. (2015). 'Letter of European development banks to the President of the European Commission' 23 April.

Blanc-Brude, F., Goldsmith, H., and Välilä, T. (2007). *Public-Private Partnerships in Europe: An Update*. Economic and Financial Reports, 2007/3. Luxembourg: European Investment Bank.

Bozier, P., Chirita, R., Gargani, F., MacGray, D., Newman, L., Oboardi, R., and Rytel, M. (2013). *Ex-post Evaluation of EPEC (The European Public-Private Partnership (PPP) Expertise Centre): Final Report*. Available online at: http://ec.europa.eu/smart-regulation/evaluation/search/download.do?documentId=10565237 (accessed 15 January 2017).

Budina, N., Brixi, H.P., and Irwin, T. (2007). 'Public-private partnerships in the new EU member states. Managing fiscal risks'. World Bank Working Paper No. 114. Washington, DC: World Bank.

Bussière, É., Dumoulin, M., and Willaert, É. (eds.) (2008). *The Bank of the European Union: The EIB, 1958–2008*. Luxembourg: European Investment Bank.

Button, M.L. (ed.) (2006). *A Practical Guide to PPP in Europe*. Old Woking: City & Financial Publishing.

Carty, A. and Nemoz, M. (2010). 'PPP: the European Investment Bank and European PPP Expertise Centre'. In D. Lee, F. Clegg, and M. Roper (eds.), *Global Guide to Public-Private Partnerships*. London: Allen & Overy, pp. 303–11.

Clifton, J., Diaz-Fuentes, D., and Revuelta, J. (2014). 'Financing utilities: how the role of the European Investment Bank shifted from regional development to making markets', *Utilities Policy*, 29: 33–5.

Clifton, J., Diaz-Fuentes, D., and Gomez, A. (2017). 'The European Investment Bank: development, integration, investment?', *Journal of Common Market Studies*, 56(4): 733–50.

Cram, L. (1997). *Policy-making in the European Union: Conceptual Lenses and the Integration Process*. London: Routledge.

Davies, J. (2006). iRisk transfer in private finance initiatives (PFI): an economic analysis'. Working Paper No. URN 06/843, Industry Economics and Statistics Directorate (IES).

Dudkin, G. and Välilä, T. (2005). *Transaction Costs in Public-Private Partnerships: A First Look at the Evidence*. Economic and Financial Report, 2005/03. Luxembourg: European Investment Bank. Available online at: http://www.eib.org/attachments/efs/efr_2005_v03_en.pdf (accessed 4 June 2019).

EIB (European Investment Bank) (1998a). '1997: European Investment Bank launches job-support action plan and strengthens its commitment to EMU', *EIB Information*, 96(1).

EIB (European Investment Bank) (1998b). 'The EIB and public-private partnerships', *EIB Information*, 97(2): 4–6.

EIB (European Investment Bank) (2003a). 'The EIB's role in promoting long-term growth through investment in TENs and major R&D projects: memorandum to Ecofin'. Available online at: http://www.eib.org/attachments/general/events/eib_ecofin150703_en.pdf (accessed 31 May 2019).

EIB (European Investment Bank) (2003b). The growth initiative: further report to ECOFIN'. Available online at: http://www.eib.org/about/news/eib-contribution-to-eus-growth-initiative-ecofin-7-october-2003-luxembourg.htm?lang=-en (accessed 31 May 2019).

EIB (European Investment Bank) (2008). 'European PPP Expertise Centre (EPEC)'. Factsheet. Available online at: http://www.eib.org/epec/infocentre/documents/03 per cent20EPEC-per cent20factsheet_enper cent20_6_.pdf (accessed 5 May 2019).

EIB (European Investment Bank) (2009). 'EIB statute'. Available online at: http://www.eib.org/attachments/general/statute/eib_statute_2009_en.pdf (accessed 26 April 2019).

EIB (European Investment Bank) (2010). 'Public-private partnership expertise gets a boost'. *EIB Info*, 139(3): 11.

EIB (European Investment Bank) (2018). *Investment Report 2018/2019: Retooling Europe's Economy*. Luxembourg: EIB.

English, L.M. (2005). 'Using public-private partnerships to deliver social infrastructure: the Australian experience'. In G. Hodge and C. Greve (eds.), *The Challenge of Public-Private Partnerships: Learning from International Experience*. Cheltenham: Elgar, pp. 290–304.

EPEC (European PPP Expertise Centre) (2009). *The Financial Crisis and the PPP Market: Potential Remedial Actions*. Available online at: http://www.eib.org/epec/resources/epec-credit-crisis-paper-abridged.pdf (accessed 25 May 2019).

EPEC (European PPP Expertise Centre) (2010). *Statistical Treatment of Public-Private Partnerships: Purposes, Methodology and Recent Trends*. Luxembourg: EPEC. Available online at: http://www.eib.org/epec/attachments/epec-eurostat-statistical-treatment-of-ppps.pdf (accessed 18 January 2019).

EPEC (European PPP Expertise Centre) (2011). *State Guarantees in PPPs—A Guide to Better Evaluation, Design, Implementation and Management*. Available online at: http://www.eib.org/epec/resources/epec-state-guarantees-in-ppps-public.pdf (accessed 25 May 2019).

EPEC (European PPP Expertise Centre) (2019). *PPPs Financed by the European Investment Bank from 1990 to 2018*. Available online at: http://www.eib.org/attachments/epec/epec_ppps_financed_by_eib_since_1990_en.pdf (accessed 27 January 2020).

European Commission (2003). *Guidelines for Successful Public-Private Partnerships*. Available online at: http://ec.europa.eu/regional_policy/sources/docgener/guides/ppp_en.pdf (accessed 5 May 2019).

European Commission (2005). 'Communication from the Commission to the European Parliament, the Council, the European Economic and Social Committee and the Committee of the Regions on public-private partnerships and community law on public procurement and concessions. COM(2005) 569 final.

European Commission (2011). *Stakeholder Consultation Paper on the Europe 2020 Project Bond Initiative*. Available online at: http://ec.europa.eu/economy_finance/consultation/pdf/bonds_consultation_en.pdf (accessed 25 May 2019).

European Court of Auditors (ECA) (2018). 'Public private partnerships in the EU: widespread shortcomings and limited benefits', 9, Luxembourg: Publications Office of the European Union. Available online at: https://www.eca.europa.eu/Lists/ECADocuments/SR18_09/SR_PPP_EN.pdf (accessed 25 November 2019).

Evans, J. and Bowman, D. (2005). 'Getting the contract right'. In G. Hodge and C. Greve (eds.), *The Challenge of Public-Private Partnerships: Learning from International Experience*. Cheltenham: Elgar, pp. 62–80.

Finnemore, M. and Sikkink, K. (1998). 'International norm dynamics and political change', *International Organization*, 52(autumn): 887–917.

Föcking, J. (2000). *Die Darlehenspolitik der Europäischen Investitionsbank*. Dissertation. Frankfurt am Main: Goethe Universität.

Gavin, M. and Rodrik, D. (1995). 'The World Bank in Historical Perspective', *The American Economic Review*, 85(2): 329–34.

Goldsmith, H. (2005). *The EPEC Proposal. Building Europe's PPP Knowledge Bank. Presentation to the ISLTC Club Technical Meeting*, 13 October. Luxembourg: EPEC. Available online at: http://www.isltc-club.org/doc/20051013_Presentationper cent20 per cent20-per cent20Theper cent20EPECper cent20Proposal.ppt (accessed 8 May 2019).

Gourvish, T.R. (2006). *Britain and the Channel Tunnel*. London: Routledge.

Great Britain (H.o.L.S.C.o.E.A.) (ed.) (2010). *Private Finance Projects and Off-balance Sheet Debt*. Volume II: *Evidence*. HL Paper 63-II. London: The Stationary Office.

Available from http://www.publications.parliament.uk/pa/ld200910/ldselect/ldeconaf/63/63ii.pdf (accessed 8 May 2019).

Hackett, T. and Barrett, T.C. (1996). 'The EIB and the financing of European infrastructure'. *Project Finance International (pfie.com)*, 107.

Hager, W. (1996). 'European infrastructure finance'. *Project Finance International (pfie.com)* 104.

Heald, D. (2003). 'Value for money tests and accounting treatment in PFI schemes', *Accounting, Auditing & Accountability Journal*, 16(3): 342–71.

Hebson, G., Grimshaw, D., Marchington, M., and Cooke, F.-L. (2002). 'PPPs and the changing public sector ethos: case study evidence from the health and local authority sector'. Working Paper No. 21. Available online at: http://www.leeds.ac.uk/ESRCFutureofWork/downloads/workingpaperdownloads/Paper21.pdf (accessed 25 August 2019).

Hodge, G.A. (2006). 'Public-private partnerships and legitimacy', *UNSW Law Journal*, 29(3): 318–27.

Hodge, G.A. and Greve, C. (2019). *The logic of public-private partnerships: the enduring interdependency of politics and markets*. Cheltenham: Elgar.

Holland, Steward (2010). 'Financial crises, governance and cohesion: can governments learn up?'. In J. Richardson (ed.), *From Recession to Renewal: The Impact of the Financial Crisis on Public Services and Local Government*. Bristol: Policy Press, pp. 51–69.

Hurst, C. and Perée, E. (1998). 'International financial institutions in the 21st century'. In EIB (ed.), *International Financial Institutions in the 21st Century*. Luxembourg: EIB, pp. 10–29.

JASPERS (Joint Assistance to Support Projects in European Regions) (2016). *JASPERS: 10 Years of Support for Cohesion Policy*. Available online at: http://www.eib.org/infocentre/publications/all/jaspers-10-years-of-support-for-cohesion-policy.htm (accessed 15 February 2020).

Kaunert, C. (2010). *European Internal Security: Towards Supranational Governance in the Area of Freedom, Security and Justice*. Manchester: Manchester University Press.

Kingdon, J.W. (1995). *Agendas, Alternatives, and Public Policies*, 2nd ed. New York: Longman.

Koen, V. and van den Noord, P. (2005). Fiscal gimmickry in Europe: one-off measures and creative accounting'. OECD Economics Department Working Papers No. 417. Paris: Organisation for Economic Co-operation and Development.

La Motte, R. de and Hall, D. (2003). *The European Commission's Guide to Sucessful Public-Private Partnerships—A Critique*. Available online at: http://www.epsu.org/sites/default/files/article/files/EC-PPPs-crit-final.pdf (accessed 5 January 2020).

Lankowski, C. (1996). 'Financing integration: the European Investment Bank in transition', *Law and Policy in International Business*, 27: 999–1026.

Liebe, M. and Howarth, D. (2020). 'The European Investment Bank as policy entrepreneur and the promotion of public-private partnerships', *New Political Economy*, 25(2): 195–212.

Lonsdale, C. (2005). 'Post-contractual lock-in and the UK private finance initiative (PFI): the cases of national savings and investments and the Lord Chancellor's Department', *Public Administration*, 83(1): 67–88.

Lonsdale, C. and Watson, G. (2007). 'Managing contracts under the UK's Private Finance Initiative: evidence from the National Health Service'. *Policy and Politics*, 35(4): 683–700.

Martimont, D. and Pouyet, J. (2008). 'To build or not to build: normative and positive theories of public-private partnerships', *International Journal of Industrial Organization*, 26(2): 393–411.

Maystadt, P. (2005). 'Speech for: Istituto per gli Studi di Politica Internazionale closed workshop on the Italian road to Lisbon'. Philippe Maystadt, President of the EIB, Milan, 25 November. Available with the authors.

Mazzucato, M. and Penna, C. (2016). 'Beyond market failures: the market creating and shaping roles of state investment banks', *Journal of Economic Policy Reform*, 19(4): 305–26.

Moslener, U., Thiemann, M., and Volberding, P. (2018). 'National development banks as active financiers: the case of KfW'. In S. Griffith-Jones and J.A. Ocampo (eds.), *The Future of National Development Banks*. Oxford: Oxford University Press, pp. 63–85.

Mertens, D. and Thiemann, M. (2019). 'Building a hidden investment state? The European Investment Bank, national development banks and European economic governance', *Journal of European Public Policy*, 26(1): 23–43.

National Audit Office (2007). 'Improving the PFI tendering process: report by the Comptroller and Auditor General, Session 2006–2007'. HC 149 2006–2007. Norwich: TSO.

Reeves, E. (2010). 'Mind the gap: accountability and value for money in public private partnerships'. Departmental Working Papers No. 2010–34. Milan: Department of Economics University of Milan. Available online at: http://ideas.repec.org/p/mil/wpdepa/2010–34.html

Riess, Armin (ed.) (2005). 'Innovative financing of infrastructure—the role of public-private partnerships'. EIB Papers No. 10 (1). Luxembourg: European Investment Bank.

Robinson, N. (2009). 'The European Investment Bank: the EU's neglected institution', *Journal of Common Market Studies*, 47(3): 651–73.

Roslychy, L.L. and Spanjaard, J. (2002). 'The European Investment Bank: a European institution subject to EU policy?' Prepared by Amsterdam International Law Clinic. Available online at: http://www.odg.cat/documents/enprofunditat/Organismes_multilaterals/bei_bankwatch3.pdf (accessed 7 April 2016).

Saussier, S., Staropoli, C., and Yvrande-Billon, A. (2009). 'Public-private agreements, instituutions, and competition: when economic theory meets fact', *Review of Industrial Organization*, 35: 1–18.

Smyth, B. (2013). 'Public-private partnerships and structural funds'. Presentation at high level conference, Investing in Europe's regions and cities, Brussels, 13 May. Available online at: http://cor.europa.eu/en/news/events/Documents/finance_smyth.pdf (accessed 15 February 2017).

TFEU (2008). 'Consolidated version of the treaty on the functioning of the European Union', *Official Journal of the European Union*, C 115: 47–199.

Thomson, C., Goodwin, J., and Yescombe, E.R. (2005). *Evaluation of PPP Projects Financed by the EIB: Synthesis Report*. Luxembourg: European Investment Bank.

Vecchi, V., Hellowell, M., della Croce, R., and Gatti, S. (2017). 'Government policies to enhance access to credit for infrastructure-based PPPs: an approach to classification and appraisal'. *Public Money and Management*, 37(2): 133–40.

World Bank Group (Independent Evaluation Group) (2015). *World Bank Group Support to Public Private Partnerships*. Washington, DC: International Bank for Reconstruction and Development / The World Bank.

14

Do We Still Need Regional Development Banks Today (and Tomorrow)?

An Inquiry in Light of their Role in Funding Sustainable Infrastructures

José Antonio Alonso and José Cuesta

1. Introduction

This chapter addresses the question of whether Regional (RDB), Sub-regional, and Inter-regional development banks[1] are relevant today in a world facing daunting developmental challenges and where developing countries seems to have at their disposal a larger and diversified set of international financing options. Are these institutions adapted or adapting to the needs of more sophisticated shareholders in more liberalized and enlarged financial markets? Do they have the technical, financial, and governance capacities to address the massive gaps and challenges for implementing sustainable and inclusive development strategies at national and international levels? If there are imbalances, what are those, why do they exist, and what priority changes should expectedly improve the performance and delivery of RDB? We try to explore some of these questions in light of the RDB contributions to fund the increasing demands on infrastructure earmarked by the ambitious Agenda 2030.

The need for RDB is a straightforward question that does not have a straightforward answer. While past and recent successes and failures of RDB have been reviewed elsewhere,[2] such assessments do not benefit from an analytical exercise constructing a counterfactual of absence of RDB in the last seventy years. Even

[1] Under the general acronym of RDB, we consider either Regional/Continental development banks, such as the African Development Bank (AfDB) or the Inter-American Development Bank (IADB), Sub-regional development banks such as the Latin American Development Bank (CAF), the Central American Bank of Economic Integration (CABEI), or the Caribbean Development Bank (CAB), and Inter-regional banks, such as the Islamic Development Bank (ISDB).

[2] For most recent reviews, see Griffith-Jones et al. (2008), Alonso (2015), Humphrey (2015), Ocampo (2015), Sagasti (2015), CGD (2016), and Prizzon et al. (2017), among others, some of which including also MDB.

José Antonio Alonso and José Cuesta, *Do We Still Need Regional Development Banks Today (and Tomorrow)?: An Inquiry in Light of their Role in Funding Sustainable Infrastructures* In: *Regional Development Banks in the World Economy.* Edited by: Judith Clifton, Daniel Díaz-Fuentes, and David Howarth, Oxford University Press (2021).
DOI: 10.1093/oso/9780198861089.003.0014

though we do not question the impacts of RDB USD 45 billions' worth of new commitments[3] or decades of on-the-ground support for multiple sectoral reforms, it is not possible to conclude that a leaner multilateral investment and development banks architecture; an increasing role of bilateral donors and bilateral development finance institutions (DFI); a stronger South-South cooperation; or a more successful global public-private partnerships would have delivered a yet stronger developmental record?

In the absence of a good predicting model, precise future scenarios, and counterfactuals, answering the proposed question on the relevance of RDB runs the risk of becoming a debating club exercise. We follow a different strategy. We assess the arguments claiming that RDB are called to play a substantive role—in fact an increasingly substantive role—in future development. We summarize these arguments in the following hypothesis, adapted from CGD (2016): if RDB did not exist, we should re-invent them. The hypothesis goes like this: seventy years of experience place RDB in a privileged position to confront the current global challenges which a few—some modest, other substantial—reforms. Next, this hypothesis is assessed against a critical developmental challenge affecting today's world and most likely to remain in the future: the massive mobilization of resources required for financing of huge gaps in sustainable infrastructure investments that exist in the developing world. This exercise is followed by a discussion on what conditions need be in place for RDB to be truly playing a pivotal role in confronting such challenge—and perhaps others—in the future.

2. The if RDB did not exist, we should re-invent them hypothesis

RDB and their past relevance

RDB have an unambiguous capacity to combine financing, technical, and country expertise, and to set standards on quality and development impact. Moreover, they have a privileged position to deal with supranational issues and the coordination of international policy responses (Eccles and Gwin 1999; CGD 2016). RDB encourage governments' ownership and catalyse resource pooling, financial leverage, analytical capacity, and technical support to borrowers. They benefit from preferred creditor status and decision-making arising from weighted voting rights. In addition, they display a fair amount of innovation in mobilizing and

[3] This figure includes market-based and concessional new commitments for 2014 among four major 'legacy' RDB, that is, the AfDB, the Asian Development Bank (ADB), the European Bank of Reconstruction and Development (EBRD), and the IADB (Nelson 2018). Data for infrastructure refer to 2013, including ISDB, AfDB, the CAF, the European Bank for Reconstruction and Development, the IADB, the European Investment Bank (EIB), and the ADB.

disbursing financial resources. Eloquently, 'if the MDB no longer existed today, the international community would have to reinvent them' (CGD 2016: x).

RDB were originally created to overcome market failures, resulting in financing gaps—as in infrastructure—absent markets—as in the provision of regional public goods (RPG)—or too small markets—as medical research for diseases in poor countries. In addition to market failures, these banks can also play a complementary role to the private sector by leveraging and mobilizing financial resources and hedging the risks faced by private investors such as political and regulatory risks. Additionally, their capacity to mobilize financial resources is especially relevant in contexts of procyclical private capital flows, where resources abound during booms but are interrupted or rationed at high cost during recessions (Ocampo 2015). By financing sectors including social and environment sectors, they provide access to funds that countries may have difficulties in accessing in private capital markets at all or at favourable terms. Furthermore, RDB have played an important role in promoting regional economic and physical integration, facing cross-border issues, and supporting development plans in border regions or financing infrastructures in trade corridors. RDB—in addition to multilateral development bank (MDB)—also provide high-quality knowledge to improve project design, implementation, and evaluation (Humphrey 2015).

The capacity of RDB to mobilize financial resources is based on a very simple (but very effective) business model. RDB—and MDB more generally—obtain their net income from interest payments on outstanding loans and from investments in capital markets. These profits bolster reserves. Interestingly, member countries commit a certain amount of resources, based on their relative share of the total capital of the institution. They only pay a small portion in cash, though, but the commitment is sufficient to allow RDB to raise funds by issuing bonds in international markets with lower risks than other borrowing countries. They add a mark-up to cover adminsitrative costs and lend the amounts raised to their borrowers. With very low gearing ratios, RDB display a strong mobilizing muscle, diversified borrower portfolios, and technical expertise (Humphrey 2017). Often, RDB also provide an additional financing 'window' with loans on highly concessional terms to a selective list of eligible countries. This concessional window is financed by periodical replenishments of capital by donors, given that returns from this financing are too low to follow a commercial bank logic.

In short, RDB (and MDB) use various ways, both directly and indirectly, to provide finance to developing countries. They do so by (i) multiplying the effective contributions of their shareholders through maket operations; (ii) helping countries to build sound public finance and boost their fiscal revenues; (iii) attracting private investment to areas with low profitability or high risk; and (iv) pooling risks and resources from different providers oriented to tackle complex isues with a long-term perspective. Additionally, by bundling loans with technical assitance, capacity building, policy advice—or outright conditionality—and institutional reform components, RDB and MDB also ensure that client countries are in the best possible position to repay their debts (Sagasti 2015). They offer non-concessional loans to middle-income countries and some creditworthy low-income countries on market-based terms; as well as concessional assistance with interest below market rates to low-income countries. This means that contrary to commercial banks, RDB differentiate their type of financing by clients' income levels rather than exclusively the associated risks of an specific project (CGD 2016; Nelson 2018).

Compared with bilaterals, RDB have an advantage in terms of scale, as most of them can mobilize more resources than most bilateral donors. Additionally, they leverage public capital to and voice from their major shareholders without the level of direct political influence from bilateral relationships (CGD 2016). In fact, they allow for more consensus on shared social, environmental, and fiduciary standards than bilateral donors do. Moreover, MDB and RDB are considered more effective and efficient than bilateral donors: they are more aligned to country priorities, are more prone to use country systems, have less conditionality, mobilize larger funds, show greater predictability, and have a strategic focus with a stronger long-term perspective (Davies and Pickering 2015). A survey on forty developing countries concluded that multilateral lending is preferred over bilateral lending (Davies and Pickering 2015).

Compared with other MDB, RDB present three main advantages: (i) they operate in more limited geographical contexts, which let them to have closer relationships with governments and social actors in the area, cumulate better knowledge about the developmental issues of the countries involved, and build more adapted and tailored responses to these issues (Birdsall and Rojas-Suárez 2004); (ii) they encourage a more genuine feeling of ownership by regional shareholders and give greater voice to developing countries borrowers, which is particularly useful in the case of small and poor countries that consider global MDB too big and too distant; and (iii) they are able to establish closer and more direct relations between shareholders and their constituencies, more likely relying on informal peer pressure rather than imposing conditionality (Griffith-Jones et al. 2008).

By contrast, RDB with limited geographical focus (i.e. Sub-regional development banks) have some disadvantages vis-à-vis other MDB. In this regard, Sub-regional development banks operate in a more reduced scale; have less diversified portfolios; and, consequently, they usually face higher spreads and lower credit ratings.[4] These challenges are partially compensated by lower transaction costs, more resolute and quick procedures, less conditionality and greater autonomy. RDB have gained a privileged position to invest in cross-border issues. Traditionally, they have played an important role in nurturing and supporting

[4] For example, in accordance with Fitch Ratings, while the IADB has triple-A rating, the CAF has AA–, the CAB has AA+, and the CABEI has A+.

processes of regional integration, mainly through investing in infrastructures, strengthening capital markets, and supporting regional programmes. That is the case of the European Investment Bank (EIB) and the European Bank of Reconstruction and Development (EBRD) in Europe, the Latin American Development Bank (CAF) in the Andean Community, the Caribbean Development Bank (CAB) in the Caribbean Community and the Central American Bank of Economic Integration (CABEI) in the Central America Integration System among others. As Berg (1998) points out, regional organizations can make crucial contributions where national capacity in economic management is weak, something that is common across many developing countries.

Additionally, RDB have played an important role in the provision of RPG. Historically, countries are reluctant to borrow for projects whose benefits extend beyond their borders. CGD (2016) argues that member countries typically fear that international public good (IPG) activities divert resources away from country specific needs prioritized in their national developmental plans. Similarly, international aid eligible countries arguably fear that donor contributions to finance IPG are not fully additional to ongoing contributions to international aid. Left alone, countries and bilateral donors do not have the incentives—nor finances—to invest in IPG initiatives such as regional and global monitoring systems, drought resilience initiatives, or pandemic rapid responses.

RDB have helped the international community—often led by the World Bank—design, collect, and collate basic development data on poverty, growth, inequality, financial inclusion, environmental resources, living standards, and so on. For example, the African Development Bank (AfDB) has collaborated with other international and national partners to develop a consensus strategy to measure monetary poverty in North African countries; the Inter-American Development Bank (IADB) is a founding member of multi-stakeholder technical commissions to measure well-being in several Latin American countries; and the Asian Development Bank (ADB) monitors East Asian local currency bond market yields and risks.

RDB have also played a large role in fostering large scale policies and programmes. They have traditionally supported International Monetary Fund (IMF)-led macroeconomic reforms and World Bank-designed sectoral policy reforms; contribute to regional trade agreements and cross-border investments in infrastructure and expansion of regional power markets (CGD 2016). For example, the IADB manages a regional infrastructure integration fund (the Fund for Integration Infrastructures, or *Fondo de Infraestructuras de Integracion, FIRII*, in Spanish) that supports cross-border projects designed to reduce transportation and logistics costs. This is expected to expand trade and reduce the estimated 50 per cent of unfulfilled intra-regional trade potential due to insufficient regional infrastructure and trade regulatory architecture (IADB 2011).

These institutions have also contributed to the development of new ideas for aid delivery (such as output-based aid), and for social policies (such as conditional cash transfers). Have also spring boarded innovative initiatives on systematic impact evaluation, climate financing, and muster the rollout of philanthropic donations such as the Advanced Market Commitment (which creates a market for pharmaceutical products that treat diseases primarily affecting the poor; Levine et al. 2005). These initiatives have contributed to a financial, analytical, and technical capacity that any donor agency on its own would have not been able to provide. They have done so with a certain degree of objectivity in the allocation of resources and policy interactions than bilateral donors—which give more weight to national interest in the definition of their priorities. For all these reasons, it is clear that RDB have played a relevant role in development during the last seven decades. They have filled important gaps in the existing development finance architecture and have enlarged the available options of public finance for developing countries. Would have other alternatives delivered more impactful contributions? We cannot know for sure but their contributions have clearly provided a meaningful push for development.

Todays' challenges

Are the expertise, capacity, and privileged position gained by RDB still relevant today? Today's world is dramatically different from when RDB were created. The developing world now accounts for half of the global gross domestic product—two-thirds, if considering borrowing countries (CGD 2016). Developing countries today face less severe financial market failures and can gain access more easily and in better conditions to international capital markets. In fact, the rapid and sustained growth in the Peoples' Republic of China (PRC) and other emerging Asian economies in the last twenty-five years marks a departure from previous decades. Rapid growth in the PRC and India is responsible for a dramatic fall in global extreme poverty, which declined by 1.2 billion as the world's population has increased by two billion since the 1990s (World Bank 2016). Unlikely countries such as Cambodia, Peru, or Tanzania have ranked atop the world's fastest growing economies in the last ten years (World Bank 2016).

In part because of this increased global prosperity, RDB shareholders' needs have also been changing. The split between reconstruction countries and financers after the Second World War and between rich creditors and developing world borrowers since the 1960s and 1970s have led to a more heterogeneous landscape. Some shareholders are no longer major borrowers from any development bank, such as Chile or Uruguay; others have become in prominent global financiers, such as the PRC and some Arab countries; and some are simultaneously donors and recipients, such as the BRICS (Brazil, Russia, India, China, and South Africa), and other middle-income countries (Colombia, Peru, Argentina, India, Indonesia, among others). This naturally has implications for their development agendas, demands for governance reforms, and distribution of financing.

Some of these changes in the international context have put the RDB business model under pressure. In the last decade, the number of available financiers has increased, the variety of mechanisms of development financing has widened, and the capacity for developing countries to access capital markets has improved. Many developing countries (including Sub-Saharan African countries) have successfully issued sovereign bonds in international markets; and many of them have received financing from new providers (such as the PRC) and new multilateral institutions (such as the New Development Bank (NDB) and the Asian Infrastructure Investment Bank (AIIB)). The enlargement of the financial options suggests either the non-financial terms and conditions of traditional RDB (and MDB generally) have lost part of their attractiveness and/or the financing needs of developing countries are far greater than MDB lending can address (Prizzon 2017).

An ample group of RDB (and MDB more generally) have assumed the logic of country 'graduation', preserving the access to concessional instruments (sometimes through specialized 'windows') to those countries under an income threshold. There is the assumption that as countries rise up the income ladder, their increasing national resources will turn the international public financing virtually unnecessary. However, not always does domestic revenue mobilization expand at appropriate rates in these countries, which means that their demands for international non-concessional public financing can be expected to increase, sometimes beyond MDB capacities for lending. As a consequence, traditional RDB (and MDB generally) are not able to play a sufficiently catalytic role in middle-income countries (Rogerson 2017). This imbalance was coined as the 'missing middle' of development finance by Kharas et al. (2014). In spite of what the logic of graduation suggests, many middle-income countries still need access to appropriate international funding to help them tackle both national and global challenges. New issues—climate change, migrations, knowledge divide, energy transition, or technological innovation—will strain their financial capabilities; while a greater emphasis on the provision of IPGs will force such countries to find new ways of financing those goods (Alonso 2016).

The combination of emerging challenges and increasingly acute traditional issues call for ever more relevant RDB. An advantage of RDB to look optimistically into the future is their capacity to re-invent themselves; move into new sectors; introduce financial innovations; broaden their range of services; and modify conditions for access to their resources (Sagasti 2015). That resilience and culture of adaptation is more necessary when facing an increasingly uncertain future. Such capabilities alongside resource mobilization are also relevant in the face of the unprecedented ambitions of the Agenda 2030 (Alonso 2015).

We therefore conclude that in a context of increasing heterogeneity among developing countries, capacities and business model of RDB make them relevant in the context of current and future development challenges. Accordingly, the best future arrangement would be a system in which MDB are complemented with a dense network of RDB. However, another question immediately arises: do these institutions have imbalances that need to be addressed so they can effectively confront the emerging challenges of a changing world? In the absence of counterfactual and credible future scenarios, we focus instead on demonstrating the claim that RDB are essential to take on the huge investment gaps in building sustainable infrastructure in the developing world, as the Agenda 2030 demands.

3. RDB and financing infrastructure

Infrastructure as an increasingly necessary condition for development

Empirical evidence has long confirmed the positive impact of infrastructure in development (Estache and Garsous 2012). Although the analysis is sensitive to ways in which infrastructure is measured or the econometric procedure followed, empirical results confirm positive links between infrastructure and growth, access to social services, and social and territorial cohesion (Romp and De Haan 2007; Irmen and Kuehnel 2009; Calderon and Serven 2014). Ultimately, improving the economic and social infrastructure within a country is a strategic component of any development process. In the short run, investment in infrastructure boosts aggregate demand, spurs growth, and creates jobs. Over the longer term, its impact will be felt in higher productivity efficiency and international competitiveness, as well as in higher levels of territorial integration and social cohesion.

Moreover, the relevance of investing in infrastructure has recently increased for four concrete reasons. First, the high level of integration and interdependency among countries means that the stock and quality of infrastructure have a direct influence on the process of international economic convergence and private sector competitiveness. Second, it is difficult to achieve and sustain significant improvements in social and territorial inclusion without promoting a good provision of infrastructures that allow people, wherever they live, the appropriate level of access to social services. Third, the world's population will increase by 1.5 billion between 2015 and 2030—mostly in urban settings—which will demand a major increase in infrastructure investments. Finally, overcoming environmental challenges will demand a massive investment in green infrastructures to allow countries to make the transition to sustainable development strategies, based on clean technologies, renewable sources of energy, and sustainable patterns of production, consumption, and transportation.

Table 14.1 Annual additional financing requirements to achieve the SDGs (USD billion)

	Greenhill and Ali (2013)	SDSN (2015)	UNCTAD (2014)
Education	38	194	250
Universal health coverage	37	69–89	140
Water and sanitation	27	42–45	260
Sustainable energy	434–934	321–347	370–690
Energy Access	34		
Renewable Energy	400–900		
Food security	50.2	148	260
Social protection			
Transport Infrastructure		189	50–470
Telecommunication		396	70–240
Protection of Ecosystems		11–28	
Emergency response		8–23	
Climate Change			420–780
Mitigation			360–680
Adaptation			60–100
TOTAL	586–1,086	1,378–1,459	1,900–3,100

[a] *Source*: authors based on Grennhill and Ali (2013); Sustainable Development Solutions Network (2015) and UNCTAD (2014).

Not surprisingly, the 2030 Agenda for Sustainable Development has emphasized the crucial role that investment in infrastructures must play in the achievement of the Sustainable Development Goals (SDG). Given their ambition, achieving the SDG will require a massive mobilization of resources, technical capacities, and political will both at national and international levels. A number of analyses have been carried out recently to replicate the SDGs financing gap analyses of fifteen years ago. For example, Greenhill and Ali (2013) looked at five sectors estimating that they would require very significant infrastructural investments of around USD 1 trillion. They warned that these 'are likely to be under-estimates' (Greenhill and Ali 2013). The Sustainable Development Solutions Network (2015) raises this figure to USD 1.3 to 1.4 trillion and UNCTAD (2014) to USD 1.9 to 3.1 trillion (see Table 14.1). A large part of the resources required for achieving the SDG will have to be oriented to improving and 'greening' the stock of infrastructures, particularly in developing countries (Bhattacharya et al. 2012).

Because investment in infrastructure involves a great mobilization of resources, this sector does not make it a suitable area for substantive bilateral Official Development Assistance (ODA). Neither does it for private capital alone, given the important imperfections of private international markets, especially in the provision of long-term funding. For these reasons, RDB (and more generally MDB) are called to play a crucial role in financing infrastructures in developing countries. Additionally, future technological progress and innovative financing mechanisms could facilitate a more significant role for the private sector in this field. In fact, the way in which infrastructures are financed, provided, regulated, and managed has dramatically changed in the last three decades. These changes have been a result of the intense process of innovation and technological change and have tended to give more room to private agents in the provision and management of infrastructures.

The role of RDB in financing infrastructure investments

Building appropriate infrastructure requires a huge financial effort. It also brings multiple opportunities for countries. These opportunities include expanding local capital markets; enlarging the project portfolio of national and foreign investors; enhancing economic growth and employment; and testing new forms of prtnership between public and private sectors. Given the importance of this area, the Group of Twenty (G20) created a Working Group on Investment and Infrastructure under the Chinese presidency. This working group immediately decided to scale up the MDB finance in infrastructure and signalled the salience of that strategy by issuing a Joint Declaration of Aspiration on Actions to support infrastructure in the coming years. Similarly, the 2030 Agenda emphasizes the need for developing countries to fill the infrastructure gap in order to achieve the SDG. Additionally, as the UNCTAD (2014) points out, between two and three times the current investment in infrastructure would be necessary to meet the needs defined by the 2030 Agenda, particularly in energy, water, and sanitation (Figure 14.1).

None of the existing analyses suggests that the financing gaps will be filled by international public funds alone. According to Miyamoto and Chiofalo (2016), most of the resources spent in infrastructure in 2014 were provided by official domestic resources coming from the developing countries; close to a third of resources were contributed by the private sector; and only a small proportion (around 7 per cent) was financed by development partners. These proportions vary across countries' income group, with development partners, as expected, playing a more active role in the case of low-income countries. By type of investment gap, Greenhill and Ali (2013) estimate that 75 per cent of the renewable energy financing gap will have to be filled by private finance. This is in stark contrast to the current financing situation. In the estimate of Bhattacharya et al. (2012) for greening infrastructure, 60 per cent of annual investment is currently financed by domestic government budgets; 20–30 per cent by the private sector; 5–8 per cent through ODA and other official flows (OOF) (from MDB); and about 3 per cent from other developing country governments. UNCTAD (2014) shows that the participation of the private sector varies significantly by sector and country. For example, private sector finances as much as 80–100 per cent of the

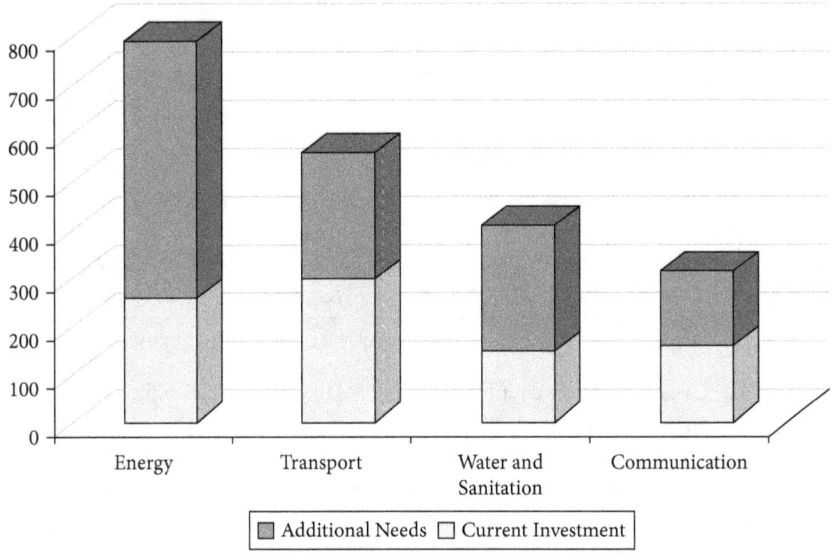

Figure 14.1 Current annual investment and additional needs in infrastructure in developing countries (USD billion)
Source: Authors based on UNCTAD (2014).

provision of power in some countries, but does not exceed 20 per cent on climate change adaptation. At the same time, the contribution of the private sector to investment in transportation reaches 60–80 per cent in some developed countries, but the ratio decreases to 30 and 40 per cent in developing countries.

When looking at flows from development partners, some 56 per cent come from concessional funds; the other 44 per cent were non-concessional. Both flows mobilized close to USD 60 billion. It is important to underline that more than a half of these resources (51 per cent) were channelled by MDB, with an additional contribution of RDB. The list is headed by the World Bank Group. It contributed some USD 13.8 billion in 2014. The ADB was the largest RDB contributor to the investment in infrastructure in that year, with USD 5.5 billion. Smaller contributions came from the IADB, AfDB, the EIB, the CAF, the Islamic Development Bank (ISDB) and the EBRD (Figure 14.2). On the other hand, of the largest bilateral contributors, Japan, Korea, Germany, and France stand out.

Moreover, RDB show particular specialization in infrastructure investments. For example, this sector represents around a third (37 per cent) of the World Bank Group's investment; with even lower ratios in the case of the bilateral donors, with some few exceptions (such as Korea or Japan). However, that share raises to over 50 per cent in the cases of the ISDB, the AfDB, the ADB, and the Arab Bank for Economic Development in Africa (BADEA), and about 40 per cent for the IADB and the CAF (see Humphrey 2015; Miyamoto and Chiofalo 2016).

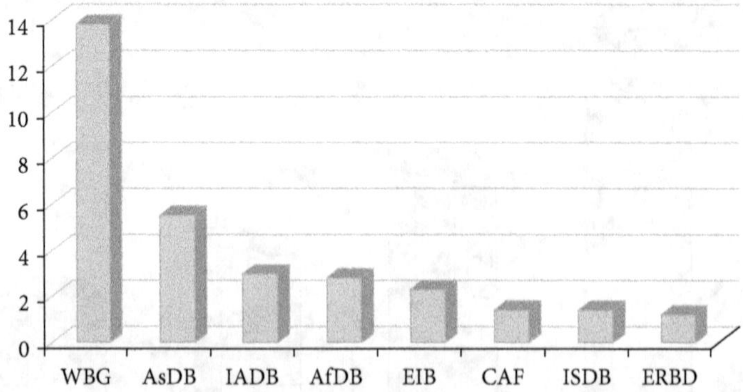

Figure 14.2 Largest investors in infrastructure: MDB (2014) (USD billion)
Source: Miyamoto and Chiofalo (2016).

The weight of the RDB among the providers of financing for infrastructure in developing countries has increased in the last decade. The amount of resources mobilized by the MDB to infrastructure doubled between 2005 and 2014, with an annual growth rate of 10 per cent, led by the contributions of the World Bank Group. Most of the investment by MDB (43 per cent) is oriented to transportation, 38 per cent to energy, 15 per cent to water and sanitation, and, finally, 3 per cent to communication infrastructures (Miyamoto and Chiofalo 2016). In terms of recipients, the bulk of the investment (close to 43 per cent) was targeted at upper-middle-income countries; 38 per cent at lower-middle-income countries; and the remaining 19 per cent at low-income countries.

A look at the sectoral specialization of RDB financed through Official Development Assistance (ODA), and OOF, reveals several relevant features (Figure 14.3). First, ISDB and AfDB are the most oriented RDB to investing on infrastructure, while EBRD, CAB, and IADB have a more diversified portfolio. Second, the bulk of resources oriented to infrastructure go to transportation and energy, followed by water, and, only marginally, communications. Third, AfDB and ADB specialize in transportation and energy, while IADB, CAB, and EBRD in transportation, and ISDB mainly in energy.

Mobilizing private resources

The activities of MDB are not limited to government financing but include the maintenance of instruments specialized in supporting the private sector involvement in development investment. In fact, according to Organisation for Economic Co-operation and Development (OECD) data, 40 per cent of all official financial cooperation with the private sector in 2015 was managed by the World Bank through the International Finance Corporation (IFC) and the Multilateral

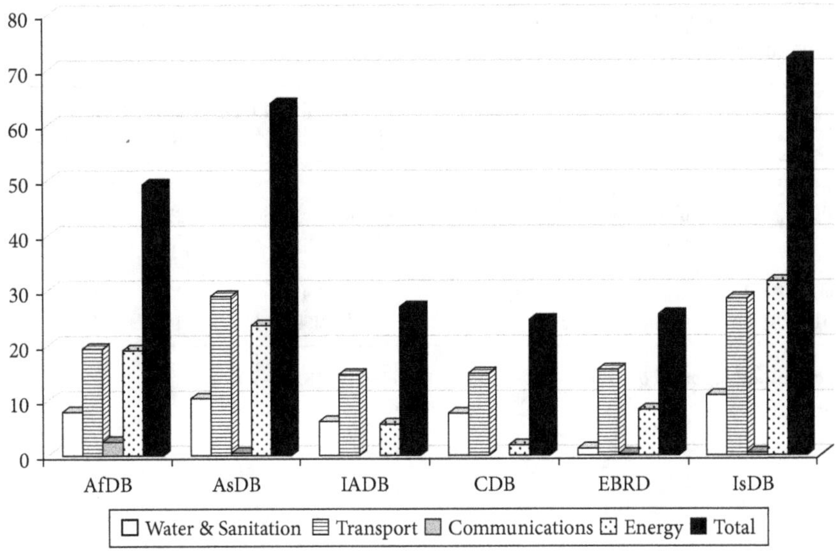

Figure 14.3 RDB specialization in infrastructure (ODA and OOF, USD billion, average 2013/15)
Source: Authors based on OECD data.

Investment Guarantee Agency (MIGA), while an additional 25 per cent was channelled through RDB (ADB, AfDB, EBRD, EIB, and IADB) and 35 per cent was contributed by bilateral DFI (Benn et al. 2017).

In the last decade, international finance institutions (both multilateral and bilateral) have strengthened their specialized lines oriented to mobilize private capital in developing countries (Center for Global Development 2016). Through different financial instruments (such as guarantees, syndicated loans, equity investment, or simply co-financing) many RDB are paying increased attention to crowding-in private resources in developing countries, particularly through blended figures. Although this field remains little explored, there are two estimates that offer a tentative account of the private resources mobilized with official support: one of them by the OECD and the other by a group of MDB led by the World Bank. Although these two estimates are based on surveys of the responsible institutions, they adopt different criteria and methodologies for calculation, which affects both the spectrum of instruments considered and the criteria adopted for attribution of resources mobilized. While the results of these exercises are not directly comparable, they point to the relevance of private resources mobilized by official funds. Specifically, the OECD estimate for 2017 indicates a mobilization of private resources of USD 38.2 billion: RDB contributed with 37.7 per cent of these resources (Table 14.2). Regarding the instruments used, guarantees were revealed as the mechanism that yielded greater capacity for resource mobilization (44 per cent of total), followed by syndicated loans (12 per cent),

Table 14.2 Mobilization of private resources directed to developing countries through blended financing

Study	Institutions	Year	Volume mobilized (USD billion)	Contribution from RDBs (percentage)
OECD, 2016 OECD, 2019	Bilateral and multilateral DFIs and development agencies	2012–2015 2017	20.2 (annual average) 38.2	32.4 37.7
World Bank, 2018	Bilateral and multilateral DFIs	2017	Direct: 19.1 Total: 59.4	47,4 46,6

[a] *Source*: Authors based on OECD (2017 and 2019) and IFC (2018).

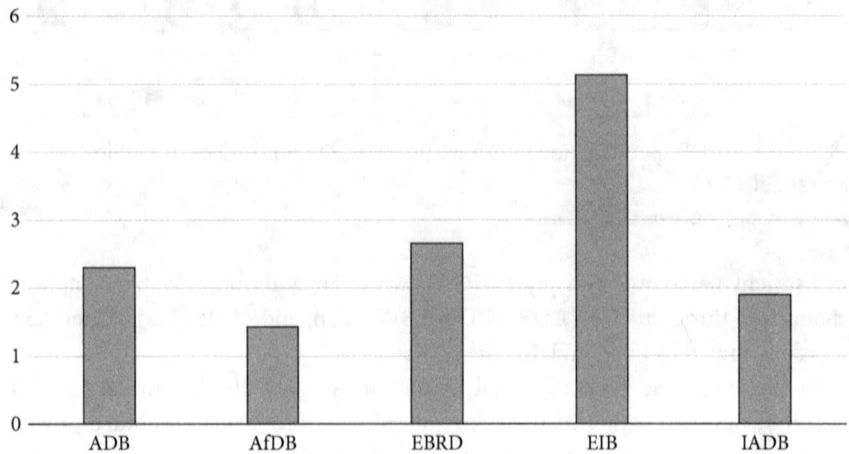

Figure 14.4 Mobilization of private resources by RDB (2017) towards developing countries (USD billion)
Source: Authors based on OECD (2017, 2019).

and direct investment (6 per cent). The two European RDB are those with greater capacity for mobilizing resources, followed by ADB and IADB (Figure 14.4).

The estimate by the group of multilateral banks confirms the magnitude of resources mobilized in 2017 at USD 19.1 billion in regard to direct mobilization and USD 59.4 billion when referring to total mobilization (including indirect funding). Importantly, about 47 per cent of these resources were mobilized by RDB. The European RDB (the EIB and, with less capacity, the EBRD) are confirmed to be the institutions with greater capacity for mobilizing private resources in aggregate terms, but the ISDB, the IADB, and the ADB equally show a high capacity for non-direct forms of leveraging (Figure 14.5). It is worth mentioning that most of these private resources mobilized by RDB are linked to the investment in infrastructures. Here the situation is very different across institutions: all

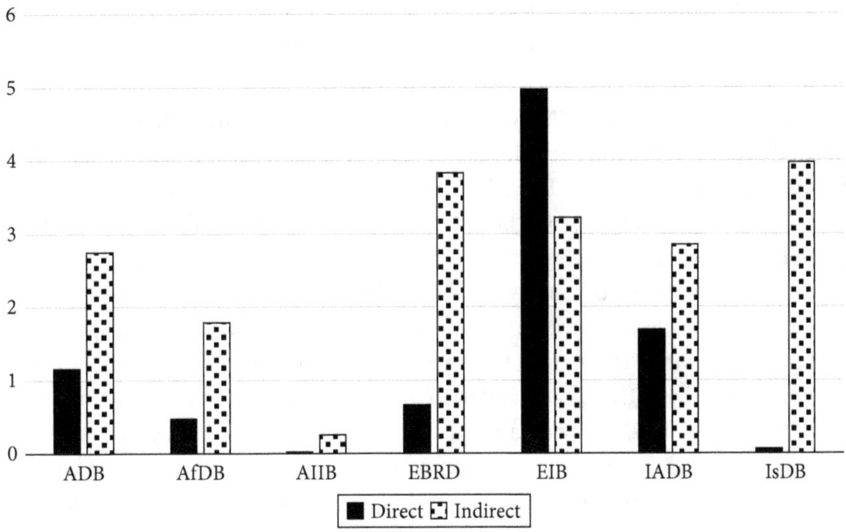

Figure 14.5 Private resources mobilized by RDB towards developing countries (2017) (USD billion)
Source: IFC (2018).

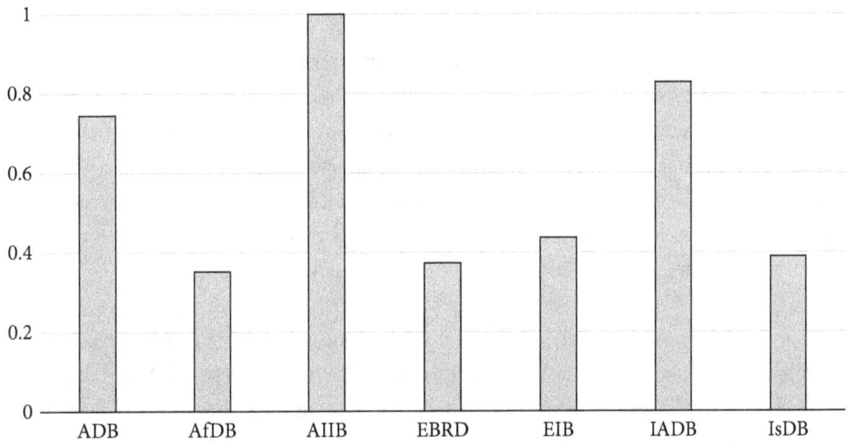

Figure 14.6 Share of private resources mobilized by RDB oriented towards investing in infrastructures (%)
Source: IFC (2018).

private resources mobilized by AIIB are oriented to investment in infrastructures (in accordance with the bank specialization); the share is close to 80 per cent for the IADB and ADB, and the share is around 40 per cent for the rest of the RDB considered in the study (Figure 14.6).

4. Limitations of the RDB in the process of scaling-up the investment in infrastructures

Having established that RDB have played an important role in both financing and diversifying infrastructure investments in the developing countries, the question that remains is whether RDB are in a strong position to respond to the massive mobilization of resources and the emerging sustainability challenges associated with the 2030 Agenda.

We offer two competing answers. First, RDB will remain crucial in filling the gap between needs on infrastructure and resources provided by private sector and domestic public funds. The fact that two new RDB have been created in the last few years (the BRICS NDB, and the AIIB) is testament of this argument. RDB (and MDB in general) provide a good way to overcome the market failures that characterize the private provision of infrastructure. Second, RDB will not be able to properly play this role, at the required level, without adopting important reforms. In fact, those same new RDB (and others not so new, such as the CAF) provide some insights on the innovations in structure and procedures that traditional RDB could face up.

Indeed, RDB experience as a financer of investment in infrastructure reveals, at least, four important shortcomings. First, they present some limitations in their capacity for mobilizing resources at the magnitude that will be required in the following fifteen years. Shareholders (particularly non-borrower ones) are very reluctant to support processes of capital increase of RDB; in fact, they tend to reject any increase in the paid-in capitals. Public budget restrictions among shareholders partly explain this attitude. Additionally, partnering countries are afraid that capital increases might modify relative shares and political weight aspirations in the RDB governance structure and decision processes. As a consequence, only exceptionally have there been operations of capital increase in multilateral finance institutions (some of them during the last decade).

Furthermore, RDB are particularly risk-averse in their lending policies, in general, and investments in infrastructure, in particular, which limit their resource mobilization muscle. This is because they usually involve remarkable risks, particularly in developing countries. Infrastructure investments often constitute complex projects, with difficult processes of planning and design, and long periods of maturity. RDB exhibit high-equity loans ratios that double (or even triple) those of their private counterparts (30–40 per cent against 13–17 per cent, respectively). Humphrey (2015) suggests that in 2013 RDB could have increased their collective portfolio by an additional USD 200 billion if their equity loans ratios had been about 20 per cent (rather than 30–40 per cent). It is the 'desire of non-borrower shareholders to avoid a call on their callable capital' that explains this over-cautious policy (Humphrey 2015).

The second important problem relates to RDB bureaucratic and lengthy business practices. Such practices bring additional costs and time to the negotiation process. Obviously, there is a potential trade-off between quality control and supervision, on the one hand, and the speed at which decisions are adopted, on the other. There are complex processes and requirements in almost every single stage in the process. For example, in 2013, as the World Bank admits, the International Development Association and the International Bank for Reconstruction and Development took twenty-eight months to move a project from the initial identification to the first disbursement. The process of approval of a sovereign loan takes fourteen months for the World Bank, thirteen for AfDB, eleven for ADB, and six for IADB (Humphrey 2015). Non-sovereign loans are approved more quickly, yet between a lengthy process between six and twelve months. Procurement is also fraught with complex processes, which typically require demanding and highly specific procedures. Furthermore, RDB apply environmental and social safeguards that frequently add more time and hassle to the negotiation process, particularly in the field of infrastructure. Interestingly, some of the new RDB (e.g., the CAF and the AIIB) aim at a leaner bureaucracy and more agile procedures, with reduced procedures and time required for implementing a loan. They actively portray such improvements as fundamental advantages of their business models.

The third constraint is the relatively limited capacity that the RDB have shown for adopting a diversified and effective menu of financial instruments for mobilizing additional resources for infrastructure. That is the case, for example, of the limited use of loan guarantees, despite their potential multiplicative effect on resources mobilized. RDB could take into account the life cycle of risks, focusing their scarcer capital (through short maturity loans, guarantees, or equity) in those stages of the project with higher risk and then selling out their participation to the private sector once the risk is lower and the project generates revenue. Other unexploited possibility consists of risk-sharing facilities. Such options include loan syndication or co-financing arrangements that bring external resources into private sector transactions, which RDB could administer in order to back up a portfolio of loans or some complex project. Some RDB use these instruments (e.g., the ERBD), but many others do not.

Finally, the fourth problem is related to the RDB ability to identify good projects to be financed. Sometimes the problem for developing countries is not to find funds for their projects, but to generate well-designed fundable projects. Many borrowers need financial and technical support for the design and formulation of good projects. Most of this support is typically managed through non-re-imbursable resources, basically grants. However, RDB typically have very tight conditions to allocate grants and they frequently use trust funds for project preparation. Given the resulting high costs associated with the design and formulation of a complex project in infrastructure, the required funds are not always available to ensure a robust preparation of projects. Bhattacharya et al. (2012) argue that the lack of project preparation facilities constitutes a major gap in infrastructure investments; and this gap has perverse distributive effect, as it affects mainly to the poorest countries.

5. 'Re-inventing' RDB: what needs to change to make RDB still relevant?

The contributions of RDB to international development are unquestionable and their expertise, capacity, and experiences of great value in todays' world. They are called to play a significant role in supporting countries to make the Agenda 2030 a reality by helping to mobilize finance, tackle cross-border problems, and look for innovative responses to complex issues. However, they are also subject to concrete limitations—in terms of their ability to mobilize funding, disincentives--financing of middle-income countries versus low-income countries, and long-due changes—for example, when it comes to internal governance.

There are still huge gaps in infrastructure financing and financing of IPG, which are estimated in the tune of USD 1.5 trillion (UNCTAD 2014) and USD 150 billion annually (CGD 2016), respectively. Bridging these gaps is increasingly important for development: infrastructure bottlenecks have become a critical constraint for sustainable growth following the rapid growth of the PRC and its increasing demand in the developing world. At the same time, when growth is globally slowing down, investing in infrastructure has been often a strategy for immediate growth (vis-à-vis a longer term strategy of investing in human capital, R&D, or truly diversifying the economy's sources of growth). If done smartly, it can be also a way to invest in long-term, climate friendly technology promoting green growth (Bhattacharya and Kharas 2016; CGD 2016).

RDB are particularly qualified to address issues related to RPG, given the complexity and the supranational scope of these kinds of goods. However, RDB have difficulty in doing that properly, given the country-based nature of their lending and leveraging model (based on their signature in instruments of sovereign loans). Overcoming these limitations would demand reform and a complementary search for new policy approaches. A way to face these limitations would be to complement the existing country-focused business model aimed at supporting client countries with a new business model focused on financing RPG (the 'two-track MDB business model' suggested by Kaul 2017). In this last case, finance should be oriented to fill the gap between what countries can do in certain RPG and what would be necessary to meet the systematic requirements of these kinds of goods.

The creation of new RDB indicates as much success of previous development banks as frustration from emerging economic powerhouses in the Global South with the capacity of existing institutions to deliver change. The very fact that the PRC and other major borrowers are creating new MDB focused heavily on infrastructure (the AIIB; the NDB) is arguably testament to the relevance of this type of bank in the current context. Yet, it is also proof of the limitations of the legacy of RDB in confronting by themselves the emerging challenges described above. They have been slow to adjust to today's realities; to reflect in their governance structures the increasing economic power of some of their borrowers; and to lighten their stifling bureaucracy and costly delays in procedures (CGD 2016). While it is hard to predict when—and to what extent—such reforms will take place, there is little evidence suggesting that they might materialize in the short run and that all involved shareholders share an overall consensus view on how to bring them about (Ocampo 2015).

An important component of this process of reform should be oriented to increasing the financial capacity of the RDB, even though shareholders reject a capital increase. Humphrey (2017) suggests some interesting avenues for overcoming this dilemma. All of them are oriented to relaxing the constraint that shareholders' capital imposes on RDB lending activities. In this line three proposals sound particularly interesting: (i) reviewing the procedures for defining capital adequacy for an MDB, as current criteria used by rating agencies and regulators are clearly restrictive; (ii) analysing the benefit and costs on going sub-triple-A, as other RDB operate very effectively under the triple-A rating without reputational costs (e.g., the CAF); and (iii) issuing subordinate debt to institutional investors, seeking low-yield and low-risk assets, as well as creating a subordinated and separate share class within MDB ownership structure for institutional investors (a procedure employed by the Trade and Development Bank). All these lines of reform, although initially intended for MDB, could be applied to RDB towards increasing their financial potential.

The magnitude of the current development challenges, particularly those related to building sustainable infrastructure, can justify the existence of multiple RDB operating in each region. The relevant question is how they should operate jointly or at least in a coordinated way. Currently, MDB and RDB operate in overlapping areas and countries, with limited coordination between them and sometimes with clear competition for the same resources and partners. The duplication of efforts dents the efficiency of the multilateral system as a whole, while different systems of procurement and reporting represent a burden for borrowers. The demand for more coordination and better division of labour between MDB and RDB is a demand as often repeated as it is unfulfilled.

Not surprisingly, despite the obvious case for an increasing role, the importance of RDB and MDB more generally in international financing has declined over the last two decades (Alonso 2015). Except for the two years immediately before and after the crisis of 2007, the provision of net credits has followed a rather stagnant trend. This suggests that countries might find it difficult to obtain this type of financing, preferring instead to resort to that provided by the market, whether in the form of private credit or of bonds. Overcoming such a tendency requires RDB to actively reduce the level of complexity of their bureaucratic procedures; be less legalistic and conservative; be more innovative in financial instruments; and be less risk-averse in a field that is changing very quickly.

The emergence of new RDB (e.g., AIIB or NDB), together with the increasing profile of others (e.g., the CAF or the IADB), particularly in infrastructure investment, provide traditional RDB with a good incentive (and guide) to adopting the required reforms. They are more specialized than traditional RDB, which have broader mandates. This specialization in part contributes to maintaining a single business window instead of the 'two-windows' model that traditional RDB have. This might favourably impact on their willingness to take risks, test innovations, abandon the logic of graduation, and avoid a 'one-size-fits-all' strategy for diverse projects.

A good sign is the re-iterated public commitment to change by most RDB in the Global Infrastructure Forum held in 2016 and again in 2017. In the 'Joint Declaration of Aspiration on Actions' to support infrastructure, MDB re-affirm

> their commitments to work together to scale up their support for sustainable infrastructure investment, including for project preparation, enhance its quality and to attract private sector capital, subject to the constraints of investment demands as well their own guidelines, governance and mandates.
>
> (See http://www.g20.utoronto.ca/2016/mdbs-joint-declaration.pdf)

These commitments were re-iterated in the 2017 'Principles to Crowd-in Private Sector' finance. MDB have recently published the first 'Joint MDB Report on Mobilisation of Private Finance'. That report shows that out of USD 163 billion of private finance mobilized in 2016, USD 68 billion went into infrastructure.

Based on this discussion, we *cannot* conclusively answer the question of whether RDB are still needed today and tomorrow. We have addressed a different question: what need RDB be doing now to ensure they will continue to be relevant developmental institutions in the future? Seeing the glass half full one can argue that while there are some important issues to be addressed, they are offset by the increasingly important roles RDB are called to play in multiple areas (financing of infrastructure, IPG, countercyclical financing to low-income countries). The glass half empty highlights that RDB still need to get their act together, adjust and up their game in two particular critical areas (CGD 2016): (i) financing programmes with substantial spill-overs at the global level, primarily on agriculture, energy, climate change, health, and development data and research that cannot be easily structured or priced as traditional country operations; (ii) support a substantial increase in financing sustainable infrastructure by the RDB over the next decade—from increasing business efficiency, shifts of priority countries, increasing contributions from shareholders—which CGD (2016) estimates at USD 200 billion a year, a remarkable increase from the current USD 50 billion a year.

References

Alonso, J.A. (2015). 'The role of multilateral development banks: international aid is not enough'. Caretas Annual Meeting WB-IMF Special Report.

Alonso, J.A. (2016). 'Beyond aid: reshaping the development cooperation system'. In J.A. Ocampo (ed.), *Global Governance and Development*. Oxford: Oxford University Press, ch. 4.

Basile, I. and Jarrett, D. (2019). 'Blended finance funds and facilities: survey results 2018'. OECD Development Co-operation Working Paper No. 59. Available online at: https://www.oecd-ilibrary.org/docserver/806991a2-en.pdf?expires=1582556731&id=id&accname=guest&checksum=21AEEF3DE227AD76E2C3D30EE6DB7F41

Benn, J., Sangaré, C., and Tomas, H. (2017). 'Amounts mobilised from the private sector by official development finance interventions'. OECD Development Co-operation Working Papers No. 36. Available online at: https://www.oecd-ilibrary.org/docserver/8135abde-en.pdf?expires=1582554976&id=id&accname=guest&checksum=4BC09ECAD1A29CC63345C8D47AA3F988

Berg, E. (1998). 'World Bank and African Development Bank Roles'. ODC's Multilateral Conference of the Future of MDB Concessional Lending, Sweden.

Bhattacharya, A. and Kharas, H. (2016). *The Role of Regional Development Banks in the New Global Agenda*. Washington, DC: Brookings.

Bhattacharya, A., Romani, M., and Stern, N. (2012). 'Infrastructure for development: meeting the challenge'. Policy Paper, June. Grantham Research Institute on Climate Change and the Environment and G24.

Birdsall, N. and Rojas-Suárez, L. (2004). *Financing Development: The Power of Regionalism*. Washington, DC: Center for Global development.

Calderón, C.A. and Servén, L. (2014). 'Infrastructure, growth, and inequality: an overview'. Policy Research Working Paper No. 7034. Washington, DC: World Bank.

CGD (Center for Global Development) (2016). *Multilateral Development Banks for This Century's Development Challenges*. Washington, DC: Center for Global Development.

Davies, R. and Pickering, J. (2015). 'Making development co-operation fit for the future: a survey of partner countries'. OECD Development Co-operation Working Papers No. 20. Paris: OECD Publishing.

Eccles, S. and Gwin, C. (1999). *Supporting Effective Aid: A Framework for Future Concessional Funding of Multilateral Development Banks*. Washington, DC: Overseas Development Council.

Estache, Antonio and Garsous, Grégoire. (2012). 'The impact of infrastructure on growth in developing countries'. IFC Economic Notes, Note 1, April.

Greenhill, R. and Ali, A. (2013). 'Paying for progress: how will emerging post-2015 goals be financed in the emerging aid landscape'. ODI Working Paper No. 366. London: ODI.

Griffith-Jones, S., Griffith-Jones, D., and Hertova. D. (2008). 'Enhancing the role of regional development banks'. G-24 Discussion Paper Series No. 50. New York: UNCTAD.

Humphrey, C. (2015). *Infrastructure Finance in the Developing World: Challenges and Opportunities for Multilateral Development Banks in 21st Century Infrastructure Finance*. Intergovernmental Group G-24. Seoul, Korea: Global Green Institute.

Humphrey, C. (2017). 'Maximising the financial potential of multilateral development banks- without a capital increase'. In Annalisa Prizzon, Chris Humphrey, Inge Kaul, Kiyoshi Kodera, Alastair McKechnie, and Andrew Rogerson (eds.), *Six Recommendations for Reforming Multilateral Development Banks: An Essay Series*. London: ODI.

IADB (Inter-American Development Bank) (2011). 'News releases: Canada, Mexico and the United States announce contributions of USD 13 to an IADB-managed regional infrastructure integration fund', March 28. Available online at: http://www.iadb.org/en/news/news-releases/2011-03-28/regional-infrastructure-integration-fund,9322.html

IFC (The World Bank) (2018). 'Mobilization of private finance by multilateral development banks and development finance institutions, 2017'. Available online at: https://www.ifc.org/wps/wcm/connect/4366950e-b757-4190-8074-7db86e2860a7/201806_Mobilization-of-Private-Finance_v2.pdf?MOD=AJPERES&CVID=mfmjKJZ

Irmen, A. and Kuehnel, J. (2009). 'Productive government expenditure and economic growth', *Journal of Economic Surveys*, 23(4): 692–733.

Kaul, I. (2017). *Providing Global Public Goods: What Role for the MDBs*. London: Overseas Development Institute.

Kharas, H., Prizzon, A., and Rogerson, A. (2014). *Financing the Post-2015 Sustainable Development Goals: A Rough Roadmap*. London: Overseas Development Institute.

Levine, R., Kremer, M., and Albright, A. (2005). *Making Markets for Vaccines: Ideas to Action*. Washington, DC: Center for Global Development.

Miyamoto, K. and Chiofalo, E. (2016). 'Official development finance for infrastructure: with a special focus on multilateral development banks'. OECD Development Co-Operation Working Paper No. 30. Paris: OECD.

Nelson, R. (2018). 'Multilateral development banks: overview and issues for Congress'. 6 July. Washington, DC: Congressional Research Service. Available online at: https://fas.org/sgp/crs/row/R41170.pdf

Ocampo, J.A. (2015). 'The future of international financial institutions'. Caretas Annual Meeting WB-IMF Special Report, October. Available online at: https://franciscosagasti.com/site/wp-content/uploads/2015/10/A-FMI-Ingles.pdf

Prizzon, A. (2017). 'Why do countries want multilateral development bank? Views from recipient countries'. In A. Prizzon, C. Humphrey, I. Kaul, K. Kodera, A. McKechnie and, A. Rogerson (eds.), *Six Recommendations for Reforming Multilateral Development Banks: An Essay Series*. London: ODI.

Prizzon, A., Humphrey, C., Kaul, I., Kodera, K., McKechnie, A., and Rogerson, A. (eds.) (2017). *Six Recommendations for Reforming Multilateral Development Banks: An Essay Series*. London: ODI.

Rogerson, A. (2017). 'Gradation, not graduation: why and how MDB financing of middle-income countries needs an overhaul'. In A. Prizzon, C. Humphrey, I. Kaul, K. Kodera, A. McKechnie and, A. Rogerson (eds.), *Six Recommendations for Reforming Multilateral Development Banks: An Essay Series*. London: ODI.

Romp, W. and De Haan, J. (2007). 'Public capital and economic growth: a critical survey'. *Perspektiven der Wirtschaftspolitik*, 8(s1): 6–52.

Sagasti, F. (2015). 'Multilateral development banks. A lasting institutional innovation'. Caretas Annual Meeting WB-IMF Special Report, October. Available online at: https://franciscosagasti.com/site/wp-content/uploads/2015/10/A-FMI-Ingles.pdf

Sustainable Development Solutions Network (2015). 'Investment needs to achieve the sustainable development goals: understanding the billions and trillions', November. Available online at: https://irp-cdn.multiscreensite.com/be6d1d56/files/uploaded/151112-SDG-Financing-Needs.pdf

UNCTAD (United Nations Conference on Trade and Development) (2014). 'Investing in the SDGs: an action plan'. *World Investment Report*. New York: United Nations. Available online at: https://unctad.org/en/PublicationsLibrary/wir2014_en.pdf

World Bank (2015). *The State of Social Safety Nets 2015*. Washington, DC: World Bank.

World Bank (2016). *Poverty and Shared Prosperity: Taking on Inequality*. Washington, DC: World Bank.

Index

For the benefit of digital users, indexed terms that span two pages (e.g., 52–53) may, on occasion, appear on only one of those pages.

The manufacturer's authorised representative in the EU for product safety is Oxford University Press España S.A. of el Parque Empresarial San Fernando de Henares, Avenida de Castilla, 2 – 28830 Madrid (www.oup.es/en or product.safety@oup.com). OUP España S.A. also acts as importer into Spain of products made by the manufacturer.

www.ingramcontent.com/pod-product-compliance
Lightning Source LLC
LaVergne TN
LVHW011821200926
848484LV00005B/1269
* 9 7 8 0 1 9 8 8 6 1 0 8 9 *